POLITICS AND GOVERNMENT IN AFRICAN STATES
1960–1985

POLITICS & GOVERNMENT IN AFRICAN STATES 1960-1985

Edited by PETER DUIGNAN and ROBERT H. JACKSON

CROOM HELM
London & Sydney

Hoover Institution Press
Stanford, California

© 1986 Peter Duignan and Robert H. Jackson
Croom Helm Ltd, Provident House, Burrell Row,
Beckenham, Kent BR3 1AT
Croom Helm Australia Pty Ltd, Suite 4, 6th Floor,
64–76 Kippax Street, Surry Hills, NSW 2010 Australia

British Library Cataloguing in Publication Data
Politics and government in African states.
    1. Africa — Politics and government — 1960–
    I. Duignan, Peter. II. Jackson, Robert H.
    320.96   JQ1875.Al
    ISBN 0-7099-1475-X

Hoover Press Publication 348

First printing, 1986

90 89 88 87 86   9 8 7 6 5 4 3 2 1

Library of Congress Cataloging-in-Publication Data

Politics and government in African states.

    Bibliography: p.
    Includes index.
    1. Africa, Sub-Saharan — Politics and government —
1960- . I. Duignan, Peter. II. Jackson, Robert H.
DT352.8.P65 1986   320.96   86-20177
ISBN 0-8179-8481-X
ISBN 0-8179-8482-8 (pbk.)

Phototypeset in English Times by
Pat and Anne Murphy, Highcliffe-on-Sea, Dorset
Printed and bound in Great Britain
by Billing & Sons Limited, Worcester.

CONTENTS

PREFACE

The history and politics of individual African states in recent years have attracted much attention. But few scholars have attempted to assess the enormous, often violent and revolutionary, changes that have come to black Africa since independence. Although there are numerous specialized books on individual countries or regions, there are but a handful on the area of the continent south of the Sahara. For this reason we asked distinguished country or regional scholars to contribute chapters on their areas of expertise.

This volume deals with the politics and governments of African states since independence. Authors were asked to consider the formal structure of government at the time of independence and to trace changes to the present. Contributors have dealt with the state machinery, the civil service, the parastatals, defense and police forces, party structure and political opposition, and trade unions. The economics of African states were dealt with insofar as they affected politics and government.

A companion volume is in preparation that will deal with the economics of independent Africa. Professor Douglas Rimmer of Birmingham University, England, is writing this study.

We wish to thank the Director of the Hoover Institution, Dr. W. Glenn Campbell, and the Institution's Research Projects Committee for providing a special grant for this study. Numerous colleagues have read chapters of the book and we thank them collectively for they are too numerous to name individually.

All opinions expressed and any errors that may remain are, however, the responsibility of the authors.

INTRODUCTION

Peter Duignan

When black Africa set out on the road to independence, there was a mood of confidence in the air. Freedom would bring peace, prosperity, and an end to colonial oppression. The optimistic forecasts made by African independence leaders found a steady response in academe and the news media. By the early 1980s, however, the pendulum of public opinion had swung the other way — and with good reason. Countries as varied as Angola, Ethiopia, Nigeria, Uganda, and the Sudan had experienced, or were going through, the turmoil of civic strife. Parliamentary democracy had widely given way to one-party rule or military dictatorship. In retrospect, even the colonial regimes have gained a certain measure of respect; Nigerian historian Johnson U. J. Asiegbu found it possible to contrast the "patriotism and probity, . . . self-discipline and other remarkable ideals of public responsibility with the bad and dishonest example, . . . the criminal wastage, the fraudulent and selfish mismanagement of the continent's resources practiced by the new 'predatory elites' in post-colonial Africa."[1]

The economic promises of independence often proved equally disappointing. Farming was often beset by unwise controls, inefficient marketing, neglect, mistaken priorities, and civil war. By 1984 the farmers' problems had been made worse by widespread droughts that were said to threaten at least twenty million people with starvation and many more with sustained shortages of food. Poor returns on exports, high import costs, and inflated currencies worsened by declining food production left much of Africa in jeopardy.

This is not to say that Africa's postcolonial record has been uniformly bleak. Most of the newly independent countries initially achieved at least modest progress; some (including Ghana, Kenya, the Ivory Coast, Gabon, Cameroon, Nigeria, Rhodesia [later known as Zimbabwe] and South Africa) had high growth rates. But beginning in the 1970s the picture darkened, and sub-Saharan Africa as a whole began to slide into a condition of profound crisis from which it has yet to emerge.

Of course, expectations were too great at the time of

1

independence, for Africa contained more of the world's poorest countries (twenty-eight) than any other region in the world. (The continuous neglect of agriculture, droughts, inefficient governance, and civil unrest had led to large-scale food imports — a condition almost unheard of during the late colonial period.)

African states have built up huge public debts and now face balance-of-payments crises. Some states have made genuine attempts at reform. Starting in 1983 Ghana, for example, began a sustained effort at economic stabilization. The Ghanaian authorities embarked on a campaign to deregulate prices and reduce external payment arrears by net cash payments and the consolidation of debts. But even here, unfavourable weather conditions, transportation difficulties, and other troubles delayed recovery and caused the government's reforms to fall short of their objective. By 1984 many states were effectively bankrupt and were surviving only because of international charity. Furthermore, conditions appeared to be worsening. In 1984 Africa received the lowest prices for its goods in thirty years; it had to pay more for its imports (food, oil, and manufactured goods) than it took in for its exports. In much of the continent, growth is not only slowed but has become negative. In the face of a continued and rapid population expansion, many African states will have a lower per capita income in the 1980s than they had in the 1960s at the time of independence.

Approximately twenty-five years after the first state became independent, Africa south of the Sahara has the fastest population growth in the world. And Africa still has the highest illiteracy rate (75 percent), the lowest life expectancy (forty-seven years), and the most impoverished countries (twenty-eight) of any region in the world. The future seems even bleaker. The World Bank's 1984 report predicted a 0.1 to 0.5 percent decline in per capita product for the next ten years. There will therefore be more people but less to share.

The dreams and hopes at the time of independence have largely been abandoned; people have become generally alienated from their governments and pessimistic about their futures. How can we account for the decay in the performance of African governments since independence? To understand the problems of Africa today we must look first at decolonization and the colonial legacy and then at the causes of Africa's loss of peace, prosperity, and civic culture.

The End of Empire

The full story of decolonization remains to be written, but some reasons for the rapid demise of empire are already clear.[2] Within one decade, the flags of Great Britain, France, and Belgium were hauled down. Outside South Africa, white rule survived only in Rhodesia and the Portuguese colonies, and during the 1970s even these remaining bastions crumbled. The colonial powers failed to cooperate with one another in their common defense. The colonial cause no longer appealed to the mass of the people in the metropolitan countries — especially since a long and bloody world war had recently been fought specifically in the name of freedom, self-government, and hostility to racism. The ideological initiative during and after World War II passed to the critics of colonialism, who were supported (with different motives) by both the United States and the Soviet Union. The colonial rulers encountered bitter and sustained criticism in the metropolitan parliaments, the media, the universities, the churches, and even within the ranks of their own colonial services. In consequence, the colonial overlords became increasingly apologetic. They compromised, and each reform and concession led to new demands.

The imperial powers faced more practical considerations. Empire had ceased to pay, either militarily or economically. Both the British and the French recognized this. The French, for example, seemed only to have compounded their wartime losses by expensive colonial campaigns. The war in Indochina imposed great sacrifices on their country. No sooner were they rid of the Indochina commitment than they found themselves faced with a serious struggle in Algeria. By 1959 the French government was maintaining a half-million soldiers in North Africa. As a result, France was reduced to temporary military impotence in Europe and was no longer able to make its promised contribution to NATO. The loss of Indochina in 1954, however, in no way injured the French economy. Contrary to predictions made by impenitent colonialists, the French got over the disappearance of their East Asian empire just as quickly as the Dutch got over the loss of their possessions and investments in Indonesia. It appeared that imperial might was incompatible with a balanced budget or with true grandeur on the European continent. The rulers lost the will to rule (with the exception of the Portuguese, who hung on until 1975).

At the same time, the colonial subjects began to organize;

African nationalism demanded self-determination. During the 1920s, the 1930s, and the 1940s, opposition to colonial rule had centered on African welfare societies and on congresses composed mainly of professionals and white-collar workers. The demands of this opposition were quite moderate. During the 1950s, however, a new generation of politicians entered public life — men and women to whom politics became both a vocation and a livelihood. They set up parties that had a wide appeal, and they often acquired ideological support that the colonial powers could not counter. In addressing their fellow subjects, nationalist leaders frequently made extravagant promises — promises that became political liabilities once independence was achieved. Party speakers in the villages often prophesied that political freedom would lead to freedom from all earthly woes; land and houses, education and social services, and even train fares and bus rides would become free. African nationalism was sometimes tinged with the messianic millennial strains that had distinguished earlier religious radicalisms of Christian inspiration in Africa.

African leaders often spoke with two voices. Sometimes they talked of modern states ruled on the principle of "one man, one vote" and equipped with all the white man's political and technological know-how. At other times they conjured up a golden past and took advantage of the conservative villagers' distrust of colonial-sponsored improvement schemes. African nationalist propaganda, however, was successful in temporarily creating African nationalists. Countless numbers of African villagers or city laborers became conscious of political problems and began to search for secular solutions to the ills of their world.

After Ghana became independent in 1957, the process of decolonization rapidly accelerated. By 1968 the Union Jack had disappeared from Africa. The French tried to hold on to Algeria in a bloody guerrilla struggle. They realized, however, that they could not, at the same time, deploy their army south of the Sahara, and by 1960 they had relinquished political power in all of black Africa except Djibouti. The Belgians followed suit in 1960. The Portuguese (the weakest of all the European colonizers) fought a protracted war against partisans who were largely supplied from sanctuaries in the newly independent African states. Militarily, the Portuguese did fairly well, but politically, the guerrilla war became a disaster. The Portuguese army, disheartened by many years of struggle, turned against its political masters. In 1975 the Portuguese finally withdrew from Africa, and in 1979 Rhodesia passed out of white control. Only white-ruled South Africa and Namibia remain as a legacy of European imperialism. (See Table 1.)

Table 1: Dates of Independence of Black African States

Sudan	1 January 1956
Ghana	6 March 1957
Guinea	2 October 1958
Cameroon	1 January 1960
Togo	27 April 1960
Mali	20 June 1960
Senegal	20 June 1960
Madagascar	26 June 1960
Zaire (formerly Belgian Congo)	30 June 1960
Somalia	1 July 1960
Benin (formerly Dahomey)	1 August 1960
Niger	3 August 1960
Upper Volta	5 August 1960
Ivory Coast	7 August 1960
Chad	11 August 1960
Central African Republic	13 August 1960
Congo (Brazzaville)	15 August 1960
Gabon	17 August 1960
Nigeria	1 October 1960
Mauritania	28 November 1960
Sierra Leone	27 April 1961
Tanzania (as Tanganyika)	9 December 1961
Rwanda	1 July 1962
Burundi	1 July 1962
Uganda	9 October 1962
Zanzibar (now part of Tanzania)	10 December 1963
Kenya	12 December 1963
Malawi	6 July 1964
Zambia	24 October 1964
The Gambia	18 February 1965
Botswana	30 September 1966
Lesotho	4 October 1966
Swaziland	6 September 1968
Equatorial Guinea	12 October 1968
Guinea-Bissau	10 September 1974
Mozambique	25 June 1975
Cape Verde	5 July 1975
Sáo Tomé and Principe	12 July 1975
Angola	11 November 1975
Djibouti	27 June 1977
Zimbabwe	18 April 1980

Source: Austin, *Politics in Africa*, p. 150.

The Colonial Impact

The ultimate effects of Western colonization remain subject to a bitter dispute that does not hinge on, for instance, the specific experience of the Belgians or French, but on the wider question of European capitalism's role in Africa. Critics of colonialism stress the negative aspects of the imperial experience. They point out its coercive aspects, such as the widespread use of forced labor for railway building, porterage, and road construction. They enlarge on the horrors of "red rubber" (that is, the rubber forcibly collected by Africans in the early days of Belgian colonization in the Congo). In general, they emphasize the destructive effects of European colonization on indigenous culture and on indigenous state systems. (Other critics argue that European colonization also had certain positive aspects, for instance, it diffused new industrial techniques.) Nevertheless, these censors are convinced that any advantages that may have derived from the colonial experience were acquired at an excessive price. Others go further still. They state that Europe actually "under-developed" Africa — that relatively peaceful and prosperous societies were debased by foreign conquest and became dependent fragments of industrialized Europe's rural periphery. Some anti-imperialists argue that colonialism retarded the natural development of Africa. They claim Africa would have been better off if colonialism had never taken place.

We take a position that is in certain respects in line with the views of Karl Marx on British rule in India. Marx believed that the British had unwittingly benefited India by transferring a broad range of social, administrative, military, scientific, and technological skills to their imperial possession. Likewise, we see the European colonizers as the unwitting state builders of modern Africa. With a few exceptions (such as Lesotho or Somalia) the newly independent countries are, for the most part, colonial artifacts. European colonization was part of a wider process in which the West imposed its military and administrative institutions, its technology, its science, and its worldviews on a vast congeries of Iron Age states and statelets and on scattered rural communities with little sense of cohesion.

As for the argument that African states would have been better off free from imperial rule, one has only to look at the backwardness, poverty, and misrule of Liberia (never under colonial governance) and Ethiopia (ruled only briefly by Italy) to see the falsity of this thesis. For all their failings, the European rulers were conquerors with a difference. Unlike African warlords, Europeans brought entirely new methods of economic production, new ways of governance, and new ideas to Africa. The languages of colonialism — English, French, Portuguese — also became the languages of science, modern education, government, and — ultimately — anticolonialism. In addition to being state builders, the conquerors were Africa's railway, road, and city builders par excellence. Colonization engendered far-reaching economic change; it was accompanied by population growth, itself occasioned by the introduction of improved medical services, a vast increase in the variety and yield of food crops, improved forms of sanitation, the spread of inexpensive soap and inexpensive clothing, the development of municipal sewerage systems, and a host of other services that helped to preserve and extend human life.

A. Adu Boahen, an African scholar, has aptly summarized the impact of colonialism in an essay otherwise critical of the imperial legacy

> The . . . positive legacy has been the infra-structure of roads, railways, harbours, and airports. In many independent African states, a large number of roads have been widened, resurfaced or tarred, or straightened; but not many miles of new roads or railways have been added since independence . . . [Another] positive impact is urbanization. There is no doubt that many urban centres in Africa, and even the very capitals of some of the independent African states, owe their foundation or rapid growth to the colonial impact . . . [Also] we have seen the emergence of two classes unknown in traditional African society: a literate middle class and a predominately illiterate working class. A [further] permanent feature has been the transfer of power within the African society itself. The process of decolonization has meant not only the overthrow of colonial rule, but also the transfer of power from the traditional ruling aristocracy to the new middle and lower classes . . . Independence has not revived the powers of the great kings of precolonial and colonial Africa. Still another significant contribution has been the introduction of cash crops and cash economy, and the consequent entry of African economy into the orbit of world economy.[3]

For better and for worse, colonialism brought about deep-seated change. The imperial system stands out as one of the most powerful engines for cultural diffusion in the history of Africa. Its credit balance outweighs its debit account. Colonialism helped to erode Africa's isolation and brought Africa into the world economy; colonial rule transmitted new skills, new techniques, new ways of thought, and new methods of governance. Colonialism also brought in its wake a vast range of new problems and new stresses. For better or for worse, old Africa was never to be the same again.

Independent Africa

The leaders of the African independence movements and their well-wishers abroad assumed that the demise of colonialism would result in peace and prosperity. But independence did not bring the paradise that the politicians had promised. The fault was not completely attributable to the new leaders however. At independence, sub-Saharan Africa was rich in diversity and poor in resources. It had ca. 1500 ethnic communities divided among forty-two states. It was composed of large countries like Nigeria, the Sudan, and Zaire and small countries like Gambia, Togo, and Swaziland. Some countries possessed mineral wealth (South Africa, Zambia, Zimbabwe, and Zaire); a few had discovered oil (Nigeria, Cameroon, Angola, and Gabon). With few exceptions, African economics were, and are, small in scale, characterized by low average incomes and small populations. Most people worked (and continue to work) in agriculture (70 percent), and only about 30 percent were urban. The economies depended (and still depend) on the export of two or three primary commodities.

Africa has a difficult climate, poor soil, and a harsh physical environment. Less than 9 percent of the continent is covered by jungle or tropical rain forest. As cultivators increasingly encroach on the forest land even this area is diminishing. Africa's major climatic troubles do not spring from too much rain but from too little. About 40 percent of the continent is dry land or desert; close to another 40 percent is savannah; the remainder is covered by forests of different varieties. Approximately 75 percent of sub-Saharan Africa experiences scanty or irregular rainfall; about 90 percent of the surface suffers from major climatic disabilities.

Africa also has poor soils. They are delicate, easily leached, lack organic materials, and quickly lose their fertility. Arable land and land under permanent crops constitute a small proportion of the total land area (perhaps 7 percent). Even on this selected land, the farmers' lot is usually hard. Most African cultivators must cope with deficient transportation and marketing facilities, unfavorable climate, lack of capital and opportunities to borrow on their land, sharp fluctuations in world prices for African products, and inequitable systems of taxation.

Since independence nature has dealt harshly with Africa. There have been severe droughts (1973–74, 1977–78, 1982–84), locust invasions, cattle plagues, plant diseases, tropical illnesses, and a host of other problems afflicting men, beasts, and crops. The geography of the continent, its great size (three and one-half times the size of the United States), dispersed populations, and lack of year-round navigable rivers and natural harbors have also been barriers to development. The falls and escarpment profile of the coastline and the rifts in the mountains constitute enormous obstacles for transportation and the provision of government services. Africa was, and is, a poor continent. At independence there was no vast wealth to be divided, rather, there was great poverty to be overcome.

The new states of Africa all lacked educated, skilled people, used land-extensive (rather than intensive) farming systems, were ethnically diverse, and were politically fragile. Since independence, population growth in Africa has been among the highest in the world. All the new African states faced enormous human difficulties and constraints to development that most of their leaders and outside academic observers failed fully to take into account. According to the World Bank report, *Accelerated Development in Sub-Saharan Africa*, the most serious of these constraints were "undeveloped human and material resources, difficult climate and geography, rapid population growth, alien unassimilated political institutions, and insecure political legitimacy."[4]

The scarcity of trained manpower was a critical problem from the beginning. (See Table 2.) Expatriate employment was as high as 62 percent in Zambia and as low as 13 percent in Nigeria. University-trained manpower was low; about 75 percent of university teachers and administrators were expatriates. Similarly, foreigners dominated government and technical positions. Africanization had begun too late to enable Africans to fill most senior government posts at the time of independence. In states where independence

Table 2: Expatriate Employment in Africa as a Percentage of Total Employment of Trained Manpower in Early Manpower Surveys

Country	Date of Independence	Year of Survey	Percentage
Botswana	1966	1967	42
Ivory Coast	1960	1962	45
Kenya	1963	1964	48
Malawi	1964	1966	18
Nigeria	1960	1964	13
Swaziland	1968	1970	35
Tanzania	1961	1965	31
Uganda	1962	1967	21
Zambia	1964	1965	62

Source: *Accelerated Development in Sub-Saharan Africa: An Agenda for Action* (Washington, D.C.: The World Bank, 1981), p. 9.

was achieved by civil war rather than by peaceful negotiations, the situation was even worse. Doctrinaire Marxists in Guinea-Bissau, Angola, and Mozambique drove out or frightened away the white populations. In Zaire the revolt of the army, the *Force Publique*, caused almost the entire Belgian cadre (over 10,000) and the white settlers to leave. (Some returned later, however.)

These four states — Guinea-Bissau, Angola, Mozambique, and Zaire — had fewer educated African people in government or business than most African states at the time of decolonization. Upon achieving independence, they experienced the immediate breakdown of both the colonial state and the economy. The Republic of Guinea's road to African socialism proved equally thorny; Guinea's economic problems and political difficulties quickly worsened after the French withdrawal in 1960. During the 1970s, African prosperity (such as it was) declined further, owing to the effects of droughts, sharply increasing oil prices, declining prices for African raw-material exports, ill-considered governmental policies, and — in some cases — the departure of expatriates.

At the time of independence large-scale trade and industry in Africa was largely managed and owned by foreigners. Before independence university education for Africans had been limited. (Only about 20,000 Africans were enrolled in universities in 1958.) Secondary education had been similarly limited. (About 3 percent of the school-age population was in high school in 1960.) There were also shortages of skilled labor, businessmen, and entrepreneurs.

Even though much had been done to improve health conditions in Africa in the 1950s, there was still a grave shortage of health care. There was one physician for every 50,000 people in black Africa. Rural areas were especially neglected. Life expectancy was the lowest in the world (thirty-nine years, as compared to forty-two years for other Third World countries). Child death rates were proportionately high (thirty-nine per thousand as compared to Third World average of twenty-three per thousand). After independence, Africa significantly improved its literacy rate and life expectancy and lowered the death rate of children. Literacy improved to 28 percent, life expectancy rose to forty-seven years, and children's death rate dropped to twenty-five per thousand. These figures represent the new states' most significant achievements.

Poor health conditions low life expectancy, underdeveloped human resources, and the lack of managerial and technical cadres were among the many handicaps that the new African nations started off with. Nevertheless, they had high expectations. The new states soon came under the rule of a single party or of the military, and most opted for central planning and government-owned corporations (parastatals).

The Economy

Experts continue to differ bitterly on the merits of private versus public enterprises. Whatever the merits of this controversy, neither socialists nor capitalists deny the importance of trained technical, entrepreneurial, and managerial cadres. All these were in short supply in newly independent Africa, and the new ruling parties were in no position to provide them. Under such conditions, prudence would have suggested a slow policy in the expansion of public enterprise. But the euphoria induced by independence and by socialist or quasi-socialist ideologies (inherited in part from the former colonial powers), plus the advice given by itinerant foreign experts, all helped to popularize a variety of socialist or semi-socialist solutions.

Marxism-Leninism found acceptance in Angola, Mozambique, Guinea-Bissau, and Ethiopia; more eclectic varieties of socialism prevailed in Guinea, Tanzania, and — for a time — in Ghana. Although experiences differed considerably, by and large, all states that tried rapidly to transform their societies by means of socialist solutions eventually suffered a decline in their GNP, a loss of civil liberties, and a decline in the legitimacy of the ruling elites. These failings were not confined to socialist states, however. Countries like Zaire or Zambia that avoided the socialist label also slid into economic turmoil.

The reasons for the decline of these African states are complex, but there can be no doubt that they all had a difficult start. Most of them began with dual economies; that is, subsistence economies supplemented by small islands of production for the market. West Africa (at least in countries near the coast and 200 kilometers or so inland) had a fairly developed peasant sector that produced export crops. (The interior states largely produced for themselves and for local barter.) Central, East, and Southern Africa also had dual economies; the Europeans dominated mining and agriculture, and (except in Uganda) African farmers produced little for the market.

In 1960, 70 to 80 percent of African farms were worked only for subsistence. The new governments therefore faced major obstacles in inducing Africans to produce for the market by taking on new crops and risks. Little was known about methods to improve farmers' productivity; basic scientific information about the land and the climate and about what would grow and sell was also widely lacking. Given Africa's poor soils, harsh climate, and numerous parasites and diseases, this kind of knowledge was essential.

To make matters worse, roads, railways, ports, and communication systems were scarce (except near the coast or in mining areas). Governments should have given the problems of agriculture and infrastructure first priority, but only a few (for instance, Malawi, Botswana, and the Ivory Coast) did so.

In economic terms, Africa is both rich and poor; it is rich in potential resources, but it is poor if its level of economic development is compared with that of Western Europe or North America (or even with that of Asia and Latin America). Much of Africa's wealth derives from a limited number of economic islands, which cover ca. 5 percent of the continent's land area and produce ca. 85 percent of its total economic output. These islands are found in Nigeria, the Ivory Coast, Cameroon, Kenya, Zaire, Zimbabwe, Namibia, Zambia, and — above all — in South Africa. The developed regions in these countries are usually situated on the coast, along fertile river valleys, in ore-bearing regions, or in fertile highlands.

Great potential wealth resides in Africa's unexploited hydro-electric power. Africa is also a major producer of petroleum, coal, uranium, copper, iron, gold, diamonds, platinum, chrome, nickel, and many other minerals. To date, mining operations have barely scratched the surface, and an enormous amount of geological survey work still needs to be done. Mineral deposits are distributed unevenly throughout the continent, however. Gold production centers mainly on the Republic of South Africa. Petroleum is found in Algeria, Gabon, Nigeria, Libya, and the Cabinda district of northern Angola; copper comes from Zambia and Zaire; iron comes from Liberia and Sierra Leone; and bauxite comes from Guinea. Foreign skill and foreign capital are still essential to the exploration and extraction of this wealth, and both are in short supply. The importance of mining will nevertheless continue to grow during the 1980s, especially in southern Africa.

The African industrial revolution began in South Africa. South Africa constitutes the continent's industrial giant, accounting for the greatest proportion of its iron and steel production and for most of its more sophisticated industries. About 40 percent of Africa's industrial output, 60 percent of its electricity, and 80 percent of its steel is of South African origin. Alone in sub-Saharan Africa, South Africa commands a great economic infrastructure complete with large ports, industrial research facilities, skilled labor, and the ability to turn out a vast range of sophisticated goods — from rockets to modern mining machinery. Economically, South Africa has dominated (and will continue to dominate) the southern portion of the continent. Manufacturing industries have spread to other areas, however. As in southern Africa, the first ones to do so have been agricultural processing, textiles, and light consumer industries, all of which gradually tend to become more sophisticated enterprises. Outside South Africa, Zimbabwe, and Nigeria, the role of manufacturing remains a minor one, but its role will increase in the future.

Even in 1984 about 70 percent of Africa's people are still farmers. This situation makes the failure of governments to develop agriculture a particularly irresponsible and depressing omission. African GNP growth rates were positive between 1960 and 1970, but per capita food production declined by 20 percent between 1960 and 1980. As a result of this steady decline in agriculture and of several severe droughts, there are grain shortages in many countries. The FAO claims that twenty-four African countries face emergency food situations. Comestibles must be imported, but the declines in production for export crops and in prices for Africa's exports limit the ability of states to pay for food imports.

The present food crisis is a result not only of a series of droughts, but of government policies, internal conflicts, and governmental neglect of peasant producers. It is not true, as some writers have claimed, that colonial administrators pushed the production of export crops over those for internal consumption.[5] By and large, the development of export crops under colonialism was accompanied by expansion of food crops. When export crops were produced in addition to food crops, they initially represented a net addition to farm output. Although production of cash crops, such as cotton, sisal, cocoa, and palm-oil, enormously increased from 1880 to 1960, food production kept pace with population growth. (Ground-nut production in Senegal was an exception, for it led to a decline in food production and the importation of rice.) The Colonial Pax, improved transportation systems, the introduction of new food crops, the spread of better agricultural methods and tools, and agricultural extension work enlarged the food supply in colonial Africa. In 1960 food imports accounted for less than 3 percent of total supplies to tropical Africa; today they account for 30 percent or more. Mozambique now has to import two-thirds of its food; Ethiopia has to be fed by Western relief.

Domestic production of food crops enabled the expanding population to be fed during the colonial period, and, at the same time, crops for exports also increased dramatically. Since independence, however, there has been a decline in food production (about 1 percent a year), an increase in population (2.5 percent to 4 percent a year), a decrease in the volume of exports, and decline in prices for goods exported. Much of this decline can be traced directly to government policies. All too often, planners — including expatriate experts — assumed that, by fair means or foul, the agricultural sector should provide the surplus required to finance urban and industrial development. Hence, in many cases African governments both underpaid and overtaxed the farmers. In contrast to colonial governments, African governments neglected agriculture during their attempts to industrialize and to support highly paid bureaucracies. Government marketing boards often paid producers at rates below world market prices, thereby discouraging cultivators from growing food and export crops for sale. Instead, many villagers retreated into the accustomed subsistence economy — a decision rendered more reasonable by the weakness of marketing organizations, the shortage of fertilizers and agricultural implements, and other afflictions.

To make matters worse, central planning authorities — interested mainly in industrial development and urban prosperity — often overregulated and overcontrolled the farmers' lives. Because of insufficient knowledge of farmers' needs, these organizations provided too few services to allow them to increase their productivity. Tanzania's massive resettlement scheme (five to seven million people moved), for example, resulted in a disastrous drop in agricultural productivity. (In 1974 just under 20 percent of the population lived in *ujamaa* (collective) villages; by 1976 over 90 percent of the population lived in villages of this type.) A general decline in law and order, or wars and coups, sometimes caused people to flee to the cities and abandon their homelands. The failure to maintain roads, canals, and bridges also played a role in decreasing farm productivity. In summary, the root causes of the present agricultural crisis were: civil wars, poor management, corrupt or reactionary cadres, pressure on peasants to join cooperatives, poor producer prices, and chaotic distribution systems.

Africanization of the economy devolved into a disaster for many countries — most notably Uganda, Zaire, Angola, Mozambique, and Guinea-Bissau. Shops, stores, and plants were confiscated and then looted. Production, restocking, and investment ended once the initial goods were gone. (Multinationals fared better because, even if nationalized, they basically continued to manage themselves.)

There was no real plan for Africanization; the economy created by the colonial state was often dismantled or allowed to decay. In Zaire, Angola, and Mozambique suburbs formerly inhabited by whites were vandalized and allowed to disintegrate. Sometimes such destruction resulted from rage or envy; at other times it resulted from ignorance. The unintended consequences of independence have been the deterioration or dereliction of the colonial estates out of neglect and the inability to maintain houses, roads, canals, and equipment.

The ideology of African communism and socialism also contributed greatly to the decay of the colonial state and economy. Most African governments took on too many responsibilities —

Table 3: Sub-Saharan Africa and the World: Basic Data

	Population, mid-1979 (millions)	GNP per capita average annual growth rate (percentage) 1960–1970	GNP per capita average annual growth rate (percentage) 1970–1979
Sub-Saharan Africa	343.9	1.3	0.8
Low-income	187.1	1.6	−0.3
Nigeria	82.6	0.1	4.2
Other middle-income	74.2	1.9	−0.5
South Asia[a]	890.5	1.5	1.5
All developing countries	3,245.2	3.5	2.7[b]
Low-income	2,260.2	1.8	1.6[b]
Middle-income	985.0	3.9	2.8[b]
All industrialized countries	671.2	6.1	2.5[b]

	Per capita growth, 1970–1979 (percentage) Agriculture	Per capita growth, 1970–1979 (percentage) Volume of exports	Adult Literacy rate, 1976 (percentage)
Sub-Saharan Africa	−0.9	−3.5	26
Low-income	−1.1	−4.5	26
Nigeria	−2.8	−2.8	—
Other middle-income	−0.5	−0.4	34
South Asia[a]	0.0	0.6	36
All developing countries	0.1	−1.5	57
Low-income	0.1	−3.1	50
Middle-income	0.6	1.9	72
All industrialized countries	0.2	5.2	99

	Life expectancy at birth, 1979 (years)	Death rate of children aged 1–4, 1979 (per thousand)
Sub-Saharan Africa	47	25
Low-income	46	27
Nigeria	49	22
Other middle-income	50	22
South Asia[a]	52	15
All developing countries	56	11
Low-income	57	11
Middle-income	61	10
All industrialized countries	74	1

[a] Bhutan, Bangladesh, Nepal, Burma, India, Sri Lanka, and Pakistan.
[b] 1970–1980.
Source: World Bank data files.

central planning, running state corporations and nationalized companies, and overly regulating the lives and work of their people. There were too few experienced bureaucrats and managers, and the political elites lacked the skills and capacities to run the economies. Bureaucracies expanded enormously, but they simply robbed or inefficiently expended the states' revenue (especially by giving high salaries to senior officials). Businessmen were not encouraged, and peasant producers were discouraged. Africanization and socialism primarily enriched the political elite. After the 1960s most governments failed to increase production and saddled the people of Africa with negative growth rates.

African Bureaucracies

African bureaucracies have grown enormously in the past twenty-five years; they have consumed too much of the gross domestic product by employing too many people and paying senior officials salaries too high for the resources of the state. During the colonial period, senior officials' salaries were set at a high level (although not as high as those of U.N. officials) in order to attract and keep able people. Black nationalists erred greatly in insisting on retaining the colonial salary structures in order to appear equal to Europeans. The period after independence witnessed a rapid expansion of the bureaucracy and the growth of state-owned corporations (parastatals). This growth of the state-system, which paid salaries totally out of proportion to state resources, was a primary cause of Africa's economic stagnation.[6]

At independence, African governments typically started off determined to develop their countries. Partially because of the colonial legacy, they looked to the state, rather than the private sector, to end the conditions of poverty and low productivity. The best road for many of them was that of African socialism, complete with central planning and state regulation and ownership. These attitudes and ideology led directly to the growth of an expensive, expanding, inefficient bureaucracy, which further weakened the private sector and discouraged agricultural growth.

These bureaucracies were ill-equipped to develop their nation's economies. They were widely lacking in knowledge, skill, experience, and risk-taking ability. There was often no countervailing private sector against which the performance of the state might be measured. There was no political opposition to restrain the bureaucracy and make it accountable. Ministries and parastatals became almost autonomous bodies, uncontrolled by anyone in the central government. As a result (except in South Africa), they became corrupt and inefficient. Each year government staffs expanded (about 7 to 8 percent a year), acquired higher salaries, and consumed much of the state's revenue.

Salaries to officials — especially senior officials — represented the largest single element of recurring expenditures. Government salaries in Africa accounted for a much higher share of total government expenditure than did those of most other regions of the world. In fact, the expenditure share of African government salaries is about twice as high as that of the world as a whole. (Salaries represent about 30 percent of government expenditures in Africa.) Furthermore, salaries for civil servants in Africa are extraordinarily high in relation to per capita income. For example, even in 1963–64 the ratio was 82:1 in Kenya, 96:1 in Tanzania, and 130:1 in Nigeria. (In the United States it is about 6 or 7:1.) As a result of high salaries, bureaucrats not only appropriated a high percentage of the state's resources but also ignored the avowed aim of equality inherent in African socialism. And the large number of lower-paid officials also posed problems for the treasury and for morale. Senior-level salaries might be thirty to forty times higher than those of entry-level positions. Officials at still lower levels were part of the problem because there were so many of them doing nonproductive work. Much of their working time was devoted to trying to move up the bureaucratic ladder rather than to trying to improve the economy or the efficiency of government. In Africa (as elsewhere) officials fought for more power for their ministry or parastatal and for a bigger share of state revenue.[7]

African bureaucracies therefore placed a drag on economic development in at least two ways. They consumed too much of the state's revenue (thus limiting funds for development), and they impeded the private sector's growth by owning too much and by overregulating the economy by such means as collectivization, marketing boards, licensing boards, and import controls.

It is not correct to trace most of the faults of African bureaucracies to the former colonial rulers. The colonial state was similarly authoritarian in approach, and it paid its officials relatively high salaries. By and large, however, the European official presence and the highly salaried establishment was small, efficient, experienced, and rarely corrupt. The state had a limited mission during the colonial period.

In contrast, independent Africa expanded the size of its bureaucracies and enormously increased the role of the state. The size of government increased manyfold. Kenya went from a civil service of 45,000 in 1955 to 170,000 in 1984. Senegal employed 10,000 in 1960 and over 70,000 in 1984. It was not just the civil service that grew; teachers and employees of parastatals increased tenfold. In Ghana there are over 80 parastatals; Kenya has over 100; Zambia has 150; South Africa has around 300. In Africa, the people employed directly and indirectly by the state amount to possibly 50–55 percent of all working-age people. (In South Africa, the figure is around 40 percent.)

Political scientist David Abernethy estimates that state employment has grown about 160 percent since 1960, and agricultural productivity has declined about 20–25 percent. He sees some positive benefits from this growth of government (Africanization, stimulus to education, social mobility, and so forth). But Africans have paid a high price for these real or assumed benefits. Given the costs of civil wars, coups, loss of civil liberties and democratic governance, abuse of ethnic groups, and the costs of bureaucracies in salaries, perquisites, and bad government, the ordinary citizen of Africa is worse off today than he was in 1960.

In numerous publications, P. T. Bauer has demonstrated that government controls and ownership have been among the main barriers to material progress in Africa. Foreign aid and development planning have contributed to the politicization of life in most African states. (For example it was large-scale aid that allowed Julius Nyerere to carry out the forced removal and collectivization of ten to eleven million people in Tanzania.)

Planners, both in the developed Western countries and in the Third World, assumed that these ills might be cured or alleviated by the provision of foreign aid. The history of foreign aid remains to be written. The final verdict has yet to be given. But clearly, foreign aid has nowhere come up to the donors' and recipients' original expectations. Foreign aid has been provided for a wide variety of reasons — many of them contradictory in purpose. The advocates of foreign aid have pleaded that it would serve as a means of developing backward economies, as reparation for real or assumed sins committed by the West against the peoples of the Third World, as a device for stopping communist revolutions, as a bribe to gain allies, and as an instrument for increasing Western exports. In fact, foreign aid may have (and in many cases has) been counterproductive, in that foreign aid was apt to strengthen local bureaucratic lobbies, promote prodigal and unprofitable expenditure, encourage the diversions of funds into the private bank accounts of the newly privileged, or even accelerate inflation. Even at the best of times, foreign aid failed to follow a consistent plan; the provision of funds fluctuated in accordance with shifting political circumstances, and, overall, there was too little insistence on accountability to make aid truly effective.

Corruption became endemic in Africa. Corruption, of course, has not been limited to Africa, but in countries like Ghana, Nigeria, or Zaire the disease became so serious that it threatened the operation of government. The military coup that seized power in Nigeria in late 1983 owed much of its popularity to public disgust at the prevalence of corruption in government. But in Nigeria, as elsewhere, military governance has proved no remedy against corruption and inefficiency. Rather, corruption seems to be linked to the growth of the state sector and to the increasing temptations open to civil servants to provide licenses, permits, and contracts in return for cash or other reciprocal favors. Corruption has hit countries as varied as Tanzania (subject to Nyerere's paternalistic form of socialism), Zambia (wedded to Kaunda's humanism), and Mozambique (subject to a Marxist-Leninist form of governance).

Nevertheless, Africa's international trade has gained in importance over the last thirty years. Between 1938 and 1970 total exports from Africa increased in value nearly fifteen times, and volume increased nearly tenfold. Whatever their political complexion, however, African countries continue to encounter serious obstacles in selling their goods abroad. Exporters have to cope with rapid price fluctuations, foreign tariffs, and growing competition from substitutes — such as aluminium for copper and synthetic fibers for wool. The developed countries increasingly trade among themselves in both primary products and manufactured goods. There are also the perennial problems of shortages of skilled manpower and capital, lack of entrepreneurial initiative (or its discouragement by government owing to bureaucratic graft), interference and regulation, and (occasionally) outright confiscation. Foreign aid (much of it misapplied or misspent at the source or in the field) has not helped. The Western countries could best assist Africa's economic development by reducing their own tariffs for manufactured products and primary resources — thereby benefiting both their own consumers and the world at large.

Politics

Africa is organized into a variety of states that differ widely in economic, military, and demographic strength. Militarily, South Africa is by far the most powerful country of sub-Saharan Africa; it is followed in importance by Nigeria. Ethiopia ranks third in military strength (although not in economics). By international standards, however, even the strongest African states do not rank highly in economic strength or military force. In the world at large, even the giants of the continent are secondary powers.

As we have seen, most of the new states have become authoritarian. At present parliamentary systems survive in only a handful of African states, including Botswana, Kenya, South Africa, and Zimbabwe. The remainder are one-party states or military dictatorships. Since 1960 there have been only six examples of regular constitutional succession in all of Africa: Gabon (1967), Liberia (1971), Kenya (1978), Botswana (1980), Senegal (1980), and Cameroon (1982). Four of these examples occurred at the death of a ruler and the other two followed voluntary resignations. Crisis followed elections in Liberia and Cameroon, however. Somalia twice removed and replaced its president and prime minister peacefully and legally. In 1984 only four countries in Africa — Gambia, Kenya, Morocco, and South Africa — had newspapers that were not owned or directly controlled by the government. At present, most African states lack an independent judiciary able to protect their citizens against arbitrary government interference. (The exceptions are Kenya, Nigeria, Ghana, South Africa, and Zimbabwe.)

With a few exceptions (such as Botswana, Lesotho, and Somalia), the new states are ethnic mosaics, and their politics hinge to a considerable extent on interethnic relations. Power is frequently concentrated in the hands of dominant ethnic groups — Afrikaners in South Africa, Amhara in Ethiopia, Tutsi in Burundi. Wealthy, or reputedly wealthy, minorities have often received short shrift from their neighbors. In the 1960s Arabs were largely eliminated from Zanzibar; Ibo were at one time persecuted in northern Nigeria; Indians were expelled from Uganda and harassed in Kenya and Tanzania. In 1983 Nigeria expelled two million foreign workers. Whites were driven from Zaire, Angola, and Mozambique. The dominant whites in South Africa have come under fire for the undemocratic nature of their regimes. According to Amnesty International's annual surveys, however, dictatorships like the former Central African Empire, Equatorial Guinea, Uganda, and Guinea-Bissau have accumulated much worse civil liberties records than South Africa.

Since independence Africa has been torn by wars, civil strife, massacres, mass expulsions, and liberation struggles. There have been some twenty major wars (mostly civil wars) and forty-two coups since 1958; it is unlikely that peace and national integration will be achieved in the 1980s. By 1984 twenty states were ruled by one-party systems and one-party dictatorships, and twenty-one were under military dictatorships. (Kenya has one-party rule, but single-party elections are real political exercises in that country.)

Political fragility in Africa has been demonstrated by coups, civil wars, genocide, one-party governments, and military dictatorships. The new leaders have given priority to short-term political objectives and have neglected economic realities. People have fled (or have been driven by strife) from the new states; as a result, at present about half (five million) of all refugees in the world live in Africa.

Civil wars and military governments inevitably increased the amount spent on arms. Interstate rivalry and national wars of liberation added to the economic burden of militarization; Africa now has the second largest arms expenditure per capita in the Third World. (The Middle East spends the most.)

Institutional adaptation occurred, but it usually had disastrous and expensive consequences. First to be abolished was parliamentary, constitutional government (that is, a parliament, multiple parties, independent bureaucracies, judiciaries, civil liberties, and the rule of law). It was replaced by one-party rule, military dictatorship, or tyranny. Local government, administration, medical care, education, attitudes, and private business were also adapted to so-called African realities, but these adaptations were usually accompanied by a severe drop in efficiency, honesty, and a sense of service for the common good.

Some of the great losses in this process of institutional adaptation were the subregional, functional, and supranational bodies that the colonial governments had established. The most important ones were the federations of French West and Equatorial Africa, the Federation of Rhodesia and Nyasaland, and the East African Community and Common Market. Their destruction (justified or not) diminished the extent of interterritorial cooperation.

By 1984 several wars were being fought in Africa. More than a million men were under arms. Hundreds of thousands had been killed in Rwanda, Burundi, Uganda, the Sudan, Ethiopia, and Equatorial Guinea. Wars were continuing in Angola, where the ruling Marxist Movimento Popular de Libertação de Angola (MPLA) was being kept in power by over twenty thousand Cuban troops and hundreds of East German and Russian advisers. There were widespread dissensions in the north and in the Cabinda enclave. In the south, the pro-Western Uniao Nacional para e Independéncia Total de Angola (UNITA) was conducting a bitter guerrilla struggle (aided by South Africa) against government forces supported by Cuban troops. In Namibia, guerrillas of the South West African People's Organization (SWAPO), based in southern Angola, were battling South African troops. By 1980 a lengthy civil war — waged by the Patriotic Front of Robert Mugabe and Joshua Nkomo against a white-supported government — had just concluded; something like 30,000 Zimbabweans (black and white) had perished, and there was widespread misery in the countryside. Amin's eight-year-old regime fell in 1979 to the Tanzanian army and Ugandan guerrillas, but unrest continued in the country; banditry went almost unchecked, and government oppression and killing continued. Near anarchy prevailed in Mozambique.

In Eritrea, guerrillas have been fighting since 1961 to achieve independence from Ethiopia. About forty thousand Arab-backed guerrillas are arrayed against an Ethiopian army of two hundred thousand supported by twenty thousand Cuban troops and thousands of Soviet advisers. Somali guerrillas are still contesting Ethiopia's Ogaden Province; Arab states are supporting the partisans, and a mixture of Soviet and Cuban personnel are guiding the Ethiopians. Although the Somali lost the war in 1976, they are reported to once again control part of the Ogaden, and it seems likely that the struggle will continue well into the 1980s. An uneasy peace presently exists in war-torn Chad.

Instability has become endemic to many parts of Africa. Although the tapestry has its bright spots as well as its dark ones, civil liberties barely exist in most African countries, and political opposition groups are often arrested, imprisoned, banned, or exiled. A number of African governments could not stay in power without foreign assistance. Mobutu of Zaire depends on Moroccan and Senegalese troops to hold on to Shaba Province; the MPLA in Angola would be gone if it were not for Cuban guns.

Wars and coups have had many causes — ethnic rivalry, religious differences, liberation movements, Marxist ideology, irredentism, secessionist movements, military opportunism, and even pure adventurism. Whites clashed with black nations in southern Africa at least until 1984, when a form of détente ended South Africa's attacks on her neighbors. The less well-publicized ethnoreligious conflicts that have afflicted the southern borderlands of Islam have been even more bitter. In the Islamic Republic of Mauritania during the 1980s blacks have called for increased political representation. In the southern Sudan, after a bloody civil war during the 1960s, discontent against Muslim rule from Khartoum has continued to smoulder, and it leads to sporadic violence. In Chad, a black government was ousted by Muslim northerners supported by Libya in 1983, only to fall to another group supported by France. To give just one example, of the general increase in military strength during the 1950s, the Federation of Rhodesia and Nyasaland relied on a defense force numbering no more than 7,000 men. Three decades later, the three African successor states — Zambia, Zimbabwe, and Malawi — together maintained nine times that number under arms. Throughout Africa there has been a good deal of ethnic discontent occasioned by arbitrarily drawn colonial boundary lines that continue to divide members of the same ethnic community. These conflicts are likely to continue during the 1980s; they may become even more severe.

Africa has also suffered from interstate tensions. The peacetime armies created by the European colonizers were small in size. After gaining independence, however, Africa armed rapidly — mostly for internal security reasons. Unfortunately, these armed establishments have usually rested on a slender economic base.

As mentioned, the tapestry has some bright patches. In 1979, for instance, Africa happily got rid of three bloodstained and sadistic tyrants: the Emperor Bokassa I, head of the then Central African Empire; Francisco Macias Nguema, life-president of Equatorial Africa; and Idi Amin, life-president of Uganda. After two decades of great reluctance to indulge in self-criticism, a number of African leaders felt sufficiently secure to discuss in public a hitherto almost unmentionable subject — human rights violations committed by black governments.

In dealing with the less-developed countries, scholars have unfortunately been inclined to ignore or downplay the problems of political authority and effective rule. Most countries in Africa are not cohesive political communities; they lack effective authoritative, legitimate governments. Many Westerners have assumed that well-intentioned outsiders, by means of aid and technical assistance, could induce economic growth and thus achieve political stability. In fact, the last decade has seen a widespread decline of political order.

The reasons for this decline were complex. More and more Africans moved into the cities, where people could be organized into parties and trade unions more easily than in the villages. Communications improved. The motor truck, the transistor radio the cheaply printed newspaper, and the school all contributed to the growth of political consciousness. At the same time, popular expectations increased. The growth of the state machinery and the intrusion of the state into economic life also heightened ethnic tensions. As long as the state concerned itself only with raising taxes and arresting criminals, a villager could make his living no matter who controlled the government. But once the state began to control trade by means of marketing boards, prices by means of planning commissions, and credit by means of state banks, control of the state machinery itself became a matter of economic survival. Rival ethnic communities therefore acquired a pressing interest in the command of political power. As more and more was expected of the government, it increasingly became a target of criticism for alienated students, intellectuals, and military officers who were convinced that they had not obtained their due share of political or economic benefits.

The Failures of African Leadership

Since independence African peoples — both rulers and ruled — have widely been inclined to disregard both public morality and democratic rights. Many of Africa's leaders and their parties or clients have proved to be ineffectual, overly ethnic in orientation, and corrupt. The military rulers have seldom been an improvement. All too often, Africa's rulers have behaved as if public goods were private property. Friends, relatives, and clients have received appointments, favors, and high salaries to the detriment of the common good.[8]

As we have seen, all the states faced problems at the time of independence: poverty, lack of skills, high rates of illiteracy, unemloyment, underdevelopment, and too few schools, teachers, hospitals, doctors, and clinics. Yet there were some exceptions to this culture of poverty. For instance, at independence the Gold Coast (Ghana) had a good-sized reserve of money, a well-trained bureaucracy, and an honest judiciary. In Ghana and in many other states, however, Africa's new leaders met their challenges by opting for state control, military or one-party dictatorships, and excessive regulation. They intensified some colonial economic procedures (marketing boards, parastatals, import-substitution industries) with bigger, less efficient bureaucracies and greater state control and regulation. The new leaders sought economic growth and independence by way of Africanization, but they failed in their endeavours and often rendered their countries dependent on a kind of international dole.

Africanization was promoted at the expense of efficiency and integrity. The public sector grew; the private sector declined. Development plans became fashionable, but they were seldom successful because the planners knew too little and often diverted resources to their own pockets. Import-substitution schemes were tried in order to protect local industries and encourage industrialization. These often failed to produce efficiently, and they cost the taxpayer higher taxes and high prices for the goods produced. Many leaders became politically intolerant and authoritarian; members of the opposition were imprisoned or exiled.

African traditions of gift-giving, hospitality, and protection of kin definitely contributed to practices that, in a modern setting, appeared corrupt. Older traditions of probity — cemented by age-old kinship links and traditional religious beliefs — weakened, but the new Western values were sometimes rejected when they clashed with self-interest. Corruption and inefficiency became root causes of coups and killings. In the first fifteen years of independence, Africa suffered 114 government changes, and forty states changed governments by coups.

Gone is the enthusiasm of the first years of independence; in its stead are frustration and indolence. Mass electoral participation in Africa has neither given the masses significant amounts of practical power not allowed them to dictate to the elite.[9] And voting has certainly not increased their material well-being.

According to Ruth Collier, "post-independence electoral policy varied according to colonial inheritance and the nature of intra-elite factions."[10] The pattern of political change after independence largely derived from experiences during decolonization and the states' position in a colonial zone or region. If a state had a strong party it soon dominated the opposition and established one-party rule. Former French African states formed plebiscitary regimes and eliminated all electoral competition. In ex-British Africa, the one-party system retained some electoral competition.[11] In states that had no dominant party operating within a multi-party system, military coups followed soon after independence.

The poor performance of many African governments can be traced to regime factions. That is, the political elites did not possess effective legitimized authority, and this circumstance affected the capacity of the state to forcefully carry out its public policies. The required resources were not only material, but organizational, symbolic, and coercive. Because most African states lacked these resources, they were unable to build or to execute development schemes.[12]

The following chapters elaborate at much greater length on these observations and distinctions, as well as many others, in the aim of exploring African politics and government in a cross section of countries since the end of colonial rule. Sub-Saharan Africa is obviously an exceedingly elaborate political tapestry of some 41 states. The course of political life has varied significantly from one country and region to the next, and individual states have begun to acquire their own distinctive identities and histories. We have organized the chapters of this book on a country and regional basis (except for Lusophone Africa) in an attempt to capture something of this diversity. At the same time, however, most of these countries also have a great deal in common, as we have indicated, beginning with geography and history and extending to culture, social structure, and many other facets of life which have undoubtedly had an important role in shaping the contemporary African political experience. The following chapters have also been planned and written in accordance with a conceptual framework that aims at disclosing as much as possible of this common political experience. The conclusion attempts to draw together the major themes that emerge.

Notes

1. Johnson U. Asiegbu, *Nigeria and Its British Invaders, 1851–1920* (New York: Nok Publishers International, 1984), p. xxlx.
2. See Crawford Young, "Decolonization in Africa," in L. H. Gann and Peter Duignan, *The History and Politics of Colonialism, 1914–1960*, vol. 2 (Cambridge: Cambridge University Press, 1970), chap. 13 and Prosser Gifford and William Roger Louis, *The Transfer of Power in Africa: Decolonization, 1940–1960* (New Haven: Yale University Press, 1982). For our own interpretation, see L. H. Gann and Peter Duignan, *Burden of Empire: An Appraisal of Western Colonialism in Africa South of the Sahara* (Stanford: Hoover Institution Press, 1977 printing). For contrasting views, see, for instance, Walter Rodney, *How Europe Underdeveloped Africa* (London: Bogle 1' Cuverture Publications, 1972), or Ann Wilcox Seidman, *Outposts of Monopoly Capitalism: Southern Africa in a Changing Global Economy* (Westport, Conn.: L. Hill, 1980).
3. A. Adu Boahen, "The Colonial Era Conquest to Independence," in Gann and Duignan, *History and Politics of Colonialism*, p. 521. Colonialism is often portrayed by the metaphor of "the steel frame." This can be very misleading, however, if it is assumed that colonial administration was a large, totalitarian operation. In fact, in most territories it was a tiny and rather unobtrusive enterprise that depended very greatly on the impression rather than the substance of power. The European layer of colonial domination was remarkably thin: it was a "thin white line", as A. H. M. Kirk-Greene puts it. In the 1930s, at the peak of the high colonial period, French Africa had a population of over 18 million and was ruled by fewer than five thousand colonial officials. The Belgian Congo with a population of about 9 million, was ruled by 2,500, whereas Nigeria, with 20 million, was governed by fewer than 1,400. Following World War II the total complement of colonial positions expanded dramatically in response to the era of the welfare state. Ghana, however, with an area the size of Oregon and a population of some 4 million at the time of independence in 1957, was never governed by more than 2,500 British officials, of whom only about a tenth were commissioners and police officers. Sudan, the largest territory in Africa with a population of 9 million at independence in 1956, had a political service of 7,000, of whom only 1,000 were British. The density of government was higher in the Belgian Congo, but there were only about 10,000 Belgians in administration, magistrature, and the army in 1960.

Colonialism depended, almost more than anything else, on the competence, duty, and dedication of its administrative service. Almost to the very end of the colonial era, however, these were staffed overwhelmingly by Europeans at the crucial decisionmaking levels. And when independence arrived, or shortly thereafter, the Belgians and Portuguese packed their bags and departed from Africa. The chief means of running the state — its most important human capital — was lost precisely at the moment when it was most needed, during the difficult period of transition to self-government. The British and the French, however, stayed on in some numbers for several years.
4. See *Accelerated Development in Sub-Saharan Africa: An Agenda for Action* (Washington, D.C.: The World Bank, 1981), pp. 1–12 and L. H. Gann and Peter Duignan, *Africa South of the Sahara: The Challenge to Western Security* (Stanford: Hoover Institution Press, 1981), chaps. 1 and 2.
5. See Jennifer Seymour Whitaker, "Africa Beset," *Foreign Affairs*, vol. 62 (Spring 1984): 746–76.
6. This section draws on David B. Abernethy, "Bureaucratic Growth and Economic Stagnation in Sub-Saharan Africa" (Paper prepared for the 1984 Annual Meeting of the American Political Science Association at the Washington Hilton, August 30–September 2, 1984).

7. Ibid., pp. 8–10.

8. See John R. Cartwright, *Political Leadership in Africa* (New York: St. Martin's Press, 1983); Robert Jackson and Carl G. Rosberg, *Personal Rule in Black Africa: Prince, Autocrat, Prophet, Tyrant* (Berkeley: University of California Press, 1982); Ruth Berins Collier, *Regimes in Tropical Africa: Changing Forms of Supremacy, 1945–1975* (Berkeley: University of California Press, 1982); and Richard E. Bissell and Michael S. Radu, *Africa in the Post-Decolonization Era* (New York: Transaction Books, 1984).

9. See Collier, *Regimes in Tropical Africa*, chap. 6.

10. Ibid., p. 153.

11. Ibid., p. 154.

12. Ibid., p. 166.

1 WEST AFRICA: NIGERIA AND GHANA

A. H. M. Kirk-Greene

Introduction

When Britain handed over power to her first tropical African colony in 1957, the Gold Coast was widely recognized as Britain's model colonial possession on the continent. It had more schools and health services per capita and a better road system than any other British territory in Africa. It also boasted a robust, non-plantation, peasant economy, a prosperous middle class, a distinguished history of higher education, an able administrative elite, and a widespread respect for representative institutions. These attributes together placed the Gold Coast (in Lord Hailey's authoritative judgment) in the most prominent position among British African dependencies in terms of progress made toward the attainment of "political self-government."[1]

When Ghana celebrated its twenty-fifth anniversary on 6 March 1982, however, the country was experiencing its sixth change of regime under its tenth head of state. (Three heads of state had been executed before a firing squad, and the most famous of them had died in exile.) It had just experienced its fourth military coup d'état. Refugees, exiles, emigrants, and political prisoners were numbered in hundreds of thousands. The economy, crippled by years of escalating national debts, had seemingly stagnated to the point of no return. (Accra urged its once exultant embassies to celebrate a purposely low-profile silver jubilee.)

In contrast, twenty-one years after achieving independence, neighboring Nigeria — early on nicknamed the Giant in the Sun and later widely recognized by the sobriquet Africa's Giant — had overcome a secessionist movement, healed the wounds of a civil war, and seen its number of universities quadruple and its student population increase tenfold. It had a revenue budget of 12 billion (as compared to a budget in the mere millions at independence in 1960). Lagos had been lavishly hosting dozens of international conferences for some time.

The intent of this historical assessment at the end of two decades of independence is not to contrast Nigeria's meteoric rise to the

Table 1: Outline of Political Chronologies

	Ghana		Nigeria
6 March 1957	Independence (CPP: Kwame Nkrumah)	1 Oct. 1960	Independence (NPC/NCNC: Abubakar Tafawa Balewa)
1 July 1960	Becomes a republic		
24 Feb. 1966	Kotoka coup (NLC) overthrows Nkrumah	1 Oct. 1963	Becomes a republic
		15 Jan. 1966	Military under Ironsi takes over government
17 April 1967	Ankrah succeeds Kotoka		
22 April 1969	Afrifa succeeds Ankrah	29 July 1966	Gowon succeeds Ironsi
1 Oct. 1969	Return to civilan rule under Kofi Busia (PP)	6 July 1967–12 Jan. 1970	Nigerian civil war (Biafra)
13 Jan. 1972	Acheampong coup (NRC)	29 July 1975	Murtala Mohammed succeeds Gowon
27 April 1972	Death of Nkrumah in exile	13 Feb. 1976	Obasanjo succeeds Murtala Mohammed
5 July 1978	Akuffo (SMC) succeeds Acheampong	1 Oct. 1979	Return to civilian rule under Shehu Shagari (NPN)
4 June 1979	Rawlings I coup (AFRC)	1 Oct. 1983	Installation of Shehu Shagari for second term
24 Sept. 1979	Return to civilian rule under Hilla Limann (PNP)		
		31 Dec. 1983	Buhari coup
31 Dec. 1981	Rawlings II coup (PNDC)	27 Aug. 1985	Babangida coup

Notes:

CPP	= Convention People's Party		PNP	= People's National Party
NLC	= National Liberation Council		PNDC	= Provisional National Defense Council
PP	= Progress Party			
NRC	= National Redemption Council		NPC	= Northern Peoples' Congress
SMC	= Supreme Military Council		NCNC	= National Convention of Nigerian Citizens
AFRC	= Armed Forces Revolutionary Council		NPN	= National Party of Nigeria

status of economic giant and acknowledged leader of black Africa with Ghana's dramatic plunge from a position of initial external admiration and great internal expectation to an abyss of bankruptcy. To do so would be to ignore Nigeria's present grave economic problems painfully symbolized in its decision to celebrate the 1984 anniversary of independence in a low-key manner unknown since the dark days of the Biafran war. Rather the object of this essay is to indicate the fluctuations of fate and fortune to which West Africa's two major independent states have been subjected and to draw attention to the differing ways in which common or comparable problems have been handled by the two governments. Further, we seek to understand why there have been

Table 2: Selected Basic Indicators for Ghana and Nigeria, 1979

Country	Area (in sq. km)	Population (millions)	Life expectancy	Per capita (GNP)	Average annual growth in GNP	Average annual rate of inflation 1970–1979	Average annual growth of agriculture 1970–1979	Percentage of labor force in agriculture 1960	1979
Ghana	239,000	11.3	49 yrs.	$400	−0.8%	32.4%	−0.2%	64%	54%
Nigeria	924,000	82.6	49 yrs.	$670	+3.7	19.0	−0.3	71	55

Source: *Accelerated Development in Sub-Saharan Africa*, World Bank, 1981.

more "Ghana tragedies" than "Nigerian triumphs" among independent African nations in the quarter-century since that heady midnight hour of March 5, 1957. In other words, why has the continent experienced the horror and shame of Amin's Uganda and Nguema's Equatorial Guinea, the brief but bloody glory of Bokassa's Central African Empire, war-torn Sudan and Ethiopia, sinister Zaire and gruesome Guinea (together ranked near the bottom of the list by Amnesty International in terms of human rights), indigent Tanzania and the one-man Malawi, crippled and dependent Mozambique, bizarre and coup-drunk Togo, Dahomey-Benin and Upper Volta, and erupted Chad? We must first identify what has happened before we can attempt to diagnose why.

This essay, then, is less a synchronic political or economic comparison of Ghana and Nigeria than a diachronic comparison of the history of the two countries since independence. We seek to elaborate upon and understand two sharply polarized scholarly assessments of West Africa — to contrast Ken Post's optimistic assessment that "the inner reality is a basic political — indeed, philosophical — question: how may a decent life be ensured for the citizens of the State, and in ensuring this decent life, how may effciency be balanced against the Rule of Law and protection from arbitrary action?"[2] with John Dunn's blunt verdict (delivered less than a generation later) that, when one evaluates the performance of West Africa's rulers in the postcolonial period, "sadly, the blame is simpler to allocate than the praise."[3]

GHANA

It was Kwame Nkrumah — founding father, first prime minister and finally inaugural president of Ghana from 1951 to 1966 — who inspired David Apter to introduce to the African scene the Weberian concept of the charismatic leader.[4] Within three years of the ousting of Osagyefo the Savior, the military who had overthrown him felt satisfied that, by eradicating Nkrumaism and proscribing all those who had been associated with his philosophy, they could not only bring about the rebirth of Ghana, but eradicate the nightmare of 1957–1966 and ensure that it could never happen again. At the end of 1983 — fourteen years and nine heads of state later — Ghana appeared to be as far from regeneration as ever. Already, mass memory (proverbially short) reveres the seemingly legendary years of Nkrumah's romantico-spectacular leadership, when West Africans could hold their heads high and be proud that they came from Ghana. Yet in 1969 the Ankrah-Afrifa military regime had little doubt about who should be its candidate for prime minister of the putative Second Republic. Professor Kofi Busia — a quiet intellectual, a long-time leader of the opposition to Nkrumah, and a one-time administrator brought up in the British colonial tradition of order and good government — epitomized the opposite of everything the flamboyant Golden Boy of Africa had stood for: here was the embodiment of democratic championship and unobtrusive leadership.

But Ghana's Second Republic was even more short-lived than its first, and from 1972 to 1979 the country was once again under military rule. The back-to-civilian-rule election of 1979 was a concession wrung from the stonewalling General Acheampong and his equally reluctant successor, General Akuffo, by the determination of a bold bourgeoisie to end military rule. On the very eve of this election the army intervened once again. Flight-Lieutenant Jerry Rawlings postponed rather than canceled the impending general election. Three months later, in the wake of a rigorous and often insensitive "house-cleaning" exercise aimed at purging the country of corruption in high places, he handed back power. Nevertheless, the incoming President of the Third Republic, Dr. Hilla Limann (perhaps considered safe because he was so unknown and so inexperienced in politics), was left in no public doubt that he was head of state by grace of Jerry Rawlings, who would always be watching from the wings. The military (and Jerry Rawlings) were back in control within two years — as of December 31, 1981. Five recorded (and several rumored) coup attempts have taken place since then. This, added to Ghana's record of six heads of state dead within a decade, suggests that the country has yet to solve its fundamental problem: how to make the activities of the head of state coincide with the best interests of modern Ghana. Equally important is the question of who can fill the top position to the satisfaction of the nation.

The Legislature

Ghana has demonstrated a phenomenon familiar to independent Africa — namely a shrinking of the arena for meaningful participation and a constriction of the freedom of electoral choice.[5] This de-democratization has occurred in the commonplace West African progression of multiparty system to one-party state and eventually military rule. After securing the withdrawal of the military, the nations in Africa which have endured this type of contraction of political choice have not generally tended to revert to the one-party system. (The one-party system has now become regarded as the start down the primrose path to dictatorship.) They have instead tended to embrace the previously calumnified multiparty system — either the increasingly out-of-favor Westminster model (adopted by Ghana in 1979, Zimbabwe in 1980, and Uganda in 1981) or the American-style presidential constitution (adopted by Nigeria in 1979). As the voting figures continually proved, one-party rule made nonsense of genuine participatory democracy in Ghana's First Republic. What was significant was not the rising percentage of votes supposedly won by the president, but the decreasing number of electors who cared to cast a (progressively meaningless) vote: in the three pre-independence elections, the all-victorious Convention People's Party (CPP) never succeeded in securing the votes of more than 35 percent of the electorate.

To accept the label of opposition in the legislature increasingly became a mark of both personal courage and devotion to a lost cause. Busia in exile and Danquah in detention (where he was to die) were not only Ghanaian exemplars of the futility of taking an opposing position to the regime in power, they were also symbols of the pan-African political adage, "Those who are not publicly for us must privately be against us." In all of Africa the penalty for such treason has been severe. Ghana's Regional Assemblies — recommended by the Bourne Commission of 1955 as a viable compromise between the National Liberation Movement's fear of ethnopolitical domination and the CPP's insistence that the country was too small to sustain a federal structure — barely survived the advent of independence; they were almost immediately dismantled to make way for a strictly unitary state. Nkrumah's imaginative plan to redesign the legislative arena in a way that would do away with confrontational Government and Opposition benches was as much a blow directed against the concept of opposition as a move against the confines of a colonial legacy. His growing tendency to dominate the cabinet — with or without his loyal inner circle of Gbedemah, Botsio, Edusei, Dzewu, and Baako — was reflected in the Accra joke (reminiscent of the Irishman who began his letters with "P.S.") that the first item on the agenda was always "Any Other Business." The fact that we know much less about the role of the legislature in the short-lived Second and Third Republics is in itself an implication of their limited efficacy.

The Legal Profession

Since the nineteenth century the legal profession in Ghana has enjoyed a respected reputation.[6] The first West African to be called to the British Bar was from Ghana. (This was in 1867, eighty years before an East African lawyer qualified!) It was the legal profession that provided much of the impetus for the founding of the National Congress of British West Africa (NCBWA) in 1920 and of the country's first major political party, the United Gold Coast Convention (UGCC), in 1947. Members of the same profession were dismayed by Nkrumah's forcing through of the Preventive Detention Act in 1958, disgusted by his capricious dismissal of the chief justice, Sir Arku Korsah, in 1963 (for having brought in an acquittal verdict unacceptable to the president), and aghast at the callous detention of one of their number (the venerable Dr. Danquah, leader of the pioneer UGCC). The legal profession proved to be a more effective brake on the later excesses of Nkrumah's leadership than the emasculated political opposition, which by then was largely in disarray or exile. Similarly, it was the legal profession which, in 1977, played a notable role in bringing pressure to bear on General Acheampong (and on his successor, General Akuffo) to cancel the referendum allegedly favoring a joint military-civilian Union Government and to promote a time-table for a return to civilian rule. It was the wanton murder of three senior members of the judiciary in 1982 by soldiers dissatisfied with the judgments handed down after the trial of their comrades in Armed Forces Revolutionary Council (AFRC) that publicly manifested the creeping breakdown of law and order in the second Rawlings government. In 1983 Rawlings began a socioeconomic campaign (with identifiable overtones of class war) against the Ghanaian bourgeoisie. The legal profession, which was then in the vanguard of the middle class's trade union, the Association of Recognized Professional Bodies (ARPS), became an obvious target of the witch hunt for suspected antistate activities.[7] Lawyers were singled out by the Citizens' Vetting Committee for "re-education" in their civic duties (notably payment of taxes) and were humiliated by having their names published in the press.[8] On their own initiative the Accra-Tema workers "dissolved" the judiciary in July 1983 and one of the sans culottes-style Workers' Defense Councils unilaterally declared the "abolition" of the chief justice and announced the introduction of a popularly elected, indigenously derived legal system.[9]

Political Parties

When we turn to political parties, the sombre Ghanaian spectacle of institutional decline and fall once again darkens the picture. Ghana was the birthplace of the mass party in West Africa — that exciting and vigorous movement which for instance in Tanzania and Guinea, stood the conventional game of politics on its head. This movement told the people that politics was not the exclusive prerogative of the old-style UGCC bourgeois elite, it belonged to everybody (including the "standard six" educated, and "verandah boys" elements). The mass party movement promised that the British colonial masters would be swept out of the country on a tidal wave of popular protest and "Positive Action", culminating in "Self-Government Now" and total "Freedom". There could be few headier slogans to animate the masses than Nkrumah's call to "Seek Ye First the Political Kingdom and All Things Will be Added unto It."[10] In the 1950s the vibrance of mass party politics was palpable as the New Jerusalem took shape out of the receding mists of colonialism. To anyone who attended the superbly stage-managed CPP rallies, there could be no doubt that the vehicle of national salvation was the new kind of political party. As the slogan had it, "The CPP is a Party of the People" and "The CPP is Ghana and Ghana is the CPP." The opposition did its cause little good by resorting to violence and bombing during the 1956 general election. After a momentary reprieve resulting from the regional structure introduced as a compromise between federation and the unitary state, the opposition was gradually squeezed out of effective existence. (See Table 3.) The so-called entrenched clauses of the constitution bequeathed by the departing British were shown to be unenforceable in the face of the majority wishes of a sovereign parliament.[11]

When Ghana returned to civilian rule in 1969, the party, which

Table 3: Political Parties and Elections in Ghana, 1951–1964 (seats won)

Date	CPP	UGCC	NLM	NPP	Ind	Others
1951	34	2	—	—	2	—
1954	71	—	—	12	16	5
1956	71	—	12	15	2	4
1960	(Presidential)	Nkrumah: 89.1%		Danquah: 10.9%		
1964	(One-Party State)	For: 2.78 million		Against: 0.02 million		

NLM = National Liberation Movement

had been tarred with the Nkrumah brush, fared badly. Gbedemah's National Alliance of Liberals (NAL) gained a mere 30.4 percent of the votes, as compared to 58.7 percent for Busia's Progress Party (PP). The PP total represented more than twice the number of votes won by the CPP in the 1956 election. In 1979, Ghana made its third attempt to install a parliamentary democracy. By this time, because of continuing national decline and domestic misery, the Nkrumah link had become romanticized into an advantage rather than a liability. As a result the People's National Party (PNP) which was "unabashedly"[12] lineally descended from the CPP secured seventy-one out of 140 seats. (The Busia-associated Popular Front Party (PFP) won only forty-two.) (See Table 4.)

Table 4: Political Parties and Elections in Ghana, 1969 and 1979 (seats won)

Date	PP	NAL	PNP	PFP	UNC	ACP	Ind	Others
1969	105	26	—	—	—	—	1	8
1979	—	—	71	42	13	10	1	3

UNC = United National Convention
ACP = Action Congress Party

Ghana is not the only example in West Africa of the lamentable fact that the political party (and especially the mass party) — once the centerpiece of the anticolonial movement and the pride of the new Africa — has withered away like leaves in the dry season. The mass party has yielded to the state as the dominant national institution of postcolonial Africa.[13] And yet, whatever the pessimist — confronted by the ubiquity of life-presidents, one-party states and preventive detention legislation — is prompted to think about the democratic process in independent Ghana, he cannot doubt the continuing faith of the electorate in the fundamental legitimacy (if not always the sanctity) of the ballot box. In the popular mind in Africa, elections still count as the elections in Nigeria, Kenya and Zambia — all enthusiastically held in the final months of 1983 — amply demonstrate.

In Ghana, there have only been a few avenues for legitimate dissent against the state. Manoeuvering room for official opposition parties has been limited. In the wake of strikes, the activities of trade unions have been as tightly controlled by independent Ghanaian governments as they were by the colonial administration.[14] No Peasants' Revolt has yet emerged. Traditional rulers have been too preoccupied with sheer survival to stage a comeback. In the 1970s it was the professional classes — doctors, lawyers, academics and students — who most often spearheaded the opposition to the dictatorial state. To read the *Legon Observer* (the journal associated with Ghana's intelligentsia) was the best way to keep one's finger on the political pulse. Since Rawlings II, the heat has been turned on these Recognized Professional Bodies, by the Workers' Defense Committees (called Peoples' Defense Committees in the rural areas). These two committees, as the chosen instruments in Rawlings' "holy war" to extirpate corruption and liquidate the venal, acted out their role of the heavy mob. In particular, they seemed to relish their assaults upon the elites-to-be, the students. As a result of the swingeing budgetary provisions of 1983 (which, for example, increased the Accra–London air fare by 600 percent overnight) the students suddenly switched from supporting Rawlings' revolutionary ethos to condemning his penal economic decrees.[15]

As a last resort there was always a military option. A. A. Afrifa, the articulate coup collaborator of 1966, rationalized military intervention by asserting that in a one-party state it was really the only way to remove an unpopular government.[16] (Military governments of course, also have their own difficulties in securing legitimacy.) In the twenty-five year political history of modern Ghana, the military shares the limelight with Kwame Nkrumah. Among the founding fathers of independent Africa, Nkrumah's name will be remembered longer than that of many of his peers. As time goes by, the good that he did for Ghana and Africa may outlive the negative reputation he earned in his later period. Nothing, however, can erase from Ghanaian history the fact that twice as many military as civilian heads of state ruled Ghana in the first twenty-five years of its so-called democratic independence. When Nkrumah was unexpectedly overthrown in 1966 Ghana became one of Africa's first giants to fall to the military. Because of its giddy alternation of administrations over the succeeding fifteen years, and because of the novelty of the Rawlings phenomenon, Ghana earned a place in black Africa's political history as a case study of the military's capacity for a nonstop round of entry, exit, and encore.[17] It could well be that the Ghana-Liberia model of the enlisted men's coup and the inclusion of NCOs in the membership of a National Revolutionary or Redemption Council will become the pattern of military intervention in an Africa now inured to — and hitherto conventionally perhaps led by generals and colonels.

The Bureaucracy

Under Ghana's First Republic, the bureaucracy was undermined not so much by its purposeful politicization (both in the district commissioner cadre of the regional administration and from time to time at the ambassadorial level of the foreign service)[18] but by the flight of a number of Ghana's ablest civil servants to international organizations. The loss of men like A. L. Adu, J. S. Annaw, R. K. Gardiner, C. O. Mattei and Daniel Chapman was symptomatic of a deeper malaise. Acheampong's decision to place military personnel in charge of civilian offices constituted another blow to the ideals of the civil service. The initial impact of Rawlings II threatened the roots of the classic bureaucratic elite. Ghana's backbone now became Rawlings' bête noire. No longer does the public service — once the cynosure of every Ghanaian high-school graduate — invariably rank high in career ambition. Neither Ghana nor Nigeria has yet faced up to the implications for its national bureaucracy inherent in the kind of question that reputedly causes anxiety in the world of international finance and commerce: "If you were a Ghanaian/Nigerian, would you be prepared to negotiate a loan or contract with your country?"[19]

Parastatals

For Nkrumah, the road to independence lay not only in securing the keys to the political kingdom, but in multiplying parastatal organizations so as to gain control of all public and private enterprise. The parastatals were, and are, extravagant, incompetent and nepotistic. Despite the arguable relevance of doctrinaire public sector *dirigisme*, they have become millstones around Ghana's economic neck. They constitute a burden from which the country has been utterly unable to release itself. The first military regime thoroughly lambasted the state corporations, but fifteen years later their successors could still point to the astonishing level of mismanagement and corruption that, for example, characterized the Cocoa Marketing Board. Like Tanzania, with its hundreds of statutory corporations, Ghana has endured, but not yet learned, how counterproductive it is to attempt to govern by means of parastatal patronage. (Perhaps there is some truth behind a witty African malapropism which willfully confuses parastatals with parasiticals.)

Armed Forces

Although it was in its tenth year of military rule, in 1977 the proportion of Ghana's population serving in the armed forces was still less than 2:1,000.[20] Paradoxically, the charge that colonial administrations were preoccupied with the maintenance of law and order can be applied with equal justice to independent African governments, when one considers the percentage of their budgets allocated to defense and security. Ghana has developed its own military academy at Teshie and deliberately weakened Commonwealth training links. Concomitantly, it has found more varied sources of military supplies — especially weapons. The effect of a whole spectrum of foreign training methods and different calibers of weapons on any idea of establishing a unified and coordinated Pan African High Command or continental fire-brigade force has yet to be tested. It is a logistical problem that no general staff would welcome. (There is also evidence to suggest that the armed forces recruit a lower quality of officer than does the bureaucracy. Although some sort of military rule for Ghana seems to be an inescapable reality, few arts graduates elect for a career in the regular army. Under both the Nkrumah and Limann regimes, the once-unobtrusive secret security men became a public (often ugly) feature of daily life in Ghana.

Socioeconomic Conditions

On the surface, independence has brought with it a considerable enhancement of the physical infrastructure and social amenities in Ghana. New roads and buildings, factories and airports, schools and hospitals, and the Volta and Kainji Dams, leap to the eye as substantial accomplishments. (In contrast to the preceding colonial period where there was penny-packet development and much bush.) To a considerable extent, this welcome expansion reflects a manifold increase in the budgetary provision for it. Development however, properly consists of more than skyscraper office blocks and luxury hotels; in the race for physical prestige, the social content of true development often seems to be left behind.

We have implied that years of gross mismanagement of the economy have resulted in one of independent Ghana's insurmountable problems. Ghana's saga is rendered sadder by the historical comparative approach followed in this volume. Cocoa production, once the mainstay of Ghana's prosperity, fell from 340,000 to 277,000 metric tons between 1973 and 1977. During the same five years, the GDP annual average declined by 0.7 percent.[21] (For subsistence crops, the situation is even worse.)

Ghana, of course, is not the only country in Africa that is unable to feed itself (an alarming situation to which the UN Food and Agriculture Organization (FAO) has drawn much-needed attention).[22] Despite sporadic domestic exhortations about "green revolution", "Operation Feed Yourself" campaigns, and periodic public lip service to the supposed primacy of agricultural production, productivity levels have plummeted in Ghana (just as they have in other parts of independent Africa). In the sometimes-mistaken urge to build big, to urbanize and to industrialize at any costs, agriculture has often been ignored. In national development plans, agriculture is the poor relation. There are few countries in Africa in which the peasant farmer has as much to show for twenty-five years of "this thing called independence" as his urban cousins. The neglected yam and plantation farmer, however, can at least eat what he grows.

Julius Nyerere estimated that in Tanzania only five percent of the people could be said to have benefited economically from independence. This estimate may apply equally well to West Africa. That some Ghanaians are better off economically since independence is an undeniable and overdue recognition. It is no less axiomatic that many are worse off; indeed many are far worse off. An alarming flight from agricultural pursuits, urban drift, unemployment, precipitous inflation, and civil disorder have wrought great economic hardship. (In 1983, for instance, the price of one egg in Accra was six cedis, the official minimum daily wage was twelve cedis, and one decent daily meal for a family of five was estimated to cost 150 cedis.) There is triple-digit inflation. Since 1974 real wages have fallen by 80 percent.[23] Even the professional class has been forced to moonlight in order to live; the respectable beggar has become a familiar part of the Ghanaian street scene. As a Ghanaian academic privately put it, "Accra's professional beggar has made way for the begging professional." That there have been economic gains from independence is undeniable, but it is equally undeniable that these gains have been narrowly distributed.

The rapid rise in Ghana's population has compounded the human tragedy resulting from falling "standards of surviving." Ghana's vital statistics are daunting. The World Bank estimates that its population will double (to 23 million) by the year 2000. By the end of 1982, well over a million Ghanaians (ca. 10 percent of the population) had been compelled to leave the country in order to find employment (or sometimes merely to survive). An alarmingly high proportion of these emigrants were people in whose education the nation had substantially invested. Many were attracted by the allure of a booming oil economy in Nigeria. Tragically, in 1983 Ghana was obliged to open its borders and absorb more than a million of its own nationals who had been expelled by Lagos as illegal immigrants.

Ethnicity

Although ethnic tensions have not pervaded the politics of Ghana as perniciously as they have in Nigeria, Ghanaian society is by no means free from these stresses. Ghana has a common culture (Akan) and its two major languages (Fanti and Twi) are spoken by more than half of the population and are mutually intelligible. Nevertheless, suspicion, envy, and irredentism have often caused political divisions and threatened to split the security forces. Of the newly independent states of West Africa, however, Ghana was conspicuously (up to 1966) reflecting a positive sense of nationality ("we are Ghanaians"). (In contrast, Nigerians were still thinking primarily in terms of "we Yoruba" or "you Northerners.") In Nigeria it was the events of mid-1966 and the rise to power of Gowon that brought the minorities onto center-stage after a political generation of waiting in the wings. Similarly in Ghana it was the emergence in 1979 of the northerner Hilla Limman as the successful presidential candidate that at last allowed the long-forgotten northern peoples in upper Ghana their chance to play a full part in national decisionmaking and to be appointed to public office in a fairer power-sharing proportion.

Higher Education

One important index of administrative viability in the new nations of Africa has been the state of higher education. In Ghana the major source is the national university. In 1957 Ghana's Legon was nine years old, and characterized by a strong "gowns-and-grace" Oxbridge tradition (a phenomenon that stopped visiting American academics dead in their tracks as they searched for relevance). Today there are universities at Legon, Kumasi, and Cape Coast, together they have a student population of ca. 10,000. Under Nkrumah (and later under the military regimes of Acheampong and Rawlings II), the universities were assailed intellectually and, at times, assaulted physically. Campus life has suffered recurrent attacks of student radicalism, faculty harassment, teaching short-ages, impoverished library resources, empty bookstores and falling academic standards. There have been alternate bouts of convoca-tion and closure, degrees and demonstrations. In 1982 the authorities admitted that 30 percent of its Ghanaian professors had resigned; by 1984, only 25 percent of the normal teaching staff was in residence.[24] For the nth time, the universities were closed by the government.

NIGERIA

If Ghana's major problem-solving needs are to curb its leadership excesses and cure its economic woes, those of Nigeria (up to the 1980s) might arguably be described as ethnic centrifugalism and national integration. Since independence, public life in both coun-tries has been characterized by galloping corruption (respectively recognized as *kalabule* and kickback). The slump in the world oil market beginning in 1981, and the resultant stringent controls that OPEC imposed on the output of its members have since made the economy the number one problem in Nigeria as well as Ghana. Nevertheless, if one can overlook the ultimate blot of a civil war (and the United States demonstrated a hundred years ago that national strength can in fact be forged from such a war) one can justify the claim that Nigeria experienced a relatively greater amount of political stability and economic growth than Ghana during the 1960s and 1970s.

In constitutional terms, it can be argued that Nigeria has moved further from its colonial legacy than any other West African territory. The leap from Westminster and prime minister to Washington and president took place without the intermediate stage of a one-party system common to most independent African countries. The regional antagonisms of the First Republic, followed by the outbreak of civil war in response to secession, persuaded the Constitutional Drafting Committee of 1975 (perhaps prompted by the military head of state's desire to find a system of government that would eliminate any need for political parties) to opt for the executive presidency (rather than from the ceremonial presidential system in place in Nigeria since 1963).[25] Competitive regionalism *à l'outrance* was blamed for the collapse of the First Republic. The regional tail was allowed to wag the federal dog (albeit often quite legally). The prime minister tended to be seen (although often far from accurately) as the puppet of the Northern Peoples' Congress (NPC) and as enjoying no more than the attributed status of the northern premier's "lieutenant in Lagos."[26] In the First Republic, big-tribe chauvinism and debilitating socio-economic inequities in the distribution of power and authority were permitted to flourish at the expense of the national concept of one Nigeria.[27] As if to symbolize its disapproval of this previous constitutional imbalance, the leadership succession during the nearly fourteen years of uninterrupted military rule included an Ibo, a Yoruba, a "minorities man" and a Hausa/Fulani. (Terms of office, however, ranged from nine years for Gowon to barely six months each for Ironsi and Murtala Mohammed.) In the elections of 1979 and 1983 neither of the veteran political leaders of the First Republic who survived the assassination of their state house colleagues in 1966 (Chief Obafemi Awolowo and Dr. Nnamdi Azikiwe) succeeded in his bid for the presidency. Given the attraction of the political past in Nigeria's magnetic field, the electorate of fifty million preferred to entrust the working out of a new political system to a new man — Alhaji Shehu Shagari.

Local government is specifically excluded from the focus of this study. Nevertheless, in any analysis of change and continuity in independent Africa's inaugural quarter-century it would be a scholarly dereliction not to make at least a passing reference to Nigeria's traditional rulers. These rulers have been gradually reduced to a primarily ceremonial role by a combination of positive legislation (particularly under the military) and slow democratization. In some cases, these measures have consisted of a revision of land control. In Kano's case, under the administration of the People's Redemption Party (PRP) after 1979, mere district heads were upgraded to emirate rank (as a brusque move against the status of the Emir of Kano). "They only bring me out in public when they want to impress a visitor with a durbar", confided one such chief during the military years.[28] Yet to confuse the Second Republic's lack of a House of Chiefs with the abandonment of chiefly power, or prematurely to discount the importance and the continuing power (if no longer the constitutional authority) of the traditional ruler in contemporary Nigeria, would still be an act of social naiveté, if not political suicide.

Legislature

Inevitably, the shift from the Westminster-style parliament inherited in 1960 to the neo-American presidential system adopted in 1979 resulted in certain discontinuities in the structure and process of the legislature.[29] These results were most conspicuous in the role of the Senate. This body was transformed from a toothless House of Representatives — which often included undistinguished failures from the "real" world of electoral politics — to an active, proud, and prickly body that quickly established a record for minutely scrutinizing (and occasionally reversing) legislative proposals. So scrupulously did it vet the presidential nominations to high office that its first act in October 1983 was to send back all Shehu Shagari's carefully balanced cabinet recommendations, pending the notification of the proposed portfolios. Subsequently, the Senate declined to approve 15 percent of these nominations without further investigation of their qualifications.

Only a cynic would claim that the principal continuity in the elected state legislatures has been their infinite capacity for self-reproduction — from three in 1960 to nineteen in 1980 more states had been created, there was a potential for twice that number by 1990 — see below. The creation in 1979 of elective state governorships was also important to the reformation of the legislative process and of legislative personnel. (Between 1979 and 1983 the prestige of these governorships increased greatly in the eyes of both ambitious aspirants and canny electors.) In the 1983 general elections, more than 10,000 candidates competed for over 2,000 legislative seats. By the end of that same year, 300 local government bodies were due to return an elected majority of councilors.

Creation of States

A fundamental aspect of the changed political scene in Nigeria since independence has been the deliberate redesigning of its framework. In 1963 a fourth region, the Midwest, was carved out of the Western Region to join the Northern and Eastern Regions as one of the four component parts of the Federation of Nigeria. In 1967, on the eve of the Eastern Region's secession as the Republic of Biafra, the Federal Military Government reconstituted the four regions into twelve states (without, however, making any substantial boundary changes). By doing so, it fulfilled one of the fundamental objectives of the principal minorities' movements of the 1950s (notably the Middle Belt and Calabar-Ogoja-Rivers (COR) State movements) and reversed the recommendation of the Willink Commission (set up on the eve of independence to inquire into and allay the fears of the minorities). Agitation for the creation of more states erupted in the "wild, wild West" even before the civil war was over, but, despite the inclusion of a decision on this crucial matter in General Gowon's postwar program for a return to civilian rule by 1976, no action was taken. It was not until after Gowon's overthrow that General Murtala Mohammed set up the Irikefe panel to consider and report on the validity of the demands for the creation of more states.[30] At the end of 1975, the government announced an increase in the number of states — from twelve to nineteen. Although boundary changes were made this time, the old North-South division principle remained undisturbed.

By this time, however, any hope for the stability of an ultimate, one-time state-creating operation could be no more than a dream. None of the political parties seeking electoral support in 1979 dared write off the possibility of the creation of more states. Much of 1982 was given over to state-lobbying and parliamentary recommendations. The economic crisis in the oil world, and Nigeria's consequent austerity measures, annulled the president's premature promise that if any new states were to be created it would happen before 1983. Meanwhile, the Senate had recommended a total of over thirty new states. ("The exact number does not matter", explained one legislator in private, "so long as it is more than the USA has.") In its 1983 manifesto, the winning National Party of Nigeria (NPN) stated that although it believed the creation of new states would bring the government closer to the people, "this cannot be a once-and-for-all exercise."[31] After the general election, it seemed possible that the creation of more states would become the dominant political issue of the second period of Nigeria's Second Republic. (What the establishment of another score of states would mean to the observance of the constitutional provisions of the "federal character" of Nigeria (see below) remained to be assessed.) The return of the military at the end of 1983 however, effectively terminated all movements for new states; they were defined as "political" and promptly banned.

The "Federal Character" of Nigeria

The constitution of the Second Republic was imbued with the freshly legalized concept of the "federal character" of Nigeria. In essence, this constituted an attempt to defuse what was considered to be Nigeria's greatest threat to survival under the First Republic — a cut-throat competitiveness along geoethnic lines that undermined national integration. The new constitution sought to facilitate national integration by applying the twin principles of equality (that is, no citizen could be discriminated against because of his or her provenance, religion, beliefs, or sex) and equity (that is, no federal institution could be dominated by one group or sector of the country).[32] To insure recognition of this federal character, the constitution provided for the appointment of at least one representative from each state to a seat in the cabinet. It also provided that the appointment of ambassadors and recruitment to the armed forces (but, curiously, not to the police force) would reflect the composition of the country. Other provisions included the allocation of federal scholarship awards[33] and the necessity for the president-elect to secure both a plurality over his rivals and 25 percent of the vote in at least two-thirds of the states. The principle of the federal character was repeated in the electoral laws, which required every political party to manifest a genuine and tangible national presence and to exercise a truly national appeal. As time went on, it became clear that problems might arise from demands to extend the concept of the federal character to determine admission into federal training institutions, universities, parastatals and even the private sector. If the principle were to have been reduced to a matter of simple mathematics, the primacy of merit would have been at risk. Nevertheless, the concept of the federal character of Nigeria could be considered to have been a novel and necessary safety device for the new Nigeria.

Political Parties

At independence Nigeria had three major political parties. Each party was dominant in its regional homeland but virtually ineffective outside of it. The three parties consisted of the Northern Peoples' Congress (NPC), led by the Sardauna of Sokoto; the National Convention of Nigerian Citizens (NCNC), led first by Dr. Nnamdi Azikiwe and subsequently by Dr. Michael Okpara (Eastern Region) and the Action Group (AG), led by Chief Awolowo (Western Region). (From 1964 on the NCNC also dominated the Midwest.) By the end of 1965 there were eighty-one registered political parties. Major minority parties included the United Middle Belt Congress (UMBC), Northern Elements Progressive Union (NEPU), National Independence Party (NIP), the Midwest Democratic Front (MDF), and the Northern Progressive Front (NPF). Although the federal government reflected a multiparty system, the three regional governments virtually constituted one-party states. Attempts like those by the AG (in 1959) and the NCNC (in 1964) to storm the North, or by the NPC (in 1962–63) to establish a presence in the Midwest, resulted in spectacular failures. The first upset to this triangular alignment came in 1962, when the AG split over an issue of domestic tactics. Eager to liquidate Awolowo's threatening hegemony over the Yoruba, the NPC helped a caretaker administration in the West and then supported the breakaway Nigerian

Table 5: Parties and Elections in Nigeria, 1951–1964 (seats won)

	NPC	NCNC	AG	UNIP	NEPU	UMBC	NNDP	MDF	Ind.	Others
Federal										
1954	84	56	23	—	—	—	—	—	7	11
1959	134	89	73	—	—	—	—	—	—	16
1964	162	84	21	—	—	—	36	—	5	4
Regional										
1951 North	(overwhelming)	—	—	—	—	—	—	—	—	—
East	—	65	—	4	—	—	—	—	—	—
West	—	30	45	—	—	—	—	—	—	—
1953 East	—	72	—	12	—	—	—	—	—	—
1956 North	100	—	4	—	9	11	—	—	7	—
West	—	32	48	—	—	—	—	—	—	—
1957 East	—	64	13	5	—	—	—	—	2	—
1960 West	—	33	79	—	—	—	—	—	—	10
1961 North	156	—	—	—	1	9	—	—	—	—
East	—	106	15	—	—	—	—	—	20	5
1963 Mid-West	—	53	—	—	—	—	—	11	—	—
1964 West	—	2	15	—	—	—	73	—	—	4

Notes:

NPC = Northern People's Congress
NCNC = National Council of Nigeria and the Cameroons (later National Convention of Nigerian Citizens)
AG = Action Group
UNIP = United National Independence Party
NEPU = Northern Elements Progressive Union
UMBC = United Middle Belt Congress
MDF = Midwest Democratic Front
NNDP = Nigerian National Democratic Party

Table 6: Parties and Elections in Nigeria, 1979 and 1983

1979	NPN	UPN	NPP	PRP	GNPP	NAP
Presidential	34%	29%	17%	10%	10%	—
Seats Won:						
Gubernatorial	7	5	3	2	2	—
Senate	36	28	16	7	8	—
House of Representatives	168	111	78	49	43	—
State Assemblies	487	333	226	144	157	—
1983						
Presidential	48%	31%	14%	4%	2%	1%
Gubernatorial	Other data					
Senate	incomplete					
House of Representatives	or					
State Assemblies	unreliable					

National Democratic Party (NNDP) of Chief Samuel L. Akintola. The lines were further redrawn for the 1964 general election (the first since independence), when the NPC renounced the NCNC, its former partner at the center. Subsequently, the election became a bipartite contest between two alliances: the Nigerian National Alliance (NNA – NPC + NNDP + MDF) versus the United Progressive Grand Alliance (UPGA – NCNC + AG + NPF). The breakdown of law and order in the Western Region after Akintola's fraudulent election victory in October 1965 led directly to the attempted coup of January 15, 1966 and the consequent military takeover. Following these events, all political parties were banned.

The ban was officially lifted in 1978. Informal soundings and covert understandings worked out behind the scenes at the sessions of the Constituent Assembly took shape in 1978 as putative political parties.[34] Out of more than fifty political associations, only five were ultimately recognized as parties by the Federal Electoral Commission (FEDECO) and permitted to contest the 1979 elections. Four of the five new parties — the National Party of Nigeria (NPN), the Unity Party of Nigeria (UPN), the Nigerian Peoples' Party (NPP), and the Peoples' Redemption Party (PRP) — were led by leaders of major political parties of the First Republic; the leader of the Great Nigerian People's Party (GNPP) had held ministerial office under Abubakar Tafawa Balewa in the 1960s. (Lineal political descent was thus plainly discernible.)

At the time of the 1983 general election this picture had changed only minimally, a sixth party, the Nigerian Advance Party (NAP), entered the list. Attempts to create a Progressive Peoples' Party (PPP) out of the four other parties to challenge the NPN on a single ticket failed because it could not be decided whether Awolowo or Azikiwe was to be the sole presidential candidate. As a result, the UPN, the NPP and the breakaway factions of the PRP and the GNPP never got beyond the loose formation of a Progressive Peoples' Association (PPA). In addition, FEDECO, which had previously refused to recognize the breakaway factions of the PRP and GNPP as new parties, denied the application of these groups and the NPP to merge into a new PPP. These controversial decisions had the effect of disqualifying a number of contestants and creating many last-minute shifts in party affiliation. As expected, President Shehu Shagari increased his personal backing on a nationwide basis. His party's success in securing twelve of the governorships (as compared to seven in 1979), a comfortable majority in both houses of the National Parliament (as compared to the need for a working accord with the NPP in 1979), and the loosening of the UPN grip on the Yoruba strongholds was gained by massive rigging.

In addition to the controversies that erupted over a number of the declared results (some of which bordered on the unbelievable), the 1983 elections resulted in the elimination of the minority parties GNPP, PRP and NAP. The first two had been riven by factional infighting before and during the electoral campaign; the PRP had suffered the loss of its leader, Malam Aminu Kano who died only a few weeks before the presidential election.[35] The NAP had never established itself as a serious contender; there were those who thought its grounds for recognition by FEDECO had been stronger in 1979 than they were in 1983. Whether the eclipse of the minor parties would or would not have also resulted in the end of the radical left was a conundrum left unsolved by the return of the military.

The morning after the elections of 1983, however, Nigerians were already thinking ahead to 1987.[36] Advocates of a three-party system were not unaware of the tragic triangular party war of the First Republic. Those in favor of a two-party system did not look forward to a replay of the North-South antagonism of the 1960s. Voices arguing for a de jure one-party state in the wake of the massive NPN victory quickly had their knuckles rapped by the president himself. (The NPN victory was by no means a landslide.

Awolowo actually increased his following and wrested Kwara State from the NPN, the NPP made inroads into Niger State; and the PRP defiantly held on to Kano, the heart of Hausaland). It seemed more likely that internal fragmentation in the NPN would increase, and that there would be dissension over the critical issue of who would win endorsement as the presidential candidate in the context of "zoning". That is how effectively the NPN would be able to enforce party discipline in order to honor its reaffirmed commitment to the allocation of the four designated top political posts — president, vice-president, chairman of the party, and president of the Senate — to the four geopolitical areas of the country on a rotational basis (to reflect the federal character of the country and to disarm accusations of "northern hegemony in perpetuity")? The return of the military, however, rendered all such speculation moot.

The Military

In a consideration of the military rule in Nigeria, three things stand out. All are best described by a comparison with the Ghana experience. First, in Nigeria the military were continuously in power for thirteen and three-quarter years (more than twice as long as the civilian government immediately following independence). In contrast, Ghana experienced half-a-dozen alternating military and civilian regimes over the same twenty-year period. (Continuity of the Nigerian type may well be a less unsettling experience than the alternating exchange of civilian and military regimes.) Secondly, Nigeria did not undergo a radical, left-wing military takeover like that of the Rawlings regime. (The Nzeogwu spectre of January 1966, when this puritanical Ibo officer momentarily took power in Kaduna, constituted the closest threat to something like this.) Thirdly, in 1979 the military in Nigeria honorably handed power back to the civilians in strict accordance with the 1975 program (although, admittedly, the predecessor Gowon regime had reneged on its promise to do so in 1976) and departed from the political scene with a relatively respectable reputation. In Ghana, Rawlings justified his brusque intervention in June 1979 by asserting (correctly) that senior officers had tarnished the honor of the military by their brazen corruption. (The resultant breakdown in normal disciplinary relations and command structures between officers and enlisted men has arguably been every bit as harmful to the reputation of the Ghanaian military — as evidenced by their subsequent wanton disregard for innocent civilians' lives.) Actually, the incidence of corruption within the officer cadres of the military was of equal concern to the Nigerians as to the Ghanaians, the public strictures of General Gowon — and the surprisingly high number of Nigerian officers who were cashiered for peculation — confirm this. In any case, the wheel turned full circle on December 31, 1983, when the army once more seized power and added Nigeria to the mounting total of Economic Community of West African States (ECOWAS) countries in which democracy had yielded to militarism.

The Bureaucracy

The quality of some of Nigeria's top civil servants — especially in light of their awesome responsibilities — has been continually impressive. Their successful roles in keeping the nation from falling apart during a civil war, and in keeping it going for much of the military period, have been truly remarkable. It is their quantity, however, that takes one's breath away. In 1960 less than 20,000 civil servants had been employed by the federal government and three regional governments combined; by 1984, (even after 10,000 had been removed by Murtala Mohammed's "Operation Dead-woods" and 55,000 by the Buhari purges) 100,000 were still employed by twenty administrations.[37] The Udoji Commission of 1975 reaffirmed the superiority (in status and salary) of the administocracy over the technological elite. In the 1970s the opening of the Staff College at Badagry, the Nigerian Institute of International Affairs (NIIA) in Lagos, the Institute of Policy Studies at Jos, and several seminars convened at the Institutes of Administration in Zaria and Ife finally brought the civil, military and academic elites closer together. On the eve of the withdrawal of the military, the Lagos "super-permanent secretaries" made their most dramatic break with their ethos and their education by speaking out publicly against the political class and indicating an unambiguous preference for the military. The military, they argued, let them get on with their jobs without interference and without the need that politicians had to play to the public gallery.[38] Nigeria has eschewed the Indian model of a superior cadre in its relations between federal and state civil services. It has also rejected the East African model, by opting for a static rather than a peripatetic Staff College. Nevertheless, senior state bureaucrats have sometimes been reluctant to be sent on a course to Lagos and have often been sensitive to the built-in "heaven-bornness" of their federal counterparts.[39] Nor did the Ministry of External Affairs professionals take kindly to the "amateurism" of the NIIA during the Obasanjo regime (and soon settled the score once the civilians returned to office).[40] Nigeria has contributed more than its share of top-level international civil servants, including A. Adedeji (Economic Commission for Africa or ECA), S. Adebo, G. Amachreen and O. Yolah (all in various UN agencies), P. Onu (Organization for African Unity or OAU), T. Elias (International Court of Justice or ICJ) and Emeka Anyaoku (Commonwealth Secretariat).

Parastatals

The performance quality of statutory corporations has not been received any more enthusiastically by Nigerian than by Ghanaian consumers. For instance, in the period of widespread power cuts in the 1970s, the acronym NEPA was redubbed, to read "No Electric Power Again." The government had to call in the army to clear the docks for the Nigerian Ports Authority (NPA). The Nigerian Airways "Jumbo" symbol has been called a "white elephant." The chairman of the Presidential Commission on Parastatals summed it up well in one of the last meetings of the Senate, when he remarked, "Only God can solve the problems of NEPA" (The Nigerian Electric Power Authority). As General Buhari was to comment at a university commencement ceremony in 1984, Nigerians suffered from "the stigma and discomfort of a country where nothing works." But at least there has been no socialist ideological rationalizations of state enterprises, and Nigerian businessmen (capitalists to the core) have been too shrewd to allow anything as injurious to their talents as a single National Trading Corporation to be set up. The need for statutory corporations that would employ staff who could not measure up to the stricter standards of a colonial-controlled civil service could be justified on the eve of independence, when accelerated Africanization was essential. As illustrated by the 1966 public revelations of inefficiency, indifference, tribalism and nepotism, however, standards once lowered are not easily restored, whether at the level of top management or board membership, or simply in routine jobs. In West Africa, parastatals have yet to attract the best people or elicit the best performances from them.

Security Forces

The percentage of federal goverment revenue spent on defense rose from 9.6 percent in 1961 to 39.0 percent in 1970 (during the Biafran war), it then decreased to 16.1 percent in 1978 (although by this time revenue had increased a thousand percent over that of 1970.)[41] It was the civil war that caused the abnormal rise in Nigeria's military strength (from 10,000 men under arms in 1966 to 250,000 three years later). Demobilization was slow after the civil war, and it was another ten years before the army was reduced to a number that Lagos then considered to be its optimum strength — approximately 140,000. An accurate breakdown of the army is almost impossible to calculate. The open convention of the budget in the 1960s, which enumerated X brigadiers, Y colonels and Z other ranks has been replaced by a clam-like, one-line "Salaries" item.

The Nigerian army, which at the time of independence had earned a good name for itself as part of the OAU peacekeeping force in the Congo, did not distinguish itself as an efficient, effective fighting force in the Biafran war of 1967–1970. (In his memoirs, General Obasanjo even castigated the top military brass for the incompetence of their strategic leadership in the operations against Onitsha.)[42] By the time of the war, however, the Nigerian army had already been torn apart (in 1966) by its own murders, desertions, and indiscipline. Nevertheless, Nigeria's signal failure to mount a credible peacekeeping operation in Chad in 1982 had political, rather than military, causes — including cabinet indecisiveness and lack of support for Nigeria by some of its African friends. Neither the air force nor the navy have shown themselves operationally significant. The Nigerian police force came off second best in the Maitatsine religious riots in Kano in 1980 and in Maiduguri in 1982. It sustained heavy losses, and the Ministry of Defense had to call in artillery and aircraft to restore the situation. As one senior officer privately observed, had an incident like this (which resulted in 4,000 deaths) occurred before independence, it would have brought down the governor (and probably the home government as well). The Defense Academy at Kaduna (supplemented by the specialist schools at Jaji and Jos) at present handles the training of Nigeria's officer corps. Although the army provides jobs for many unemployed youth, except in the technical branches it is not yet considered an attractive career for the better educated. The Ministry of Defense has expressed concern over the inability of the army to recruit the requisite representation from all the states to fulfill the federal character requirements. The martial races tradition of the colonial period has proved hard to erase.[43]

The Economy

The performance of the Nigerian economy during the first two decades since independence was subsequently dwarfed by the tremendous impact of oil. By 1980 Nigeria had become the sixth largest producer of petroleum in the world, a position reached within ten years of its emergence as an oil-producing country. Over 95 percent of federal revenue was derived from oil. In black Africa oil came to mean Nigeria, and Nigeria to mean oil (just as it has meant Texas in the United States and Alberta in Canada). Export crops were virtually abandoned, and subsistence farming was neglected. Urban drift grew alarmingly; immigrants came to the cities from both inside and outside the country (above all, from Ghana). The dimensions of the oil boom were such that one gained the impression that it was easier to construct a new highway or put up a fresh headquarters office in Nigeria than to repair one recently built. With production at over 2 million barrels per day at $40 a barrel, Nigeria — and many Nigerians — became rich beyond imagination.

This buoyant economy persisted until 1982, when the world oil market suddenly underwent a far steeper decline than it had in any

Table 7: End-Use Analysis of Imports to Ghana and Nigeria, 1965 and 1980 (percentage of total imports)

	Ghana		Nigeria	
	1963–65	1978–80	1963–65	1978–80
Nondurable consumer	45.5%	24.1%	39.2%	20.6%
Durable consumer	9.7	5.3	8.1	7.9
Raw materials	24.9	39.5	23.7	22.9
Capital equipment	14.0	25.0	27.6	48.5

Source: Douglas Rimmer, *The Economics of West Africa*, 1984.

Table 8: Selected Nigerian Exports, 1960–1980 (percentages of total exports in value)

	1960	1970	1980
Cocoa beans	21.7%	15.2%	2.2%
Cotton	3.7	1.5	minimal
Groundnuts	13.5	5.0	minimal
Hides and skins	2.5	0.6	minimal
Oil	2.6	58.2	96.3
Palm kernels	15.4	2.5	0.1
Rubber	8.4	2.0	0.1
Timber	4.1	0.7	minimal
Tin	3.6	3.9	0.1

Sources: Anthony Kirk-Greene and Douglas Rimmer, *Nigeria Since 1970*, 1981; Douglas Rimmer, *The Economies of West Africa*, 1984.

of its previous cycles. The price of oil fell by 25 per cent, and Nigeria's daily output was cut to two-thirds. After a year of crisis meetings, OPEC could insure its survival only by imposing grudgingly agreed-upon quotas and price ceilings. Under this accord, Nigeria (which had held out for and secured special consideration in 1983) was restricted to the production of 1.3 million barrels per day at a selling price of $30 a barrel. In 1983–84 Nigeria was able to earn only half the revenue it had earned in 1980 — much less than the amount upon which its ambitious National Development Plan had been predicated. Austerity succeeded inflation, which by 1982 was over 20 percent in Lagos (and subsequently closer to 40 percent). Development was trimmed, and belts had to be tightened all around. After the mid-1983 election, even before Shehu Shagari was sworn in, the first thing the victorious NPN did was to promise that the economy, and agriculture in particular would be the first priority of the new administration. (On the eve of the election it had announced that its aim was self-reliance in food crops). A stronger Ministry of Agriculture was created, and a professional presidential adviser on agriculture was appointed. A siege economy went into operation.

Unfortunately, all these measures amounted to shutting the stable door after the horse had bolted. Within hours of his announcement of the "most austere" budget that Nigeria had ever known, Shehu Shegari was overthrown. Although the military attributed their intervention inter alia to the chronic state of the nation's economy, other than quitting OPEC, they had few

Table 9: Nigeria's Oil Statistics, 1966–1982

Year	Average barrels per day (millions)	Annual total (millions)	Average price per barrel (US $)
1966	0.4	152	?
1969	0.5	197	2.2
1970	1.1	396	2.3
1971	1.6	569	3.1
1972	1.8	665	3.4
1973	2.1	750	4.8
1974	2.3	823	14.7
1975	1.8	651	12.2
1976	2.0	758	13.8
1977	2.1	766	14.6
1978	1.9	695	14.2
1979	2.4	840	20.7
1980	2.1	753	35.2
1981	1.4	526	38.8
1982	1.3	472	35.7
1983	1.2	452	30.0
1984 (estimated)	1.3	470	28.0

Sources: Anthony Kirk-Greene and Douglas Rimmer, *Nigeria Since 1970*, 1981; Douglas Rimmer, *The Economies of West Africa*, 1984; *Financial Times* (London), 23 January 1984.

Table 10: Central Government Functional Expenditure for Ghana and Nigeria, 1978

Country	Defense	Education	Health	Housing	Social Welfare	Agriculture	Roads
Ghana	5.3%	15.6%	7.3%	0.0%	9.7%	12.2%	5.1%
Nigeria	17.9	9.6	2.2	3.2	1.1	2.6	13.9

In 1982–83 the amount allocated in the Nigerian Federal budget (out of a total budget on recurrent expenditure of ₦ 4658.7 million) was ₦ 660.8 million to defense, ₦ 387.3 million to police, ₦ 549.4 million to education and ₦ 34.1 million to agriculture. For capital expenditure, the figures were ₦ 450.4 million to defense and ₦ 88.8 million to police (out of a total budget of ₦ 5308.8 million).

Sources: *Accelerated Development in Sub-Saharan Africa*, World Bank, 1981; *Africa South of the Sahara*, 1983–1984.

immediate economic options beyond continuing the discredited civilian regime's policy: maintaining oil production, freezing wages and cutting back jobs in the public sector, seeking a massive loan from the IMF (if need be accompanied by devaluation of the grossly over-valued naira), liberalizing imports, and ending the subsidy of petroleum within the country. In a nutshell, the economy was in a chronic mess. By 1983 Nigeria — the eagerly courted big spender of the mid-1970s — had become a notorious debtor in the banking world and a bad name in international trade circles.

Population and Ethnicity

"One African in every four is a Nigerian" and "Nigeria is the fourth biggest democracy in the world" were the proud boasts of the Federal Office of Information in 1983. But since no acceptable census had been undertaken in Nigeria since 1962–63 (and even that was considered highly suspect at the time), this self-advertisement constituted a claim that was hard to grasp and harder to prove. Estimates of Nigeria's population range from 80 million to 120 million people. FEDECO's questionable total of 65 million registered voters in 1983 would imply a population of 120–150 million (given that in Nigeria, as in much of Africa, over half the population is under 18). A figure of 85 to 95 million is a more acceptable one. The World Bank projects 172 million for the year 2000 and doubles that for twenty years later.[44] Political passion (rather than administrative incompetence) has prevented Nigeria from taking a genuine census since independence.[45] General Gowon's administration was deeply harmed by the charade of its 1973–74 census, which reported an increase in inhabitants from

Table 11: Population Figures for Ghana and Nigeria, 1953–1983 (millions)

Ghana		Nigeria	
1950	4.2	1953	30.42
1960	6.73	1963	55.64
1970	8.56	1973	79.76
1980	11.5	1983	84.7 (est.)

55 million to 80 million within a decade. General Murtala Mohammed wisely eschewed a census count before the return to civilian rule. It is, however, difficult to understand how a government worthy of the name can even think about planning ahead without knowing the size of its population.

If Ghana has guaranteed itself a place in every textbook on the subject of the military in African politics, any textbook on ethnicity would be incomplete without data from Nigeria. For all their claims to open access, Nigerian political parties from 1951 to 1966 were strictly constituted along ethnic lines. Nigeria became the arena of ethnic politics par excellence. Although the Biafran allegation of genocide against the Ibo people was shown to be over-inflated propaganda, ethnically motivated animosity and bitter competitiveness was serious enough to induce the Second Republic to introduce the deliberate device of the federal character (see above). This measure was intended to defuse the situation and prevent any repetition of the ethnically aggravated divisiveness of the First Republic. In the Second Republic, the common Nigerian rationalization of the 1960s and the 1970s,[46] "We are being discriminated against by them and they are preventing us from getting a proper share of amenities and offices", began in the 1980s to be replaced by arguments that explained how the creation of more states would allow greater economic development and better social services. In Nigeria, as in Ghana, it is probably patronage rather than ethnicity that is still the major determinant of sociopolitical success. Although, at present, patron-client relationships are still generally as influential as considerations of class in these countries, it is questionable — in industrializing Nigeria and in currently anti-elitist Ghana — how much longer this will remain so.

Religion and Education

Denominational religious statistics are elusive. Census superintendents, sensitive to charges of divisiveness, generally fight shy of them. They are also often inflated by convert-conscious church chroniclers. A safe assumption would be that there has been an increase in the practice of both Islam and Christianity since independence (at the expense of the practice of African traditional religions ATR). Few ATR children leave school without at least nominal conversion to Islam or Christianity. Adult conversions

Table 12: Education Statistics for Ghana and Nigeria, 1960 and 1980 (percentage of age group)

Country	Primary		Secondary		Tertiary	
	1960	1980	1960	1980	1960	1980
Ghana	38%	69%	5%	36%	minimal	1%
Nigeria	36	98*	4	16	minimal	2

Source: World Bank, *Accelerated Development in Sub-Saharan Africa*, 1981; *World Bank Development Report*, 1983.

Note: *This figure does not agree with UNESCO estimates, which are around 68 percent.

(although they by no means match the dubious rate of the Sardauna of Sokoto's personal evangelistic campaigns of the early 1960s, when tens of thousands of pagans publicly adopted Islam) continue to be a feature of Nigerian life. Independent Nigeria has never indulged in inter-denominational strife. (The Biafrans claimed a *jihad* against the Christian minority, but this accusation made no sense in light of the predominantly Middle Belt, Christian composition of the federal army. Similarly, the pogroms of 1966 were ethnically, not religiously, inspired.) But Nigeria's reputation for freedom to worship and religious equality — reaffirmed in the 1979 constitution — was jolted by the outbreak of religious violence by the millenarian "maititsine" movement viewed by most Nigerian Muslims as heretical in Kano in 1980, in Borno and Kaduna states in 1982, and in Yola in 1984.

At independence Nigeria had two universities. Two decades later it had twenty-four, eight of them state-owned. At present there are nearly 200,000 students and 10,000 university and polytechnic teachers. The Joint Admissions Matriculation Board had 165,000 applicants for 100,000 university places in 1983. (There were 31,000 applicants for lawschool alone!)[47] In the same year the federal government awarded 3,000 post-graduate scholarships (in addition to those awarded by state scholarship boards). Although there has been much encouragement of the natural and applied sciences, the arts and social studies still retain their preindependence popularity among school and university students. There are over 2 million pupils in secondary schools in Nigeria, and 15 million pupils in primary schools who are part of the ambitious, costly and successful University Primary Education (UPE) scheme initiated in 1975. The UPE program accounts for the majority of school age children in Nigeria, and it is now ready for rigorous evaluation.[48] Despite the heavy investment in teacher training, teaching remains a strikingly unpopular career — as the continuing recruitment of expatriate (until 1982, primarily Ghanaian) teachers shows. University teachers have demonstrated a new tendency to leave the campus and take up posts in public life — as, for example, federal ministers, state commissioners, secretaries to the state government, advisers to the governor, and politicians. The National Youth Service Corps, which requires twelve months (well-paid) service from every Nigerian student before he or she is allowed to take up employment in the country, has overcome an initial cool response from students in 1975 and now elicits enthusiasm from many of its "Corpers." An objective assessment of the contribution of the National Youth Service Corps (NYSC) to national integration (a goal toward which the Federal National Schools have already made significant progress) might prove a worthwhile exercise. A rationalization of the numerous universities would also be advisable; establishing a few selected centers of excellence would be preferable to scrambling for the same teaching facilities at every university. The new military government has already presented the universities the unwelcome news that their budgets are to be slashed and their total number reduced by the enforced amalgamation of more than half of the federal technological universities.[49] A clear answer has not yet emerged to the fundamental question of whether the presence of more universities in Nigeria has fostered a broader sense of national unity or simply increased individual state loyalties.

CONCLUSIONS

Writing in the aftermath of self-government, Ken Post foretold that, if the new rulers give way to "self-interest and love of power for its own sake, the result will be certain misery, probable anarchy, and the condemnation of posterity."[50] Writing after the experience of two decades of independence, Richard Rathbone felt that in Ghana "there is a widespread cynicism about national politics and politicians" and "the wholesale success of the urban minority . . . has been essentially parasitic." Gavin Williams and Terisa Turner foresaw that postmilitary Nigeria would repeat the civilians' "failure of politics", that is, it would fail to demonstrate "either the will or the capacity to tackle the sources of political instability."[51] J. F. Ade Ajayi, one of Africa's leading historians, in a retrospective assessment of the expectations of independence, wrote that education "soon ceased to be the dominant factor in the access to power . . . more important were the ability to monitor and manipulate governmental patronage and the historic rivalries of different ethnic and communal groups."[52] For one of Africa's leading economists, Adebayo Adedeji, the nagging question for Ghana and Nigeria (and other countries in Africa) was incontrovertibly plain: "How have we come to this sorry state of affairs in the postindependence years which seemed at the beginning to have held so much promise?"[53] Barbara Okeke felt that Rawlings's withdrawal in September 1979 was nothing short of "a revolution betrayed."[54] The Nigerian historian, E. A. Ayandele held that his country's independence movement had already been traduced by what he stigmatized as its "collaborative elite."[55] Most recently, Professor Ajayi has soberingly argued that, rhetoric aside, the search for democracy is obviously not particularly high on the African leaders' lists of priorities. "They are more likely to argue," he realistically concludes, "that in the initial stages of nation building following decolonization, other problems such as national integration, establishing effective organs of management in a government, and coping with an unstable world economic system must feature on the agenda ahead of the search of democracy."[56] Presumably, in both new nations, the Revolution is yet to come (if that is really where salvation lies).

Many of West Africa's iconoclastic intellectuals are too young to have ever set eyes on the veteran nationalists they scorn so knowingly. If there has been betrayal, it can be argued that it is primarily an economic and moral one. Despite the claims of a younger generation of radical critics, there was no more appropriate, effective, or timely slogan for nationalist strategy in the 1950s than Kwame Nkrumah's "Seek Ye First the Political Kingdom." It is in the pathetically patchy distribution of socioeconomic rewards (as opposed to the personal acquisition of untold wealth) that the independent governments of Africa have most glaringly failed to deliver the goods (except, of course, to themselves and their clients). Independence has failed to meet the legitimate expectations generated by its promoters. The application of the slogan "Life More Abundant for All" has been reduced to the fortunate few.

Blame should by no means be exclusively attributed to the ruling elite. As part of the Third World, Africa has been caught up in the maelstroms of the international market economy. Crops, metals and oil, are all products susceptible to cataclysmic cycles of glut and scarcity. The dismal economic record of many African states is often a result of a failure to diversify and manage the economy in the wake of a profligate, sometimes wayward, dissipation of previously existing assets. Many African governments have contributed to the failure to achieve an acceptable level of economic self-determination by their wilful neglect of agriculture. (The success stories of India, China, and much of Southeast Asia — all of which have far larger populations and far less arable land than Africa — bear witness to the fact that careful agricultural planning can enable Third World countries to feed themselves.)

As a result of the new political alignments of the second half of the twentieth century, Africa has been prey to and often a willing pawn of, the whims and strategic needs of the major powers. If 1984 produces a centennial replay of the Scramble for Africa, this time the foreign powers may be there by invitation, not intervention.[57] The new imperialism, in contrast to the old colonialism, may no longer be the sole prerogative of excolonial powers — or even of non-African nations. It may be an African power that will establish new "spheres of influence." The new imperialism will not need a structure of plumed proconsuls. It could be just as neatly effected by the giving or withholding of aid or arms. The feature that will distinguish the domination of 1984 from that of 1884 may well turn out to be its ideological input. To place instant blame for disappointment and disaster on the colonial legacy is itself the worst manifestation of that psychological inheritance.[58] Nevertheless, total independence is a long way off (if indeed total independence is achievable by any modern nation in the context of the interlocking political economics of the twentieth century). External influence and internal economic mismanagement have together contributed to and culminated in domestic political instability in Africa. Over the past twenty-five years, these two factors have inflicted undeserved misery on long-suffering populations and have devalued the worth of human life. In statistical terms, the total number of people killed in these twenty-five years has probably exceeded that caused during the whole period of the colonial regime.

A quarter of a century is a long time in the history of modern Africa; it is almost the same length of time that most of Africa has been independent. Transformation has been substantial. If Nadine Gordimer's "honored guest"[59] were to revisit West Africa, he would often be hard put to reconcile his memories of then with the vivid actualities of now. Stubborn continuities have mingled with abrupt discontinuities. Political sovereignty is assertive — on occasion, abrasively so. Economic independence may be rather an outworn idea, given the complexity of international market forces; economic interdependence is probably a more realistic modern goal. In a cultural sense decolonization still has a way to go. Some inherited institutions have survived; others have succumbed, although understandably some have been Africanized. If the New Jerusalem has not yet materialized, the alternative is not necessarily a Vale of Tears. In countless respects, achievements and progress have been enormous. The meaning of democracy itself may have undergone changes. (Has it not done so in the West since the Greeks coined the word?) There is no reason why its interpretation, practice, or priority should remain a Western preserve. The neo-mythical faith in the legitimacy (if not always the sanctity) of the ballot-box persists unabated in Africa. Nevertheless, with the exception of the offshore island of Mauritius in 1981, no African country has yet experienced what India under Indira Gandhi did in 1977 — the phenomenon of an incumbent administration, defeated at the polls, gracefully conceding victory to the opposition. The fact that for nearly thirty years there has never been a parliamentary change of government (in mainland black Africa) does not bode well for democracy.

Perhaps the greatest discontinuity in Ghana, Nigeria and much of the rest of Africa (especially the northern half) has been the about-face in the role of the military.[60] The military has moved from serving as guards of honor and acting as national frontier defense force to occupying center-stage as the single most influential force on the political scene. In contrast to yesterday's governors-general, no contemporary president (whether or not his country has experienced a coup) can dismiss the military factor from his political decisions and live to tell the tale.

This chapter is not meant to be a single comparison between Ghana and Nigeria. Nevertheless, comparisons are useful for specific illustrations, and they are particularly inescapable when it comes to conclusions. Any historical review of the performance records of the neighboring countries of Ghana and Nigeria in their quarter-century of independence, inevitably necessitates some kind of comparative framework.

Distinct differences between these two prima facie comparable countries can be found both in their colonial histories and in their subsequent methods of postcolonial self-determination. Their different statuses were recognized by the colonial power; after 1886 Britain made no attempt to unite the two countries in some putative West African federation and never obliged one colony to be governed by the pace or policy of the other. At independence, their differences were very marked. Ghana manifested a sense of palpable national unity and exuded an air of "we are Ghanaians." Nigeria unambiguously trinitarian was still merely groping for evidence of a wish for national integration. In Ghana, patriotism and loyalty were concentrated in the person of the prime minister, designated "Mr. Ghana"; in Nigeria, patriotism and loyalty were neither focused on, nor directed toward, the prime minister but were divided among its three regional premiers. Economically, socially, and politically, Ghana started off with greater prosperity, resources and expectations than Nigeria. Although both the new republics succumbed to military intervention within six weeks of each other in 1966, Ghana was spared the trauma of civil war. In any case, by 1966 their paths of leadership had long since diverged. Abubakar Tafawa Balewa was everything Nkrumah was not. In the 1970s, when both countries were under military regimes, Nigeria progressively distanced itself from the Ghanaian way of doing things. Finally, appalled by the barbarity of a head of state who could order the execution of three of his predecessors, Nigeria simply felt it had had enough and withheld Ghana's oil supply. Whereas in the 1960s Accra was the hub of "Pan-African" ideas and ideals, in the 1970s that center emphatically shifted to Lagos.

Ghana's collapse into poverty and Nigeria's rise to prosperity over the first two decades of their independence provide startling economic contrasts. Nevertheless, there are similarities as well as dissimilarities in the politico-economic configurations of contemporary Ghana and Nigeria. Monoculture remains a trap for the indifferent or the short-sighted, whether it be in cocoa or oil, and there is no African country in which agriculture can be permanently relegated to the status of a despised alternative to industrialization. In both countries, institutionalized corruption has run rampant, ethnic polarity has been more in evidence than not, and national integration has remained an unachieved goal.

One question continues to dishearten even the most enthusiastic and empathetic observor of contemporary Africa. Granting that the quality of human dignity was thought to have been better since the ending of colonial rule, why do the statistical records of independent Africa suggest that the value of human life has been grossly debased? J. F. Ade Ajayi's recent verdict on contemporary Africa is that "life has become more uncertain."[61] In Chinua Achebe's view, existence in Lagos today is like life at the battle-front.[62] A character created by a Nigerian novelist laments, "When the Europeans ruled us, few people died. Now we rule ourselves, we butcher each other like meat-sellers slaughtering cows."[63] In its attempt — twenty years after independence — to identify Africa's most urgent goals for the next twenty years the OAU Monrovia Symposium concluded that Africans must give priority to the issues of freedom and justice. "Only yesterday the birth of a State that respected basic freedoms was one of the most important demands in the struggle for independence: has this erstwhile dream turned into a nightmare?"[64]

To attribute Ghana's continuing decline to Kwame Nkrumah's priority — "Seek Ye First the Keys of Political Kingdom" — is a fallacy of hindsight. It is in what has been done with those keys — the wrong doors they have opened or forced open, rather than in their change of ownership — that the trouble has lain. Nigerians had little liking for Nkrumah's suppression of opposition through harsh Preventive Detention Acts or for his overweening Pan African ambitions. Abubakar Tafawa Balewa's reply to Nkrumah's invitation to get on the Pan African bandwagon ("Let us first put our own houses in order") was symbolic of Nigeria's preferred way of doing things. That is exactly what Nigeria did between 1960 and 1979, even if it needed a civil war to complete the process. (Rawlings's superficial 1979 "house-cleaning" exercise in Ghana meant something else and, in any case, came too late.)

In 1983 the initial impetus of Nigeria's Second Republic, when compared to the stagnation and corruption of Ghana's Second and Third Republics, seemed to offer political scientists a chance to test their hypotheses concerning differing levels of development in comparable Third World countries. It would be unfair to set up identical rigorous measuring rods as if the two economies were equal; oil constitutes a unique factor in the development of any country. Nevertheless, the steadily sinking Ghanaian economy and the "positive and frightening decline in [Ghana's] international importance and respect"[65] represent real tragedies for independent

Ghana. No alibi can cover up a quarter-century of abject mis-management; no excuse is comfort for the knowledge that a country has seen better days. Alert to the signals of its own recessions of 1978 and 1982 (setbacks rendered all the sharper by the previous prosperity of its petronaira golden age), Nigeria's Second Republic at first showed a greater readiness to eschew doctrinaire precepts and enforce austerity. But debtor Nigeria was not able to claim superiority over bankrupt Ghana for much longer.

It may be argued that December 31 will replace March 15 as the dreaded *dies irae* of West Africa's tumultuous political calendar. On December 31, 1983 — a reformist military regime seized power in Lagos — two years to the day after a similar junta seized power in Accra. As the *Economist* headline put its, "Down goes democracy in Nigeria."[66] As a result of this turn of events, the chance to use conditions in these two new West African nations as a model for comparative analysis was shattered. With the suddenness of a tropical storm, the picture dramatically changed, and the roles of Ghana and Nigeria were — if not reversed — at least leveled. The Nigerian coup of December 31, 1983 had multiple causes. These included a desperate determination to do something about the downward spiraling economy; impatience with the widespread acceptance of kickback and corruption; suspicion about the validity of the summer's general elections;[67] and a desire to pre-empt a far bloodier coup by the lower ranks, who were angered by the profligacy of politicians in power. The coup's causes, however, are of less relevance to our present discussion than is the coup's effect on our attempt to evaluate the political history of Ghana and Nigeria at the end of their first quarter-century of independence.

By New Year's Day, 1984, there was no longer much difference between the critical conditions of Ghana and Nigeria. They were both bankrupt states in massive debt to the world, and both were (for the umpteenth time) under the control of military leaders who were disgusted by mismanagement and despaired of democracy. General Buhari's diagnosis of "the crisis of confidence now afflicting our nation"[68] was echoed on the same day by Flight-Lieutenant Rawlings's condemnation of Ghana's neglect and indiscipline, which had "eaten into the fabric of our society."[69] Both leaders pointed to this collapse of management to justify the necessity for their corrective intervention. Both identified the same causes for their countries' calamities. Both declared a plague on all politicians. As long as Nigeria had been blessed with huge oil revenues, it could make successful use of the patronage system and could overlook (or at least overcome) the threat of instability that confronted Ghana. But one can afford to sweep problems under the carpet only if one is confident that there will always be a carpet. Once the petronaira bubble burst, Nigeria began to resemble woebegone Ghana — a country destabilized by economic monoculture and its own managerial recklessness. Now the lamentation for Accra was echoed by the dirge for democracy in Lagos; "Adieu! Sweet Nigeria" had become the antiphon of "Alas! Poor Ghana."[70]

The new head of state, General Buhari, translated Rawlings's 1979 warning to the incoming political class, "I am waiting and watching you" into a no-nonsense "I have watched you and do not like what I have seen" action. He wasted no tears in mourning the departure of the politicians and said that his administration had no immediate plans to bring them back.[71] He emphasized that his priorities were to put the economy to rights and to rebuild the nation. A hundred days later, neither ruler had any cause to regret his diagnosis. Buhari referred to "irresponsible and recalcitrant behavior."[72] Rawlings maintained his theme that at the end of nearly twenty years of "sham democracy and political sovereignty, very few of us at any level of authority can now say [we are] in a position truthfully and honestly to be satisfied with the condition of this nation."[73] In the program of either contemporary [1984] Ghana or Nigeria, a return to civilian rule enjoys no priority.

How stand these two West African states in late 1984? Economically, both long-bankrupt Ghana and newly austere Nigeria in common with the rest of the continent are experiencing the dual impact of global recession and their own mismanagement. Ghana's incompetence in the handling of her cocoa industry has been as crippling to her long-ailing economy as has Nigeria's oil squandermania to her erstwhile prosperity. Although both countries are now inured to the far from rare humiliation of international debtor status, Nigeria's reversal of fortune has been of shorter duration and is hence, all the more dramatic and damning. In the art of economic survival, it is Ghana's plan that has won the approval of the IMF as "well-conceived, feasible and realistic" in the short term.[74] Nigeria, on the other hand, does not look as if it can bring itself to accept the IMF's customarily stringent conditions. At the end of 1984 a prolonged period of belt-tightening seemed to be in store for both countries. If Ghana has already seen its worst time economically, Nigeria's may be yet to come.

Politically, by the end of 1984 there were indicators that the hard-line leftist ideology of the Rawlings regime might be developing some cracks. The earlier belief that Rawlings II was a different phenomenon from Rawlings I began to assume positive shape. In Nigeria, Buhari's demonstration of his ability to last out his first year has strengthened his credibility. Every day he remains in political power increases the nation's now-or-never chance to salvage its economy from bankruptcy. His "War Against Indiscipline" (WAI) has a patriotic objective as well as a personal thrust. Yet in neither Ghana nor Nigeria does there seem to be much hope for a sudden economic upturn. The probability of a return to democratic institutions in the near future is even more remote. Whereas at the end of 1983 one could discern the outline of a Nigeria that had begun to overcome its political divisiveness (although *en revanche* it has lost its way socioeconomically) and of a Ghana that was getting better if only because it was impossible to imagine it getting worse, at the end of 1984 one is left with the unambiguous picture of two nations in a profound and continuing crisis — economic, political, social, and moral.

On the last day of the eerily Orwellian year of 1984, even the empathetic observer may ruefully wonder if there is really anything to distinguish melancholy Ghana from tatterdemalion Nigeria. Both countries have long left their age of innocence behind them. After having had only a few short-lived civilian regimes in each country, how much longer can these two West African nations go on pretending that they are major states and deserve to be taken seriously in the international arena without proving it? As both countries deteriorate economically, is it possible to believe that their political leaders really care, provided they can keep their own private jets, London villas, and Swiss bank accounts? If, in 1985, Nigeria suddenly becomes no different from Ghana (that is, if both countries are now to be characterized by economic chaos, political collapse, social catastrophe, sinking international reputations and futures marked by the signs of an indefinite period of military authoritarianism and severe austerity), what does the unglamorous record of the first quarter-century of Ghana's and Nigeria's independence portend for the future of Africa's new nations? After only twenty-five years, Nigeria and Ghana have experienced a steep decline from the delirious euphoria of the 1960s through the developmental enthusiasm of the 1970s to the dark disenchantment with development economics and the debt traps of the 1980s. If the fates that have befallen black Africa's first new nation and the continent's one-time giant are representative, what can the later, lesser, new nations hope for in terms of stability, good government, and social justice?[75] The crystal ball is opaque — like the harmattan sky. The establishment of a liberalized economy is proving to be as elusive as the achievement of a liberal democracy. Many economies across the continent are quietly regressing into a precolonial subsistence-and-barter mode, characterized by human withdrawal and agricultural atavism. The faults lie not only in domestic irresponsibility, but also in global constraints.

Nevertheless (leaving aside the suggestion of a period of "benign neglect" as Africa's best hope),[76] if the new African nations genuinely want to become an integral and respected part of the wider international community, they need to learn that — like charity — stability, good government, and social justice begin at home. A few years ago, writing sadly but soberly about West Africa's sorry record of postcolonial performance, John Dunn concluded that "only the peoples of West Africa can learn how to make their rulers responsible to them."[77] It is a lesson West Africans have yet to learn. If, in the long run, Ghanaians and Nigerians may only choose which of two bogeymen they prefer — authoritarian generals or corrupt politicians — it is because the search for a leadership selflessly committed to democracy and good government has so far proved singularly elusive for these two West African states.

A generation ago in the age of decolonization, the enlightened maxim was that "good government is no substitute for self-government." In the present age of postdecolonization, may not Africans themselves soon be arguing that self-government per se is no substitute for good government, and hence demand more from independence.

Postscriptum: Since this was written Nigeria has suffered another military coup (August 1985) and Ghana has increased the signs of a positive economic recovery under way.

Notes

1. Lord Hailey, *An African Survey*, (rev. ed.) (New York: Oxford University Press, 1957), p. 316.
2. Ken Post, *The New States of West Africa*, (Baltimore, Md.: Penguin Books, 1968), p. 178.

3. John Dunn, ed., *West African States: Failure and Promise*, New York: Cambridge University Press, 1978), p. 216.

Instead of citing standard texts here, attention is best drawn to the notes to the Dunn chapters, which provide a sound commentary on and evaluation of the classic accounts of the political history of Ghana (pp. 222–24) and of Nigeria (pp. 244–45) up to ca. 1976. Since these works were published, few books on the political history of the subsequent republics have appeared; the principal exceptions are, for Ghana, M. Oquaye, *Politics in Ghana, 1972–1979* (Accra: Tornado Publications, 1980) and Naomi Chazan, *An Anatomy of Ghanaian Politics, 1969–1982*, (Boulder, Colo.: Westview Press, 1983) and, for Nigeria, Oyelaye Oyediran, ed., *Nigerian Government and Politics under Military Rule*, (Lagos: Macmillan Nigeria, 1979); Anthony Kirk-Greene and Douglas Rimmer, *Nigeria since 1970*, (London: Hodder and Stoughton, 1981); and B. J. Dudley, *An Introduction to Nigerian Government and Politics*, (Bloomington, Ind.: Indiana University Press, 1982). Each carries a useful bibliography.

4. David E. Apter, *The Gold Coast in Transition*, (Princeton, N.J.: Princeton University Press, 1955), especially the second edition (1972) with its new Chapter 16, "Ghana — A Retrospective View." For categories of African leadership, see also the important contribution by R. H. Jackson and Carl Rosberg, *Personal Rule in Black Africa*, (Berkeley: University of California Press, 1982).

5. The concept was developed by Nelson Kasfir in his book *The Shrinking Political Arena*, (Berkeley: University of California Press, 1976).

6. See Björn M. Edsman, *Lawyers in Gold Coast Politics*, (Stockholm: Almqvist International, 1979).

7. See "Ghana's 'Holy War' Goes On." *Scotsman*, (August 25, 1983): *West Africa* (1983): 2976; Association of Recognized Professional Bodies, "Statement on Ghana," (Accra, 20 December 1982, mimeographed).

8. See, for example, "The 'Hardworking and Successful' Lawyers," *People's Daily Graphic* (Accra), May 23, 1983, pp. 4–5, with schedules of names, tax assessed and paid or not, and remarks, and *West Africa*, (1983): 1811 and 2976.

9. *West Africa*, (1983): 1603; "Cadre School at Legon," ibid., pp. 1880–81. A useful presentation of the structure and function of the original People's and Worker's Defense Committees is contained in the PNDC publication, *Ghana: Two Years of Transformation*, (1984), pp. 19–21. The recent restructuring of these Defense Committees towards the end of 1984 hints at an ideological estrangement between Rawlings and his Marxist mentors (notably the Tsikata dynasty), possibly brought about by the perceived neocolonial ascendancy of the IMF in the determination of Ghana's economic policy. *West Africa*, January 7, 1985; *The Times*, January 24, 1985; *Africa Confidential*, February 1985, pp. 3–4.

10. Dennis Austin attributes the source of this subsequently immensely popular, but hard to pin down, maxim to the CPP's general election in *Politics in Ghana, 1946–1960*, (New York, Oxford University Press, 1964), p. 131.

11. Although a comparable device was an integral part of the Lancaster House Agreement of 1979, a parallel fate could, quite legally, befall the reserved white seats in the Zimbabwean parliament.

12. The description is that of Chazan, *An Anatomy of Ghanaian Politics*, p. 286.

13. See Crawford Young, *Ideology and Development in Africa*, (New Haven, N.J.: Yale University Press, 1982).

14. For an excellent case study, see Richard Jeffries, *Class, Power and Ideology in Ghana: the Railwaymen of Sekondi*, (New York: Cambridge University Press, 1978).

15. See the memorandum submitted to the chairman of the PNDC by the Central Committee of the National Union of Ghana Students, (Kumasi, December 14, 1982, mimeographed).

16. A. A. Afrifa, *The Ghana Group*, (London: Cass, 1966), p. 31.

17. For this formulation, see A. H. M. Kirk-Greene, *"Stand by Your Radios":
Documentation for a Study of Military Government in Tropical Africa*, (Leiden:
Afrika-Studiencentrum, 1981), p. 11.

18. See W. Scott Thompson, *Ghana's Foreign Policy, 1957–1966*, (Princeton,
N.J.: Princeton University Press, 1969), pp. 250–6.

19. The World Bank's favorable response to the PNDC proposals as "realistic"
is analyzed in the editorial in *West Africa* (1983): 2783. See also the article by Nii K.
Bentsi-Enchill on the politics of Ghana's IMF-inclined economic policy in *West
Africa*, (1984): 654–55. An excellent unpublished analysis of the economic situation
is to be found in the notes for an address given at the Overseas Development
Institute on December 8, 1983 by His Excellency the Ghanaian High Commissioner
to London, K. Dadzie. (Personal communication).

20. In 1977 156.9 million cedis were allocated to defense (out of a total recurrent
expenditure of 3,017 million cedis).

21. Chazan, *An Anatomy of Ghanaian Politics*, p. 176.

22. "I fear that many African nations, if they do not take action to encourage a
drop in fertility rates, are speeding headlong to disaster." Director-General of the
FAO, *Scotsman*, July 24, 1984. See also the World Bank's controversial report
Accelerated Development in Sub-Saharan Africa: an Agenda for Action, (Published
for World Bank, Washington, D.C.: Oxford University Press, 1981). A useful
analysis of the implications of this report is to be found in the special issue of the
IDS Bulletin (University of Sussex), 14, no. 1, 1983. In the grim words of the
preamble to the OAU "Lagos Plan of Action" of 1982, "Africa is unable to point
to any significant growth rate or satisfactory index of general well-being in the last
twenty years." A comparative analysis of the World Bank proposals and the OAU's
counterprogram has been undertaken by R. S. Browne and R. J. Cummings of
Howard University, (Lawrenceville, Va: Brunswick Publishing Co.).

23. See "Ghana's Worsening Malaise," *West Africa* (1983): 2234–35, and
"PNDC + PDCs ÷ IMF = ?," *West Africa* (1984): 654.

24. Report from Accra, *West Africa* (1984): 1288.

25. For a summary of the history of the constitutional changes between 1947 and
1979, see B. O. Nwabueze, *A Constitutional History of Nigeria*, (London: Hurst,
1982).

26. The English translation has always seemed to me far more slighting than the
Hausa original, *wakili nawa*, (my wakil or representative).

27. The formula of paradox was introduced into the Nigerian literature by
Richard L. Sklar in his perceptive exposition, "Contradictions in the Nigerian
Political System," *Journal of Modern African Studies* 3, no. 2 (1965): 201–13.

28. Personal information (Zaria 1979), unattributable.

29. The best study of the 1979 constitution is B. O. Nwabueze, *The Presidential
Constitution of Nigeria*, (London: Hurst, 1982).

30. The report was not made public; only a government white paper was
published.

31. *Election Manifesto of the National Party of Nigeria* (Lagos, 1983), Section
16. See also two unpublished papers by Dean E. McHenry "Attitudes toward State
Creation in Nigeria" and "Disaggregating Governmental Units" (Presented to the
African Studies Association annual conference, Los Angeles, 1984).

32. The distinction is drawn in A. H. M. Kirk-Greene, "Ethnic Engineering and
the 'Federal Character' of Nigeria: Boon of Contentment or Bone of Contention?"
Ethnic and Racial Studies 6, No. 4 (October 1983): 457–76. But, as I used to tell my
students at Ahmadu Bello University, one of the ultimate tests of Nigeria's federal
nature will be the day an Ibo runs for MP of Sokoto and wins. That the thought
took some root is apparent in A. D. Yahaya's preface to Billy Dudley, *Introduction*

to Nigerian Government and Politics, 1982, p. 7. The results of the election of 1983 make that day appear no nearer than it did in 1964!

33. Although this aspect of the federal character is implicit rather than explicit, the figures are revealing; see the data assembled in the article "Postgraduate Patterns in Nigeria," *West Africa* (1982): 1260-62.

34. In addition to the standard texts listed in Note 3, important studies recently published include Abubakar Yaya Aliyu, ed., *Return to Civilian Rule* (Zaria, 1982), and Haroun Adamu and Alaba Ogunsanwo, *Nigeria: The Making of the Presidential System — 1979 General Elections* (Kano, 1983); Richard Joseph, "Class, State and Prebendal Politics in Nigeria," *Journal of Commonwealth and Comparative Politics*, 21 (1983): 21-38; Sayre P. Schatz "Pirate Capitalism and the Inert Economy of Nigera," *Journal of Modern African Studies* 22 (1984): 45-57; and two unpublished papers by Larry Diamond, "The 1983 Nigerian Elections: Electoral Fraud and Democratic Failure" and "The Political Economy of Corruption in Nigeria", (Presented to the African Studies Association annual conference, Los Angeles, 1984) and his article on the reasons behind the Buhari coup in *Foreign Affairs* Spring 1984, pp. 905-27. See also the essays in C. S. Whitaker, ed., *Perspectives on the Second Republic in Nigeria*, Occasional Papers, (University of California — Los Angeles 1981). The origins of the Nigerian Civil War are to be the theme of a Third World case study for the Open University, edited by Gavin P. Williams.

35. In this connection, researchers will welcome the forthcoming publication of a bio-bibliography of Malam Aminu Kano by Moses Omoniwa, Kashim Ibrahim Library, Ahmadu Bello University, Zaria.

36. See, for example, Alaba Ogunsanwo's essay "The Political Battle for 1987," which was written in late 1983 and appeared in the January issue of *Spectrum* (Lagos, 1984).

37. According to the *Daily Times* (Lagos), as many as 21,000 came from Bendel State alone. See *West Africa* (1984): 1416.

38. See A. A. Ayida, "The Nigerian Revolution, 1966-1976," (Presidential address delivered to the 13th annual conference of the Nigerian Economic Society, Enugu, April 1973).

39. The most recent studies of the bureaucracy in Nigeria by Nigerian academics include 'Ladipo Adamolekun, *Public Administration: A Nigerian and Comparative Perspective* (New York: Longman, 1983); M. J. Balogun, *Public Administration in Nigeria: A developmental approach* (1983); and A. Adebayo, *Principles and Practice of Public Administration in Nigeria* (New York: Wiley, 1981).

40. See Clem Baiye, "Change of Batons at NIIA," *West Africa* (1983): 2506-7.

41. P. N. C. Okigbo, *Nigeria's Financial System: Structure and Growth*, (Harlow: Longman, 1981), pp. 17 and 33.

42. General Olusegun Obasanjo, *My Command* (Ibadan: Heinemann Nigeria, 1980), p. 43 and Linday Barrett, "Nigeria: The Pattern of Military Rule: III," *West Africa* (1984): 1488.

43. See A. H. M. Kirk-Greene, " 'Damnosa Hereditas': Ethnic Ranking and the Martial Races Imperative in Africa," *Ethnic and Racial Studies* 3, No. 4, (October 1980): 393-414.

44. World Bank, *Accelerated Development in Sub-Saharan Africa*, p. 112.

45. In his article, "The Numbers Game and Ethnic Politics in Nigeria," *Spectrum* (Lagos), January-February 1984, pp. 44-50, Emeka Aniagolu gloomily concludes that since Nigerians cannot be relied upon to undertake a reliable census themselves, "let us contract it out to the United Nations."

46. The theory was propounded in my *The Genesis of the Nigerian Civil War and the Theory of Fear*, SIAS Research Report, no. 27, (Uppsala; Scandinavian Institute of African Studies, 1975).

47. *Nigeria Newsletter*, no. 142 (June 30, 1984): 13. See also Nigerian Universities Commission, *Twenty Years of University Education in Nigeria* (Lagos, 1984).

48. World Bank, *Development Report*, 1983. The quoted figure of 98 percent in school must, however, be suspect.

49. *West Africa* (1984): 1376.

50. Post, *New States of West Africa*, p. 181.

51. Respectively, in Dunn, *West African States*, pp. 30–32 and 172.

52. J. F. Ade Ajayi, "Expectations of Independence," in *Black Africa: A Generation After Independence*, special issue of *Daedalus* (Spring 1982): 5.

53. Adebayo Adedeji, in OAU/IILS, *What Kind of Africa by the Year 2000?*, (Geneva, 1979), p. 62.

54. B. Okeke, *4 June: A Revolution Betrayed*, (Enugu: Ikenga Publications, 1982). See also E. Babatope, *The Ghana Revolution from Nkrumah to Jerry Rawlings* (Enugu: Fourth Dimension Publishing Co., 1982).

55. E. A. Ayandele, *The Educated Elite in the Nigerian Society*, (Ibadan: Ibadan University Press, 1974), chap. 3.

56. J. F. Ade Ajayi, "Is Failure of Development in Africa Due to the Absence of Democratic Institutions and Freedoms?" (Unpublished seminar paper, Ibadan University, 1984). It was because African scholars of this widely respected caliber now feel able to write openly of what they recognize as the "dismal record" of their own political leadership that I overcame my own initial reluctance to undertake the writing of this pessimistic and personally painful critique of the performance of a country with which I have been closely and happily associated for thirty-five years. Without their lead, I would not have agreed to discuss the Nigerian record with such frankness. A similar sense of impatience seems to have motivated Richard Rathbone, a leading historian of modern Ghana, who, in his unpublished paper "Some Thoughts on West Africa Since Independence" (African Studies Association of the United Kingdom annual conference, York, 1984) condemned British and American scholars for their "long and decent tradition of relative flummery in which a post-colonial liberal conscience has hindered attempts at objectivity, a position that neither adds understanding nor in the long term helps the country and its inhabitants."

57. For an elaboration of this theme, see A. H. M. Kirk-Greene, "Centennial 1984: a Second Scramble for Africa?" *Contemporary Review* 243, no. 1414 (November 1983): 232–39.

58. This concept of an alibi was advanced by J. K. Galbraith in his 1977 television lectures, "The Age of Uncertainty."

59. In her novel of this name (1971), a retired colonial civil servant returns after some twenty years to Central Africa.

60. This regional pattern is graphically demonstrated in one of the maps in Claude S. Phillips, *The African Political Dictionary*, (Santa Barbara, Calif.: ABC-Clio, 1984), p. 195.

61. Ajayi, "Expectations of Independence."

62. His comment was made in a widely acclaimed TV program "Nigeria: The Squandering of the Riches," shown on BBC in January 1984.

63. Buchi Emecheta, *Destination Biafra*, (New York: Allison and Busby, 1982), p. 88.

64. *OAU/IILS Symposium Report*, Conclusions.

65. The judgment is that of Richard Rathbone in Dunn, *West African States*, p. 29.

66. *The Economist*, January 2–9, 1984, front cover. For an early public statement what had been privately in the minds of many see Femi Aribisala, "An Appraisal of the 1983 Presidential Election," *Spectrum* (Lagos), November 1983, pp. 7–18.

67. For two recent Nigerian critiques, see Shehu Othman, "Classes, Crisis and Coup: The Demise of Shagari's Regime." *African Affairs* 83, 333 (1984) 441–61, and Alaba Ogunsanwo, "The Nigerian Polity: Democracy, Stability, Political Structures and Processes" (Paper presented to the African Studies Association annual conference, Los Angeles, 1984).

68. Broadcast to the nation, January 1, 1984; reproduced in full in *West Africa* (1984): 56–57.

69. Nationwide broadcast by the chairman of the PNDC to mark the second anniversary of his return to power, January 1, 1984; quoted in extenso in *West Africa* (1984): 21–22. The celebrations were reported to be even more austere and low-key than those of the previous year. *Ibid.*, p. 141.

70. The latter lament was the title of *The Times* lead editorial marking Ghana's 27th anniversary, March 6, 1984. The event was described as "an occasion full of melancholy . . . a case study of the things that can go wrong in Africa . . . [an example of] how a confused left-wing 'revolution' can transform a critical situation into an unmitigated disaster." Two recent important analyses are Richard Crook, "Bureaucracy and Politics in Ghana," in Peter Lyon and James Manor, eds., *Transfer and Transformation: Political Institutions in the New Commonwealth* (Leicester: Leicester University Press, 1984), pp. 185–213 and Richard Jeffries, "The Political Economy of State Collapse in Ghana" (Paper presented to the African Studies Association of the United Kingdom annual conference, York, 1984).

71. Quoted in *Nigerian Newsletter*, April 25, 1984.

72. Broadcast to the nation, April 6, 1984.

73. Independence Day broadcast by the chairman of the PNDC, March 6, 1984: quoted in extenso in *West Africa* (1984): p. 586. See also the commentary by Nii K. Bentsi-Enchill, "Masses or Asses?", *West Africa* (1984): 597–98.

74. Quoted in *West Africa* (1983): 2783.

75. See the conclusions of the distinguished Indian economist Deepak Lal in his book *The Poverty of Development Economics* (Albuquerque, N. Mex.: Transatlantic Arts, 1983). See also the editorial "100 Years Later — What Kind of Independence?", *Development and Co-operation* (Bonn) 3 (1984): 3 and Ajayi, "Failure of Development." A similar disenchantment with African leaders' betrayal of democratic development inspired Ken C. Kotecha and Robert W. Adams' *African Politics: The Corruption of Power* (Lanham, Md: University Press of America, 1981). See also Dennis Austin, "Things Fall Apart." *Orbis* (Winter, 1982): 925–47; Timothy Shaw, "The African Condition: Prophecies and Possibilities," *Yearbook of World Affairs* 1983, pp. 139–51; and Douglas Anglin, "Independent Black Africa: Retrospect and Prospect," *International Journal* (Spring, 1984): 481–504.

76. The proposal derives from a 1984 conversation with Professor Bolaji Akinyemi of the University of Lagos.

77. Dunn, *West African States*, p. 216.

2 CAMEROON, TOGO, AND THE STATES OF FORMERLY FRENCH WEST AFRICA

Victor T. Le Vine

This essay discusses the politics of ten independent west African countries: Senegal, Mauritania, Mali, Burkina Faso (formerly Upper Volta), Guinea, the Ivory Coast, Benin (formerly Dahomey), Niger, Togo, and Cameroon. All but Togo and Cameroon were once members of the colonial administrative federation of French West Africa; the latter, German colonies before 1916, were thereafter administered by France as mandates of the League of Nations and from 1946 to 1960, as trusteeships of the United Nations. All ten countries use French as their official language; all have been deeply influenced by French legal, political, and cultural tradition; and all still maintain important commercial, cultural, political, and financial links with France. On closer inspection, of course, these ten countries are quite dissimilar in many respects — ethnocultural composition, economics, political structures, and internal politics — but their shared characteristics, derived largely from their common colonial heritage and contemporary ties with France, permit us to make valid comparisons and generalizations about them.

THE COLONIAL PERIOD

At its zenith during the period between the first and second world wars, the French overseas empire was physically as large, though not as populous as the British empire. The African component of France's empire included most of the western third of the continent. Only the Spanish Sahara, the four west African British territories (the Gambia, Sierra Leone, the Gold Coast, and Nigeria), and Liberia, Portuguese Guinea, and Spanish Equatorial Guinea interrupted the pattern of French control in the region.

France's north African holdings (Morocco, Algeria, and Tunisia) were *Afrique blanche* (white Africa), of which Algeria was the centerpiece. Algeria was the only colony where the French, normally a stay-at-home people, settled in large numbers. The anticipated destiny of Afrique blanche — at least until 1954 — was to become part of the *métropole*. (As a matter of fact, Algeria — at least administratively — came to be considered a part of the *métropole*, as distinct from Tunisia and Morocco, both of which were protectorates.) In French colonial mythology, Afrique blanche was something special; its peoples, Islam notwithstanding, had historically been as Mediterranean as the French. It was hoped that they could be assimilated to the values, ways, and institutions of French civilization with relative ease.

Afrique noire (black Africa), south of the Sahara, was different in French eyes, not only racially but also culturally. The Arab term for sub-Saharan Africa, *bilad as-Sudan*, land of the blacks, captures some of the racial arrogance that the French — despite their protestations to the contrary — shared with their Arab cousins. Although there was some early and promising experimentation with the policy of assimilation (for example, the grant of French citizenship to the black and *métis* (mixed-blood) inhabitants of the four Senegalese communes of Dakar, Rufisque, Goree, and St. Louis in the nineteenth century), by the 1920s and 1930s a majority of Frenchmen (and certainly the French government) undoubtedly shared the view that most of the populations of what had become French West and French Equatorial African were unassimilable. At the least, they were considered too culturally backward to be eligible for French citizenship. The prevailing policy of "association" unambiguously distinguished between the very few *assimilés* and *evolués* ("assimilated" and "evolved" Africans who were entitled to the privileges of French citizenship according to carefully specified gradations of evolution and assimilation) and the vast majority of *indigènes* (natives who were subject to a formidable array of administrative controls, servitudes, and penalties that served to accent their "backward" character). The corvée (a form of forced labor thinly disguised as a labor tax), hut taxes, the *Indigénat* (a broad-ranging code of administrative prescriptions and penalties), and a French colonial civil service that kept close watch over those activities of the traditional authority systems that were still permitted to operate accentuated the essential differences between the French rulers (and their native auxiliaries) and the indigenous populations.

Despite the unattractive features of the French colonial system, it must nonetheless be said that France's dominion in black Africa, once uncontested French rule had been established, was probably no worse and no better than that maintained in their African territories by the British, the Portuguese, and the Spanish. The worst French excesses occurred in Cameroon and French Equatorial Africa; elsewhere French rule was sometimes even benign. Where sympathetic and intelligent Frenchmen operated France's version of the (British) indirect rule system, as in the Sahel, bonds of affection and respect were frequently forged between Frenchmen and Africans.[1] At its best, French colonial rule was relatively color-blind, as in the Senegalese communes; at its worst, it exacted a terrible toll in human lives and suffering, as in southern Cameroon, the French Congo, and Gabon, where corvée labor was massively employed on railroad projects.[2] Moreover, after the First World War, the special cases of Togo and Cameroon, former German colonies, were placed under French administration under the terms stipulated for mandates of the League of Nations. In both cases, the French — albeit reluctantly — agreed to something previously unheard of in colonial history: nominal supervision of their colonial administrations by the international community. Although the League's oversight had little effect on the day-to-day administration of the Togo and Cameroon territories, it did focus international attention on the worst of the colonial abuses (as in Cameroon) and thus probably helped to mitigate the harsher aspects of French rule.

DECOLONIZATION, 1940 to 1960

The Second World War launched the process that brought the French empire to its end. By 1962, when Algeria gained its independence after a bloody eight-year rebellion against French rule, the only French colony left in Africa was the minuscule Territory of the Afars and the Issas (formerly French Somaliland) on the continent's eastern horn, and in 1977 it finally became the sovereign state of Djibouti. The beginning of the French empire's end probably dates to January 1944, when General de Gaulle convened in Brazzaville the governors and governors-general of France's African colonies. The purpose of the meeting was to discuss these territories' future political evolution. Although the conference undoubtedly opened the door to decolonization, that was not, according to Roger de Benoist, the direction the conferees themselves wished to take:

Aware of the fact that colonization could no longer perpetuate itself as it had before the Second World War, the French officials took whatever measures were needed to satisfy immediate [African] demands: they thought that that would be enough to stifle any slight inclinations toward independence . . . In fact the participants of the conference fixed precise limits on the political evolution of the colonies. If these limits were exceeded, it was due to the historical dynamism of the struggle for independence.[3]

All the conferees understood that postwar France would need its African colonies to recover from the ignominious defeat and occupation by Germany; the willing cooperation of the growing African educated and commercial classes was essential. The recommendations of the Brazzaville conference, conservative though they were, nevertheless found eventual expression in France's 1946 constitution and the flood of colonial legislation it triggered. Significantly, eight elected black African representatives attended each of the two French constituent assemblies in 1946, and Leopold Sedar Senghor, the Sengalese poet, *agrégé*, and politician, even served as the *Constituante*'s unofficial rhetorician, responsible for the proper prose forms in the new constitution.

The period between 1946 and 1960 (the year in which most francophone African states became independent) was remarkable for several reasons. First, the African deputies in the French parliament worked closely with metropolitan deputies (largely from the French left) to push through legislative reforms that radically changed the relationship between France and her colonies. These reforms included (1) abolition of forced labor and the special regime of administrative penalties (the *Indigénat*); (2) elimination of distinctions in status between citizens and subjects; (3) extension of the right to vote to hundreds of thousands of black Africans and greater black African representation in French metropolitan assemblies; and (4) creation of the Economic and Social Development Investment Fund (FIDES) to subsidize overseas development programs. Needless to say, reform of the franchise would have been meaningless without the first two reforms; as it was, the popular franchise became pillars of decolonization and provided the votes that legitimized African politicians' demands for increasing measures of territorial self-government. The figures speak for themselves: in 1945, the registered voters eligible to cast ballots for representatives to the first French constituent assembly numbered (in the ten

territories) only 129,900 on the second (or African) electorial roll
and 56,800 on the first (or French) roll. Twelve years later, those
registered to vote in the 1957 territorial assembly elections
numbered 12,445,200 on a single (or common) roll, an increase
66.6 times that of the combined 1945 registration![4]

The second major development of the 1946–1960 period was the
irrevocable — and certainly unintended — passage of France's
African wards from French to African hands. At least until 1946,
virtually all significant political and economic decision making
regarding the African colonies occurred in Paris or, where administrative discretion permitted (as was often the case), decisions were
made by colonial civil servants in the territories. The creation of
local assemblies (and, later, of territorial executive councils,
regional councils, and executives — all eventually with African
majorities) and the presence of African representatives in France's
national legislature and supra colonial institutions (the French
Union and, after 1958, the French Community) provided the political arenas within which Africans demanded and achieved increasing measures of local autonomy. By 1958 so much authority had
devolved to the African assemblies that most of the ten territories
had become dyarchies — in which responsibility and power was
shared by French and African officials — rather than colonies.

Third, the new forums for the expression of African demands
not only brought to the fore an entire generation of nationalist
politicians, but also stimulated the birth and growth of literally
hundreds of political parties ready to take advantage of the
elections that fed personnel into the new institutions. By the time
independence was achieved, the number of these political parties
had in most territories been reduced to a handful (through electoral
attrition, mergers, disintegration, proscription, and so on). But,
during the mid-1950s, the political arena was crowded with parties
of every stripe, and several inter-territorial parties, movements,
and groupings emerged as well. (A complete list of political parties
and groups active in the ten territories between 1945 and 1960 has
yet to be compiled; a preliminary estimate puts the number at close
to 500, including at least 100 in Cameroon and 80 in the Ivory
Coast. This estimated total also includes several transterritorial
parties, the most important of which was the Rassemblement
Démocratique Africaine [RDA]. The RDA, formed in 1946, came
to have branches in nine of the ten territories.)[5]

The new institutions and the political opportunities they

represented encouraged the growth of a wholly new generation of African politicians and created these countries' postindependence leadership groups. With very few exceptions, leaders were not revolutionaries, anxious to rid themselves of the colonial presence at any cost, but establishmentarians, formed by and within the emerging political systems.[6] As a consequence (disregarding a few exceptional cases), decolonization was accomplished peacefully and with relative ease. As a matter of fact, until 1958, most leading francophone African politicians did not seek their territories' outright independence from France, but, like their French counterparts, instead sought some sort of autonomy within a loose French commonwealth of nations. When General de Gaulle put the question to a vote in 1958, only Guinea chose immediate independence over association within a new French Community. Almost everywhere else, independence was achieved by cordial negotiations between the territories' African leaders and the French government. The two exceptions were Togo and Cameroon, the trusteeships of the United Nations. Their independence was the result of sometimes passionate interaction between the U.N., France, and leading local African politicians. (Cameroon bears the unhappy distinction of being the only sub-Saharan ex-French colony to become independent to the sound of rebel gunfire. The dissidents, eventually crushed by a combined Franco-Cameroonian military effort, were members of an outlawed Marxist party that had unsuccessfully tried to seize power in 1955. They had vigorously and unavailingly lobbied the U.N. for open elections prior to independence.)

The francophones' spectacular march to independence was also affected by extraordinary changes on the international scene and in France itself. On the international level, particularly within the U.N., a growing anti colonial consensus was led by both the United States and the Soviet Union. This newly powerful movement resulted in the creation of the U.N.'s trusteeship system, under whose terms administering powers agreed to move former mandates toward internal self-government or independence. France accepted trusteeships for Togo and Cameroon and, as a consequence, Togo became something of a catalyst for decolonization in the rest of francophone Africa.

Immediately after the war, France had hoped to regain most of her overseas colonies relatively intact, but events in France and the empire soon destroyed that hope. The French political left, which gained strength after the war, actively sought decolonization. When the Socialists came to power (as in the governments of Leon Blum and Paul Ramadier, 1946–47, and Guy Mollet, 1956–57), notable steps were taken toward that end.[7] Then, too, France was forced to fight an increasingly costly, and eventually losing, war against the Indochinese rebels led by Ho Chih Minh. The traumatic wounds of that loss (in 1954) were still unhealed when another bloody anti colonial conflict started in Algeria. The Algerian war, and the crisis of public and military confidence it generated, resulted in the collapse of the Fourth French Republic in 1958 and General de Gaulle's return to power. De Gaulle eventually ended the Algerian war (leading to Algerian independence in 1962), set up the Fifth Republic, and took the final steps that led to independence for most of Afrique noire in 1960.

INDEPENDENCE: TRANSITIONS

The first francophone black African state to become independent was Guinea, in 1958. Guinea had defiantly voted *"non"* in the September 1958 general referendum on de Gaulle's new constitution, the only territory in Afrique noire to do so. In effect, it opted for immediate independence, and an angry de Gaulle (who took rejection with ill grace) brutally cut off almost all French ties with the new state, despite attempts by Guinea's charismatic young President, Sékou Touré, to mollify the French leader. If Guinea's fate had been meant as an example to the other francophone African leaders, it did not quite work out that way; they soon realized that they would would could have close ties with France and independence as well. Their choice was thus both simple and painless.

Cameroon, under special U.N. status, led the way (January 1, 1960), followed by Togo (also under U.N. auspices) on April 4. Senegal and Mali, temporarily united (January 17, 1959, to August 20, 1960) as the Mali Federation, declared the union's independence on June 20, 1960. Four others followed suit in August or September, with Mauritania bringing up the rear on November 28. Following the break-up of their federation, Mali and Senegal each declared its independence (Mali on September 22, 1960, and Senegal on August 20, 1960.

All ten new states attained independence with constitutions and institutions modeled more or less closely on those of France's Fifth Republic. All became republics and, with the exception of Mauritania (which chose to make Islam the state religion), all adopted an officially secular outlook on politics. All adopted constitutions that created (1) national legislatures based on universal adult suffrage, (2) legal and judicial systems resembling those of France, and (3) executive presidencies directing governments nominally ratified by parliament, but in fact wholly responsible to the president. The resemblance to the French system was certainly more than nominal: the text of several of the African constitutions, especially in sections dealing with the presidency, followed the French document almost word for word. Again, the choice was both easy and understandable. Actively schooled in the French political tradition and habituated to French legal and institutional norms and forms, the African leaders were not likely to reject the political culture in which they themselves had been nurtured. Most attractive, of course, were the provisions for a dominant presidency, a model consonant with both the African leaders' personal admiration for de Gaulle and their preference for strongly centralized leadership and control.

French, of course, remained the official language of government, and the ten countries' school systems continued with instruction in French (usually from the later elementary grades), used syllabi based on French models, and (with the exception of Guinea) hired considerable numbers of French teachers, particularly in the secondary schools and the institutions of higher learning. To be sure, the new ministries of culture and education hastened to produce texts and syllabi that reflected the change to nationhood, but it took almost ten years for the new civic cultures to begin to take hold throughout the ten states.[8] Even today, some twenty-five years after independence, the ten countries' high schools and (particularly) universities still strongly reflect their French origins. For example, Cameroon's national University of Yaounde awards degrees cognate to those awarded in France and organizes its curricula, courses, and faculties along French lines. Its professors look chiefly to France for intellectual leadership and inspiration, and its best graduates vie for the limited number of postgraduate scholarships to French universities, institutes, and *grandes écoles*. And beyond the schools and universities, the ten countries' educated elites continued to live the often tense counterpoint between their francophilism and their assertion of an African identity. On the one hand, France remained their stylistic model for manners, entertainment, literature, and ideas. On the other, their need to develop specific African forms for the new political and social cultures prompted demands for the rejection of alien ways and spurred a search for usable African roots, heroes, cultures, and histories. To this day, the problems posed by this dilemma remain largely unsolved.

The passage to independence also created some totally unforeseen difficulties. Almost universally, achievement of independence generated nationwide celebrations of extraordinary scope and intensity; more people participated in that political event than any other, before or since. Further, and more important, the coming of independence was accompanied by almost millennial — and hence totally unrealistic — expectations of its benefits. Once freedom had been gained many believed, the new leadership would quickly solve the old, intractable problems of poverty, unemployment, official corruption, lack of economic opportunity, intertribal conflict, and the like. Given the general tone of nationalist rhetoric, which tended to ascribe most problems to the evils of French colonialism and subservient status, such hopes were hardly surprising. Unfortunately, these problems, which had been charged to embarrassable colonial regimes before independence, remained just as intractable thereafter, but now African governments had to deal with them. The high level of optimism with which the new governments began their work tended to fade once it became apparent that they were unable to meet the high expectations of performance. Moreover, many of the new leaders found it very difficult to accomplish the stylistic shift required by independence: the political talents needed to wage successful oppositional politics were not necessarily those appropriate to rulership, the responsibilities of power, and the tasks of national construction.

Many of the ten countries' subsequent political troubles may have germinated in that unhealthy, early gap between popular expectations and government performance.[9] The honeymoon tended to last about three to five years; Afrique noire saw its first military coup d'etat in Togo in January 1963, followed the same year by coups in Congo/Brazzaville (August) and Dahomey (October). By mid-1966, the Central African Republic and Upper Volta had increased the list to five. The infection eventually struck Mauritania, Mali, Niger, Chad, and Guinea and scarred the Ivory Coast, Cameroon, and Gabon. As of 1984, only the latter three states had never experienced a successful military coup d'etat; each, however, has seen at least one attempted coup by elements of its military.

The common elements in the ten states' passage to independence should not, however, be permitted to conceal their diversity, unique circumstances, and striking differences. One major set of differences can be found in the character of the ten states' first generation of leaders, that is, the men who agitated for greater measures of self-government, negotiated independence, and took power after the French departure. By and large, they were not revolutionaries or radicals by disposition or experience, although sometimes their rhetoric certainly made them sound as if they were. But in other ways these establishmentarians were a quite disparate lot. Their differences became obvious in their styles of governance and the ideas they brought to rulership. Some were avowed socialists, determined to create more or less militant, mobilized political systems. President Leopold Senghor of Senegal espoused a mixture of mild socialism and a visionary philosophy of black cultural assertion (*négritude*) and his first prime minister, Mamadou Dia, favored an activist socialism that would transform the country and the Third World.[10] Next door, in Mali, Modibo Keita sought to make his nation the epitome of socialist progress; his impatience with the slow pace of change in Senegal may have been partly responsible for the sudden collapse of the Mali federation, a union originally designed to forge a single, model socialist state.[11] Sékou Touré of Guinea was an avowed Marxist who came to his beliefs through the trade union movement (in contrast to Senghor, who learned his socialism in Paris's intellectual and university circles). Touré probably took his country further toward a centralized, fully mobilized state than any of his contemporaries; unfortunately, his socialist vision eventually foundered on the twin rocks of an inefficient, corrupt government and a brutal family dictatorship.[12]

Others offered more pragmatic and less ideological ruling styles, for example, Togo's Sylvanus Olympio, a bilingual businessman; Dahomey's Hubert Maga, a former teacher and civil servant; and Niger's Hamani Diori, also a former teacher and civil servant. In the Ivory Coast, one of the deans of francophone African politics, Félix Houphouet-Boigny, almost completely rejected ideological trappings, preferring instead to lead his country down an unabashedly capitalist path. Some adopted almost bureaucratic ruling styles: Mauritania's, Mokhtar Ould Daddah, an attorney;

Upper Volta's Maurice Yaméogo, a former civil servant; and Cameroon's, Ahmadou Ahidjo, a former government radio operator. Keita and Touré's relatively radical brand of socialism led them to close collaboration (and an ill-fated political union) with west Africa's Marxist *enfant terrible*, Kwame Nkrumah of Ghana. Keita and Touré established warm relations with the world socialist camp (the USSR, China, and others) and became members of the so-called Casablanca group (Morocco, Alergeria, Egypt, Libya, Mali, Guinea, and Ghana). The Casablanca group (so named after the pact signed in Casablanca on January 7, 1961) espoused radical international causes, supported Patrice Lumumba in the Congo, and advocated a rapid advance toward the political union of all African states. The rest of the francophone states, including those in equatorial Africa, preferred participation in the more moderate Monrovia (later, Lagos) group, whose thesis regarding African unity through gradual, functional (but not political) integration won the day when the Organization of African Unity was created in Addis Ababa in 1963.

The founding fathers, for all their stylistic and personal differences, did agree on the desirability of establishing strong central governments. Each national group set about creating institutions that would perpetuate its tenure in office and make it virtually impossible for opponents to come to power by legal means. One path taken by the new leaders combined constitutional amendment, the multiplication of restrictive political statutes (for example, censorship laws), and the creation of elaborate security apparatuses. The net effect was the establishment of a form of presidentialism even more powerful than the original Gaullist model. By March 1963, all ten of the states had installed such "reinforced" presidencies.[13]

The other, and complementary, route was the creation of so-called single-party systems. Four of the ten states had come to independence with what amounted to single-party systems: Guinea, Mali, the Ivory Coast, and Niger. Guinea's single party, the Parti Démocratique de Guinée (PDG), was enshrined in the 1958 constitution as the country's dominant political institution. The PDG's annual congress was to promulgate government policy, the party was to supervise all aspects of government, and all deputies to the national legislature were to be elected from the single list drawn up by the party leadership.[14] (In practice, of course, it was Sékou Touré and his closest associates who actually ran the government and made policy; in most cases the PDG congress simply ratified Touré's proposals.) Both Mali and Niger became de facto single-party systems in 1959, and the Ivory Coast had been one since 1957, when Houphouet's Parti Démocratique de Côte de'Ivoire (PDCI) swept away all opposing parties in that year's elections. The Guinean device of a constitutionally sanctioned national list of parliamentary candidates was subsequently adopted by the Ivory Coast, Dahomey, Upper Volta, and Niger (all four soon after August 1960) and, later, by Mali (1960), Togo (1961), Mauritania (1961), and Senegal (1963). Only Cameroon remained officially a multiparty system, but, since 1962, when President Ahidjo forced the remaining parties to unite with his Union Camerounaise (UC), no other party has dared to challenge the UC's supremacy. Unquestionably, the point of the exercise was not only the conquest of power but also its maintenance. Ahmed Mahiou, writing about the advent of single-party systems in francophone Africa, put the case bluntly:

> There is a close relationship between (the process of) *taking charge* of independence and the advent of the single party. In effect, the coming of independence involved the total transfer of powers and responsibilities . . . to the new sovereign state . . . Thus, it is precisely because the governing party seeks sole exercise of these powers and responsibilities that it sets out to eliminate all opposition. The single party thus appears not as a means by which to gain independence, but as a means of *assuming* it. (Italics in original.)[15]

How effective were the single-party systems in achieving the aims of their creators? No simple answer will suffice. The single party was meant to organize all political life within one institutional arena. Auxilliary organizations — of youth, women, trade unions, professionals, and so on — were founded to bring defined social and occupational categories into the national political fold. Certainly, as the only officially sanctioned political organization, the party soon became a favored avenue for anyone seeking preferred access to the scarce resources at the disposition of the regime: jobs, government contracts, development projects, schooling, and political careers, among others. One became a party member, paid party dues, or voted, for good and sufficient reasons. By mobilizing the country's human resources, the single party was designed to ensure support for the tasks of national construction as set by the regime and to develop stable loyalties to government leaders. The parties, however, never managed to achieve either the full mobilization or the support and loyalties the founders had hoped for. Admittedly, during the first three to five years after independence the founding fathers almost invariably enjoyed a great deal of popularity and civic support, and the ranks of their single parties swelled with eager members. Thereafter, the record is less heartening. With the conspicuous exceptions of Senegal, the Ivory Coast, and Cameroon, the other single parties gave way to military regimes and their single parties (as occurred in Togo and Dahomey), were simply abolished by new military leaders (Mauritania, Mali, Niger, and Upper Volta), or, as in Guinea, became the lifeless tools of an increasingly dictatorial elite. Cameroon, Senegal, and the Ivory Coast were exceptions not because the parties in these countries achieved full mobilization and loyalty, but because the regimes performed relatively well, particularly in the management of economic affairs. The success of a single party — as an instrument of popular mobilization and organization — probably depends much less on the zeal of its leaders and officials than on the overall performance of the regime. A regime that can deliver a reasonable amount of general prosperity can apparently induce its citizens to tolerate a single-party system. Even a regime faced with considerable economic uncertainty and forced to decree unpleasant austerity measures, as in Senegal, can retain popular confidence if its leaders are seen as honest men trying to make the best of a poor situation. Abdou Diouf, whose Parti Socialiste won 111 of the 120 seats in the February 1983 parliamentary elections, apparently benefited from just such trust.

On another level, however, the single parties were quite successful: together with state institutions of repression, the parties played an important role in preventing the organization or expression of overt opposition to the regimes in power. Further, in an unanticipated development, the single parties also contributed to the emasculation of formerly vigorous, deliberative, national parliaments. Once effective national decision making had been removed to the councils of the single party (in effect, to the national leadership circle), the francophone parliaments atrophied or simply became annual ratificatory conventions for policies made elsewhere. They could also (as in Cameroon during the latter years of the Ahidjo regime) become comfortable pasturages for super-annuated but faithful and deserving public figures.[16] In the final analysis, however, the single parties could ensure neither the constant loyalty of citizens nor the founding fathers' continued enjoyment of power. In one respect the single parties may even have hastened their founders' downfall: by suppressing dissidence and effectively preventing organized opposition from forming, the parties made it more than likely that, when dangerous opposition did arise, it would do so clandestinely and, more frequently than not, from essentially uncontrollable quarters — the military and police. Moreover, the absence of legal opposition within the single-party system made it much harder to check corruption.

INDEPENDENCE: CHALLENGES

The aura of extraordinary enthusiasm and optimism that accompanied independence dissipated once the real, and seemingly irreducible, problems faced by each new state became clear. Certainly, making nations of collections of people with parochial loyalties — to family, clan, and ethnic group — was no easy task. In the process, each national government had to establish its authority, persuade the citizenry of its legitimacy, and mobilize the country's resources, both human and physical, for the tasks of national construction. If this were not enough, each state also had to find its own way in the international community of potential friends, allies, and enemies into which it had been born. International links, in many cases, were critical to political and economic survival. How did the states respond? The year 1985 will mark 25 (or more) years since independence, and, although the states' domestic records offer little encouragement to the early optimists, they do reveal several highly interesting examples of political and economic experimentation and adaptation. Some of the experiments were dead ends, some made bad situations worse, still others were inconclusive, and a very few were crowned with conspicious, though modest, success. Responses to the international environment were similarly varied, although (with the exceptions of Guinea and Mali) the links with France tended to remain strong throughout.

French political scientist Jean-François Médard has argued that most African states are now examples of what he calls *l'état mou*, an almost untranslatable term that refers to weak states in which the structural and institutional foundations are in place, but, because the basic questions of power, legitimacy, and authority remain unanswered, the whole remains unstable, flaccid, and soft.[17] Characteristically, l'état mou often finds itself either unable or ineffective in coping with internal crises. Given the record since 1960, Médard may be correct. Needless to say, this state of affairs is not what the founding fathers had in mind; indeed, their first steps were designed to achieve national cohesion and control by strengthening the political and institutional center of the state. The desire for control led to the establishment of powerful, "reinforced" presidencies; the creation of single-party systems; amendments to constitutions; and the gradual transformation of inherited structures into handmaidens of the new centers of power and authority. In one respect, these changes were probably inevitable, particularly those that altered the constitutions and structures acquired at independence. The French undoubtedly intended — and the African founding fathers initially agreed — for the new states to be created in the image of France's Fifth Republic, a multiparty system with (to be sure) a strong presidency. In France, however, the electorate and parliament played critical, determinative roles. Once in office and faced with a multitude of unresolved problems, the African founding fathers chose to consolidate their power by curtailing opposition (frequently seen as unproductive, harmful, or disloyal), reducing the electorate to bystanders entitled to cheer but not to choose (Nelson Kasfir calls this "departicipation"), and emasculating or transforming any institutions (legislatures, consulative councils, or judiciaries) likely to contain uncooperative elements. In addition, in all ten states, the full panoply of state structures was quickly erected: ministries, administrative boards, bureaus, local governments, and government-run enterprises (parastatals, particularly in Guinea and Mali) emerged almost immediately. Everywhere, government became the primary employer, and operating budgets swelled to accommodate the increasing amounts needed for official salaries and perquisites. In short, the founding fathers' response to the problem of establishing authority was *étatisme* — the creation of dominating, centralizing states. Except in Senegal, Cameroon, and the Ivory Coast, neither a massive public sector nor a powerful central apparatus could guarantee internal stability or the survival of the founding regimes.

All ten states are plural societies, that is, all comprise a variety of well-defined social groups commanding strong primary loyalties. Most common is ethnic (or tribal) diversity, though other powerful forces (such as religion, language, race, and even region) attract social allegiance and frequently coexist with ethnicity. The classic task of nation builders is to transform or, if that is impossible, to harness, these parochial, primordial ties to new, larger, all-inclusive loyalties. The founding fathers had mobilized ethnic sentiment on behalf of nationalist causes before independence, and they recognized that unchecked competition between parochial groups for scarce political and economic resources could wreck all their plans for national development. As a result, they acted quickly to find the means to manage, if not altogether control, such potentially damaging diversity. Their record of accomplishment, and that of their successors, is both spotty and inconclusive, demonstrating that even the most sensitive of their formulas were and are fragile.

Guinea's attempted solution to the problem was the most radical. To promote ethnic integration, the PDG-controlled Council of Government approved, on December 31, 1957, a ministerial order that formally abolished "the chieftaincy of cantons called 'traditional chieftaincy' all over the Territory of French Guinea." In its place, Touré offered himself and the PDG as the new symbols of national unity. The move was at first popular, because most Guineans were prepared to believe, as Touré claimed, that the chiefs had been irredeemably tainted by excessive collaboration with the colonial regime. In any event, the decision did in fact help "to destroy an important symbol of ethnic particularism," although it did not, as later events were to demonstrate, destroy ethnicity as a factor in Guinea's internal politics.[18] During the first years after independence, Guinea enjoyed remarkable interethnic harmony. Guinea's revolution began to sour, however, when the PDG regime failed to deliver on its promises and a succession of real and imaginary plots shook the country. A fearful Touré increasingly turned to his fellow Malinké (and, ultimately, to members of his family) for advice and support. In 1971–72, following a brief but humiliating invasion by a small group of dissident Guineans and Portugese regulars, the regime announced the discovery of the so-called Fulani plot, attributed to the country's largest ethnic minority. The most prominent victim of the subsequent persecution of Fulanis was Diallo Telli, a former minister and previous secretary-general of the OAU, who was deliberately starved to death in Conakry's notorious Boiro prison camp.

At the other end of the spectrum, Cameroon, Senegal, the Ivory Coast, and perhaps (in recent years) Togo represent relative success stories. Cameroon contains almost two hundred ethnic groups and has politically significant religious (Muslim-Christian), regional (north-south), and linguistic (English- and French-speaking) divisions. Throughout his long tenure as president (1960–1982), Ahmadou Ahidjo, a northern Muslim Fulani, rather successfully followed a policy of regional balance (a code phrase for ethnic-religious-regional-linguistic equilibrium). Key positions in the country's ruling elite as well as political and economic benefits were carefully distributed. Ahidjo's regime may have been authoritarian, even brutal at times, but even his most zealous detractors did not deny the political skill with which he maneuvered Cameroon's social constituencies into peaceful cooperation and maintenance of a steady rate of economic growth. Only after Ahidjo had resigned the presidency was the ethnic-regional factor in politics brought forcibly to the surface: on April 6–7, 1984, the largely northern (and Muslim) presidential guard, hoping to bring Ahidjo back to power, launched a bloody attempt to remove President Paul Biya, himself a southerner and a Christian. The attempt failed because most elements of the army — including northerners — remained loyal to Biya and the regime. The event's impact on interethnic relations in Cameroon, however, has yet to become fully clear.

In Senegal the most important social divisions are not ethnic (the Wolof, Serer, Fulani, Tukolor, and Diula are the largest of over thirty groups) or religious (Muslim, about 78 percent; Christian [mainly Roman Catholic], about 4 percent). Rural-urban conflicts (approximately 33 percent of the population lives in coastal urban areas, chiefly in and around Dakar, the capital) are more significant, and especially important is the hostility among the four major Islamic brotherhoods (*tariqa*) to which about 98 percent of the country's Muslims belong. Because it virtually monopolizes the growing and marketing of Senegal's main crop, peanuts, the second-largest tariqa, the Muridiyya (or Mourides, with 500,000 members) wields a disproportionate influence. The single most important political legacy President Senghor left his successor, Abdou Diouf, upon his retirement in 1980 was a record of mutual accommodation and cooperation between the state and the tariqas.[19] The alliance he forged between Christians and Muslims (Senghor was a Catholic), between the sophisticated world of Dakar and the religious fundamentalists of the hinterland, was remarkable for both its duration and effectiveness. It brought Senegal's most powerful traditional magnates behind Senghor and gave him the weight (as well as the time and the means) to cope with the fissiparous, ideologically divided, modern political sector. Diouf, a Muslim, continues the relationship, but he must now deal with possible ethnic troubles in the Casamance (the region south of Gambia) and problems with the English-speaking Gambians, federated with Senegal since February 1, 1982. The new union, in fact more a confederation than a federation, was created in the wake of a bloody attempted coup in Banjul put down — at the request of Gambia's President Jawara — by Senegalese troops. The difficulties have come in trying to integrate the weak, but traditionally protected economy of Gambia with that of Senegal, itself in some difficulties because of several consecutive years of drought and decline in the earning power of its exports.

In the Ivory Coast, the last of the great francophone founding fathers, Félix Houphouet-Boigny has been in power since 1957. By judiciously distributing shares in the country's prosperity, he has co-opted the major ethnic groups and their leaders into a relatively stable (though occasionally internally contentious) system of reciprocal self-interest.

Finally, Togo probably qualifies as a partial success not because the old hostility between the southern, largely Christian Ewe and the northern Kabire has disappeared, but because the country's (Kabire) ruler, General Gnassingbe Eyadema, by guile and coercion, has kept the Ewe too busy making money to aspire to overthrow his regime. The Ewe have good reason to dislike Eyadema: after all, it was he who organized the 1963 "noncom's coup" and he was one of the group of soldiers that killed the popular Ewe president, Sylvanus Olympio. That coup and Olympio's murder brought an end to Ewe political supremacy and the death of Ewe hopes for creating an ethnic state with their tribal members in neighboring Ghana. Eyadema combines considerable political skill and a talent for ruthlessness with a liking for ostentatious international display. He has benignly encouraged the commercially enterprising Ewe to make the most of Lomé's status as a free port and to use the country's exploitable agricultural and mineral resources to good advantage. This tactic appears to have worked.

Togo is undeniably prosperous and the Togolese, in contrast to the Ghanaians next door, are quite well fed. Many Ewe still grumble about "northern domination," some still talk openly of the good old days under Olympio, and a very few (most in exile) swear revenge and plot Eyadema's downfall. On the whole, however, the Ewe are doing well economically, perhaps as well or better than they might have done under a government of their own choosing. Their dislike of Eyadema is not strong enough for the Ewe to risk their economic good fortune on an open confrontation. Someday, perhaps, if the regime falters or breaks down, but certainly not now.

The other states, Mali, Burkina Faso, Mauritania, Niger, and Benin, are all ruled at present by their militaries and appear to have taken the path of repression as a solution to their socioethnic problems. Mali, which includes people of Mande (50 percent), Fulani (18 percent), Voltaic (13 percent), Songhai (5 percent), and Berber (Tuaregs and Moors, 4.5 percent) stock, has become more socially and culturally homogeneous during the twentieth century. Traditionally distinctions that derive from previous enslavement or old caste systems still persist in some places. Nevertheless, the greatest problem has been the unhappy fate of the nomadic Tuaregs, driven south from their pasturages by the recurrent Sahelian droughts. The Tuaregs, independent and little inclined to respect outside authority, have long been an irritant to governments trying to domesticate them. Hence, it is hardly surprising that the response of the Malian government has been to confine most of them to barely habitable camps, provide the absolute minimum for their survival, and hope that God or a change in the weather will put them out of their misery.

Niger, like Mali, is a polyethnic crucible, but, unlike Mali, remains socially heterogeneous with various ethnic groups in a constant state of agitated political tension. Hamani Diori, president until he was removed by his military in 1974, engaged in a continuous, although ultimately unsuccessful, effort to balance demands and pressures from the various groups. His successor, Colonel Seyni Kountche, has had to do the same, although he has had considerably more persuasive means at his disposal. Pierre Biarnes's lucid epitome of Niger's complex ethnic situation is a good summary of problems faced not only by Niger but also by the other states of the western Sahel:

Its populations divide into two large groups of unequal importance, the nomads and the settled, who, despite constant inter-
penetration over the centuries, remain no less profoundly
different. The first group — Tuaregs, Toubous, Arabs, and
Fulani — is the less numerous, but ranges over the desert two-
thirds of the country in the north and east. The second group,
which comprises three-quarters of the population, is concentrated in the southern, more fertile, parts: The Songhai and
Zarma (Djerma) in the west, the Hausa (the largest ethnic group)
in the center, and the Kanuri in the east. Since they are primarily
Sahara dwellers, the nomads cannot . . . help feeling more and
more attracted to Libya and, above all, to Algeria, which is
developing rapidly and pushing roads in their direction . . . On
the other hand, the Hausa in the Zinder, Maradi, and Magaria
regions have always lived in close symbiosis, socially and
economically, with their coethnics in northern Nigeria, where
railroads and modern roads come within a few kilometers of
Niger's borders. Finally, the Songhai and the Zarma, who represent a bare third of the population and who occupy a limited area
of the country (including, to be sure, the region of Niamey, the
capital), are almost alone in being truly integrated with French-
speaking west Africa. In sum, the potential risks of an explosion
in Niger are considerable, and it is precisely in their attempts to
avoid these risks that Niger's successive rulers have . . . demonstrated a remarkable spirit of continuity.[20]

Mauritania and Burkina Faso, like Mali, share a considerable
measure of ethnic homogeneity. Each, however, faces some unique
complexities. Mauritania has a centuries-old division between the
so-called black and white Moors (both Arab-speaking, Muslim,
and of Berber origin, but distinguished by their life styles [nomadic
or sedentary], degree of arabization, and the extent of intermixture
with the black, non-Arabic-speaking peoples in the south). In addition, Mauritanians still make distinctions based on traditional
castes and slave status. Balance and compromise were key elements
in the response by the first (civilian) government of Mokhtar Ould
Daddah. The performance was unconvincing, however, since Ould
Daddah was himself from one of the more important *beidane*
(white Moor) clans, and he clearly favored the white Moors and
their clients over the black Moors and their clients. The 1979 coup
brought in military men who have tried to redress the balance but

have had only limited success thus far.

In Burkina Faso (so renamed in 1984), the key problem has been the position of the Mossi, for two hundred years the numerically and politically dominant ethnic group in the region. The civilian regime of Maurice Yameogo (in power from 1960 to 1965) effectively curtailed the power of the Mossi king, the Mogo Naba, but Yameogo's government was nevertheless a Mossi regime. A succession of civilian and military regimes have attempted, with varying success, to find ways of bringing representatives of the minority ethnic groups (Fulani, Djerma, Hausa, and so on) into the governing circles.

Benin (formerly Dahomey), is almost unique in that the several military interventions that began in 1963 (the first coup was headed by General Christophe Soglo), including the one launched in 1972 by junior colleagues of the present ruler (General Mathieu Kerekou) were all principally in response to incessant, virtually uncontrollable interethnic feuding. Benin has three main ethnic groups (the southern Yoruba, the south-central Fon, and the northern Bariba). The principal champions of these ethnic groups, Hubert Maga (a Bariba from the north), Justin Ahomadegbe (a Fon from the Abomey region), and Sourou-Migan Apithy (a Yoruba from the Porto-Novo area), headed the political battles. Each leader attempted to create a presidential regime in which he and his group dominated the country's politics, and each failed; each tried an alliance with one of the others against the third, and that also failed; the three then tried a somewhat bizarre three-man presidency in which each man was president for a year (1970–1972), and that did not work either.[21] Finally, a disgusted military took over and sent the three into exile in Paris — where, it is claimed, they sometimes get together amiably over drinks. Since 1972 the Kerekou regime, by legal and coercive means, has put a heavy lid on the country's tradition of interethnic conflict. Reports persist, however, that even under Benin's current Marxist dispensation, old rivalries still simmer within the regime.

The Benin/Dahomey case illustrates the third challenge faced by the ten states after independence, that is, how their regimes respond to crisis, whether generated internally or by external events. In Dahomey, the turning point was a crisis of public confidence: when all possible combinations of civilian rule failed to produce either domestic peace or effective government, the military, which saw itself as the ultimate guardian of the national patrimony, stepped in to restore order. A somewhat similar circumstance prevailed in Upper Volta in 1966, when the army was literally invited by massed demonstrators to take power from a civilian regime that had grown excessively corrupt, ineffective, and (in popular eyes) morally bankrupt. The president's own behavior apparently was the last straw. Maurice Yameogo, a Catholic, had unceremoniously sent his wife back to her village and ostentatiously married an Ivoirian beauty-contest winner, looting the public treasury to pay for an expensive honeymoon in Brazil. The enraged citizens of Ouagadougou, urged on by the local archbishop, Paul Cardinal Zoungrana, first massively repudiated Yameogo's party during the 1965 local elections and then, as Yameogo showed little inclination to repent of his sins, took to the streets against him.

If the first coup in Burkina Faso was an example of an internal crisis resolved by military intervention, the fourth coup since 1966 (on August 4, 1983), had less to do with domestic difficulties than with disagreements about the direction of internal and external policy. Admittedly, the seeming inability of the preceding military regimes to remedy Burkina Faso's chronic economic problems (due principally to a poor resource base, chronic drought, relative isolation, the annual labor flight south, and the poverty of most of its citizens) had something to do with Captain Thomas Sankara's seizure of power, but his coup was certainly not preceded by anything like a domestic crisis. An exponent of radical, *Marxisant* solutions and a friend and admirer of Libya's Moammar Khadafy, Sankara apparently took advantage of a sharp ideological split within the ruling council led by his predecessor, Major Jean-Baptiste Ouedraogo. If "crisis" there was, it was artificially created. It should be added that the "ideological" coup or coup attempt is not uncommon in Africa: one took place in Marxist Guinea-Bissau in November 1980, at least two have occurred in Congo/Brazzaville, and several recent attempted military coups against the (military) regimes in Niger and Mali have been launched for such reasons.

Another form of domestic crisis is the succession crisis, generated by the transition from one leader to another or from one regime to its successor. In a continent where change of leadership or regime is usually involuntary and, in the majority of cases, involves the military, peaceful and constitutional transition is both rare and welcome. Since 1960, there have been only eight examples of regular constitutional succession in all of Africa.

Table 1: Regular Constitutional Succession in Sub-Saharan Black Africa, 1960–1985

Date	Country	Incumbent President	Successor	Circumstances
November 28, 1967	Gabon	Leon Mba	Omar Bongo	Death of Mba
July 23, 1971	Liberia	William Tubman	William Tolbert	Death of Tubman
August 22, 1978	Kenya	Jomo Kenyatta	Daniel arap Moi	Death of Kenyatta
July 13, 1980	Botswana	Seretse Khama	Quett Masire	Death of Khama
December 30, 1980	Senegal	Leopold S. Senghor	Abdou Diouf	Senghor retires
November 6, 1982	Cameroon	Ahmadou Ahidjo	Paul Biyo	Ahidjo retires
October 5, 1985	Sierra Leone	Sioka Stevens	Joseph Memoh	Stevens returns
November 5, 1985	Tanzania	Julius Nyerere	Ali Hassan Mwingi	Nyerere retires

Note: Not included is succession by way of national elections, since, in all instances in which a new national leader took power by election, the elections themselves were either the direct consequence of an irregular overthrow of the preceding regime or were organized by the makers of the coup.

Source: *Africa Report*, 28, no. 3 (May–June 1983), p. 25.

Note that four of the cases involved the death of a president and the other four followed voluntary resignations. Yet even this salutary record is flawed: although no succession crises occurred during the actual transitions, in two of these instances (Liberia and Cameroon), a crisis did follow after some delay. In Liberia, the unfortunate William Tolbert, unable to fill his remarkable predecessor's shoes and lacking Tubman's extraordinary political skills, died during the successful military coup of April 1980. In Cameroon in November 1982, Ahmadou Ahidjo turned the presidency over to his constitutional successor, Prime Minister Paul Biya, after 24 years in power. But Ahidjo himself (who had apparently changed his mind about retiring) created a crisis that led, on April 5 and 16, 1984, to a bloody but unsuccessful coup attempt by the presidential guard.

The most recent succession crisis occurred in Guinea immediately after Sékou Touré's death on March 26, 1984, in an American hospital. The death of Touré, who had dominated his country's political life since 1957, left an enormous power vacuum. None of his colleagues (including his relatives) could fill his shoes, and they found themselves completely unable to deal with the accumulated anger and frustration of a people living under what had become a brutal dictatorship. Eight days after Touré's death, the military took over amid genuine rejoicing. In francophone Africa Senegal has experienced the only completely peaceful voluntary transfer of power from one leader to another.

I noted earlier that some of the more recent military regimes in Burkina Faso took power partly because their predecessors had been unable to find ways of dealing with the country's deteriorating economic situation, much of which has been due to the droughts that have hit the Sahel since 1968. In that sense, then, some of the Burkinese coups were in partial response to externally generated circumstances. The drought had an even more direct bearing on the military coup of April 1974, which overthrew the corrupt civilian regime of Hamani Diori. There is little doubt that the Diori regime's principal response to the drought of 1973 — to make as much personal profit as possible from the event — led directly to Seyni Kountche's putsch. It can be argued that in part the Mali coup of November 1968 was also a response to the inability of Modibo Keita's regime to deal with the country's drought-related problems, but its proximate cause was undoubtedly a set of policies that threatened to weaken the army in favor of Keita's party militias.

The Mauritanian coup of July 1978 is probably the clearest example of a response to an externally generated crisis. Without going into the details of the tangled controversy surrounding the ex-Spanish Sahara (now known as the Western Sahara), suffice it to say that Mauritania, which had controlled the southern portion of the Western Sahara (Morocco hold the phosphate-rich north) as a result of a 1975 deal with Spain, came into open military confrontation with the Algerian-backed Saharoui rebels of the Polisario Front. That war, which even involved a Polisario raid on Nouakchott (Mauritania's capital), almost ruined the country and led directly to the July coup. Subsequently, Mauritania turned its portion of the Western Sahara over to Morocco, made peace with the Polisario, and adopted a highly anti-Moroccan stance.[22]

Most of these crises, though varied as to cause, duration, circumstance, and effect, had at least this much in common: a military response was made possible in most cases because the first civilian regimes simply failed in conflict management, resource mobilization, and economic development. The gap between expectation and performance may have played a role in these failures, but, generally, they were largely the work of the new leaders themselves. Only the regimes in the Ivory Coast (which now apprehensively awaits the passing of its septuagenarian president) and Senegal (where President Adbou Diouf still rules with the apparent blessing of both his predecessor and the Senegalese people) have managed to overcome all potentially dangerous challenges and so have avoided military intervention. In Cameroon, long an exemplar of stability and progress, the military in 1984 put aside temptation and aided its civilian president in suppressing an attempted coup from its own ranks. For that, despite the bloody events of April 5 and 6, 1984, and unless Biya completely fails to restore confidence in his rule, Cameroon perhaps deserves to rank among the few states able to cope effectively with severe domestic crises. In all, however, the record of response to crisis, even from an African standpoint, is hardly encouraging, although in Guinea, Niger, and Mauritania, where the military became the political court of last resort, intervention may well have averted economic or political disaster or prevented further deterioration of a dangerous situation.

A final challenge for the ten states was entrance into the international arena. Here again, the record is mixed. One way of assessing that record, of course, is to examine the ways in which the states have dealt with the colonial legacy of their close ties to France.

Table 2: The Military in Francophone Sub-Saharan Africa

	Total Armed Forces (1983–84)	Estimated Paramilitary[a] Forces	Estimated Defense Expenditures (millions of U.S. dollars)	Military Expenditures as percentage share of GNP (1978)
Benin	3,150	1,100	23.6 (1981)	2.0
Burkina Faso (Upper Volta)	3,775	900	32.1 (1981)	3.4
Cameroon	7,300	5,000	78.6 (1982–83)	1.6
Central African Republic	2,300	1,500	20.0 (1981)	2.2
Chad	4,200	6,000	51.7 (1982)	3.4
Congo	8,700	3,000	150.0 (1981–82)	5.2
Gabon	2,200	2,800	88.8 (1982)	0.5
Guinea	9,900	9,000	79.9 (1982)	—
Ivory Coast	5,070	3,000	92.0 (1981)	2.2
Madagascar	21,000	2,500	78.5 (1982)	2.8
Mali	4,950	5,000	40.0 (1981)	3.5
Mauritania	8,470	2,500	62.0 (1982)	7.1
Niger	2,220	2,550	19.2 (1981)	0.8
Senegal	9,700	6,800	50.8 (1982–83)	2.2
Togo	5,080	750	21.0 (1982)	2.8

Sources: *The Military Balance 1983/4* (London: Institute for Strategic Studies, 1984): and *Accelerated Development in Sub-Saharan Africa* (Washington, D.C.; World Bank, 1981), table 43, p. 186.

[a] In most cases, this includes the gendarmerie. In Guinea, prior to the 1984 military coup, the figure included 7,000 members of the "people's militia."

With the exceptions of Mali and Guinea, at the time of independence the states all signed sets of political, economic, and (in several instances) military cooperation accords with France. These links, whether regarded as salutary marks of friendship or neocolonial burdens, have resulted, among other things, in a continuing flow of French developmental assistance and private capital; financial subsidies for budgets in perennial imbalance (as in Dahomey/Benin); the presence of hundreds of French technical and cultural assistants (*coopérants*); the backing of the French franc for local currencies; a more or less protected market for African products in the Common Market zone; annual conferences with every French president since de Gaulle; and French military assistance to help train army and police officers, put down armed rebels, or rescue governments in extreme distress. The use of French troops in Africa has been highly selective and somewhat confusing: France apparently intervenes militarily only to help its most recently favored clients or friends. Beneficiaries have included Cameroon's Ahmadou Ahidjo (1960–1962), Gabon's Leon Mba (1964), and Senegal's Senghor. The Central African Empire's Jean-Bebel Bokassa was overthrown by French paratroopers in 1979, and French troops were sent to Chad in August 1983 to protect President Hisseine Habre from former president Goukouni Woddeye — whom the French had previously and unsuccessfully protected from Habre. Overall, however, the French military commitment in Africa has been quite consistent since 1960. Although decisions to intervene on behalf of one or another African government frequently depend on the political circumstances of the moment, France still maintains military technical assistants and "advisers" (some of whom handle administrative matters for the host government or even command units) in all its former African territories except Guinea. (And a number of military advisers reportedly returned to Guinea following Colonel Conte's coup.) There are French bases or garrisons in four countries (Djibouti, Gabon, the Central African Republic, and Senegal), and (excluding the more than 3,000 troops sent to Chad in 1983) some 6,700 French soldiers are stationed in six countries. The latter figure, incidentally, does not include the approximately one thousand noncoms and officers posted to francophone Africa as technical assistants and advisers. Finally, France still has active defense agreements with seven countries (Djibouti, Gabon, the Ivory Coast, Senegal, Cameroon, the Central African Republic, and Togo) and has conducted joint military maneuvers with local units in six of the seven countries (the Central African Republic is the exception).[23]

France remains the primary or secondary trading partner for each of the ten countries, and French cultural influences remain strong everywhere. All ten countries have not maintained their links with France to the same extent; they range from the Ivory Coast and Senegal (both still very close in all respects to the former *métropole*) to Guinea under Sékou Touré and Mali under Modibo Keita. At one time, both Guinea and Mali pulled out of the French zone (which made their currencies virtually nonconvertible elsewhere), established close political and economic ties with the Soviet Union and the countries of Eastern Europe, and, as members of the so-called radical bloc of African states (the Casablanca group before 1963; later the bloc included Ghana, Algeria, Libya, Egypt, and Tanzania) maintained cold, sometimes hostile relations with their francophone neighbors. Of the two, Guinea had the better deal; Mali's connections to the socialist world did little to help it out of its economic difficulties. Guinea, whose economy was kept afloat by the returns from its large Western-financed and American- and European-run mining sector, used its radical ideological stance and ties to the East to play a leading role in international Third World politics, thumb its nose at the "imperialist" West, and claim the high moral ground from which Touré regularly denounced his more moderate neighbors as "lackeys of world imperialism" and "neo-colonialist enclaves." (Incidentally, the possible contradiction between creating a Marxist state and giving Western capitalists a privileged position in the economy appears not to have disturbed the Guineans.) Eventually, as economic, social, and political conditions worsened in both countries, their leaders increasingly turned to the West for help. Not surprisingly, donors anxious to wean Touré from his Eastern associations were not hard to find: since 1962, Guinea has received almost twice the official development assistance the United States has offered any other African country.

On the one hand, most of the ten states continue to maintain close connections with France, but, on the other, they have also established highly diverse trade, financial, and political relationships with other countries throughout the world. The United States, for example, is one of the principal purchasers of Ivoirian cocoa. American firms also buy most of Cameroon's oil and help in petroleum exploration and production; there are even branches of three large American banks in the country (Chase Manhattan, First Boston, and the Bank of America). The consortiums that mine, process, and export Guinea's bauxite include not only French, but also German, British, American, Italian, Japanese, and Scandinavian companies. Even Israel, officially shunned by most African states in 1973, has returned to do business in francophone Africa. Among other ventures, a major Israeli construction firm, Solel Boneh, (operating through an American affiliate) is building thousands of housing units in Cameroon. In the Ivory Coast, another Israeli conglomerate, Koor (operating through a Dutch affiliate), sells agricultural equipment and know-how. The examples could be multiplied almost indefinitely; the point is that while France still occupies a preferred position in the ten countries' international exchanges, it no longer completely dominates those relationships. In fact, since 1960, the French share of these states' export and import trade has markedly diminished.

The same pattern of diversification is evident in the countries' international political contacts. Again, France continues to play a preferred role in those contacts, although the ten have not hesitated to look elsewhere for useful friends and exchanges. In addition to Guinean and Malian ties to Eastern Europe (which, to be sure, have waned in recent years), the self-styled Marxist regime in Benin has opened active channels in that direction, and Upper Volta has cultivated new friendships with the ideologically compatible regimes of Libya and Ghana. Mauritania, a member of the Arab League and once an ally of Morocco, has found new affinities with Algeria (on the question of the Western Sahara). Guinea has formally renewed financial and political ties with France, and now seeks Western aid and investment. The American presence, long held in check by Washington in deference to French sensitivities, is now increasingly felt throughout the area, particularly in Cameroon, where both the Ahidjo and Biya regimes have welcomed American help in countering Libyan adventurism in Chad and the Saharan region. Francophone Africa was for a long time considered a private reserve for French interests; the governments of the francophone countries themselves have begun to alter that situation and now feel free to pick and choose new political friends and economic partners as self-interest dictates.

Finally, to make the record complete, mention must be made of the countries' participation in a wide range of regional, continental, and international organizations. All ten countries are full members of the United Nations, and all participate in the array of international organizations affiliated with it. All ten are associate members of the European Common Market and full members of the Organization of African Unity and its related functional organizations. Mauritania, as noted above, belongs to the Arab League, and several (Mali, Upper Volta, Niger, Guinea, Senegal, and Cameroon) send observers to the somewhat amorphous Organization of the Islamic Conference. The Council of the Entente, a loose political-economic consultative venture organized by the Ivory Coast in 1969 still functions, bringing the Ivory Coast, Upper Volta, Benin, Niger, and Togo together for annual discussions of common problems. All are members of the African Development Bank and the Economic Community of West African

States. Within the region, and with varied memberships, the ten help maintain such useful organizations as the Niger River Commission and the Organization for the Development of the Senegal River.

THE TEN COUNTRIES TODAY: THREE SUCCESS STORIES AND AN OVERVIEW

The ten countries began as French colonies and, with the exception of Guinea, all became independent states in 1960. The period from 1945 to 1960 schooled their peoples in the basics of participatory politics, formed the local leadership groups destined to become the ruling elites of the new states, and created the legal-institutional basis for the surrender of colonial power. Provided with a framework of constitutions, laws, and government structures, as well as the rudiments of a national political culture, the ten states were born in a climate of general optimism about the future. In three of these countries, Senegal, the Ivory Coast, and Cameroon, developments appear more or less to have justified that optimism; the reasons are worth exploring in summary.

When Abdou Diouf became Senegal's president in 1980, there was considerable apprehension both about Diouf's ability to fill his predecessor's admittedly large shoes and about the willingness of the country's most powerful leaders and political groups, including the army, to accept Diouf's leadership during a period of relatively severe economic stress. There was no military coup, as some had predicted, and Diouf skillfully moved to consolidate his position by co-opting the most important of Senghor's collaborators into his regime; quickly gaining the support of the country's principal Muslim brotherhoods including the dominant Mourides and their dynamic leader, Abdoul Lahat M'Bake; liberalizing the educational system; and by a controlled revival of Senegal's multiparty tradition. Some eight parties finally contested the presidential and legislative elections of February 27, 1983; although some of the losing parties and candidates claimed that electoral irregularities and fraud had deprived them of a fair count, by general admission this was the fairest and most open election the country had seen since the 1960s. Not surprisingly, Diouf defeated four other presidential candidates with 83.55 percent of the votes cast, and his party, the Socialist Party (founded by Senghor), took 111 of the

120 seats in parliament. On February 1, 1982, Senegal formally inaugurated a political union, Senegambia, with English-speaking Gambia. Long a dream of Senegalese politicians, Senegambia became a reality following a bloody 1981 attempted coup in Bathurst when Senegal intervened militarily at the request of Gambia's President Daouda Jawara.

The only genuinely worrisome aspect of an otherwise promising situation remains the economy. Badly hurt by the recurring Sahelian droughts, forced to inaugurate unpopular austerity measures because of high foreign indebtedness, and faced by the need to transform the old peanut-based colonial economy into a much more diversified and productive economic system, the country's economic outlook is none too bright. Some steps toward drastic change have already been taken: in 1982, several major dam (and irrigation) projects were under way, and the basic infracture that would permit the exploitation of Senegal's promising phosphate and iron ore deposits was in the process of being constructed.[24] Senegal has turned out to be an undoubted political success story; whether it can also turn the economic corner is open to debate.

In mid-1984 the Ivory Coast, by all comparative indexes, still had one of the most successful economies in tropical Africa. Despite a drop in the world price for cocoa (the country's most valuable export crop), some alarming deficits in the balance of payments, rising unemployment among youth, and serious social problems attending a too-rapid urban influx of rural populations, the Ivory Coast has nonetheless managed to sustain a net economic growth rate of around 5 percent and a per capita income of approximately $1,250 (in 1983), the fifth highest on the entire continent (only Libya, Gabon, Algeria, and South Africa have higher figures). After Nigeria and Zimbabwe, it is the most highly industrialized black African country, has one of Africa's most diversified economies, and boasts one of west Africa's best transport and communications networks. Although the agricultural sector has had difficulties during the past several years, there is a good deal of hope that Ivoirian petroleum resources can give the economy a needed boost. In 1982, "Espoir," the first of several major deposits to come on stream, began producing commercially important quantities of oil, and, by the end of 1983 (according to the December 26, 1983, issue of the *Oil and Gas Journal*), some fifteen Ivoirian wells were producing an estimated average of 24,000 barrels per day. That production figure represents a 118 percent increase since 1982, and, with new fields coming into production, 100,000 barrels per day in 1988 is not improbable. That will mean a sharp decline in what the Ivory Coast has to pay for imported petroleum products, an additional supply for domestic users, and, most important, an improvement of the country's balance of payments position.

It need hardly be added that the Ivory Coast's strong economy could not have been built without the pragmatic policies of its government and the stability and continuity of leadership provided by Félix Houphouet-Boigny, now nearing 80 years of age. The possible problems surrounding his succession have cast the greatest cloud over the country's political future. Houphouet has talked for years about retiring and, in 1981, even created the position of vice president, constitutionally entitled to succeed the president in the event of the latter's death, resignation, or incapacity. By mid-1984, however, he had not yet named anyone to that position fearing, it is widely believed, to precipitate open conflict among his possible successors (including Henry Konan Bedié and Philippe Yacé, the current and past presidents of the Ivoirian National Assembly, respectively). In 1985 he was re-elected president. In the meantime, Ivoirians wait uneasily, hoping that a dangerous succession crisis can be avoided when the inevitable occurs.

In some respects, the Cameroonian success story is even more remarkable than those of Senegal and the Ivory Coast, since Cameroon had much less to start out with and began independence with the burden of an active local rebellion. The rebellion was largely put down by the end of 1965 (its last remaining internal leader, Ernest Ouadie, was publicly executed in January 1970). The few remnants of what had once been the country's most dynamic nationalist party (the Union des Populations du Cameroun [UPC]) now live in exile in France. The rebellion, which had involved large areas in Cameroon's southwest departments and the major cities, failed to prevent the political union of the English-speaking Southern Cameroons (a former U.N. trusteeship under British rule) with the Cameroon Republic and the creation in 1961 of the Cameroon Federal Republic. This experiment lasted until 1972, when a new unitary state, the Cameroon United Republic, replaced the earlier arrangements. The guiding hand throughout was that of Ahmadou Ahidjo, a Muslim northerner from Garoua. By a combination of guile, ruthlessness, and persuasion Ahidjo pushed through pragmatic policies that not only co-opted most of the rebellion's leadership into his regime, coerced the legal opposition into surrender, and created wholly new sets of institutions in 1961 and 1972, but also the foundations for a growing and increasingly productive economy. In 1977 Cameroon joined the ranks of Africa's oil-producing states. By the end of 1983, Cameroon's 166 active wells were producing 114,000 barrels per day (which compared favorably to Gabon's 150,000 barrels per day), enough to satisfy the country's internal petroleum needs (about 125,000 barrels per day). The remainder was exported to the United States. The regime's oil policies are yet another example of Ahidjo's pragmatic approach to economics and politics: anxious to avoid excessive reliance on petrodollar income or to generate an oil boom psychology, he had about half the income from oil sales and exports put away in foreign banks in high interest-bearing accounts. The other half was carefully channeled back into the economy. (There is circumstantial evidence that some of this money, put into accounts under Ahidjo's name and accessible only to Ahidjo and a few of his most trusted lieutenants, were used by Ahidjo to feather his own retirement nest, to make private investments, and to reward his friends. True or not, the matter has been hard to lay to rest because Ahidjo was not publicly accountable for these funds.) Ahidjo also insisted that agriculture remain the foundation of the country's economy, and the 1981–1986 five-year plan reflects that policy.

By the time Ahidjo voluntarily retired in November 1982, the country was in excellent economic shape. Ahidjo and his colleagues were certainly very much in charge, but some undercurrents of discontent had begun to surface. Unfortunately, despite the seemingly amicable circumstances under which Ahidjo turned power over to Biya, the events of 1983 and 1984 have raised serious questions about Cameroon's political future. Apparently changing his mind about relinquishing power, Ahidjo at first tried to change the constitution to make the country's single party, the Cameroon National Union, of which he remained president, the supreme arbiter of national affairs. Failing in that, he then encouraged a conspiracy that planned a military coup to oust Biya and, presumably, would have returned Ahidjo to power. The conspiracy was discovered, and its principals were put on trial; Ahidjo himself, now in exile in Senegal, was tried an absentia and condemned to death, a sentence Biya later commuted. Then, on April 5 and 6, 1984, came the attempted coup by the presidential guard. Both civilian and military casualties were high in Yaoundé, where the attempt took place, but fortunately for Biya and the constitutional order, the military rallied to put down the rebellion. The questions raised by these events, however, remained unanswered. What could the country now expect from its military, once the forbidden door of intervention had been opened by Ahidjo and his partisans? What obligations to the army had Biya now incurred, since it had his life and regime? And could Biya, given the events of 1983 and 1984, manage to regain control and fulfill the liberalizing promise represented by his succession? The example of Abdou Diouf in Senegal provides some comfort, but Cameroon is not Senegal, and it remains to be seen if Biya has Diouf's political talents or his luck.

The seven other states have military regimes of varying degrees of effectiveness, repressiveness, and staying power. Those in Niger, Mali, Benin, and Togo have been in power at least ten years, have demonstrated a fair capacity to govern, and show little inclination to return government to civilian hands. And Benin, despite its Marxist trappings, remains almost completely oriented to Western Europe and France in its external economic relations. The remaining three regimes are difficult to categorize or to evaluate: Guinea and Burkina Faso because they are still quite new, Mauritania because not much is known about it. Of the new Guinean military regime, headed by Colonel Lansana Conte, this much is clear: it intends to dismantle the repressive apparatus erected by Sékou Touré, to reopen the country to French and Western investment and aid, and to make it possible for the more than one million Guineans who fled Touré's dictatorship to return home. In Burkina Faso, it now appears that Captain Thomas Sankara intends to reorganize the country's political institutions along the revolutionary lines developed in Libya and adapted in Ghana. Whatever Sankara does, however, Burkina Faso remains trapped by drought, its isolated inland position, and one of Africa's poorest economies. And, finally, in Mauritania, the current military regime headed by Colonel Mohammed Khouna Ould Haidalla appears to have become highly repressive in the face of serious internal troubles. The economy is in a shambles because of the drought and declining revenue from its mining sector, and the regime keeps finding alleged pro-Libyan, pro-Nasserian, pro-Iraqi, and pro-Moroccan plots against it. Arrests and detentions have multiplied, and there are now hundreds of political prisoners held under extremely harsh conditions.

The current state of the ten countries, then, ranges from economically difficult but relatively politically promising (Senegal) to desperate (Mauritania). Two (the Ivory Coast and Cameroon) have managed to sustain enviable records to economic growth and political stability, but now face uncertain political futures. Togo will probably remain something of a success story so long as Eyadema remains in power, and, as for the rest, the future remains largely clouded, given the uncertain political and economic situations described in these pages.

FRANCE: FRIEND, PATRON, OR NEOCOLONIAL EXPLOITER?

"Without Africa," wrote French president François Mitterand in 1957, "there would be no twentieth-century French history."[25] During his last press conference on January 27, 1981, former president Giscard d'Estaing shifted the emphasis: "I take care of African politics, that is, of France's interests in Africa" (*Je m'occupé de politique africaine, c'est à dire les intérêts de la France en Afrique*). The two quotations speak dramatically to the impact of France's relations with its former African colonies on both France and the francophone states. The second quote also seems to reinforce a widely held belief that the independence granted the francophone states was more formal than real and that France continues to control them through a variety of economic, political, and social means. Needless to say, such a view is not shared by francophone African leaders, particularly those whose countries have retained especially close ties to France (including the Ivory Coast, Senegal, Gabon, and Cameroon). For them, France remains a close friend, even patron, but there is no question of French control over their countries' political and economic lives. What is the evidence for both arguments, and how can it be interpreted?

First, as was indicated earlier in this chapter, during the 1950s neither the French nor the leaders of the French African territories had much enthusiasm for the prospect of outright independence for *Afrique noire*. Both saw the future in terms of continued close association: the African nations would become self-governing entities connected to France within de Gaulle's new French Community. Only Guinea demurred in 1958, and hence gained its immediate independence under a heavy cloud of spiteful French

disapproval. In any event, for the rest, the future did lead to independence, but (initially) within the Community, and terms that
guaranteed a continuation of the most useful of the reciprocal
economic and political links with France. The new arrangements
also suited de Gaulle and, apparently, his successors. French
journalist Pierre Biarnes, who has devoted most of his lifetime to
studying francophone Africa, aptly summarized de Gaulle's
design:

> Moreover, by chance, this disengagement, easily coated with
> liberal colors, happened to coincide with the aspirations of the
> African elites. With a little effort, it would thus be possible to
> keep their friendship (in any case, that of many of the top-
> ranking ones), to make them diplomatic allies, and to continue to
> sell cloth and enamelware to their countries. Occasionally, and
> more easily than before, [they could be sold] an electrical power
> station, a radio transmitter, or a radio and television station, all
> insofar as they would be prepared in turn to follow a develop-
> ment path that [France] stood ready to suggest. In short,
> [France] would continue to exercise a preponderant influence on
> these countries and would preserve its trade — in any case a large
> part of it — with them, but at much less political and economic
> cost than before.[26]

Biarnes's tone is cynical, but he does accurately convey a point of
view widely shared by French leaders at the time. De Gaulle himself
was certainly much more interested in the welfare of France than he
was in that of the francophone states, but it cannot be denied that
his design probably has worked out much more successfully than
even he expected, at least as far as the French presence in Africa is
concerned.

Various aspects of the French presence in Africa have already
been outlined in this chapter: trade, cooperation, technical assistance (particularly in education), cultural diffusion and exchange,
and, of course, military aid and assistance. Some additional details
may help make the point. For example, there are now (with the
exception of north Africa) actually more Frenchmen living in black
Africa than there were at the time of independence. This is particularly true of the Ivory Coast, where the French population has
quadrupled from about 12,000 in 1960 to about 50,000 in 1984. The
same is true of Gabon, where there are now some 27,000 French

citizens, compared to about 4,000 in 1960. The same pattern, to a lesser degree, also holds true for Senegal, Niger, and Cameroon. In all, there are about 200,000 French citizens in Afrique noire, most of them employed in the private sector. Of the total, some 13,000 are involved in technical assistance programs (mainly in education, which accounts for about 10,000), for which France pays part or most of the costs.

France remains far and away the most important trading partner of its former African colonies. In 1981 (according to the latest data) it was the principal source of imports for Cameroon (52 percent of the total value of its imports), the Congo (62 percent), the Ivory Coast (33 percent), Gabon (43 percent), Guinea (36 percent), Burkina Faso (36 percent), Mali (65 percent), Mauritania (about 40 percent), Niger (32 percent), the Central African Republic (63 percent), Senegal (38 percent), and Togo (32 percent). During the same year, France was the main client for the exports of Benin (22 percent of the total, mainly cotton and cocoa), the Ivory Coast (20 percent, mainly cocoa, coffee, and tropical woods), Niger (40 percent, mainly uranium), Senegal (19 percent, mainly minerals and fish), Mali (32 percent, mainly cotton and live meat animals), the Central African Republic (52 percent, mainly tropical woods, coffee, and industrial diamonds), and Gabon (25 percent, mainly oil).[27] In addition to bilateral trade, hardly a single major French company does not have representation in Africa. The huge CFAO trading company, Peugeot and Citroën cars, and such giant construction firms as Bouygues, Dumez, and SAE all have firm and long-standing bases in the francophone countries.

In addition, there is the financial cover provided by the French franc zone, to which all the former French territories of equatorial and west Africa (except Mauritania) belong. Mali and Guinea rejoined in 1984, and two other countries — Zaire and Sierra Leone — hope to join soon. The heart of the franc zone system is the guaranteed parity (and convertibility) of the French franc and the currencies of the CFA (Communauté Financière Africaine). Whatever the fluctuations of the French franc against other currencies, the CFA franc is always worth two French centimes, a parity guaranteed by the huge resources of the French treasury. Through its two regional African banks, the zone gives unlimited backing to local currencies, permits those in financial difficulties to borrow from the French treasury at very low rates of interest (1 percent for amounts up to 5 million French francs), and, in general, provides a financial security blanket for all commercial transactions between and among its members.

Finally, mention must be made of France's official development assistance, which in 1983 was worth over 6 billion French francs (about $1.3 billion). In addition, the French treasury is prepared to make loans as direct budgetary support, as, for instance, in 1981 when Senegal found itself unable to pay its civil servants.

It is also prepared in some circumstances to act as the guarantor for loans from the financial markets. The bulk of these loans and investments by the French government are channeled through the Fonds d'Aide et de Cooperation (FAC), which depends on the Ministry of Cooperation for its resources and has little auto-nomy. There are three branches to which it lends money — state projects, general interest projects, and interstate projects for transnational undertakings. The paying arm of the FAC is the Caisse Centrale de Coopération Economique (CCCE), which with resources of some FF3 billion a year is the second most important lender for capital projects after the World Bank — though very much smaller. The CCCE tries to concentrate on least-developed countries by according them soft loans and managing projects, especially rural development schemes.[28]

Unquestionably, all this — plus other aspects of the relationship, such as the annual francophone summits in Paris and the frequent trips to Paris by francophone heads of state, ministers, and other leaders — adds up not only to a considerable French presence in the former colonies but also to an extraordinary range of Franco-African political, economic, and cultural links. Does it, however, add up to French neocolonialism, to French control of its former colonies by other means? Evidence to the contrary is also readily available.

First, it should be pointed out that while France is the principal supplier of trade goods to francophone Africa, only the Central African Republic sells more than 40 percent of its exports to France. The main client of three oil-producing states — Cameroon, Gabon, and the Congo — is the United States, despite the fact that the French oil multinational Elf-Aquitaine is the major foreign shareholder in all three countries' oil industries. The United States is also Guinea's main client, the Ivory Coast is for Burkina Faso, and Belgium is for Mali and Benin. And if the francophone countries' import figures still favor France, it is significant that these figures nonetheless represent a net decline from those of 1970 (for example), when French imports accounted for an average 60 percent of the countries' (import) totals. France continues to enjoy a favorable balance of trade with its former African territories, but if they continue the trend toward increasing trade diversification, that advantage might well disappear during the next five to ten years. Nor is continued French commercial dominance in these countries a foregone conclusion: Asian, Latin American, North American, Arab, and (other) European firms have begun to establish themselves in what the French once considered their own private economic preserve. The four oil producers — the Ivory Coast, Cameroon, Gabon, and the Congo — have led the way in opening their economies to non-French investment and enterprises, and the other francophone states may soon follow their lead. Two good examples of this development can be found in the Ivory Coast and Cameroon, where, over the vigorous objections of the French, active branches of seven major American banks were permitted to open (in Cameroon, First Boston, Bank of America, and Chase Manhattan; in the Ivory Coast, Chase Manhattan, Citibank, Chemical Bank, Manufacturers Hanover, and Bankers Trust).

Another area in which French influence is diminishing is in the governmental machinery of the francophone states; for several years after independence, French advisers and technical assistance could be found at the top echelons of virtually every government ministry in francophone Africa; some were actually running minstries (as they had before independence) behind the acquiescent backs of newly appointed African ministers. That has now changed dramatically in view of what Biarnes calls "the irresistible ascent of the [African] bourgeoisie," in particular, the rise of one of its most significant components, the bureaucracy, which through various policies of "Africanization," "indigenization," "Cameroonization," and the like, has taken control of these states' administrative machinery.[29] There are still French advisers and "technical assistants" to be found in francophone African administrations, and their input is occasionally quite important (as, for example, in the preparation of national economic plans), but their contribution is almost always technical, not political, and their numbers are far fewer than before. In Cameroon, for example, by 1965, there were about 110 expatriate Frenchmen listed as part of the national administration (less than half the number in 1960), and, by 1981, that number had been further reduced to about 35, not including the (approximately) 200 in education, extension services, and aid projects.[30] Even the Ivory Coast, long considered France's most loyal and docile vassal, has undertaken its own "Ivoirianization" program to gradually phase down (and, eventually, out) the numbers of French *coopérants* in the country. In 1980, there were as many as 3,976 of all kinds; in 1985 there were less than 2,500, and by 1990 (according to some Ivoirian sources) almost all will have left. Undoubtedly the cost to the Ivoirian treasury (some $10 million per year for free lodgings, salaries, and other perquisites) played a role in the decision to reduce the French advisory presence, but it is clear that political pressure, particularly from the large pool of qualified (and restive) Ivoirians, was the main reason.[31]

There are many other indications that France finds it difficult to control events in its former colonies (if it ever really could), even to the point where France appears sometimes to be manipulated or embarrassed by African leaders. For example, for nearly a year, between November 1983 and October 1984, relations between the French government and that of Gabonese president Omar Bongo were extremely difficult, due mainly to the publication in France (which the French government refused to prevent) of a book by Pierre Péan (*Affaires africaines*) that was highly critical of Bongo, his family, and the French role in the country.[32] It took assiduous wooing by Mitterand to persuade Bongo to return to the French fold. Also, even though France maintains friendly relations (and extensive economic ties) with the self-styled Marxist or "revolutionary" military regimes in the Congo, Benin, and Burkina Faso, their leaders apparently conduct highly independent foreign policies, often preferring aid and advice from Eastern socialist countries to that offered by France. Thomas Sankara of Burkina Faso is a case in point: the developemt path he espouses is a modified but recognizable version of Libya's, and his closest regional friend is Ghana's Jerry Rawlings, also an admirer (if not a disciple) of Libya's Colonel Moammar Khadafy. The examples could be multiplied almost indefinitely; the point is that, by 1984, it became difficult to make a creditable case for general French control of the former colonies.

How then to describe France's role vis-à-vis its former colonies? The neocolonial case seems hardest to make, though arguably in such countries as the Ivory Coast, Gabon, and Senegal, the French presence — economic, cultural, and political — unquestionably overshadows all others. Yet, even in these three states, most frequently cited as French neocolonial bastions, neither Frenchmen nor French interests control the local political or economic scene to suit themselves or France, or only manage to do so occasionally. The many long-standing ties with France admittedly have their own momentum and dynamic, but it can no longer be argued that Senegalese, Ivoirian, or Gabonese leaders and people invariably dance to French tunes. If this is true of these three states, it is even more true of the others. Probably a patron-client relationship most closely approximates the realities of present Franco-African ties, with the reservation that patronage does not necessarily also mean French control, nor does client status mean obedience.

Notes

1. See, for example, Robert Delavignette, *Freedom and Authority in French West Africa* (New York: Oxford Univeristy Press, 1950).

2. Mario Azevedo, "The Human Price of Development: The Brazzaville Railroad and the Sara of Chad," *African Studies Review* 24, no. 1 (March 1981): 1–19.

3. Joseph Roger de Benoist, "La Conference de Brazzaville: Un acte colonial," *Afrique histoire*, no. 7 (1983), p. 9. My translation.

4. Franz Ansprenger, *Politik im Schwarzen Afrika* (Cologne and Opladen: Westdeutscher Verlag, 1961), extratextual table 2.

5. For details, see Ruth Schachter Morgenthau, *Political Parties in French-Speaking West Africa* (New York: Oxford University Press, 1964); Philippe Decraene, *Tableau des partis politiques de l'Afrique au sud du Sahara* (Paris: Presses de la Fondation des Sciences Politiques, 1963); Victor T. Le Vine, *The Cameroons from Mandate to Independence* (Berkeley and Los Angeles: The University of California Press, 1964); and Aristide Zolberg, *One-Party Government in the Ivory Coast* (Princeton, N.J.: Princeton University Press, 1964).

6. Victor T. Le Vine, "Political Elite Recruitment and Political Structure in French-Speaking Africa," *Cahiers d'études africaines* 8, no. 3 (Winter 1968): 369–89.

7. Edward Mortimer, *France and the Africans, 1944–1960* (London: Faber and Faber, 1969).

8. For a discussion of education in francophone Africa during the early years of independence, see Abdo Moumouni, *Education in Africa* (London: Andre Deutsch, 1968).

9. Victor T. Le Vine, "The Trauma of Independence in French-speaking Africa," *Journal of the Developing Areas* 2, no. 2 (January 1968): 211–24).

10. Mamadou Dia, *The African Nations and World Solidarity* (New York: Frederick Praeger, 1961). On Senghor and *négritude*, see Irving L. Markovitz, *Leopold Sédar Senghor and the Politics of Négritude* (New York: Atheneum Press, 1969).

11. William J. Foltz, *From French West Africa to the Mali Federation* (New Haven: Yale Univeristy Press, 1965).

12. For a discussion of the Guinean regime, see Claude Rivière, *Guinea* (Ithaca, N.Y.: Cornell University Press, 1977); Ladipo Adamolekun, *Sékou Touré's Guinea* (London: Methuen, 1976); and "Sékou Touré et la Guinée après Sékou Touré," *Jeane Afrique plus* 8 (June 1984), special issue.

13. Ahmed Mahiou, *L'Avènement du parti unique en Afrique Noire* (Paris: R. Pichon and R. Durand-Auzias, Librairie Générale de Droit et de Jurispridence, 1969).

14. Adamolekun, *Sékou Touré's Guinea*, pp. 93–100.

15. Mahiou, *L'Avènement du parti unique*, pp. 94–95.

16. Victor T. Le Vine, "Parliaments in Francophone Africa: Some Lessons from the Decolonization Press," in Joel Smith and Lloyd D. Musolf, eds., *Legislatures in Development* (Durham, N.C.: Duke University Press, 1979), pp. 125–54.

17. Jean-François Médard, "La Specificité des pouvoirs africains," *Pouvoirs* 25 (1983): 5–22.

18. Adamolekun, *Sékou Touré's Guinea*, pp. 126, 127–34; and Pierre Biarnes, *L'Afrique aux africains* (Paris: Armand Colin, 1980), pp. 157–81.

19. On the relationship between the Senegalese regime and the Muslim brotherhoods, see, among others, Lucy Behrman, *Muslim Brotherhoods and Politics in Senegal* (Cambridge, Mss.: Harvard University Press, 1970); and Donal B. Cruse O'Brien, *The Mourides of Senegal* (New York: Oxford University Press, 1971).

20. Biarnes, *L'Afrique aux africains*, p. 240. The translation is mine.

21. Dov Ronen, *Dahomey Between Tradition and Modernity* (Ithaca, N.Y.: Cornell University Press, 1975).

22. For details of the controversy, see, inter alia, Tony Hodges, *Western Sahara: The Roots of a Desert War* (Westport, Conn.: Lawrence Hill, 1984).

23. Robin Luckham, "French Militarism in Africa," *Review of African Political Economy* 24 (May–August 1982), esp. p. 57.

24. Sheldon Gellar, *Senegal: An African Nation Between Islam and the West* (Boulder, Colo. Westview Press, 1982), pp. 45–66.

25. Cited by François Soudan in "'Mitterand entre ses 'islamistes' et ses 'africainstes,'" *Jeune Afrique*, no. 1241 (October 17, 1984), p. 44.

26. Biarnes, *L'Afrique aux africains*, p. 61. The translation is mine.

27. These data are drawn primarily from the foreign trade statistics in *La Zone franc en 1982* (Paris: Sécretariat de Comité Monetaire de la Zone franc, 1984).

28. Mark Webster, "France in Africa: Gendarme, Banker, Project Manager," in *Africa Guide 1984* (Saffron Walden, England: World of Information, 1984), p. 48.

29. Biarnes, *L'Afrique aux africains*, pp. 22–32.

30. The 1960–1965 figure is from my *The Cameroon Federal Republic* (Ithaca, N.Y.: Cornell University Press, 1971), pp. 139–41; the 1981 Cameroon figures are from the *Annuaire National 1981* (Yaoundé: Éditions SOPECAM, 1982) and conversations with officials of the Yaoundé Office de Coopération during 1982.

31. See Lyse Doucet, "Ivory Coast: Struggle Against the 'Dependence Complex,'" *West Africa*, no. 3496 (August 20, 1984): 1678–79.

32. Pierre Péan, *Affaires africaines* (Paris: Fayard, 1983). Among other embarrassing matters, Péan revealed a variety of unsavory details concerning Bongo's wife, Marie-Josephine, and her lovers, several of whom subsequently met unpleasant fates either in Gabon or abroad. The book was banned in Gabon, but became something of a cause célèbre in France.

3 ZAIRE AND CAMEROON

Crawford Young

In 1960 Zaire and Cameroon achieved political independence within six months of each other. At the time, the air was heavy with uncertainty in both these large and important central African polities. In contrast to the auspicious and hopeful mood that accompanied the transfer of sovereignty in such neighboring African states as Nigeria and Ghana, fear and foreboding mingled with the ritual toasts to independence.

In Zaire (formerly the Belgian Congo), the uncertainties were predicated upon the sheer abruptness of the transition. Until 1956 African society had been totally submerged by the leviathan colonial superstructure that had been methodically constructed by the Belgians. The Belgian government, corporations, and Christian missions had established a comprehensive political, social, economic, and cultural hegemony. In late 1955 the publication of a cautious 30-year plan for the emancipation of the Belgian Congo by a little-known Belgian professor triggered an avalanche of furious protest within the colonial establishment.[1] The first urban elections were not held until 1957, and these were for city councils that had limited responsibilities. At the beginning of 1959, an all-Belgian study commission proposed an elaborate formula for gradual political transition that assumed ten to fifteen years of remaining Belgian rule. But the seismic shock of massive, leaderless riots in the capital city of Kinshasa (formerly Leopoldville)[2] in January 1959 caused the once omnipotent Belgian administration suddenly to lose its grip over important segments of the country and its control over the pace of events. A year later the decomposing colonial authority conceded to the burgeoning, tumultuous, and fragmented nationalist movement and granted its maximum demand — immediate independence. Thereafter, events proceeded at breakneck speed. By independence day, 30 June 1960, new political institutions (largely modeled on Belgian constitutional arrangement) had been created, national elections had been held, and a fragile coalition government had been formed. A precarious Zairian political superstructure was erected upon a colonial state whose key organs remained almost wholly European; only three of

120

the top 4,700 functionaries — and none of the military officers — were African. This transformation generated exorbitant hopes (particularly among Zairian youth) but also widespread insecurities about who would dominate and how.

In Cameroon, decolonization was also problematic (although somewhat less abrupt). Although the French recognized that the special status of Cameroon as a United Nations trust territory made its eventual independence inevitable, they did not want its political evolution to move ahead of that of their other African territories. From 1948 on, the French colonial administration was confronted by the Union des Populations Camerounaises (UPC), a militant and radical nationalist opposition movement centered in Douala and the southern zones. By 1955 the UPC and the French administration were locked in armed combat.[3] (Most of the UPC leadership resisted co-optation by the electoral machinery provided by the French in 1956.) From this point forward, French decolonization strategy was based on crushing the UPC and fostering the emergence of alternative political forces. As Joseph argues, "The politicians in Cameroon who inherited power from the French . . . were the very ones who had played no part whatsoever in the nationalist struggle — whether as radicals or moderates."[4]

When decolonization was achieved, UPC insurgent forces were operating close to the capital of Yaounde and the insurrection was far from over. The viability of a political formula for independence that excluded the radical wing of the nationalist forces was very uncertain. Additionally, the disposition of the segments of the old German colony of Kamerun (then under British trusteeship) — which were avidly claimed by most of the Cameroon political class — was yet to be decided. At the beginning of 1960, the new state of Cameroon therefore faced a doubtful future. Given its divergent colonial heritage (German, French, and British); its two official languages; and the tensions that existed between north and south, east and west, and Muslims and Christians, the apprehensions widely voiced at independence about the future of Cameroon seemed fully justified.

The patterns of political evolution in Zaire and Cameroon in the quarter-century since independence have been dramatically different. Cameroon has enjoyed a stability under autocratic rule that few would have believed possible in 1960. Its level of economic and social well-being has risen at a respectable rate, and it has a reputation as one of Africa's most effectively governed states. In contrast, Zaire entered a phase of deep crisis almost immediately after independence. This was followed by a cycle of revival and restoration from 1965 to 1973. In 1974 the country fell into a new period of decay and regression, the ultimate consequences of which are difficult to specify. In this chapter we will explore the contrasting experiences of these two polities and seek to identify the factors that have brought these remarkable divergent outcomes. Because of the size and complexity of Zaire, more space will be allocated to this country than to Cameroon. Despite this imbalance in presentation, we hope that each case will illuminate the other.

ZAIRE

At independence the new state of Zaire was an uneasy fusion of the institutional apparatus of colonial domination and a suddenly fabricated superstructure of constitutional politics. This hybrid system of government had been imposed upon a country of vast dimensions — 905,000 square miles (or three-quarters the size of India and 80 times as large as Belgium). The formula, known at the time as the *pari congolais* (Congolese wager), was a gamble that, for a prolonged transitional period after independence, the core institutions of colonial control — the bureaucracy and military — could continue to be directed and staffed by Europeans, but operate under the authority of African political institutions consisting of elected assemblies and councils of ministers. These institutional arrangements rested upon the fragile premise that, although the new African political class would hold formal power and carry out the rituals of democratic governance on the European parliamentary model, the actual exercise of rule would continue under the firm hand of an administration still dominated by Belgians.[5] While the African politicians were gaining experience in their new responsibilities, a new generation of Africans was to be carefully and methodically trained for admission into the managerial ranks of the administration and the officer corps of the armed forces. (It was not until 1959 that legal provision had been made for the admission of Africans into the top four executive grades of the civil service and for the induction of African officer-training candidates into the army.) After entry at the bottom levels of these institutional hierarchies, the Zairians were only gradually to work their way up to the key command posts within the bureaucratic and military establishments. As of 1960 only three of the top 4,600 civil servants, and none of the military officers, were African — in sharp contrast to patterns in the British and French-ruled territories.

In retrospect, this formula appears staggeringly naive. It is important to recollect, however, that after the Kinshasa riots had dissolved the myth of the omnipotence of the colonial state, Belgium had few options. A constitutional amendment would have been required to permit the transfer of conscript-manned units of the Belgian army to the colony, this was politically out of the question. The colonial constabulary was assumed to be incapable of forcefully repressing national unrest over time. Belgium was bitterly divided along linguistic, religious, and ideological lines, and could therefore muster only weak coalition governments. Painful economic retrenchment, and the necessity to close many non-productive coal mines concentrated in the French-speaking portion of the country, had produced a sullen public mood. There was strong prospective opposition to costly colonial policies, which were viewed by many as mainly of benefit to the wealthy corporations. The tremendous drain on the French economy caused by their interminable war in Algeria was a negative example of colonial policy that haunted the Belgian public and the political leadership. Across the Zaire river in Brazzaville, French President Charles de Gaulle had promised in August 1958 that independence could be had by simple referendum vote. Concomitant British moves toward decolonization had also contributed to the conviction that power transfer was inevitable. Settlement on whatever terms the nationalist forces would accept therefore appeared to be the only option.

On the Zairian side, no contending party could successfully campaign on a platform that advocated a delay for independence; it was a cause that by this time had taken on millennial overtones. There was therefore remarkable agreement on the achievement of immediate independence and on the retention — largely intact — of the Belgian constitutional model for political institutions. Neither Belgians nor nationalists, however, had a very realistic view of the problems that lay ahead.

There were several fatal flaws in the decolonization deal struck between Belgium and the Zairian nationalist leaders. Although the agreement provided spectacular opportunities for a small number of persons drawn from the subaltern white-collar ranks of public and private bureaucracies (specifically, those in the 25–40 age range who were equipped with a partial or complete secondary education), it left a much larger number of similarly situated persons (and somewhat older people with more modest educational credentials) with no opportunities at all. Real mobility in the colonial organizational structure — whether state or corporate — would obviously be possible for future generations only. Three months prior to independence, a group of soldiers issued a tract that expressed a sentiment of frustration widespread at the time:

> It astonishes us to see our African brothers forget us . . . There will be two branches of Congolese independence. First there will be . . . the class of the great Congolese leaders and their white counselors. These will benefit from all the advantages of the new independent state . . . A second dishonored wing, which will include the inferiors, the criers of 'Vive independence' . . . will be and [will] remain the servants of the first branch.[6]

This prophetic tract pinpointed the locus of initial breakdown — the armed forces. Within a fortnight the premise of prolonged Belgian tutelage over the crucial organs of the state was irrevocably shattered.

A second flaw consisted of the assumption that transplanted constitutional institutions loosely stitched to the colonial state could keep the struggle for power among the political class from becoming explosive. The complex fabric of Belgian public law was wholly inadequate to provide an adjudicative framework for the inevitable conflicts between a president whose role was modeled on the Belgian monarch and a prime minister who was theoretically responsible to a parliamentary majority — between provincial presidents (chosen by dominant coalitions in their assemblies) and central authorities. Superior forces and effective external support were the crucial arbiters of political outcomes. Constitutional exegesis was used only for legitimation of already accomplished facts — not as an authoritative device for resolving conflicts.

A third defect was an inability (on the part of both Europeans and Africans) to foresee the nature of the political competition that would arise within the electoral framework and the structural character of the political parties that would be engendered by this framework. The implicit model for the Zairian political party was a loose mélange of the European party system — characterized by enduring, institutionalized structures and clienteles and a full range of political ideologies — and the new type of African mass nationalist party (which was then at its apogee of political success and intellectual prestige).[7] The scope for the politicization of ethnicity by the electoral process was greatly underestimated in Zaire (as it was in much of Africa). The ephemeral character of leader-follower linkages, and the problematic and fluid nature of relationships among party leaders, was also unforseen. Although conceived as enduring, structured bodies that would organize and articulate the collective will of civil society, Zairian political parties proved to be formless congeries of personal clienteles — constantly subject to segmentation, defection, and recalculation to individual advantage.

Finally, the power transfer settlement failed to take into consideration the immense impact of external forces.[8] Outside actors played little direct role in the formulation of the decolonization settlement, which assumed that the fate of the new state would be determined by Belgians and Zairians alone. This premise was at once invalidated by the outbreak of crisis, with the result that the major powers (above all, the United States) and the United Nations became crucial elements in the political equation. This point was elegantly summarized by the first Zairian Ambassador to the United Nations. "Though we sat so comfortably in our sumptuous official cars, driven by uniformed military chauffeurs, and looked as though we were ruling this large and beautiful country, we were in fact ruling nothing, and a prey to whatever might happen."[9]

The essential elements of the Zairian political superstructure were a president (elected by the bicameral parliament), a prime minister (designated by the president but requiring a parliamentary majority), and a council of ministers (designated by the prime minister, but also requiring a parliamentary vote of confidence). Each of the six provinces had its own elected assembly, which in turn chose a president; the provincial president and his cabinet of ten ministers remained responsible to the assembly. In 1957 provision had been made for the election of urban and rural local councils. Seven towns elected urban councils; in 1960 the most prominent members of these councils left to take advantage of the newly opened provincial and national offices. Elected rural councils were operating effectively in only parts of the country before the independence crisis intervened.

The judicial branch of the government posed particular constitutional problems. At the moment of independence, it seemed destined — like the bureaucracy and the army —to remain under European tutelage for a prolonged period. Although the new posts opened in the political superstructure required no qualifications except literacy in French, entry into the magistracy required a doctor of law degree (which no Zairian was to hold until 1982). Therefore, it was not realistically possible to assign the highly political responsibility of authoritatively interpreting the constitution to the judicial branch. When in September 1960 a constitutional impasse ensued over the precise circumstances under which a president could dismiss a prime minister, force rather than law was the inevitable arbiter. To make matters worse, virtually the entire corps of magistrates fled during the crisis. In the words of one leading jurist at the time, "Impartial and competent observers have not hesitated to affirm that the worst catastrophe in this series of disasters had been the disappearance of the judicial apparatus in the greater part of [Zaire]."[10]

Relations between the center and the provinces were bitterly disputed in the debates over decolonization arrangements. Battlelines formed around the slogans of "unitarism" and "federalism." A passionate commitment to the unitary state was particularly associated with the parties loosely allied with Prime Minister Patrice Lumumba and his Mouvement National Congolais (MNC); this view was influenced by contemporary mainstream African nationalist thought, as espoused by such towering figures as Kwame Nkrumah of Ghana and Sekou Touré of Guinea. Unitarism was also congruent with the traditional state ideology of the colonial polity and was therefore the ideology generally preferred by the Belgian administration. The most important partisans of federalism were the Alliance des Bakongo (ABAKO), led by President Joseph Kasavubu, and the Confédération des Associations Tribales du Katanga (CONAKAT) led by Moise Tshombe. [Both of these movements assumed they could dominate their respective provincial institutions (Leopoldville and Katanga), but risked playing only a marginal role in the central government. Their 1960 perspectives were shaped by intense rivalries with other ethnoregional groups in the urban context: the assortment of Lingala-speaking up-river immigrants collectively labelled "Ngala" in Kinshasa for ABAKO, and the Kasaian immigrants who predominated in the white-collar ranks in the copper-belt cities of Shaba.] In the latter case, federalist claims were noisily supported by the European settler community (and more discreetly, but effectively, by the mining giant Union Minière du Haut-Katanga or UMHK). The unitarists saw Federalism as camouflage for the secessionist tendencies that were threatening to destroy the new state at its birth; the federalists saw unitarism as camouflage for a desire to dominate hinterland groups — to the detriment of the "sons of the soil."

The 1960 constitution was, in effect, a compromise between these two positions. The primacy of the central institutions was preserved, but the provinces were accorded an (ill-defined) autonomy by means of their elected assemblies and representative governments. In practice, this autonomy became much greater than intended; there was no effective machinery for overseeing and hierarchically controlling the provinces. The state commissioners who, according to the constitution, were intended to represent central authority in the provinces were never able to function. The breakdown of the state financial apparatus, which took place almost immediately, gave the provinces de facto budgetary autonomy. The regional administrative apparatus, including district commissioners, territorial administrators, and police also operated autonomously, unimpeded by central monitoring mechanisms. (The constitution had neither anticipated nor intended this situation.)

The party system that emerged from the May 1960 elections was weak and fragmented. Only two movements made a serious effort to organize on a national scale: the Lumumba wing of the MNC (MNC-L); and a loose coalition constructed under the patronage of the decomposing colonial administration — the Parti National du Progrès (PNP, popularly known as the Parti des Nègres Payes). As the campaign progressed, most of the members of the colonial administration realized that, given their declining influence, any effort to support a party that was under their tutelage was bound to fail. They therefore shifted their support to the local factions least belligerent to the Belgian system. The MNC-L, by means of its radical nationalist appeal and the charismatic personality of Lumumba, won the support of most of the intelligentsia within the country — and many without. Its electoral strength (thirty-three of the 137 seats in the lower chamber) was regionally concentrated in Haut-Zaire, the ethnic homeland of its leader. The other parties all originated in one of the provincial capitals (six in all) and therefore had a restricted regional base. Nine parties succeeded in winning seven or more seats in the national assembly, and fifteen won representation in parliament.

This fractured parliament made the task of forming a government difficult. A precarious, last-minute compromise awarded the presidency to Kasavubu and the premiership to Lumumba. The underlying fragility of this compromise was clearly revealed in the vote of confirmation of the Lumumba government; although the parties from which Lumumba drew his cabinet members held 94 percent of the seats in the assembly, he only obtained 54 percent of the vote of confidence.

The brief moment of euphoria created by the formation of a compromise government — and the impending celebrations — concealed unresolved tensions among the new politicians. There were significant differences between political leaders like Lumumba, who expressed his nationalism in radical and passionate terms, and those like Kasavubu, who was more cautious and less aggressive in his anticolonial language. Lumumba's flamboyant political discourse, his impulsive character, and (after independence) his cosmopolitan entourage of well-known figures of the Left made some Zairians, most Belgians, and (by July 1960) — both the American diplomatic establishment and top United Nations officials fearful and suspicious of his behavior.

Before its power was deflated in 1959, the Congolese colonial state apparatus had been a formidable machine. Soaring public revenues had permitted a rapid postwar expansion of the state, whose expenditures had increased fifteen-fold between 1939 and 1950 and had tripled again in the 1950s.[11] The older hierarchies of control and order had been augmented by technical, regulatory, and welfare services. Prices, labor, population movement, and peasant production had been subject to sweeping controls. On the eve of independence, there were 10,000 Belgians in senior bureaucratic ranks (as compared to late colonial figures of 2,500 British in similar positions in far more populous Nigeria,[12] or 760 British in the elite Indian Civil Service).[13] In 1959 the Belgian colonial state was widely reputed to be the most effective in tropical Africa in such spheres as rural health delivery and agricultural research. The sheer scale and scope of the colonial state apparatus made it especially vulnerable to decline.

On the eve of independence, Zairian civil society was rapidly changing. Barriers to African economic enterprise beyond peasant and petty commodity production were preventing the emergence of a mercantile class, but the swift expansion of a primary and secondary educational infrastructure was producing a growing white-collar petty bourgeoisie, known as *evolues*, or "intellectuals." An expanding economy was drawing one-third of the adult males into wage employment. Urban centers were experiencing explosive growth. New forms of ethnic consciousness were taking shape; the cities were becoming arenas of social competition, and some communities were becoming aware of their relatively disadvantageous access to modernity. (Political parties were playing a potent role in politicizing these new forms of consciousness.)

A final significant point to be remembered about conditions in Zaire during its last decade under colonialism is that they were unusually favorable. In retrospect, the period 1950–1960 was a veritable golden age. It was the only period of the colonial era in which sustained, broadly-based improvements were made in the well-being of most of the populace. Real wages and agricultural prices rose substantially. At the same time, intangible incomes became available in the form of access to welfare services. The severity of the coercion and sanctions imposed by the colonial government softened markedly. Forced agricultural and public works labor was reduced; later, it was eliminated. Public whipping as a form of punishment was terminated. The historic period immediately preceding the independence of Zaire was a considerable improvement over earlier phases of the colonial period, during which the country had endured the brutalities of the Congo Free State of King Leopold, the rigors of the massive forced labor practices of the 1920s, the savage wage and agricultural price slashes of the 1930s, and the ruthless war-related impositions of the 1940s.

The postcolonial political history of Zaire may be instructively divided into three periods: breakdown and crisis (1960–1965); resurgence and resurrection (1965–1973); and prolonged decay (since 1974). Following the coup by Mobutu Sese Seko in 1965, the political superstructure of the decolonization settlement was swept away. In its place, a new set of political institutions were grafted onto the colonial state legacy. In 1974 these institutions entered a phase of seemingly irreversible decline.

The decolonization was not long in coming; within five days of independence, the army mutinied against its white officers.[14] In swift succession, the administration broke down, the state lost its territorial integrity, and the constitutional arrangements became inoperative. United Nations forces occupied the territory, and cold war rivals discovered a new battleground.

The army mutiny, provoked by resentment over the fact that independence brought no change to the status of the Zairian troops, began in a camp near Kinshasa and quickly spread throughout the country. Within days, the 1,000 European officers were ousted from the command structure; a small number stayed as advisors. Their places were filled by Zairian noncommissioned officers. These officers were mainly chosen by seniority of rank, but on occasion they were elected. Because garrisons were scattered all over the country, the process of naming new commanders could only be partially influenced from the center. Prime Minister Lumumba appointed two of his political followers, who had prior military experience as non-coms, as commanders of the army: Mobutu and Victor Lundula (a relative). Mobutu split with Lumumba almost at once and was able to influence successfully the selection of unit commanders in key locations near the capital. Control, however, was highly relative; loss of the command hierarchy also resulted in the dislocation of the logistical infrastructure for provision, payment, and supply indispensable to the operation of military units.

The army mutiny panicked the European community. The situation was exacerbated by lurid tales (some of them true) of assaults by roaming bands of mutineers. The subsequent intervention of the Belgian army to protect the European residents inflamed the situation; within ten days of independence, a massive exodus of European civil servants followed that of the army officers. Because many senior Zairian clerks had long bureaucratic experience, the immediate disruptive effect on the civilian sphere was less severe. Nevertheless, this loss of human skills was to be very damaging in the long run. The European exodus effectively undermined the most basic premise of the decolonization settlement: that the colonial bureaucracy would continue to rule the country while the Zairian political class gradually gained experience.

Eleven days after independence, Katanga (the richest province) declared its secession from the country.[15] Although Belgium declined to grant diplomatic recognition to the new state, it did supply military assistance to expel the national army mutineers and to provide cover while a Katanga gendarmery was organized. Belgian functionaries remained at their posts, and the potent European corporate sector — especially the copper giant UMHK —

lent crucial support. Shortly thereafter, the diamond-producing regions of Kasai (homeland of the Kasai Luba) joined Katanga in secession; in this instance, the precipitating faction was ethnic tension between the Luba leadership and the Lumumbist alliance. By August 1960 the new state had lost the two areas that produced over half its revenues and foreign exchange and was facing the threat of permanent disintegration.

To complete the process of breakdown, the constitutional system reached an impasse on September 5, when President Kasavubu abruptly revoked Prime Minister Lumumba; Lumumba angrily riposted by securing a parliamentary vote of support. The stalemate was broken ten days later by Mobutu. Claiming to speak as commander of the armed forces, he neutralized both men. The Lumumbist alliance, unable to regain effective control in Kinshasa, regrouped in the Lumumbist bastion of Kisangani (Stanleyville), where they erected a rival national government. Lumumba himself tried to escape from his house arrest in Kinshasa in order to take charge of this rival regime, but he was captured and, in January 1961, assassinated. Complicity for this murder was shared by the Katanga and Kinshasa authorities and, indirectly, by American intelligence.[16] Meanwhile, authority in Kinshasa was exercised by a College of Commissioners installed by Mobutu, who operated under the dubious legal cover of President Kasavubu.

A far-reaching deflation of state power and capacity to govern followed the collapse of the power transfer formula. The political institutions were never able to operate as prescribed by theory. The political parties lost the ephemeral linkages with their clienteles that had been constructed in the electoral campaign and never developed institutionalized structures; they kept up an appearance of viability by means of occasional statements made in the name of a given party by one or another of its leaders. Because they lacked the ability to resolve the competing personal ambitions of their leader, nearly all the parties split into at least two wings within weeks of the elections.

The armed forces became as much a threat to state authority as an instrument of it. Their various units were, at best, uncertain weapons in the hands of the power contenders. General Lundula rallied to the Kisangani rival government; Katanga and the dissident section of Kasai had their own gendarmes; Mobutu more or less controlled units in the western part of Zaire, but especially those in the capital. Crucial to any semblance of control was the capacity to pay the troops. In this Mobutu had a major advantage, not only because he had access to the disorganized national treasury, but also because he was the beneficiary of a clandestine transfusion of funds from the CIA and, on a couple of occasions, from the U.N.

The bureaucracy in Kinshasa was not wholly paralyzed however. Segments of it continued to perform routine functions by an inertial momentum; thus was supplemented by technical assistance from the United Nations, and by the guidance of a number of Belgian functionaries who returned as advisors. At more local levels, performance was uneven; in some places, able and ingenious Zairian former clerks performed marvels of improvization. Routines were thoroughly ingrained, and normative concepts of what the state bureaucracy ought to do continues to guide behavior. The term "chaos", which has often been invoked to describe the Zairian situation in the early postindependence period, is much too strong. Nevertheless, the administration was only partially insulated from the conflicts in the political realm. Political figures at the national and regional levels sought to find niches in the state apparatus in order both to reward their following and to enhance their personal influence over its operation. Logistical problems increasingly hampered the daily functioning of this apparatus. For instance, its fleet of vehicles gradually fell into disrepair; funds to maintain its capital infrastructure — from the humble typewriter on up — were hard to procure.

Confronted with the disarray of its mutinied army, the Katanga secession, and the Belgian military intervention, the new government appealed (during the second week of independence) for American, United Nations, and Soviet intervention. The cold war environment in which the Congo crisis occurred virtually guaranteed that any perceived power vacuum would draw in the major world actors (particularly since Zairian political factions were clamoring for their aid). An uneasy international accord provided that world intervention would be through the United Nations (although the two superpowers each sought to influence the U.N. intervention according to its own perceptions and objectives).[17] The United States and the Soviet Union (as superpowers); Belgium, France, and Britain (as colonial powers with regional interests); and the diplomatically active African states — especially Ghana, Guinea, Tunisia, and Egypt — all pursued their own bilateral policies of involvement in addition to their work through the U.N.

By September 1960 the Soviet Union found itself largely excluded. The most decisive external influences were American and Belgian. Until its withdrawal in 1964, the U.N. peacekeeping force was the most potent armed establishment in the country. In sum, throughout the first years of the republic — 1960–1965 the impact of external forces, particularly at the center, was very great.

The U.N. was assigned the task of keeping the peace without intervening in internal Zairian political affairs. In reality, this mandate (even as amended by successive Security Council clarifications) proved uncomfortably ambiguous. To preserve its own disputed image of impartiality, the U.N. had an institutional interest in upholding figments of legality and in helping to restore a political framework compatible with the decolonization constitution. Thus, when Kasavubu revoked Lumumba, the U.N. upheld the legal continuity of the presidency and cooperated with those acting in the name of Kasavubu. By the parliamentary investiture of Cyrille Adoula in August 1961, it actively promoted a new constitutional regime. This settlement consecrated the triumph of the Kinshasa-based moderate alliance, which took shape with strong American support and even tutelage. It also brought to an end the existence of a rival government in Kisangani and a separatist state in southern Kasai. Subsequently, the U.N. and the United States focused their efforts on the restoration of the 1960 boundaries; in January 1963 they reversed the Katanga secession by means of U.N. military action.

During the first years of the republic the external vector may therefore be judged to have had two net effects. First, because American influence on the overall outcome was greater than that of any other single external actor, the political balance in the reunified country favored those elements that had relied on U.S. support in their contest for power. Second, because international intervention was largely channeled through the U.N., questions of formal constitutional legality assumed a relatively greater degree of importance.[18] The important role played by the U.N. in assuring the legal survival and territorial integrity of Zaire through a period of virtual institutional decomposition validates the arguments of Jackson and Rosberg concerning the major role played by the international system in sustaining the juridical state during periods when its empirical substance had collapsed.[19]

The missions and corporations were also significant factors that helped to limit disintegration during the first phase of state decline in the early 1960s. In a number of regions, well-organized Catholic (and to a lesser degree, Protestant) missions were able to supplement the state apparatus in the supply of basic services — especially in the health and education fields, but also in other areas. Capitalist enterprises were compelled to assume responsibility for the maintenance of the social and economic overheads in their zones of operation — for instance, roads, communications systems, and hospitals. In general, expatriate mission and private-sector personnel did not join the Belgian functionaries and army officers in the panic exodus; most of these operations therefore experienced substantial continuity. These numerous islands of relative normalcy scattered throughout the country provided important insulation against the total loss of state capacity.

The period from the installation of the Adoula government in August 1961 until late 1963 was marked by rising hope that the damage resulting from the failed decolonization settlement could be contained and that the state could be restored to a reasonable level of operation. Emergency programs for the purpose of completing the training of Zairian personnel in all fields of public service were well underway. The governments of the six colonial provinces, which by 1961 had all been paralyzed by factional divisions, were broken down into twenty-one smaller units, several of which were off to promising beginnings. The immediate dislocations of the 1960 crisis were subsiding, and by January 1963 the country was fully restored to its 1960 boundaries. In 1964 (with the aid of extensive U.N. technical expertise) a permanent constitution was drafted; the Adoula government won approval for it in a national referendum.

The optimism, however, was short-lived. At the end of 1963 a wave of rebellions broke out; by August 1964 these had engulfed roughly one-third of the territory.[20] By June 1964 the new crisis triggered by the rebellions brought about the collapse of the Adoula government and resulted in a surprise comeback by the Katanga secessionist leader Moise Tshombe, who succeeded as prime minister in Kinshasa. Tshombe mobilized his disbanded Katanga gendarmery into the national army, recruited white mercenaries, and obtained military aid from Belgium and the United States to turn back the insurgents. The most dramatic episode in this battle was a joint Belgian-American parachute operation in the eastern cities of Kisangani and Isiro (Paulis), primarily undertaken to free several hundred hostages who had been seized by the insurgents, but also to recapture what had become the rebel capital of Kisangani. The insurgents belatedly received a flow of Soviet and Chinese arms via Algeria, Egypt, and Tunisia; also, for several months in 1965, a Cuban contingent led by Ernesto "Che" Guevara fought with the rebels. But by early 1965 the major leaders had fled and the various rebellions had broken into many pieces. Many months were to pass before a tenuous central authority could be re-established in many of the affected areas; for instance, in the northeast quadrant of the country and in the southwestern district of Kwilu. (One insurgent pocket — in the Fizi-Baraka zone on the eastern frontier — still persisted two decades later.)

The rebellions were defeated, but at great cost. The national army performed poorly and was clearly unable to maintain order without external reinforcement. The social anger born of the bitter disappointment of a large segment of the populace (especially its youth) was translated into ferocious vengeance against those believed to have monopolized the benefits of independence: politicians associated with the Kinshasa regime and the white-collar class generally. After the defeat of the insurgents, the humiliated national army wreaked its revenge upon those suspected of complicity and, in the process, revealed its own indiscipline. No certain figures exist for the death toll, but it most certainly ran into the tens of thousands. Most importantly, these actions imprinted on the populace an indelible fear of disorder and insecurity (a state of affairs associated in the popular consciousness with the first republic era).

In conformity with the 1964 constitution, national elections were organized in early 1965, but their character and results simply confirmed the terminal malady of the first republic. Some 223 parties contested the elections; some forty-nine of them were brought together as the Convention Nationale Congolaise (CONACO) by Prime Minister Tshombe, who was intent on supplanting Kasavubu as President. Although CONACO apparently won 133 of 167 seats, the coalition was held together only by the notoriously soluble glue of venal opportunism. The fractured parliament proved unable to carry out its task of electing a chief of state; the Kasavubu-Tshombe tussle reached impasse, providing a pretext for the army high command to install Mobutu in power on November 24, 1965.

The Mobutu coup occurred at a singularly propitious conjuncture of the national psychosis, which was in a Hobbesian mood. The public realm was a zone of disorder. Immediate past experience validated the gloomy analysis of the philosopher of absolutism; in the absence of effective authority, life was "nasty, brutish, and short". Despite the controversial role of Mobutu in the 1960 crisis and the Lumumba assassination and his linkages with American intelligence, which were well-known to the intellectual class, his seizure of power was greeted with relief and acceptance. Parliament at once gave it unanimous endorsement. African states, fatigued and embarrassed by the unending Congo crisis and eager to focus their diplomatic energies on southern African liberation, also welcomed the new regime (in spite of their suspicions concerning American sponsorship or even initiation).[21]

Mobutu set about reconstructing a new state, which, in its ascendant phase in the early 1970s, appeared to be a remarkable success.[22] Three constitutive elements were interwoven in the Mobutu formula: resurrection of the bureaucratic structure and ideology of the absolutist colonial state; adoption of the hegemonic instrument designed by African nationalism (the mass single party); and institution of a web of patrimonial linkages to bring about a personal ascendancy for Mobutu. In the Mobutu design, these apparently incompatible patterns of rule combined to create the appearance of an African leviathan.

The authoritarian legacy of the colonial state provided an ample reservoir of juridical doctrine supportive of the Mobutu venture. Indeed, in a number of respects the Mobutu state resembled the personal autocracy of King Leopold II from 1885 to 1908. Centralization of power, unity of command, hierarchy of the state apparatus — these colonial state principles provided an ample base on which to reconstruct an autocratic state. The pervasive statism of the colonial era provided a normative model for the new regime. Initially, Mobutu embarked on a systematic dismantling of the political superstructure that the decolonization settlement had grafted onto the authoritarian bureaucracy. Political parties were dissolved. After a year, parliament itself was dismissed. The twenty-one provinces — by this time all paralyzed by factional divisions that reinforced the popular vision of the first republican state as an emblem of disorder — were recombined into nine.[23] Their political institutions joined the national parliament and political parties on the scrapheap; as in colonial times, their chief officers (who were routinely posted outside their regions of origin) became simply the delegated agents of the central authority. Unification, centralization, depoliticization, hierarchy, discipline — so thoroughly was the first republic discredited in the popular mind that these resurrected watchwords of the colonial order resonated favorably in the public mind.

The new regime recognized that the original legitimacy conferred on it by the overwhelmingly negative perceptions of the first republic would not persist indefinitely. The Mobutu state sought to gain a long-term legitimacy by borrowing institutional weapons fashioned in the armory of radical African nationalism. This aim was pursued by means of the creation, in 1967, of a single national party, the Mouvement Populaire de la Révolution (MRP). The party, which projected itself as "the nation politically organized," claimed to be the supreme institution of the land through which popular sovereignty was exercised. As the personal incarnation and authoritative interpreter of this general will, Mobutu led the party, appointed its key officials, and spoke in its name. All Zairians, by reason of birth, were automatic members. Conversely, the MRP claimed to embody their sovereign collective personality.

The party progressively assimilated all recognized associations into its framework. Trade unions, youth, students, women, merchants, and others were required to unify their corporate bodies into a single organization. This organization became an ancillary branch of the party and was subject to its control and discipline. Even the Catholic seminaries were forced to permit the grouping of their students into party cells at the beginning of the 1970s — a move that provoked bitter but unsuccessful opposition from the church hierarchy. By 1973 spokesmen for the regime were comparing the MRP (as a transcendantal framework) to a national church, and its leader was likened to a messiah.

Associated with the party institutions was a national ideology that claimed to have exclusive hegemony. In its first version, this doctrine bore the label of "authentic Zairian nationalism," a co-optation of the radical populist vocabulary and symbols of the martyred Lumumba. It was a sacred invocation of national unity. The humiliations of the colonial past were excoriated; MRP ideology aligned itself with the main themes of anticolonial nationalism elsewhere in Africa, insisting upon the imperative rights of the Zairian people to achieve full control over their political destiny and to determine the use and development of the natural wealth of the country. In 1970 the ideology of the regime took on a more cultural cast; Mobutu articulated an official doctrine of "authenticity." This was a vaguely defined invocation of ancestral values as a means of bursting the shackles of cultural submission imposed by the colonial state. In 1974 the national ideology was personalized; it was redefined as Mobutism, and its doctrines were to be discovered in the words and actions of the president. Although this personalized caricature of popular ideology was swiftly swallowed up in the subsequent crisis; the domestication of the vocabulary and symbols of radical anticolonial nationalism in the early years of the Mobutu regime had genuine meaning.

The third aspect of the Mobutist state was patrimonialism and personal rule.[24] The importance of this aspect was not immediately apparent; over time, however, it became clear that it was not only an indispensable complement to the institutional marriage of the colonial state legacy and African nationalist political forms, but was indeed the most important single element. The arid juridical abstractions of the colonial state legacy did not suffice to motivate the key operatives in the institutional framework of the regime or to ensure their fidelity to the ruler. Similarly, the public vocabulary of authentic Zairian nationalism did not inspire zealous performance or secure loyalty. A much more personal structure of incentives and sanctions seemed necessary in order to make the machinery of state respond to the ruler's will.

In a patrimonial state system, the political elite are tied to the ruler by bonds of individual clientship. High office is awarded in return for personal service to the ruler. Additionally, the office holder is provided substantial benefits linked to possession of the post. These include not only a generous official renumeration but also occult revenues gained through venal exploitation of office. In return, the office holder has an absolute obligation of total fidelity to the ruler and of effective discharge of his duties. Failure to render such service leads to dismissal. Those in high office are not simply servants of the state; they are primarily clients of the ruler.

The power of the ruler depends upon his ability to maintain the clients in a state of permanent dependency. They cannot be permitted to form political bases of their own. Similarly, they cannot be allowed to remain in high office too long; they might entrench themselves in some institutional bastion within the state apparatus. They are not only permitted, but encouraged, to acquire occult revenues by exploiting their positions; this practice enhances both the value of the president's gift of office and increases the clients vulnerability by laying them open to charges of corruption.

Initially, Mobutu built his regime by co-opting a broad cross-section of the political elite of the first republic. Later, he progressively eliminated those with an autonomous political base; within five years, those in top positions had been reduced to the status of courtiers. The most coveted high offices — membership in the MPR Political Bureau, appointment to the Council of Ministers, or command of a region — were all rotated at least once a year, and few people held office for more than two years at a time.

Patrimonialism was a continuing process. The pattern of incentives and sanctions by which the president maintained power over the political class was founded not only on immediate transactions but also on the long-term prospects of office holders and those who wished to supplant them. Over time, everyone could expect to be rotated out of office, but the conditions of exit were variable. Removal often meant disgrace and even jail. Of the 212 persons holding top party and governmental office between 1965 and 1975, about ten percent were transferred from the sumptuary comfort of high position to the dank austerity of imprisonment. In contrast, honorable removal from office assured transfer into prosperous mercantile activities. (An office holder could usually lay foundations for these activities while he was still in power.) Prison or exile were not necessarily permanent conditions, however, on a suitable pledge of personal fealty to the ruler, amnesty by presidential grace (or even a profitable return to high office) was always possible. To cite but one of many cases, the remarkable career of Nguza Karl-i-Bond illustrates this pattern. Although handicapped by family ties to Mobutu's archenemy, Tshombe, faithful and energetic service catapulted him to the post of foreign minister from 1972 to 1974, and again in 1976–77. He was also political director of the MPR from 1974 to 1976. In 1977 he was accused of high treason, sentenced to death, and subjected to disgusting tortures. A year later the death sentence was commuted, and in 1979 he was released to become prime minister. In 1981 he fled into exile and became a leading spokesman for the Brussels-based opposition.[25]

Viewed as a system, patrimonialism is aptly defined by Jackson and Rosberg as personal rule: "[Patrimonialism is] a system of relations linking rulers not with the 'public' or even with the ruled (at least not directly), but with patrons, associates, clients, supporters, and rivals, who constitute the 'system.' If personal rulers are restrained, it is by the limits of their personal authority and rivals, who constitute the 'system.' "[26] Personal rule did not operate in a vacuum, however. The bureaucratic-authoritarian legacy of the colonial state, and the legitimating apparatus of African nationalism — single party and exclusivist ideology — were the indispensable institutional underpinnings of patrimonialism.

The abstract doctrines of state hegemony bequeathed by colonialism were amended to incorporate the idea of personal rule. The prime icon of this ideology — the effigy of the president — was everywhere. It looked out from public billboards, all office walls, the party pins that the political class were obliged to wear in public, banknotes, postage stamps, and the front pages of the daily newspapers. The nation was metaphorically represented as a vast village whose chief was a venerated, sanctified, paternal figure. The president was adorned with various heroic titles: founding father of party and state; helmsman; supreme guide of the Zairian revolution. At the apogee of Mobuto's career, adoration of the president was elevated into a national cult. The 1970 MPR Congress solemnly declared, "One man, previously noted for his outstanding services to the country, can assure the well-being of each one of us and create the conditions propitious for the people's moral and spiritual growth, and offer them a common ideal, the feelings of a joint destiny, and the knowledge of belonging to one country."[27] The interior minister, L. Engulu, offered an even more extravagant elegy:

> In our religion, we have our own theologians. In all religions, and at all times, there are prophets. Why not today? God has sent a great prophet, our prestigious Guide Mobutu . . . This prophet is our liberator, our Messiah. Our Church is the MPR. Its chief is Mobutu, we respect him like one respects a Pope. Our gospel is Mobutism. This is why the crucifixes must be replaced by the image of our Messiah. And party militants will want to place at its side his glorious mother, Mama Yemo, who gave birth to such a son.[28]

Until 1973 this political formula appeared to be successful. Between 1966 and 1973 the bureaucratic, political, and patrimonial institutions held undisputed sway. Growing cohorts of university graduates entered the state apparatus, and those skilled in playing by the patrimonial rules were swiftly promoted. A well-executed economic stabilization programme begun in 1967 practically eliminated inflation for several years. By 1970 there was a balanced budget, a neglible external debt, and a strong currency. Mobutu had put to rest the residual suspicions associated with his first republic role, and Zaire was playing a leading role in African and Third World forums. In 1970 a ten-year program designed to achieve abundance by means of the rapid development of the vast natural resources of the country was unveiled; at the time, many believed that its goals were within reach.

The fates, however, ordained a very different destiny. In 1974 Zaire entered a prolonged phase of crisis whose end point is not yet in sight. Several events triggered the deflationary spiral, some of which were unrelated to the character of the Mobutist state. During the era of ascendancy (1965 to 1973), international commodity markets were generally favourable, reflecting the long age of prosperity and expansion in the Western capitalist world. With the exception of a brief dip in 1971–72, prices for copper, the most important Zairian export, were high, reaching record levels in 1973. In April 1974 the copper market broke, prices plunged to all-time lows, and — except for a brief recovery in 1980 — have remained in the doldrums ever since. There have been short-term price surges for some other important exports (for instance, coffee, in 1976–1978 and cobalt, in 1978–1980), but for the most part, the Zairian economy has shared the cruel blows that an adverse trade climate has inflicted on most African states. In 1973 — and again in 1979 — crises in the Middle East brought about an explosion in oil prices. The long-term decline in Zairian agriculture was never able to be remedied (even in the ascendant years), and by the early 1970s Zaire required $300 million in grain imports; since then, the need for these imports has continued to rise.[29]

Sweeping measures for the Zairianization and radicalization of the economy in 1973 and 1974 constituted a serious self-inflicted wound. During the first phase, nearly all the foreign-owned commercial and agricultural enterprises were sequestered. Subsequently, the state distributed them as free booty to the political class.[30] In the second (radicalization) phase, the state seized control of a wide range of Belgian-owned enterprises and placed leading Zairian political figures in command of these ventures. Both sets of measures were abruptly enacted by presidential fiat; no serious provision was made for dealing with the host of problems that (inevitably) followed. As a result, the economic life of the country was seriously dislocated, many of the affected enterprises were disrupted, widespread shortages occurred, and inflation began to gather a momentum which has not yet abated. When it became evident to the public at large that, despite the revolutionary rhetoric, the sole beneficiaries of these measures were the members of the political class, the painfully constructed apparatus of legitimacy suffered a major blow. The biggest single winner in this predatory class action was the president himself, who constructed an imposing mercantile and agricultural empire out of the most profitable expropriated businesses. In 1976 — partly because of external pressure from the International Monetary Fund (IMF) and Mobutu's creditors — retrocession measures were taken, and many of these enterprises were restored to their former owners. Nevertheless, great damage had already been done.

From 1973 on the soaring costs of the Mobutist state — which by 1974 exceeded 50 percent of the gross national product — overrun available revenues by large amounts. Some of these costs reflected the formidable expansion of the educational system (and to a lesser degree, the armed forces), but an important fraction could be ascribed to the exorbitant costs of the patrimonial system.[31] (Financial specialists privately calculate that under patrimonial systems roughly one-third of public revenue is diverted to patrimonial uses or is simply privately accumulated by leading political figures.)

For a time, the revenue needs of the state were met by sharp increases in rents collected from the mineral industry (made possible by the nationalization of UMHK in 1967). During the early 1970s, there was a massive influx of revenue from indulgent international lenders, who at this time regarded Third World borrowers as their salvation. By 1974 (before anyone began to take serious notice) Zaire had run up a $3 billion debt, roughly equivalent to its gross national product.

A final triggering event for the decline of the state was Zairian involvement in the Angolan civil war in 1975. Mobutu, who was then viewed as a major player on the African stage, aspired to a broker role in this crisis. (He was also anxious to prevent the triumph of the Movimento Popular de Libertação de Angola (MPLA), whose radical ideology and Soviet connections posed the threat of the existence of a hostile neighbor on Zaire's longest border.) In August 1975 several battalions of the Zaire armed forces crossed the border in support of anti-MPLA forces and by November, had nearly reached Luanda. But both they and their Angolan allies were eventually routed by Cuban and MPLA forces and compelled to flee in disarray. For Mobutu, the outcome could hardly have been more disastrous: a humiliating defeat for the army; the entrenchment of his enemies in Luanda; and the exposure of Zaire as a junior partner in the American and South African intervention.[32]

The Angolan misadventure soon had painful repercussions. Beginning in 1967 dissident Zairians — some of them remnants of the old Tshombe/Katanga constabulary, other former members of the Tshombe police force, still other simply young men driven into exile by the repressive actions of the Mobutu administration — had begun to congregate in the areas of Angola bordering southeastern Zaire. The Portuguese had armed them, using them as leverage against Zaire and at times also against the Angolan guerrillas (particularly the Frente Nacional de Libertação de Angola (FNLA). During the civil war, the MPLA had enlisted these Zairian irregular units in their cause and (with Cuban help) had improved their armament and training. In 1977 elements from this group — now labeled the Front pour la Libération Nationale du Congoor (FLNC) (better known as Katanga Gendarmes) — invaded Shaba. Although their numbers were small (ca. two thousand) and their armament light, the national army was unable to halt their advance; only the dramatic arrival of Moroccan reinforcements and French and American logistical help stemmed their progress. The FLNC units vanished when confronted by the Moroccans, but they renewed their invasion the following year. This time they seized the crucial mining center of Kolwezi before being driven out by French and Belgian paratroops.

The inability of the state security forces (in spite of their expansion, re-equipment, and widely publicized retraining) to cope with this feeble incursion punctured the mystique of strength that the regime had cultivated.[33] As the crisis dragged on, long-term vectors of state deflation became apparent. The hazards of an interaction between international capital and the patrimonial state became increasingly clear. What had been widely perceived as an investment boom in the early 1970s on closer inspection proved to have been primarily an orgy of speculative borrowing by the Zairian state. International investors had in fact shown little disposition to risk equity capital in Zaire. Multinational enterprises were much more intent on selling their technology and contracting their services with funds lent by the international banks. For the top office holders in the patrimonial state, giant development contracts and loans provided opportunities for lucrative occult commissions. The Zairian state, which assumed most of the risk, in effect guaranteed that it would extract enough revenue from the civil society to underwrite the immediate profits for the contractors and the rents for the political class.

The $250 million steel mill near Kinshasa is emblematic of the development disasters produced by this situation. It was justified by feasibility studies carried out by consulting firms linked to the contractor, operated entirely on imported scrap iron, produced low-quality steel products (that no one wanted to buy) at eight times the cost of imported equivalents, never operated at more than 10 percent of capacity, and was virtually shut down (probably for good) in 1980. Still more disastrous was the Inga-Shaba power line, which was designed to join the imposing hydroelectric capacity of the lower Zaire river to the Shaba metallurgical complex by a new and unproven technology of direct current transmission. This project was entirely financed by the Zairian state by means of external borrowing, finally cost over $1 billion (a fourfold increase over initial estimates), was completed six years behind schedule, was predicated upon an expansion in copper production that never occurred, and now delivers power to the Shaba mines at a prohibitively high cost. There is no prospect that revenues earned by the line can amortize its cost; rather, the project constitutes a huge mortgage on the resources of Zaire for many years to come.

Although efficacious for purposes of political control, over time the patrimonial devices used to assure the personal ascendancy of the president over the state apparatus revealed hidden costs. Some of these were purely financial; side-payments entail a drain on public resources that (although impossible to specify precisely) is very substantial, and only a tiny fraction of the population benefits from these diversions. Another negative result of the patrimonial system was the progressive demoralization of the state machinery brought about by the visible and large-scale corruption of the top office holders. The mercantilization of public authority, and its progressive transformation into a commodity available to the highest bidder, transformed the nature of state-society interactions. The continuous rotation of top personnel that was an essential feature of the patrimonial process inhibited the accumulation of institutional competence. This was perhaps most visible in the armed forces, where the president's preoccupation with personal control was highest. Competence was simultaneously built up by a succession of training programs and undermined by an ongoing series of purges of the officer corps. These practices eventually resulted in institutionalized incompetence in the security forces.

The international environment became much more difficult for the Zairian state during the crisis years that began in 1974. At the peak of its prosperity, the Mobutu regime enjoyed a real degree of autonomy, sought diversity in its external economic partners, and enjoyed widespread respect in African diplomatic circles. During the crisis years, Zaire was in constant receivership, limped from one external debt impasse to another, and was an object of derision on the international scene — even among its Western supporters.

These processes produced a steady deflation of the state, indicated by a dramatic decline in its probity, credibility, and competency. As could be argued, corruption had itself become the system.[34] In his celebrated speech on the "Zairian sickness" in July 1977, Mobutu himself described the state as "one vast marketplace" in which those who held any slice of power utilized it to levy an "invisible tax." More bluntly, in an anguished 1981 pastoral letter, Zairian bishops characterized the state as "organized pillage for the profit of the foreigner and his intermediaries."[35] Any sense that the state embodied some form of moral order vanished.

The decline of state integrity reinforced the decline of its competency — defined as the ability to use resources effectively for public purposes. The ability of the state to deliver valued services to its civil society steadily dwindled, especially outside Kinshasa. Except for a couple of hospitals in the capital, and the hospitals and clinics operated by missions and private enterprises, health facilities became empty shells undermined by unpaid personnel and empty medicine cabinets. Agricultural research stations became mere centers of involuted administration. The road network and the river transport system atrophied. Administrative outposts in the hinterland were primarily concerned with assuring their own continuity and performing occasional ceremonial functions.

This type of situation leads to an erosion of credibility. In her recent analysis of a similar impasse in Ghanaian politics, Naomi Chazan has stated this phenomenon very well:

> By the early 1980s it was apparent that Ghana had forfeited its elementary ability to maintain internal or external order and to hold sway over its population. Although its existence as a *de jure* political entity on the international scene was unquestionable,

these outward manifestations did raise doubts as to its *de facto* viability. The Ghanaian state thus seemed to be on the brink of becoming less distinctive and relevant. Indeed, some kind of disengagement from the state was taking place. This withdrawal was only minimally directed at physical removal from the Ghanaian context. Much more rampant was an emotional, social, and political detachment from the state element.[36]

There are important limitations to the process of state deflation. The process is uneven; it does not occur uniformly throughout the state apparatus. The effective resources of a state in decline are concentrated on those segments of its apparatus most crucial to its survival: its security police; elite units of its armed forces; presidential services; agencies that deal with the external financial and diplomatic world. The ultimate priority of an eroding state apparatus is to assure its own continuity.[37] Islands of activity persist here and there, spurred by an unusually able and vigorous public servant swimming against the currents of deterioration. The local institutions of chiefly administrations survive — with varying effects. The mission and church infrastructure acts as a significant buffer, supplying a number of services not available from the state. (In Zaire economic enterprises have also performed these functions in some areas — although much less so now than in the first republic crisis period, when the colonial capitalist infrastructure was largely intact.)

The school system is an intriguing example of institutional persistence. This may be explained by the great value attached to its product — diplomas — which have not lost their credibility as a passport to a better future for the mass of the populace. The school is able to directly extract from its clientele an indispensable minimum sum for its operations, this revenue provides insulation from the irregularity (or even lapse) of resource transfers from the state. Further, its clientele has a powerful interest in its nominal function, it need not supply education, but it must permit its pupils to meet the criteria to earn its credentials. Only religious networks seem able to operate quality schools, but even the state school system, despite qualitative decline, continues regularly to process pupils through its machinery.

As Jackson and Rosberg have already argued, the international system is a critical factor in explaining the persistence of states such as Zaire.[38] Zaire remains a visible actor on the international stage;

it completed a term on the United Nations Security Council in 1983 and dispatched elements of its handful of elite military units to Chad in 1981 and 1983. Leading world figures visit Kinshasa regularly. In recent years, these have included Pope Paul II, Vice President George Bush, and French president Francois Mitterand. Zaire is continuously reified in the global imagination by those who define policy towards it, engage in debates about it, and write about it.

More than the modicum of viability supplied by international recognition is at stake, however. Various forces in the global arena have an interest in the continuation of the Zairian state. To the public and private creditors who hold its $5 billion debt, the Zairian state is the indispensable agent of repayment. Although the external capital stake in Zaire has (in real terms) declined since independence, Western states and private capitalists desire access to Zairian minerals; the basic security conditions for their extraction can only be assured under cover of state authority. In strategic terms, Western states also have a clear interest in sustaining at least the credible facade of a Zairian state; form is more crucial than substance. Because of widely held external views that the demise of the Mobutu regime might result in the end of the Zairian state in its present form, Western actors and their African partners (in particular, Morocco) have sprung to the defense of the regime whenever it has been seriously threatened (as in the two Shaba invasions of 1977 and 1978). This attitude fosters a widespread conviction in Zaire that, however weak and inefficacious the state may prove to be in the conduct of its accustomed responsibilities, it will always be salvaged in extremis by external forces; that is, it will be propped up from the outside.

The remarkable survival skills of the Mobutu regime should also be noted. President Mobutu has mastered the art of the diplomacy of dependence with consummate ability. Zaire has held its creditors at bay with a succession of improvised accords that have generally involved the apparent acceptance of conditions that could not (or would not) be respected. Mobutu has been able nimbly to orchestrate the themes of "Mobutu or chaos" and "Zaire as faithful ally" (particularly because the United States and France have been willing to provide the ultimate guarantee of armed support).

To maintain the internal power of the regime, Mobutu makes artful use of the widespread image of powerful alien forces prepared to forestall any forcible overthrow of the rulers. He forestalls

the threat of military intervention by maintaining intimate patrimonial ties with the senior officers, a number of whom have close
affinities of family or ethnicity to the president. Command lines are
scrambled, and rivalries among top officers are encouraged. Israeli
security officers, and French Belgian, and Chinese military
advisors, work with key units. As noted in a 1982 Senate staff
report, "The 'tripwire' presence of these personnel represents the
assurance of foreign intervention during a crisis."[39]

The opposition to the regime is kept at bay by a well-calculated
combination of co-optation, corruption, and coercion. Every new
slate of ministers or Political Bureau members includes several
spectacular entries from the ranks of the opposition. This divide-
and-conquer tactic is demoralizing, and it contributes to the
environment of distrust and suspicion that characterizes opposition
milieux. The most effective formula for opposition tactics to date is
exemplified by the fate of a movement launched by thirteen parlia-
mentarians in 1980 — the Union pour la Démocratie et la Progrès
Social (UDPS). The UDPS demanded recognition as a second
party. The party gained wide visibility by resisting the seductive
inducements dangled by the president to some of its members and
by rejecting violent resistance but it remained within the country to
claim democratic rights. It could not be crushed, driven into exile,
or co-opted. Nevertheless, it failed to organize a mass constituency
or to pose a serious threat.[40] By 1984 Mobutu had succeeded in
winning over five of the instigators of the UDPS and in stigma-
tizing the party as a Kasaien regionalist movement.

In contrast to the wave of uprisings in 1964–65, the response of
the mass of the populace to the unending crisis has been resignation
and disengagement. Survival energies are increasingly directed into
the parallel (black market) economy, which exhibits surprising
vitality.[41] As one sociologist recently put it, "Despite the inefficiency, corruption, and poor performance of the formal sector, the
total economy and society of Zaire have not broken down because
the African informal sector has been vigorous and has enabled
Zairians to survive."[42] In other words, the state is to be avoided
and evaded rather than resisted.

At the upper end of the social scale, the privileged class
(consisting of the external estate of expatriate managers, bankers,
and purveyors of services and the internal politico-commercial
class) continue to overconsume the dwindling resources of the
state. The external estate and its international extensions insist as

best they can on the servicing of the foreign debt and on full payment for their sales and services. The internal politico-commercial class shows no signs of slackening its relentless pursuit of private rents by exploitation of public power. By consuming the capital of the public economy, these two groups appear to create a situation resembling the classical economist's paradox of "the tragedy of the commons." The relationship between them is summarized with particular cogency by Ilunga Kabongo, a leading intellectual.

> The system is far more sophisicated than anticipated . . . It looks very much like a spider web from whose nodal and secondary centers one moves progressively from a zone of existence to one of non-existence. The zone of existence is one in which people can, socially speaking, have more or less acceptable standards of living in modern terms and in accordance with the canons of existing ideology . . . Politically, this sector of the population makes up the real nation to which the ruling group feels more or less responsible. It is to this sector that the government addresses itself and in terms of which it governs. As one moves . . . into the zone of non-existence . . . there is no social life dominated by money or its corollaries nor specific political power vis-à-vis the ruling group. In this sense, transfer from the zone of existence to that of non-existence practically means civic and political death.

These circumstances lead many watchers in and out of Zaire to forecast an imminent social explosion. But Ilunga concludes, "The dynamite seems to be wet and the detonators too small to blow up the mountain."[43]

CAMEROON

Cameroon, which we can treat only briefly, stands in dramatic contrast to Zaire. The stability and continuity of its political life (from 1960 until a succession crisis in 1983–1984), the prudence of its economic management, and the caution of its external policies have gradually built for this nation a reputation as one of Africa's most effectively governed states. In 1983 it was the only African state with a triple A credit rating from the World Bank.[44] Its growth rate averaged 3.7 percent in the 1960s and rose to 5.4 percent annually in the 1970s. There were sharp increases in its prospects in the early

1980s, when oil production became a major factor. From a colonial backwater besieged by a radical nationalist movement in 1960, Cameroon evolved into a top-performing polity — an outcome foreseen by few. This condition of stability was threatened by serious conflicts in 1983–1984.

Cameroon's political stability was firmly grounded in the progressive imposition of an autocratic and centralized state apparatus by President Ahmadou Ahidjo. At the time of independence, this seemed only a remote possibility. The Ahidjo party, the Union Camerounaise, won only 34 percent of the vote in the final preindependence election in the former French-ruled areas and had no base at all in West Cameroon (which had been a British trust territory governed as part of Nigeria). The weakness of the new Ahidjo government was further demonstrated by the large voter abstention (40 percent) on a referendum for a postindependence constitution in February 1960, a few weeks after the power transfer.[45] There seemed a genuine risk that Ahidjo might lose the legislative elections scheduled for April 1960. Ahidjo, a northern Fulani Muslim with a low-status background, seemed to lack the personal characteristics necessary to gain ascendency over Cameroonian society.

Nevertheless, in April 1960 elections his party won an increase in its fraction of the vote — from 34 percent to 45 percent. Ahidjo began to master some of the same statecraft devices employed by Mobutu — co-optation and coercion. Smaller parties began to rally to the ruling party. By the time of the next elections in 1965, the Ahidjo movement garnered 93.5 percent of the vote in East Cameroon. In 1966 the main surviving party in anglophone West Cameroon accepted amalgamation into what subsequently became a single national party — renamed the Union Nationale Camerounaise (UNC).

At the outset, Cameroon was an amalgam of cultural elements more diverse than those of Zaire. It was a region that had been loosely drawn together by three different colonial administrations (German prior to World War I, and subsequently, French, in the eastern region, and British, in the western region). The Fulani emirates of the Muslim far north had only been lightly touched by the colonial period; correspondingly, their populations were weakly represented in the contemporary social elites. In the south, large numbers of the Bamileke had thrust themselves into leading positions in both commerce and white-collar employment. At the time of independence, Bamileke immigrants were believed to represent 70 percent of the professionals, 30 percent of the civil service personnel, 60 percent of the traders, and 80 percent of the artisans in the largest city, Douala.[46] The dynamic thrust of the Bamileke in the struggle for social ascension fostered sharp resentments among other groups. The role of a segment of the Bamileke in support of the UPC insurgency made their loyalty suspect to the regime. Added to these difficulties was the challenge of integrating two very different colonial state traditions — the French and the British. Along with the language difference, there were also differences in the administrative culture and state doctrine.

During the first two decades of independence in Cameroon, there was a steady process of unification, centralization, and integration. The Cameroonian state modeled itself upon the unitary, bonapartist doctrine of France, eclipsing the British legacy of West Cameroon. Although the state domain was honeycombed with clientele networks, its autocratic base was preserved. By 1964 the UPC insurgency was all but eliminated. In 1966 a single-party hegemony was established. In 1972 the Federal constitution (created in 1961 to induce Anglophone West Cameroon to join the country) was scrapped in favor of a unitary formula. Although it insisted upon hegemony, the state avoided confrontation with significant clusterings of social or economic power. Provided they rendered obeisance to central power, influential Fulani emirs and other powerful chiefs were not challenged in their local domains; in fact, a 1977 statute called for "restoration of the dignity of the chief." Islamic notables and the powerful Catholic missions were left undisturbed in their spheres. Economically, the capitalist strategy prescribed by the official ideology of planned liberalism made room for both the external estate and the mercantile ambitions of the Bamileke commercial class.

At the center of the system stood Ahidjo, who proved to be a shrewd, calculating, and durable patrimonial ruler. Around Ahidjo and the institutional core of the state, a hegemonic politico-administrative class took shape. Under Ahidjo orchestration this class managed the affairs of the realm and were generously rewarded for it. Two recent studies provide excellent portraits of the nature of the Ahidjo system.

From his entry into office, he had a concept at once specific and ambitious for the pursuit of state hegemony which it was his role to direct, and understood from the outset that he had to transcend the clientelistic colonial state which he inherited. Although his nomination was represented by many as a mere expedient, Ahidjo as Prime Minister in reality inaugurated a process of reinforcing the autonomy of the state which constituted a global and coherent response to a structural crisis which had persisted for more than a century.[47]

Lacking personal charisma, President Ahidjo has sought consistently to create for himself the image of patriarch, and has been remarkably successful in depoliticizing the public arena, appropriating the State as his private domain. Government affairs, as a result, remain largely technical and administrative, and the realm of politics is small. His success has been due in large part to shrewd manipulation, excellent timing, and a knack for co-opting potential opponents into his government, as well as to the will and ability to use force if necessary, for which purpose there exists an extensive network of police and secret service agents who frequently intimidate, arrest and/or detain individuals suspected of harboring anti-government sentiments.[48]

Although the Cameroonian state managed its domain far more effectively than did its Zairian counterpart, it would be wrong to view it as a monolithic and omnipotent leviathan. The proliferation of its bureaucratic apparatus, in the name of "the struggle against underadministration," was not matched by comparable increases in its efficacy. Bayart offers a cogent summation of the limitations to bureaucratic effectiveness set by incompetency.

The procedures are slow, vexatious, and confused; the legal texts are not always applied; corruption, waste, inertia are daily coin; the management of the public services is often deplorable, while budgetary regulation of their activity, purchases, and expenditures is practically nonexistent; the hierarchical structure of decisional processes is not always respected, and in general terms the administrative machinery has little hold on the underlying social realities.[49]

Also, despite the important headway made in the process of unification, the deep divisions in Cameroon society were not wholly overcome. The sudden upsurge in regional tensions that accompanied the unsuccessful coup attempt by northern elements of the presidential guard in April 1984 amply demonstrated the serious nature of these cleavages. Ahidjo's successor, Paul Biya, was a southerner. The fierce fighting that accompanied the coup effort, and the anxieties and tensions that followed it, brought north-south tensions to the surface with new intensity.

In some respects, however, the north-south division was less clearcut than it appeared. Many southerners and outside observers believed that Ahidjo was running the country with a tight-knit northern mafia. Although his power base did include some highly visible northerners (such as Sadou Daoudou and Maikano Abdoulaye), other crucial positions — like prime minister and minister of the interior (Territorial Administration) — were invariably held by southerners. Additionally, in 1975 only one of the nine ministers who had served in the thirty-one member cabinet for more than seven years was from the north. In 1982, 75 percent of the ruling party's political bureau were Christians.[50] (There was, however, a preponderance of northerners in the presidential guard.) Northerners, for their part, were convinced that their region suffered from a debilitating educational disadvantage that blocked northern access to elite roles (in the mid-1970s the north accounted for 29 percent of the population but only 4 percent of the secondary school pupils).[51] On the other hand, southerners were convinced that the north was disproportionately favored by development expenditures; the north had magnificent highways for its few cars, but the dense traffic of the south traveled over wretched dirt roads full of potholes.

Similar arguments developed between the eastern and western regions of the country. The Anglophone elites of former West Cameroon argued that their region was withering on the vine, that English was being eclipsed by French as a state language, and that earnings from the newly exploited oil wells located in their region were mainly being diverted to other regions. A close scrutiny of the distribution of leading positions in the state apparatus, however, does not sustain the Anglophone claim that they were systematically excluded from power at the center.

In general, the Ahidjo regime sought to manage the regional, linguistic, ethnic, and religious tensions of this complex society by carefully balanced representation in the organs of rule. In a closely reasoned study, one Cameroonian scholar found that the regime attempted to simplify the great diversity of the country for representational purposes by an informal practice of grouping the 200-odd ethnic groups into about thirteen ethno-linguistic clusters. This subtle formula for the political management of cultural pluralism proved to be a two-edged sword. The balanced representational quotas did assure that no significant group believed itself to be wholly excluded. But the practice also tended to structure interest articulation along ethno-regional lines. As Kofele-Kale explains:

> The ethnic arithmetic formula for distributing political power was in reality a sophisticated patronage system through which ethnic groups were transformed into pressure groups with the responsibility of articulating, aggregating and resolving particularistic interests and demands. At the head of this system was none other than Ahidjo, the *grand patron*, and below him several tiers of ethnic barons . . .
>
> Since the most direct link between the masses and their government was through a few senior politicians, it was absolutely essential that these regional/ethnic spokesmen and women hold claim to some ethnic base or at the very least to be able to convey the appearance that they enjoyed the support of their ethnic constituents. The scramble to secure, establish, and consolidate an ethnic power base contributed to the politicization of ethnic loyalties at both the leadership and mass levels.[52]

The ambiguous boundaries of these informally reorganized ethno-linguistic clusters opened up the possibility for a number of people to simultaneously identify themselves as affiliates of two (or even three) neighboring clusters, depending on the circumstances and opportunities of the moment. (These manipulators of ethnic identity were engagingly labeled "ethnic transvestites" by Kofele-Kale.)[53]

The initial smoothness of the leadership succession in 1982 seemed to demonstrate the stability of the Cameroonian political system. Ahidjo suddenly and unexpectedly resigned, apparently on the advice of his physicians.[54] According to the provisions of the presidential constitution of 1977 (amended in 1979), Prime Minister Biya succeeded automatically. Ahidjo retained the post of general secretary of the party; initially, he seems to have believed that he could nurse his health and still serve as an occult power broker.

Biya — a Catholic from south central Cameroon — had other ideas. He assumed office without incident but in 1983 began to replace a number of key inner figures with personal ties to Ahidjo by his own henchmen. By mid-1983 some northern militants, fearing that they would be gradually isolated and eliminated, began to conspire against Biya. One plot was nipped in the bud. As tensions deepened, Ahidjo established himself out of reach in France. In August 1983 he publicly broke with Biya, resigned his party office, and denounced the "police state and terror" he claimed Biya had installed.[55]

The public rupture lead Biya to view northerners believed to be associated with Ahidjo with even greater suspicion and to gradually eliminate those holding sensitive roles in the security services, especially in the presidential guard. In February 1984 Ahidjo was tried for treason in absentia; a death sentence (subsequently commuted) was imposed. These pre-emptive measures helped trigger the coup they were designed to forestall. In April 1984 about 500 members of the presidential guard mutinied, briefly seized some key Yaounde installations, and were subdued only after bitter fighting. Although Biya had clearly gained the upper hand in the immediate crisis, the trauma of these events left in its wake an uneasy feeling that an era of heightened regional tensions and uncertainties lay ahead. (At the very least, the external image of Cameroonian stability and progress was tarnished.)[56]

During the 1970s the impressive economic performance of Cameroon was largely built around a more stable agricultural base than that possessed by many other African states. Beginning in 1980 Cameroon entered the ranks of the oil producers. This has constituted a potential bonanza and a possible threat to the ruling regime. Controversy is growing over the practice of keeping oil revenues a closely guarded secret and allocating them to the presidential account. By 1983 there were large discrepancies between the officially recorded oil export earnings and foreign estimates of their real value.[57] Oil (and possibly natural gas) promise rapidly to swell state revenues in the 1980s. (The experiences of Nigeria and other countries warn of the possible perils of the rentier state.)

CONCLUSIONS

By way of conclusion, we return to the remarkable contrast in the performances of these two African states. The obvious advantages of stability stand out at once. The underlying political strategies of Ahidjo, and of Zaire during the second republic, are similar in important respects: (1) Incorporate the authoritarian legal and bureaucratic doctrine of the colonial state; (2) Build upon it the hegemonic model of the single-party political monopoly conceived by African nationalists as an indispensable integrative instrument; (3) Weave these together by means of personal rule and patrimonial controls over the political class. The patrimonial leg of this tripod of state architecture was perhaps less visible and predominant in the Cameroon case, but it was certainly present. The Zairian project, however, suffered from two fatal handicaps: first, the loss of state ascendancy and the dissipation of the inheritance of colonial control during the first republic crisis; and second, the long-term degeneration of all three dimensions of the state apparatus in the crisis years since 1974.

Once the deflation of the state machinery begins, it becomes enormously difficult to resurrect it. The civil society becomes rapidly autonomous by developing a parallel economy into which much of the populace begins to direct its energies. Over time this "zone of nonexistence" is likely to acquire its own structures; the state becomes increasingly irrelevant to its functioning. The apolitical character of this underground economic sphere provides protective coloration; its strategy for dealing with a shrinking state apparatus is one of avoidance rather than confrontation.

The synthesis of colonial state, party hegemony, and personal rule in Cameroon has thus far proven reasonably viable. At the same time, there are evident flaws that produce an element of uncertainty. The representative nature of the government places the intelligentsia in an ambivalent situation and circumscribes the regime's legitimacy. The loyalty of the mercantile classes to the regime is dependent upon the continuation of their economic success and the loyalty of youth, upon the preservation of opportunities for social mobility. The tacit acceptance of the hegemony of the regime by the popular classes is contingent upon the maintenance of its image of effective authority.

Finally, the serious tensions that erupted in Cameroon over the political succession of Biya (which at first seemed a model of legality and effectiveness) laid bare an important flaw in the patrimonial state. Key personnel in the state apparatus are bound to a given ruler by personal ties of fidelity. In a state structured like

Cameroon and Zaire, when a succession occurs while the former president is still alive, the new leader must establish his personal ascendancy by building his own network of clients and displacing those irrevocably linked to the predecessor. In the process, the delicate balances tied to ethnicity and personal factionalism are bound to be disturbed.

The clientele of a given ruler are bound to oppose his departure. (In the case of the Ahidjo resignation, few, if any, of his northern power brokers were informed of his intentions; because they at once foresaw that their own positions would be threatened; they felt betrayed and outraged. The leader himself finds it very difficult to disentangle himself from power without (justifiably or unjustifiably) being accused of fomenting conspiracy. A successor will find it tempting to consolidate his own legitimacy by bringing the abuses of his predecessor (such as divisions of public resources and acts of political repression) to light. The ruler of the patrimonial state is thus ensnared in a trap of his own making. Exile is virtually his only avenue of retirement. (To date, Leopold Senghor of Senegal is the only leader of an African single-party patrimonial state who has been able to voluntarily and securely retire within his own country.)

Nevertheless, over time the differences between Cameroon and Zaire have been very great. In my view, the prudent and skillful statecraft of Ahidjo has been the single most important factor in the contrasting outcomes of these two countries. Over this quarter-century of stable independence, some degree of institutional consolidation has doubtless occurred in Cameroon. There is, however, an underlying fragility to these systems. The shadow of state decay stretches from Kinshasa to the monumental and costly new buildings that are the emblems of the hegemonic state in Yaounde.

Notes

1. A. A. J. Van Bilsen, *Vers l'independence du Congo et du Ruanda-Urundi* (Brussels: Privately printed, 1958). I wish to acknowledge the generous support provided by the Woodrow Wilson International Center for Scholars where I was a fellow in 1983–84.

2. Between 1967 and 1971 European place names in Zaire were replaced by African designations. To avoid confusion, we will retain the present names throughout, indicating the former name in parentheses on first appearance.

3. The reason for the violence, and who provoked it, remain subject to debate. Richard Joseph, author of the best study on Cameroonian nationalism, argues that

the violence was attributable to French determination to destroy the UPC. Richard Joseph, *Radical Nationalism in Cameroun* (Oxford: Clarendon Press, 1977), pp. 265–88. On this period, see also George Chaffard, *Les carnet secrets de la colonisation* (Paris: Calman-Levy, 1965).

4. Joseph, *Radical Nationalism*, p. 2.

5. The power transfer process is covered in the invaluable yearbooks published by the Centre de Recherches et d'Information Socio-Politiques in Brussels, *Congo 1959* through *Congo 1967*; Rene Lemarchand, *Political Awakening in the Belgian Congo* (Berkeley: University of California Press, 1964): Catherine Hoskyns, *The Congo since Independence* (London: Oxford University Press, 1965); and Crawford Young, *Politics in the Congo* (Princeton: Princeton University Press, 1965).

6. *Courrier d'Afrique*, March 4, 1960. Cited in J. Gerard-Libois and Benoit Verhaegen, *Congo 1960*, vol. 1 (Brussels: Centre de Recherche et d'Information Socio-Politiques, 1961), p. 350.

7. Excellent academic analyses of African nationalism are to be found in Thomas Hodgkin, *African Political Parties* (Harmondsworth, United Kingdom: Penguin Books, 1962); Ruth Schachter Morgenthau, *Political Parties in French-Speaking West Africa* (New York: Oxford University Press, 1964); and Immanuel Wallerstein, *Africa: The Politics of Independence* (New York: Vintage Books, 1961).

8. The best treatment of the international aspects of Zairian independence is to be found in Madelaine G. Kalb, *The Congo Cables* (New York: Macmillan, 1982).

9. Thomas Kanza, *Conflict in the Congo* (Harmondsworth, United Kingdom: Penguin Books, 1972), p. 151.

10. J. Sohier, "Problèmes d'organisation judiciares dans l'Etat du Katanga," *Publications de l'Université de l'Etat a Elisabethville* (1 July 1961): p. 112.

11. *Le Congo Belge*, vol. 1 (Brussels: Inforcongo, 1959), pp. 60 and 82; Joseph Segers, "L'économie congolaises hier, demain, aujourd'hui," *Documents pour l'Action* 3, no. 15 (May–June 1963): 146–52.

12. I. F. Nicolson, *The Administration of Nigeria, 1900–1960* (Oxford: Clarendon Press, 1969), p. 260. (The date was 1948.)

13. Philip Woodruff, *The Men Who Rule India*, vol. 2 (London: Jonathan Cape, 1953–54), p. 300. There were a number of British personnel in services other than the ICS: the vast disparity between the number of British administrators in India and the number of Belgian administrators in Zaire, however, was striking.

14. The day the mutiny began, the stubborn and inflexible Belgian commanding general, Emile Janssens, summoned the Zairian noncoms in Kinshasa to a lecture session on the urgency of retaining the rigid discipline of the colonial army. He strode to the blackboard and wrote in large letters: AFTER INDEPENDENCE = BEFORE INDEPENDENCE — a blunt announcement that the army was to "continue as before." This provocative sermon helped intensify the first incidents of indiscipline into full-scale mutiny. Crawford Young, *Politics in the Congo* (Princeton: Princeton University Press, 1965), p. 316.

15. This episode is exhaustively chronicled in Jules Gerard-Libois, *Katanga Secession* (Madison: University of Wisconsin Press, 1965).

16. The most thorough account of the Lumumba assassination may be found in Kalb, *The Congo Cables*, pp. 128–96. See also *Alleged Assassination Plots Involving Foreign Leaders*, An Interim Report of the Select Committee to Study Governmental Operations with Respect to Intelligence Activities, United States Senate (Washington: Government Printing Office, 1975). By mid-August 1960 the Central Intelligence Agency had become persuaded that Lumumba was working in alliance with the Soviet Union to bring about a communist takeover in Zaire. The CIA participated in his overthrow in September 1960 and dispatched an agent to Kinshasa with a vial of poison to organize his assassination. No way was found to carry out the poison plot, and by November 1960 this scheme was abandoned. At the

time of the actual assassination in January 1961, CIA representatives were in close touch with those involved; they knew about (and in all likelihood encouraged) the plans for his transfer to Katanga (although they did not direct or participate in the action).

17. For valuable analyses of the U.N. role, see, Kalb, *The Congo Cables*; Rajeshwar Dayal, *Mission for Hammarskjold: The Congo Crisis* (Princeton: Princeton University Press, 1976); Arthur H. House, *The U.N. in the Congo: The Political and Civilian Efforts* (Washington: University Press of America, 1978); and Ernest Lefever, *Uncertain Mandate* (Baltimore: Johns Hopkins University Press, 1967).

18. For example, Mobutu sought American support for a military coup in October 1962, but was discouraged because this would have undermined American efforts to achieve their policy goals of reuniting the country under moderate leadership. See Kalb, *The Congo Cables*, p. 364.

19. Robert H. Jackson and Carl G. Rosberg, "Why Africa's Weak States Persist: The Empirical and the Juridical in Statehood," *World Politics* 35, no. 1 (October 1982): 1–24.

20. For details on this major social interaction, see especially Benoit Verhaegen, *Rébellions au Congo*, 2 vols. (Brussels: Centre de Recherche et d'Information Socio-Politiques, 1966, 1969). See also Crawford Young, "Rebellion and the Congo," in Robert Rotberg and Ali A. Mazrui, eds., *Protest and Power in Black Africa* (New York: Oxford University Press, 1970), pp. 968–1011.

21. The United States gave strong encouragement and support to the Mobutu takeover. The precise nature of the involvement, however, is yet to be elucidated. See Stephen Weissman, "The CIA and U.S. Policy in Zaire and Angola," in Rene Lemarchand, ed., *American Policy in Southern Africa: The Stakes and the Stance* (Washington: University Press of America, 1978), p. 394; and John Stockwell, *In Search of Enemies* (New York: W. W. Norton, 1978), p. 136.

22. One able analyst has compared the state-building project of Mobutu to that of Louis XIV in France. Thomas M. Callaghy, "State Formation and Absolutism in Comparative Perspective: Seventeenth-Century France and Mobutu Sese Seko's Zaire," Ph.D. diss., University of California-Berkeley, 1979).

23. Or more precisely, eight, plus the capital district of Kinshasa, which was administered as if it were a province.

24. The term "patrimonialism" was first applied by J. C. Willame, *Patrimonialism and Political Change in the Congo* (Stanford: Stanford University Press, 1972). For the general concept of personal rule as a system, see Robert H. Jackson and Carl G. Rosberg, *Personal Rule in Black Africa* (Berkeley: University of California Press, 1982).

25. His illuminating autobiographical account sheds useful light on this process, Nguza Karl-i-Bond, *Mobutu ou l'incarnation du mal* (London: Rex Collings, 1982), p. 38.

26. Jackson and Rosberg, *Personal Rule in Black Africa*, p. 19.

27. Cited in *African Contemporary Record*, 1970–71, p. B288.

28. Kikassa Mwana Lessa, "L'année 1974 dans le monde," *Zaire-Afrique* 91 (January 1975), p. 25.

29. For Zairian economics see International Bank for Reconstruction and Development, *Zaire: Current Economic Situation and Constraints* (Washington, D.C., 1980).

30. On these actions, see especially Michael G. Schatzberg, *Politics and Class in Zaire* (New York: Africana Publishing Company, 1980); Edward Kannyo, "Political Power and Class Formation in Zaire: The 'Zairianization Measures,' 1973–75" (Ph.D. diss., Yale University, 1979; and Lukombe Nghunda, *Zairianization, radicalization, rétrocession en République du Zaire* (Kinshasa: Presses Universitaires du Zaire, 1979).

31. For additional detail, see Crawford Young, "Zaire: The Unending Crisis," *Foreign Affairs* 57, no. 1 (Fall 1978): 169–85.

32. Stockwell, *In Search of Enemies*; Crawford Young, "The Portuguese Coup and Zaire's Southern African Policy," in John Seiler, ed., *Southern Africa Since the Portuguese Coup* (Boulder: Westview Press, 1980), pp. 195–212.

33. See especially Jean-Claude Willame, "La seconde guerre de Shaba," *Enquetes et Documents d'Histoire Africaine* (1978); and Idem, "Contribution à l'étude des mouvements d'opposition au Zaire: Le F.L.N.C.," *Cahiers du CEDAF* 6 (1980).

34. David J. Gould, *Bureaucratic Corruption in the Third World* (New York: Pergamon Press, 1980).

35. *Le Monde*, 28 July 1981.

36. Naomi Chazan, *An Anatomy of Ghanaian Politics: Managing Political Recession, 1966–1972* (Boulder: Westview Press, 1983), pp. 334–35.

37. This point is well documented by Nzongola Ntalaja, "Urban Administration in Kananga" (Ph.D. diss., University of Wisconsin-Madison, 1975), and in forthcoming Ph.D. dissertation at the same university by Margaret Turner, which concerns the administration of housing policy in Lumbashi.

38. Jackson and Rosberg, "Why Africa's Weak States Persist."

39. U.S. Congress, Senate Committee on Foreign Affairs, *Zaire*, 97th Conf., 2d sess., July 1982, 5.

40. The opposition strategy is defined and critiqued by one of its major intellectual figures in Dikonda wa Lumanyisha, *Massacrer pour governer* (Brussels: Club Travail et Développement, 1983).

41. The most comprehensive sociological examination of this sector can be found in Vwakyanakazi Mukohya, "Traders in Butembo" (Ph.D. diss., University of Wisconsin-Madison, 1982).

42. Anthony Oberschall, "On the Political Economy of Zaire" (Paper delivered at the annual meeting of the African Studies Association, Bloomington, Indiana, October 1981), p. 11.

43. Ilunga Kabongo, "Baffling Africa, or the Dying Gasps of a Discourse" (Paper delivered at the Conference on African Crisis Areas and United States Foreign Policy, Los Angeles, California, March 1983), pp. 10–11.

44. Howard Schissel, "Cameroon's Economy: Myth of Miracle," *West Africa* 12 (September 1983), p. 2107.

45. The best study of postindependence Cameroon is Jean-Francois Bayart, *L'Etat au Cameroun* (Paris: Presses de la Foundation Nationale des Sciences Politiques, 1979). See also Victor T. Le Vine, *The Cameroon Federal Republic* (Ithaca, N.Y.: Cornell University Press, 1971): Willard Johnson, *The Cameroon Federation* (Princeton: Princeton University Press, 1970); and Michael Prouzet, *Le Cameroun* (Paris: Libraire Générale de Droit et de Jurisprudence, 1974).

46. Johnson, *The Cameroon Federation*, p. 50.

47. Bayart, *L'Etat au Cameroun*, p. 52.

48. *African Contemporary Record* (1981–1982): 39.

49. Ibid., p. 225.

50. Ndiva Kofele-Kale, "Ethnicity, Regionalism and Political Power: A Post-Mortem of Ahidjo's Cameroon" (Paper presented to Conference on Cameroon, School of Advanced International Studies, Johns Hopkins University, Washington, D.C., April 1984), pp. 8–13.

51. Ibid., p. 10.

52. Ibid., pp. 29–30.

53. Ibid., p. 31.

54. Victor T. Le Vine, "Leadership Succession and Regime Change in Cameroon, 1946–1984" (Paper presented to Conference on Cameroon, School of

Advanced International Studies, Johns Hopkins University, Washington, D.C., April 1984).

55. *Le Monde*, 30 August 1983.

56. For a pessimistic interpretation, see the contribution of veteran African analyst Colin Legum, in *Christian Scientist Monitor*, 1 May 1984.

57. Schissel, "Cameroon's Economy," p. 2169; *African Confidential* 24, no. 20 (October 5, 1983): 7. The discrepancy reportedly exceeded $500 million in 1982. In 1984 French sources claimed that Ahidjo had secreted $2 billion in presidential accounts abroad.

4 MALAWI, ZAMBIA AND ZIMBABWE

L. H. Gann

Malawi, Zambia, and Zimbabwe — the three Central African states formerly under British rule — cover a huge area. Zambia is 290,587 square miles in extent and three times the size of Great Britain. Zimbabwe extends over 150,820 square miles and is bigger than East and West Germany combined. Malawi extends over 49,177 square miles and is comparable in size to Czechoslovakia. All these countries are landlocked. They use the ports of Mozambique but mainly depend on South Africa for most of their outlets to the sea and much of their commerce.

The modern states of Central Africa are of colonial derivation. Their predecessors — precolonial African monarchies and smaller independent communities, all technologically equivalent to early Iron Age cultures — failed to survive the colonial experience as sovereign authorities. The colonizers implanted English as the lingua franca of government, administration, and scholarship. The various empire builders shaped the frontiers and the administrative and economic infrastructures of the new states, and they gave each its separate and distinct identity. The diverse colonial legacies of these states have continued to influence them in an extraordinary fashion. These legacies therefore merit introductory discussion.[1]

THE MACHINERY OF COLONIAL CONTROL

Malawi (formerly Nyasaland) and Zambia (formerly Northern Rhodesia) were British protectorates. The British Colonial Office exercised rule by means of local governors and local executive and legislative councils that were effectively controlled by the administration. The British governed their possessions by means of a small bureaucracy; in 1953 the Northern Rhodesian civil service comprised no more than 365 Europeans and 5,577 non-Europeans. In Nyasaland the Senior Branch numbered only 779 posts; most (though not all) were held by expatriate Europeans. Junior Branch posts (including clerks, uniformed police, and prison officers) were held by 5,157 people. The military force available to the governor

162

in peacetime was negligible (not more than one African battalion in Northern Rhodesia; between one and two in Nyasaland). British governance emphasized rigid economy, orthodox finance, and balanced budgets. (In 1952 revenue in Nyasaland amounted to Ł4,052,760 and expenditure to Ł3,991,323. In the same year revenue in Northern Rhodesia, amounted to Ł23,662,000 and expenditure to Ł23,438,000.)

Zimbabwe (formerly Southern Rhodesia, later Rhodesia), in contrast, was intended to become a "white man's country" — a country to be settled and ruled by permanent white colonists. The colony originated in 1890 as the fief of a private corporation — the British South Africa Company. The company crushed all indigenous resistance to its rule and set up its own administration, mainly based on the Cape model.

Southern Rhodesia barely missed incorporation into the Union of South Africa. In 1922, faced with a choice between joining South Africa and responsible government as a self-governing colony, a small majority of the (largely white) Rhodesian electorate voted for what amounted to almost full internal autonomy. Most of the well-off whites opted for union; the poorer farmers, artisans, and white-collar workers (the same categories of people who were to oppose Southern Rhodesia's entry into the Federation of Rhodesia and Nyasaland in 1953 and favor the Unilateral Declaration of Independence, or UDI in 1965) cast their votes against the South African connection. In 1923 Southern Rhodesia became a self-governing colony with is own thirty-member legislature, prime minister, and cabinet — all answerable (in the British tradition) to the legislative assembly. The Crown retained a formal veto (not exercised in practice) over legislation affecting Africans and control over the country's foreign policy. Otherwise, Southern Rhodesia operated as a quasi-independent dominion. A restricted franchise and a restricted (mainly white) electorate made for an oligarchic political style. Parliamentary seats might be won or lost by a few votes. Election campaigns remained inexpensive. Parties depended primarily on small contributions from their members; however, powerful financial donors could not acquire an anonymous influence, and parties could not provide permanent careers to paid functionaries. The average member of Parliament was a farmer, a businessman, or a physician — a man who looked to politics for public service and prestige rather than as a means of livelihood.

Whites dominated Southern Rhodesia in an economic as well as a political sense. Whites provided most of the country's administrative, industrial, scientific, and farming skills and owned nearly half the land. Whites built a relatively balanced economy. Southern Rhodesia, formerly a primary producer dependent on backwoods farming and (mainly small-scale) mining, was developed into a partly industrialized country, possessing a strong manufacturing sector, its own iron and steel industry, and modern agricultural and mining sectors. These economic successes owed nothing to foreign aid. On the contrary, the Rhodesian settlers constituted the only community in the British empire who ever had to pay cash for the privilege of gaining self-government. (In 1923, under the terms of its new constitution, Southern Rhodesia had to compensate the Crown for the public lands taken over by the colony. In 1933 Southern Rhodesia purchased the country's mineral rights from the British South African Company, and in 1947 it purchased the railways.)

The Southern Rhodesian settlers enjoyed certain inestimable advantages. They lacked the semimessianic assumptions about the benefits of independence aroused among African villagers by many nationalist organizers after World War II — assumptions ignorantly strengthened by committed intellectuals overseas. The white Rhodesians resisted the temptation (which would have scared away outside capital) to nationalize major enterprises like the railways without paying due compensation to the owner. They also did not try to alleviate unemployment or reward party stalwarts by swelling the ranks of the civil service with political appointees. By both colonial and postcolonial African standards, public services were well-organized and efficient. Their structure reflected the wider pattern of a white backwoods ethnocracy solidly committed to the values of hard work and financial orthodoxy. Although writers like Doris Lessing (a white Rhodesian by upbringing) derided such values as philistine, they had their use in building a productive economy and an effective administration.

By 1953 the civil service numbered 12,943 persons, including 2,000 teachers. Most of the senior and medium-grade appointments continued to be filled by whites, although Africans made accelerated advances during the 1950s and 1960s. During this time the proportion of blacks attending school in Southern Rhodesia was higher than in most other African countries. By 1967 nine percent of the country's budget was devoted to African education. Southern Rhodesia's military structure was also based on a philosophy of racial supremacy. Only whites, Indians, and Coloreds, were subject to subscription. They provided the bulk of the country's military manpower, including all officers and specialists. The army was built around a small permanent cadre that administered and trained the white reservists and a small force of professional black soldiers.[2]

The Southern Rhodesian system of governance sharply conflicted with the tenets of imperial rule, which posited control through London. The initial challenge to imperial power in Northern Rhodesia came not so much from the blacks as from the local whites, who comprised the bulk of the colony's businessmen, managers, technicians, skilled workers, and the most wealthy and progressive farmers. These settlers were neither as numerous nor as permanently established as the whites in Southern Rhodesia. (In 1951 Northern Rhodesia contained 37,221 whites, as compared to Southern Rhodesia's 177,311.) Although the whites secured substantial representation for themselves in the Northern Rhodesian legislature, they never formed a majority. Most whites in the north hoped that Southern and Northern Rhodesia would eventually form a Rhodesian dominion.[3]

THE BREAKDOWN OF WHITE RULE

At the end of World War II, the Europeans in Central Africa had reached their political apogee. Sir Godfrey Huggins (later Lord Malvern), the Southern Rhodesian prime minister and a friend and ally of General Smuts in South Africa, enjoyed a reputation in Great Britain as a moderate and a reformer and was persona grata with the British establishment. The British conscience was as yet little concerned with Africa, and the average British voter cared no more about Rhodesia than about Tasmania or Prince Edward Island. Had Southern Rhodesia attempted to secure dominion status at this time, it would hardly have encountered effective opposition (provided Huggins had made some minor concessions regarding African policy).

Huggins wanted a great deal more than a Rhodesian midget dominion, however. The colony was booming; industrial production was increasing at a phenomenal rate. (The estimated net national income rose from Ł47.9 million in 1946 to Ł89.1 million in 1950.) The Rhodesian manufacturers had only a restricted home market, however, and desired federation into a larger Central African state in order to be protected from foreign competition — including that of South Africa. A Central African state would more easily be able to make transterritorial decisions concerning the allocation of priorities in transport, the provision of technical services, and so forth. A federated state would possess larger and more balanced resources than its components and could more easily secure scarce loan capital from overseas than would any one Central African territory.

The advocates of federation made an initial appeal to the great copper companies in Northern Rhodesia. They argued that a large Central African state would be well placed to initiate the large-scale hydroelectric developments essential for progress in the industry. A mildly reformist African policy of the kind advocated by Huggins and his United Party would favor African advancement in industry and thereby reduce labor costs. But Huggins and his associates did not think in economic terms alone. They were British patriots, determined to build a dominion well placed to resist two contrary threats. To Huggins, the immediate menace derived from white Afrikanerdom in South Africa. (In 1948 Smuts fell from power and the Nationalist party took over.) The second threat, (at the time, considered the more remote peril) derived from black nationalism in the north — a threat the federation was intended to counter.

In 1953 the three British Central African states joined to form the Federation of Rhodesia and Nyasaland, a loose association that placed defense and many major economic functions under the central government but left police and African affairs under the control of the constituent territories. From a purely economic and administrative standpoint, the federation was a striking success. Between 1954 and 1961 the gross national product increased from Ł338.3 million to Ł546.8 million. Gross capital formation averaged about 31 percent of the gross national product. Federal services concerned with such noncontroversial matters as meteorological research, archives, medicine, and demography performed with considerable competence. The federation also fulfilled the expectations of its founder by successfully accomplishing a variety of major development schemes.

According to its architects, the Federation was to embody a new partnership, with the whites as senior, and the Africans as junior, partners. In fact, the Federation rested on an uneasy working arrangement between Salisbury and London — between the settlers and the traditional imperial power exercised through the bureaucracy of the Colonial Office. The imperial government continued to control the rate of African constitutional advancement within the legislatures of the two northern territories. The federal Parliament, by contrast, was dominated by the traditional white Rhodesian establishment (organized into the United Federal Party, whose Southern Rhodesian affiliate also had a majority in the Southern Rhodesian legislature).

At first appearance the Federation seemed to be firmly established, but its formation actually opened the road to African independence. For the first time, Central African affairs became a major subject of concern in British domestic politics — (the British were at this time beginning to give up power in the rest of black Africa). The federal issue also deepened existing splits between the European settlers. The bulk of white businessmen and the traditional white establishment in Southern Rhodesia backed the federal experiment; the smaller farmers and white artisans opposed it, as did many officials of the British Colonial Office in the northern territories — albeit for different reasons. Above all, the federal controversy provided an enormous stimulus to African nationalism, especially in the two northern territories, were blacks looked to the imperial power for constitutional advancement similar to that of Nigeria and the Gold Coast.

In Northern Rhodesia, the first country-wide organization (formed in 1946) was the Federation of African Welfare Societies. From 1948 it was known as the African National Congress (ANC). The ANC, which was especially powerful among the Tonga and Ila along the Railway Belt, inclined toward moderation. It split in 1958 and its younger and more radical adherents formed the Zambia African National Congress; this was succeeded in 1960 by the United National Independence Party (UNIP). UNIP's immediate aim was to dissolve the Federation. It soon attained a mass membership. UNIP's president was Kenneth Kaunda, a former headmaster. He was assisted by other national officers, a permanent executive (the Central Committee), and regional organizations (twenty-four in 1961), each of which had a full-time organizing secretary appointed by and responsible to the Central Committee. UNIP also had associated Youth Brigades and Women's Brigades. Using both persuasion and strong-arm methods, UNIP became indisputably the most powerful political organization in Northern Rhodesia, especially among the Bemba of the northeast and the

Bemba migrants in the Copper Belt.

In Nyasaland, as in Northern Rhodesia, African political organization began with an ultramoderate group, the Nyasaland African Congress; this group linked a variety of welfare societies, literary societies, and social clubs into a common front. The Congress became increasingly radicalized over the federal issue and was reorganized in 1958 as the Malawi Congress Party, a mass organization led by Dr. Hastings Kamuzu Banda, an African physician partly educated in the United States and the United Kingdom. Banda appealed to a wide constituency, including labor migrants discontented with the treatment they had received in Southern Rhodesia, tenants on European estates dissatisfied with their conditions of service, cultivators angry at apparently onerous anti-soil erosion measures, and educated men and women who regarded the Federation as an obstacle on the road to African self-government. Banda succeeded in obtaining leadership on his own terms, along with full powers to personally appoint the central executive.

African resistance developed most slowly in Southern Rhodesia. A handful of Africans joined the dominant United Party; others formed trade unions and civic clubs. The first truly nationalist organization was the Youth League, formed in Salisbury in 1955. The Youth League was the first organization that sought not to amend, but to end, white rule. In 1957 it became the African National Congress, later succeeded by the Zimbabwe African People's Union (ZAPU). ZAPU was headed by Joshua Nkomo, a former welfare officer and one of Huggins's original political protégés. ZAPU eventually derived its main strength from the Ndebele. Dissidents, composed mainly of Shona-speaking Africans, split off from the party in 1963, and founded the Zimbabwe African National Union (ZANU), which was subsequently headed by Robert Mugabe, a teacher with experience in both Rhodesia and Ghana.

All Central African political parties shared certain common characteristics. Their leadership overwhelmingly derived from strong personalities rather than collegial control. They suffered from numerous organizational weaknesses associated with factionalism and fluctuating membership. (Memberships fluctuated because so many African workmen were migrant laborers.) They had to cope with financial stringency (often made worse by poor record keeping, poor bookkeeping, or financial defalcations on the part of ill-paid officials). Their ideology was eclectic; it was more indebted to pan-Africanist writers — or British Labourites like Harold Laski — than to Marx and Engels. Their propaganda inspired activists and often aroused quasi-millenarian expectations about the spiritual and material benefits to be gained from liberation.

The new parties claimed to represent the disinherited — that is, the mass of village cultivators and the new urban proletariat. Party leadership, however, did not derive from the ranks of rural and urban laborers but from white-collar professionals, especially schoolmasters. Teachers in particular had their own networks of present and former colleagues and students; these served them well in politics. They brought to their task a peculiarly didactic style and a sincere and lasting commitment to education. Most of these men and women had become involved in the organization of trade unions, civic clubs, welfare societies, and the like before they embarked on political careers. For many of them, politics became an avocation, a way of life, and a source of livelihood. Although they were opponents of the colonial tradition, they were also heirs to it. Therefore, they had strong faith in education as an instrument of social improvement and a firm belief in the power of the state as a mechanism of reform. They looked to public institutions, the civil service, their parties, or parastatal organizations to provide for the advancement of educated Africans.

The new parties soon managed to mobilize a mass membership. They skillfully internationalized their struggle. Their support abroad included members of the U.N., members of the British Labour Party, and the bulk of the liberal and left-wing intelligentsia. A new (now forgotten) evil trinity began to dominate the headlines of the progressive media. It was made up of Sir Roy Welensky, Hendrik Verwoerd, and Antonio Salazar (then prime ministers of the Federation, South Africa, and Portugal, respectively). The British conservatives became convinced that decolonization had become inevitable and that the Federation must go. Against such opposition, the Federation had no chance. After a series of complex negotiations, the African nationalists gained decisive majorities in the two northern legislatures. Their success in turn strengthened European right-wingers (drawn mainly from the ranks of farmers and artisans) in Southern Rhodesia, where the incumbent United Party lost power in 1962 and was supplanted by the Rhodesian Front. By now, all the territorial legislatures were dominated by antifederal majorities, and in 1963 the Federation broke up. In 1964 both Zambia and Malawi obtained sovereignty within the British Commonwealth. A year later, in 1965, white Southern Rhodesia (then known as Rhodesia) declared its unilateral independence (UDI).[4]

South of the Zambezi river, the UDI regime held on to power for another fifteen years. For the most part, expert opinion overseas did not expect white Rhodesia — run by farmers and provincial businessmen — to last for any length of time, especially since from the late 1960s African nationalists began to embark on a long drawn-out guerrilla campaign against it. In fact, the proponents of UDI at first resisted quite successfully. The Rhodesian economy both expanded and diversified. (Between 1964 — after the breakup of the Federation — and 1974, the gross national product rose from Rh. $668.0 million to Rh. $1,251.8 million at constant 1965 prices. Gross fixed capital formation rose from Rh. $85.5 million to Rh. $351.1 million.) The Rhodesians gained indirect, but strong, support from South Africa. They profited from bitter divisions between ZANU (sustained in part by the People's Republic of China) and ZAPU (backed by the Soviet Union). For a time it almost appeared as if the white counterrevolution might succeed.

The collapse of the Portuguese colonial regime in 1974, however, decisively changed the power equation. The Rhodesian military frontier lengthened enormously, and Rhodesian military forces increasingly became incapable of preventing guerrilla infiltration. The Rhodesian armed forces — originally manned chiefly by whites — were transformed into a largely black force. (By the late 1970s about four-fifths of the military forces consisted of Africans, and for the first time Africans began to receive commissions.) An ever-growing demand for skilled and supervisory black labor (occasioned in part by an expanding economy, the burden of conscription on whites, and growing facilities for African education) provided new and unexpected opportunities for African economic advancement. Even if the UDI regime had managed to triumph in purely military terms (an unlikely prospect) the Rhodesian Front would have failed to obtain its avowed objective — the indefinite maintenance of white supremacy.

White Rhodesia also began to resemble independent African states in other ways. In 1970 Rhodesia adopted a republican constitution. In practice, this unrecognized republic operated as a one-party states. (In the 1970 election the Rhodesian Front retained all the fifty seats on the white voters' roll; the other twenty-four seats went to Africans.) The Rhodesian prime minister, Ian Smith, enjoyed a degree of personal power almost comparable to that of Kenneth Kaunda in Zambia.

From 1973 onward the pace of guerrilla warfare quickened. As expressed in ZANU and ZAPU publications abroad, the partisan leadership was now wedded — at least in theory — to the doctrines of Marxism-Leninism. But the partisans remained divided in an organizational sense into the Zimbabwe People's Revolutionary Army (ZIPRA), which had been relatively well-trained, in the Soviet-bloc countries and later in Angola; and the Zimbabwe African National Liberation Army (ZANLA), ZANU's army, which was more numerous than its rival but less well-equipped and disciplined. Despite occasional clashes with one another, both armies grew in numbers and efficiency. They were composed of labor migrants and commanded mainly by high-school graduates. They steadily improved their political infrastructure within Rhodesia and extended the sphere of their operations. They could neither capture cities nor defeat the Rhodesian army in the field, but they increasingly disrupted the rural administrations and the rural economy.

Like all partisan wars in history, this conflict was a grim business. Although guerrilla struggles were naively glamorized during the 1960s, the realities of war — with their currents and countercurrents, their betrayals and acts of heroism, their contrasting and shifting loyalties — bore no resemblance to campus rhetoric, the language of military communiqués, or bloodless social-science jargon. The following remarks, which refer to the Greek civil war of 1943–1949, are equally applicable to the situation in Zimbabwe thirty years later.

> The civil war . . . bred its own Furies, and furnished material in abundance that would rankle in countless hearts forever. It was, in every sense, internecine and intestine: the second epithet seems peculiarly appropriate for a conflict that reputedly had more than its share of disembowelment. The violence of sectarian hatred was matched by a horrific and widespread indulgence in torture and executions, of civilians as well as combatants, more often than not in the name of freedom and justice, and accompanied by third-rate rhetoric either ethnic or ideological, according to conviction.[5]

Challenged on every front, the whites made numerous mistakes of both a strategic and a political nature. The Rhodesian high command was inclined to fight the war as a series of individual engagements devoid of an underlying strategy. Elite units such as the Grey Scouts, the Selous Scouts, and the paratroopers engaged in bitter internecine rivalry; the Rhodesian intelligence services declined in quality; the Rhodesians failed to enlist Africans in large numbers until it was too late, and failed to make adequate political concessions at a time when such concessions might still have aided their cause. Above all, white Rhodesia became increasingly dependent on South Africa, and South Africa became increasingly unwilling to bear the financial burden and the international odium of sustaining the Rhodesian regime.

In 1976, under joint pressure from Pretoria and Washington, Ian Smith finally agreed to a phased transfer of power to a moderate black government. In 1979 there was an attempt at an internal settlement, which resulted in a black government headed by Bishop Abel Muzorewa. Muzorewa, however, failed to achieve peace, international legitimacy, or the end of the international boycott. He lost any remaining credibility in 1979, when he agreed to stand down as prime minister in favor of an interim British administration (this at a time when Mozambique and Zambia had themselves become intensely weary of a destructive and costly war). New elections — held at a time when the guerrillas had obtained official legitimacy — resulted in an overwhelming victory for Robert Mugabe's ZANU party and left ZAPU and its Ndebele supporters in the position of a powerless opposition party. (Mugabe won fifty-seven of sixty-one seats set aside for the Shona-speaking peoples. The Ndebele won twenty seats.) ZANU won the 1980 election on an ultramoderate program that belied the party's previous commitment to revolutionary Marxism-Leninism. In fact, the new regime rested on a compact that reflected the uncertain military and economic balance of power that existed at the end of the 1970s. As Mugabe himself put it in a television interview, "We did not win a military victory . . . We reached a political settlement, a compromise."[6] After a bitter war that cost ca. 30,000 lives, the colonial regime ended on an apparent note of conciliation.

After they broke the colonizers' might, the three Central African states might well have considered recreating their former federation. The challenges of the past were still a reality. There was the same need to compete against South Africa, the mighty neighbor to the south whose GNP in 1981 (U.S. $75,739 billion) amounted to nearly seven times that of the three Central African states. There was much to be said in favour of recreating an economic unit larger than that of the three separate states. But just as the Federation of Rhodesia and Nyasaland had been dominated by Southern Rhodesia, a new African-run federation would have fallen under the sway of Zimbabwe.

Zimbabwe had the largest population (8,000,000 as compared to Zambia's 6,200,000 and Malawi's 6,300,000). Zimbabwe had the largest GNP (U.S. $6,238 billion in 1981–82, as compared to U.S. $3,519 billion for Zambia, and U.S. $1.53 billion for Malawi). Zimbabwe also had the most developed agriculture, the most sophisticated industries, the greatest reservoir of technical expertise (drawn in considerable measure from the white community of ca. 220,000), the best system of African education, and the largest number of African graduates (estimated at 10,000 — the majority of which had been educated at the University of Rhodesia). (Ironically, by holding out as long as they did, the whites in Zimbabwe assured that more educated blacks were available to run the country than in any of the other former British, French, or Portuguese territories at the time of their independence.)

Zimbabwe also enjoyed military predominance. The breakdown of colonial rule had entailed a vast expansion, rather than a contraction, of the local military establishments. (The Federation of Rhodesia and Nyasaland had had a peacetime strength of ca. 7,000 men in all services and an equal number of reservists. By 1982 the three Central African states together maintained nearly nine times that number.) The end of white rule left Zimbabwe with a force twice the size of the northern states (41,300 in 1982, as compared to Zambia's 14,300, and Malawi's 5,000). The three Central African states remained separate, for each of the new political establishments had a vested interest in maintaining unfettered independence.[7]

ZIMBABWE

When the guerrillas took over the reins of government in Zimbabwe, they were in a difficult position. The partisan war had ravaged large areas of the country, caused hundreds of thousands to flee from their homes, and destroyed much of the educational and administrative infrastructure in the countryside. The guerrillas had acquired experience in the use of arms and the building up of cells but not in the management of firms or government offices. They had inherited a state in which their erstwhile adversaries remained firmly entrenched in the administration and in farming and industry. Moreover, the guerrillas were divided because the ZANLA and ZIPRA forces had operated in distinct regions and had built up separate bases of support in the countryside.

Zimbabwe's constitution (adopted in 1980) tried to rebuild national entity in a formal sense. The constitution provided for a ceremonial head of state, whose functions in many ways resembled those of the British monarch. The new president, the Reverend Canaan Sodingo Banana, served as nominal commander-in-chief of the Defense Force and was responsible for appointing the prime minister (the person considered best able to command a majority in the House of Assembly). Parliament itself consisted of a forty-member Senate (including ten white members and ten black chiefs) and a House of Assembly (comprising 100 members, twenty of which were drawn from a white constituency). Effective power lay with ZANU, which commanded an absolute majority in the House, as compared to twenty seats reserved to the whites, twenty to Nkomo's supporters, and three to supporters of Muzorewa. ZANU was formally governed by congresses, but real authority resided in the Central Committee, within which Mugabe was able to consolidate his hold. This is not to say that ZANU was a monolithic bloc; while in exile, it had suffered from dissensions, and upon achieving power, its cohesion was further weakened by the infusion of exiles and ambitious opportunists. Within the party, there was a spirited ongoing debate between those who looked for a radical social solution and those who were willing to work more or less within the existing framework. By skillfully maneuvering between the opposing factions, the pragmatic Mugabe entrenched his position as head of the party, prime minister, and holder of the key portfolios of Defense and Public Services. Like Kaunda, Mugabe had a well-earned reputation for personal honesty that contrasted with the grasping ways of many in his entourage; this made it unlikely that his leadership would be effectively challenged.

As an opposition party, ZANU had firmly committed itself to the principles of Marxism-Leninism. According to Robert Mugabe's published statements, at home ZANU stood for rigid party discipline, and abroad, for unswerving hostility to American and British imperialism and "Zionist colonialism." Mugabe had ceaselessly expressed solidarity with revolutionary leaders like Castro and Mengistu and with revolutionary organizations like the PLO. Mugabe's expressed preference was for Marshal Tito rather than Marshal Stalin, but he nevertheless regarded himself as a revolutionary socialist of the purest water. Once in power, however, Mugabe felt compelled to make concessions — at least for a time. Zimbabwe has therefore continued to be a multi-party state.[8] In 1981, however, the government announced new regulations that imposed new restrictions on meetings and processions of parties other than ZANU. ZANU remained committed to introducing a one-party system, but by popular consent. According to Dr. Edison Zvobgo, the minister for local government and housing, ZANU was to be gradually transformed into a vanguard party along Marxist-Leninist lines. But the party first had to build a mass base throughout the country because the people had not as yet "received enough ideological instruction." Party spokesmen predicted that once the proper conditions had been established, conditions of membership in the restructured party would become much more exacting than before. They also predicted that the party's second congress would already witness the completion of a nucleus that would form a sizable vanguard within ZANU.[9] The Second Party Congress, duly held in 1984, was a festive occasion, attended by more than 6,000 delegates and the heads of state of Mozambique, Botswana, and Zambia. Mugabe asked the congress for a mandate to turn Zimbabwe into a one-party state in order to complete the ongoing socialist revolution.

The whites were the least troublesome minority for the new government. The most irreconcilable elements (including those who had served in elite military formations such as the Selous Scouts) emigrated. Many of the younger professionally and technically trained Europeans, who had no trouble getting jobs elsewhere, also emigrated. (By 1984 an estimated 67,000 of the 230,000 white residents had left.) Their departure posed serious problems. According to Dr. Ibbo Mandaza, the secretary for the Ministry of Manpower Planning, Zimbabwe's loss of skilled manpower was "astronomical" and the resultant shortages were "critical."[10]

But there was nothing like the mass exodus of whites that had crippled Angola, Mozambique, and Algeria at the termination of Portuguese and French imperial rule. The white minority in Zimbabwe continued to occupy an important position. They received two cabinet seats and continued to play a major part in the economy as farmers, industrial entrepreneurs, and specialists. Whites still served as officers and specialists in the armed forces (especially in the air force, because of this branch's need for high technical expertise). Whites held a substantial (although rapidly decreasing) stake in the civil service; key appointments increasingly went to loyal ZANU supporters. (By 1981 eleven Africans had been appointed permanent secretaries to various ministries.) White judges continued to preside over the higher courts. In 1982 the chief justice, the two judges of appeal, and the judge president were still Europeans. These courts continued to administer Roman-Dutch law, but in a form modified by the integration of traditional African law courts into the legal system.

Despite these concessions, white confidence diminished. There were many complaints of declining standards in public services like health. Other problems included rising inflation (27 percent at the end of 1983), widespread corruption, extensive misappropriation of public funds, and official interference with private business. The pursuit of "socialist egalitarianism" entailed a high rate of taxation. Whites were apprehensive about rural squatters, who were taking over some outlying farms, stripping them of their equipment, and diminishing their productivity. They were equally concerned about statements by ZANU militants that called for an accelerated drive toward socialism and a new order in which ZANU's Central Committee would assume executive and legislative authority in place of the cabinet and Parliament. Because they felt powerless and were anxious to conciliate the new establishment, the whites increasingly lost interest in politics; white political unity disintegrated. In 1982 nine of the twenty white members of the Republican Front (formerly the Rhodesian Front) resigned from the party and announced their intention to sit as independents. At the time of writing (end of 1984), special white representation still continued in the legislature, but these constitutional arrangements seemed unlikely to last.

For Mugabe, black dissatisfaction was a far more serious concern than white dissidence. The unrealistic hopes raised at the time of independence were soon dashed. The government raised the minimum wage for farm laborers and industrial workers, but inflation soon did away with these benefits. Little land was redistributed many goods remained in short supply, and unemployment continued to beset the economy. The government's problems were most serious in Matabeleland, where ZAPU continued to demand the allegiance of most local people. Revolutionary theoreticians and their admirers in the West had assumed that the independence campaign was a class struggle as much as a war of national liberation. They had thought that the colonialists had exaggerated the force of tribal divisions and that these divisions would become increasingly irrelevant as the anticolonial struggle went on.

Postrevolutionary realities belied these hopes. Revolutionary fever did not fuse the country's divergent black ethnic components into a new nation. The Patriotic Front, divided by conflicts between the Ndebele and the Shona-speakers and by personal struggles between proud rivals for the leadership, failed to maintain its cohesion (just as real or supposed reactionaries had predicted during the civil war). Mugabe certainly tried his best. Upon forming his new government in 1980, Mugabe first admitted several senior ZAPU officials into his new cabinet. A number of important civil service and military positions also went to ZAPU members. ZANU and ZAPU remained formally linked — as they had during the war — into one Patriotic Front. In 1981 Nkomo would have been wise to accept the presidency as a formal office and thereby consolidate the revolutionary government. But he did not, no permanent reconciliation took place, and the alliance split. The government discovered ZAPU arms caches in ZAPU-owned farms and houses, and Mugabe accused ZAPU of secretly preparing a new war.

In 1982, mistakenly convinced that Nkomo controlled the dissidents in the bush, Mugabe dismissed Nkomo and several of his colleagues from the cabinet, thereby effectively ending the governing coalition. The two groups were indeed polarized. ZANU accused ZAPU of having shirked the war of independence — of having left the bulk of the fighting to ZANU while it built up its forces on Zambian soil into regular units that would be capable of seizing power in a postindependence putsch. ZAPU accused ZANU of neglecting the special problems of Matabeleland, a region where the land was poor and little was available for redistribution. To ZAPU (especially to militants within a minority faction known as Super ZAPU), ZANU seemed an assembly of Shona-speaking trimmers. There was no genuine reconciliation. Instead, bitter fighting broke out in Matabeleland. The government deployed its security forces (including North Korean-trained units) against the dissidents and those villagers accused of lending support to the rebels. The inevitable accompaniments of guerrilla warfare and counterinsurgency — murder, torture, and rape — were once more carried out in the bush (as they had been during the civil war against the white regime). Many ZANU members went into exile; the Ndebele peasantry's antipathy to the government in Harare deepened. ZAPU split into members (mainly Mashonaland-based) who continued to give conditional support to the government, members who believed in peaceful opposition, and irreconcilable members (disowned by Nkomo) who stayed in the bush and carried out acts of banditry and reprisal against both whites and blacks.[11]

The ZAPU-ZANU cleavage extended to the armed forces. When the war ended, the government faced the difficult problem of fusing the existing Rhodesian security forces and the two guerilla armies, which together consisted of ca. 60,000 men. Since the majority of partisans were unwilling to return to farming, and there was considerable urban unemployment, jobs had to be found for them either in the administration or (mainly) the military.

In building the new army, Mugabe drew on instructors from many different sources, including Great Britain, the former Rhodesian security forces, and North Korea. (North Koreans trained the 5th Bridgade, which was to acquire an unsavory reputation for cruelty and corruption. The North Koreans subsequently left Zimbabwe.) By and large, the task of unification was carried out with success. By 1983 the army consisted of 40,000 men divided into five brigades; a sixth brigade (the presidential guard) was in the process of formation. The efficiency and loyalty of the new battalions varied greatly. The twelfth battalion, for example, disintegrated at first into warring factions. Yet later this same battalion — composed in equal measure of ZANLA and ZIPRA members — stood firm under fire against feuding guerrillas.[12]

For Mugabe, the army was more than an instrument of defense; it was also a means of nation building and an agent for social action. Mugabe therefore rejected any thought of creating a tribal army divided into ethnically distinct battalions. He also used the army for projects such as Operation Seed (Soldiers Engaged in Economic Development), in which cadres were employed for irrigation and other projects, a practice loosely based on the Chinese model. Such ventures, however, militated against the degree of military efficiency the government needed to counteract possible threats from South Africa.

The scope of public services was greatly extended. Between 1979 and 1981 the share devoted to public administration increased from Z $266 to Z $352 million. The government justified this policy on the grounds that the transition to socialism required a larger public sector and that existing services should be both democratized and made more widely available. Only in this manner would the government be able to achieve its declared objectives of redistributing national income; developing the rural areas; and creating a sharp increase in housing, office accommodation, stores, workshops, transport, and equipment.[13] The chief beneficiary of this policy was the education service, expenditure for which increased two-and-a-half times (from Z $98 million to Z $253) between 1979 and 1981. As the number of schools increased, so did the number of graduates who were entering the labor market and seeking new opportunities in public employment. To meet the expense of this expansion, the government resorted to deficit financing; shortfalls were met by some foreign borrowing but mainly by the issuing of domestic stocks and bonds.

At the same time, the machinery of government grew more complex. This development, of course, was nothing new. Long before African nationalism had become a political force, successive white governments had created an elaborate network of Statutory Commissions that attempted to combine private and public enterprise to promote farming, transport, and manufacturing industries.[14] (These statutory bodies had derived their impetus from purely pragmatic considerations, rather than from a commitment to public enterprise as such.) The Mugabe government simply expanded their scope, but it left the bulk of industrial, mining, and farming enterprises in private hands.

Nevertheless, the state bureaucracy continued to grow. (Sir Godfrey Huggin's last cabinet — formed in 1951 just before the onset of the federal era — had contained no more than seven cabinet ministers. Thirty years later, the first Mugabe administration comprised twenty-seven ministerial appointments. Between 1979 and 1984 the number of civil servants rose from 49,000 to 86,000.) The growth of government was accompanied by Africanization; appointments vacated by the natural process of retirement were largely filled with Africans. In addition, the government began to make new structural appointments. These entailed, for instance, the 1982 replacement of the country's incumbent attorney general, a European, by Godfrey Chidyauki, the deputy minister of justice. This was a serious concern for the public service and the morale of its senior officers, since the constitution had stipulated that the attorney general could be removed only for professional misconduct or corruption (and then only by means of a judicial tribunal).

The impact of these changes on efficiency varied considerably. In 1982 certain technical agencies, such as the National Archives, were still operating with accustomed competence. (Connoisseurs in these matters claimed that nonpoliticized departments could be distinguished from politicized departments because the former displayed only one portrait — President Banana's — whereas the latter showed two — the president's and the prime minister's.) But by and large the civil service had become politicized to a greater degree than in colonial days (when incumbent governments had resisted the temptation to fill public-service appointments with their own supporters). Expansion had been accompanied by a decline in standards. (This was especially problematic because ZANU's long-term socialist program could be expected to make ever-increasing demands on public services.)

There were other difficulties. At the end of the civil war, industrial equipment and rolling stock had depreciated. Antiquated equipment needed replacing. Educational, health, and agricultural services had been deliberately disrupted. Guerrilla warfare had created a bitter legacy of personal enmities, not only between whites and blacks but also (and perhaps to an even greater degree) among blacks.

The country did enjoy certain advantages that initially seemed to justify ZANU's optimism. Under the new order, Zimbabwe obtained international recognition and foreign aid. Merchants and civil servants were able to dispense with the elaborate schemes for evasion and deception required to beat the international boycott. During the UDI period, Zimbabwe's industries had both expanded and diversified. During the years 1965–1980, manufacturing had risen from 18.6 percent to 22.5 percent of the gross national product, and agriculture (especially European agriculture) had made a successful shift from tobacco to food crops. The government resisted the temptation to expropriate the relatively productive European farms that accounted for the bulk of the country's crops. During the immediate postwar period (1979–1981), the country's GNP actually expanded (from Z $1,312 million to Z $1,710 million at 1969 market prices) and substantial gains were made in both agriculture (from Z $137.8 million to Z $219.1 million) and manufacturing (from Z $307.0 million to Z $539.9 million).

In a mood of remarkable optimism, the government launched an ambitious Transitional National Development Plan in 1982. This plan required substantial changes and massive new expenditure at a time when the population was expanding and inflation was running at about 20 percent. ZANU's hopes were destined for disappointment. In 1983, for the first time since independence, the GNP began to decline. Sluggish world markets, foreign-exchange shortages, inflation, diminishing demand for local manufactures, and persistent droughts all added to the country's difficulties. Zimbabwe also spent heavily on defense and education, but agriculture and rural development remained relatively underfunded. (The 1983–84 budget provided for an estimated expenditure of Z $2,709.4 million. Of this, an estimated Z $382.4 million was earmarked for defense; Z $414.1 million for education and culture; Z $118.0 million for agriculture; and Z $32.1 for lands, settlement, and rural development.) Overall, services not directly linked to economic production (including defense, education, health, and public administration) continued to take up half the country's recurrent expenditure. The public debt had risen to nearly Z $1,000 million by 1983. The cost of servicing this debt amounted to something like 30 percent of the estimated value of Zimbabwean exports, and there was no prospect of securing sufficient amounts of foreign exchange.

In the face of these difficulties, the government made a number of concessions to private business. The 1983–84 budget tilted the balance in favor of taxes on consumption rather than income. (The tax structure inherited from the UDI regime had provided for consumption taxes amounting to 44 percent of the total taxes and income taxes amounting to 56 percent. The new budget almost reversed the proportion — to 55 percent for consumption and 45 percent for income taxes.) The budget trimmed subsidies and cut spending on long-cherished development projects like land resettlement.[15] The authorities planned for an annual growth rate of 5 percent in the agricultural sector; growth was to be achieved by reversing existing trends toward declining employment in farming, initiating new resettlement and irrigation schemes, and developing small-scale industries in the rural areas. At the time of writing, agriculture — especially European agriculture — continued to do well. The white farmers — long denounced by progressive scholars and political activists as functionless parasites — enabled Zimbabwe to actually export food at a time when many other

African countries were experiencing shortages and even famine.

The rest of Africa could learn from Zimbabwe's successes in agriculture since independence. First they encouraged white farmers to stay (4,400 of 5,000 remain) and offered land and services to black farmers as well. The result: a thriving, profitable farm sector — even during three years of drought. Zimbabwe not only fed itself it also exported food. In fact in 1983–84 agricultural exports accounted for about 65 percent of the states' export earnings. African peasant farmers are encouraged to stay on the land; they are provided efficient services and fair prices for their goods. Most African states have acted just the opposite — urban consumers were favored, farmers were neglected and paid below the market prices for their products. Good prices encourage farmers; but they also need good agricultural services, seeds, bags, prompt payment for their crops and further training in advanced agricultural practices. This Zimbabwe is doing. Would that all African states would follow this approach.

Manufacturing — at the time still under private ownership — was expected to be the leading sector (despite pervasive personnel shortages in engineering, management, and administration). Foreign investors were also reassured by a cabinet reshuffle that shifted Dr. Herbert Ushewokunze, a radical, from the crucial Ministry of Home Affairs to the less influential Ministry of Transport and that consolidated Mugabe's position within his cabinet.

Zimbabwe also achieved some success in its commercial policy. In 1983 Zimbabwe managed for the first time to substitute the European Economic Community (EEC) for South Africa as its chief trading partner. In that year, the EEC accounted for just under one-third of Zimbabwe's foreign commerce. Nevertheless, much to the government's displeasure, South Africa remained Zimbabwe's main individual trading partner, and 75 percent of Zimbabwe's foreign commerce continued to move through South African ports. South Africa remained essential as Zimbabwe's sole supplier of fuel and petroleum products, and was its main outlet for railway transport at a time when shortage of rolling stock had occasioned a major transport crisis in Zimbabwe.

To correct this dependency, Zimbabwe did all it could to strengthen the Southern African Development Coordinating Conference (SADCC), formed in 1980 by Angola, Botswana, Mozambique, Tanzania, Zimbabwe, and Zambia to promote regional cooperation and to reduce these states' common reliance on South Africa.

The SADCC received a great deal of financial help from the Western countries; its members pledged themselves to support specific regional projects, and Zimbabwe assumed particular responsibility for food security. But the SADCC experienced great difficulties in coordinating the divergent interests of its member states; projects proved to be more difficult and expensive to implement than anticipated; private finance for industrial development proved hard to secure; and SADCC lacked an effective mechanism to enable donors and recipients to cooperate effectively.

Not surprisingly, Mugabe could no more eliminate the Pretoria connection than Ian Smith could. The Zimbabwean prime minister insisted that his country was in no position to provide operational bases for the ANC guerrillas operating against South Africa. Nevertheless, Zimbabwe conducted a vigorous diplomatic campaign, not only against South Africa but also against Israel and the United States. Although Zimbabwe failed to condemn the shooting down of a Korean airliner by Soviet planes in 1983, it did denounce U.S. action in Grenada. Zimbabwe's socialist style abroad has thus made up for its lack of socialist achievement at home (without at any time endangering the U.S. aid that has continued under the Reagan administration, however). But vigorous diplomacy, international recognition, foreign assistance, and a cautious policy of socialism by instalment have not succeeded in preventing the gradual erosion of the Zimbabwe economy by the mid-1980s. ZANU's Second Party Congress, with its program for greater state involvement in all sectors of the economy and its commitment to socialism, was ill-designed to reassure those who dread the prospect of Zimbabwe going the way of Angola or Mozambique.

ZAMBIA

Zambia achieved independence under happier circumstances than its southern neighbor. When the country attained sovereignty in 1964, it was in excellent financial shape. (Revenue amounted to Ł56,081 million; expenditure amounted to Ł45,291 million.) The country's economy had expanded considerably during the federal period. There was a well-filled treasury, a reasonably stable currency, an efficient civil service, a free press, and a working parliamentary system that gave representation to several parties.

The country was in a position to feed itself, an achievement made possible both by the efforts of a small number of expatriate white farmers (no more than 700 at the time of independence) employing modern methods and by those of indigenous cultivators (especially Tonga and Ila small-holders along the so-called Railway Belt). Zambia benefited greatly from high prices for its main mineral exports — especially copper — and during the first few years following independence, Zambia's gross national product rose in an impressive fashion (at a rate of 9.5 percent per annum).

Zambia also enjoyed the more intangible benefits derived from the unstinting support of liberal academicians and aid-giving agencies in the West, an advantage shared by most other newly independent African states. Corruption in newly independent Africa was at first an almost taboo subject.[16] Inter-African violence also widely escaped academic scrutiny. (The shooting of African rioters at Sharpeville in South Africa in 1960 became an international scandal; in contrast, only a few specialists took any note of Zambia's suppression of the dissident Lumpa Church in 1964, when Zambian security forces killed more than ten times as many people as had been shot in South Africa.)

From the beginning, Zambia also faced a certain amount of regional unrest. Regional and black ethnic separatism were minimized, however, because of the commanding position held by the Copper Belt and the desire of all the provinces to share the wealth of this region. Ethnic and regional dissensions found expression in a number of separate parties; the African National Congress represented mainly the Tonga and the United Party spoke for the Lozi. Nevertheless, UNIP held a commanding lead, and the very multiplicity of black ethnic groups prevented the formation of effective ethnic separatist movements. The army, which numbered just over 4,000 men in 1970, was too weak and relatively too unconscious of its separate identity to stage a coup of the West African variety. Aid flowed in from abroad, and Zambians made determined attempts to reduce their economic dependency on the white-ruled south. (Italian engineers built an oil pipeline to Dar es Salaam; the People's Republic of China provided assistance for building a railway from the Copper Belt to Dar es Salaam so that Zambia would no longer have to rely on the Rhodesian system.) Secondary industry grew apace, and Zambia also increased its own sources of power. The school system expanded strikingly.

This is not to say that all was well in the land. The Tan-Zam

Railway (completed in 1975) failed to live up to its planners' expectations, and Zambia's dependency on the southern transport system continued. Zambia's decision to provide sanctuaries for guerrillas and to join in the international boycott against Smith's Rhodesia exacted a heavy economic price. Existing trade patterns were disrupted, inflation accelerated, bloody dissensions broke out among the Zimbabwean guerrillas on Zambian soil, and Rhodesian forces retaliated against partisans in Zambia. Villagers continued to drift into the cities; there was growing unemployment, a severe shortage of skilled manpower, and a striking disparity between the incomes of copper miners and those of the cultivators in the countryside. The government made a determined attempt to Zambianize the key posts in the administration and economy. (By 1968 Zambians accounted for 71 percent of administrative and executive posts, 59 percent of technical and related positions, and 19 percent of professional jobs outside the teaching profession.)[17]

The new governing elite made heavy use of government patronage for personal advancement; therefore, efficiency in many public services began to decline. In 1970 Kaunda himself complained that since independence Zambia had been forced to cope with both a sharp drop in labor productivity and a serious increase in wages and prices. Absenteeism in industry, drunkenness, and nepotism had increased rapidly, and investment had suffered.[18] Nevertheless, as long as copper remained king — providing the government with a steady and growing source of revenue — these troubles all seemed ultimately manageable.

The country's politics were thus inextricably tied to the mines. Originally, the government had denied that it would require public ownership of the mines. But, beginning in 1969, UNIP began to take an increasingly *étatiste* position — one that conformed to the current orthodoxies of development economists, who sought the secret of prosperity in the triple expansion of education, manufacturing industries, and central planning. In doing so, Kaunda was particularly influenced by the Tanzanian model and by his personal admiration for Julius Nyerere. Nyerere had called for a new form of African socialism, and his admirers inside and outside Africa expected him to provide "a model for all Africa and indeed the wider world."[19]

In the early 1970s the Zambian government established far-reaching controls over banking, the mass media, insurance, trade, and various other enterprises. The mining industry was nationalized in stages. Actually, the new partnership between the state and the great corporations was not unwelcome to the companies. According to H. F. Oppenheimer, one of the great South African mining magnates, the new arrangement provided the companies with liquid funds derived from compensation payments that enabled the corporations to broaden their field of operations elsewhere.[20] The Zambia Industrial and Mining Corporation (ZIMCO), a government-owned corporation, became the main instrument for controlling a large parastatal sector — including such bodies as the Industrial Development Corporation (INDECO), the State Finance and Development Corporation (FINDECO), and the National Hotel Corporation. Under nationalization a host of new positions became available for political patronage, thereby decreasing efficiency. Additionally, nationalization could not cope with the previously unforeseen problem of falling copper prices. By 1974 copper (the source of some 98 percent of all Zambia's export earnings) had drastically decreased in value; inflation had caused costs to spiral, and the two great state-owned mining concerns were operating at a loss. Zambia's prospects were made even more dismal by the fact that (for many uses) copper had to compete with aluminium on the world market. (Advances in the development of synthetic substitutes for copper posed an even greater long-term threat.)

Other nationalized concerns fared no better. At the time of independence, it was widely assumed that great state-owned corporations could not fail to out-perform petty shopkeepers devoid of both capital and managerial skills. Indeco Trading, a large state-owned concern, was turning a much lower profit than small African village trading concerns run by men with little formal education and a minimum of capital. Indeco performed poorly because state managers earned high salaries and lived well. Their projects routinely received favors for credits, supplies, and state contracts. Nevertheless, Indeco incurred heavy losses because of inefficiency, high overheads, and lack of adaptability in marketing. A commission of inquiry on the parastatals appointed in 1980 unearthed a sad tale of heavy debts, forged checks, misappropriated funds, inefficient management, and any number of other irregularities.[21]

Agriculture also underwent many vicissitudes. In theory, farming should have received first priority in a country in which (as of 1974) two-thirds of the population lived on the land. Yet, during the first ten years of independence, food imports doubled in value. In 1970 the country found, to its humiliation, that maize had to be imported from Rhodesia. According to Andrew Roberts, a historian of modern Zambia, the government did spend a good deal of money on farming, but these funds were largely wasted because of excessive reliance on complex machinery, inadequate technical training, inefficient marketing and the gross mismanagement of credit facilities.[22]

Agriculture suffered further from shortages in storage facilities, the lack of skilled manpower outside the European sector, inadequate transport facilities, and the continuing exodus of young and able-bodied people to the cities. Moreover, falling prices put a high premium on the use of efficient farming methods, and these were most readily mastered by the few hundred white farmers in Zambia. According to the anticolonial orthodoxies put forward in the 1950s and 1960s by such writers as Thomas Franck, Boris Gussman, and Patrick Keatley, the settlers were the "New Bourbons" of Africa; they were guilty of "racial neurosis" and of enjoying an all-too-comfortable existence at African expense. Their expertise, however, continued to play a valuable part in the postcolonial market economy. The trouble was not that too many privileged white parasites remained on the land or in industry, but that too many of them had departed. They were partly replaced by competent African farmers. But ordinary villagers became increasingly reluctant to stake their livelihood on the land; many of the most ambitious and best-educated left for the cities to find better jobs in industry or mining or to obtain further education that would qualify them for bureaucratic employment.

This is not to say that Zambia has achieved nothing. (Between 1979 and 1981 maize output rose from 700,000 to 1,000,000 metric tons; sugar rose from 880,000 to 1,000,000 metric tons.) Overall, however, agriculture remained the planners' orphan. This situation was reflected in the allocation of funds for national development plans. The crucial Second National Development Plan for 1972–1976 allotted only 152.2 million kwacha (out of a proposed total of 1,956.4 million kwacha) to land and agriculture.

Since independence, Zambia has strikingly increased its public sector. Public consumption increased from 11 percent of the gross national product in 1960 to 27 percent in 1976; at the same time, Zambia diminished its gross rate of domestic saving from 41 percent of the gross domestic product in 1960 to 28 percent in 1976.

The expansion of the public sector has been accompanied by a rapid growth in the educational system. Between 1964 and 1979 enrollment in schools rose by over 200 percent; familiarity with English increased substantially after 1965, when English became established as the language of instruction in all schools. The government failed to encourage adequately the acquisition of practical skills however. By 1981 there were 1,068,314 students in primary schools, 98,862 in secondary schools, 4,485 in teacher-training colleges, and 3,603 at universities; in contrast, there were only 5,487 students in trade and technical schools.

In Zambia, as elsewhere, the new educated elite had a natural stake in the expansion of the public sector. Its members were awarded more and more positions in government service, municipal employment, and the parastatals. In the Copper Belt these persons became popularly known as the *abapamulu* (those on top) in contrast to the *abapanshi* (the lowly ones who lived on a laborer's wage). The new elite advocated the rapid Zambianization of the civil service. They widely supported Zambian humanism, whose aims became identified with the creation of a one-party state that would supposedly eliminate internal dissent (but that in practice facilitated the distribution of political spoils).

In 1972 a national commission designed a new constitution; its adoption in 1973 inaugurated the Second Zambian Republic. Under the new dispensation, Kaunda's powers were further strengthened. As president of the Republic of Zaire, he was head of state and commander of the armed services. In addition, he served as chairman of ZIMCO, thereby acquiring powers that went far beyond those once exercised by traditional colonial governors. Kaunda was made president of both UNIP and the Republic; in his dual capacity, he became responsible for appointing the secretary-general of the party, the prime minister, the attorney general, the director of public prosecutions, and justices of the Supreme Court, including the chief justice. No limits were set on the presidential term of office. Senior cabinet and senior UNIP posts became interchangeable. Thus the prime minister was an ex officio member of UNIP's Central Committee, and the party's secretary-general served as an ex officio member of the cabinet.

UNIP's Central Committee consisted of only twenty-five members, twenty of which were to be elected by the party's General Conference. In practise, the General Conference exercised little influence. Real power rested with the president and his close entourage within the Central Committee and its subcommittees. These organs were responsible for security and defense, elections and propaganda, economics and finance, political and legal matters, appointments and disciplinary questions, social and cultural questions, and rural development. All Central Commitee and subcommittee members owed their appointments to the president and were required to be full-time officials of UNIP's national headquarters. Within the political system as a whole, the ruling party stood supreme. As the Central Committee's guidelines put it, "The supremacy of the Central Committee over the Cabinet is derived from the position of the Party vis-à-vis other institutions in the nation."[23] The cabinet, which was appointed by the president, therefore played a subordinate role — as did the National Assembly and a purely decorative House of Chiefs. On a lower level, UNIP developed a whole network of subordinate organizations: cultural clubs, rate-payers associations, bodies concerned with adult education (the Fight Illiteracy Association), and even funeral committees that looked after the ceremonial internment of their members.

The one-party state outlawed all formal opposition. Parliament became no more than a rubber stamp. (Of 135 members in 1983, more than half were ministers, ministers of state, or provincial governors who were dependent on the president's good graces.) The armed forces — poorly administered and generally inefficient — seemed unlikely to stage a putsch. The paramilitary formations — divided into self-sufficient units with their own armored vehicles and helicopters and numbering between 5,000 and 6,000 men — were more combat-worthy and disciplined than the army. The president used these units to insure his supremacy. The paramilitary formations were in turn supported by the Special Branch and a nationwide network of informers that also helped to keep a lid on dissidence.

Nevertheless, disagreements persisted both inside and outside the ruling party. UNIP was divided between advocates of moderation like Humphrey Mulemba, UNIP's secretary general and a wealthy businessman, and advocates of "scientific socialism," like Grey Zulu, minister of defence and a man committed to the expansion of Soviet and East German aid for the military and the security apparatus. Outside the party ranks, the trade union movement served as a potential counterweight to UNIP. The two most important unions were the Zambian Congress of Trade Unions (ZCTU) and the Mineworkers' Union of Zambia (MUZ). The miners occupied an especially strong position. Their pay compared favourably with that of most other workers. Because of the mining industry's strategic importance in the economy, and the government's dominant position in mine ownership, miners had considerable bargaining power. Workers in general, however, did not necessarily see eye to eye with the new bourgeoisie (politicians, civil servants, and teachers), whose life style and income strikingly contrasted with the antimaterialistic rhetoric of Zambian humanism. The ruling party also encountered opposition from churchmen, who commonly sided with the workers.

Zambian humanism, with its emphasis on African democratic socialism, had worked well enough as long as the economy expanded, salaried jobs increased, and rapid promotion gave educated people the sense of living in an open society. The authority of the party had been sustained in the early years by the apparent threats to Zambia's security and the challenge to blacks posed by Smith's declaration of UDI in Rhodesia. The slump in the Zambian economy, the loss of the original enthusiasm engendered during the independence campaign, the pervasive inefficiency and corruption, and the contrast between Zambia's anti-South African rhetoric and the government's willingness to deal with South Africa in practice all brought about a growing mood of disillusionment. Disenchantment spread to many social groups, including industrial workers and miners discontented with their pay packets, cultivators dissatisfied with the prices paid for their produce, and professional people and businessmen who felt that their interests were being neglected by the government. Hostility to the ruling party began to find expression among a growing number of sacked or disillusioned politicians. These people forged a new reserve army of dissidence, one which, moreover, had more political and practical administrative experience than Kaunda's African opponents had in the early days of independence.

This dissidence appears hard to stamp out, particularly because the world recession is continuing to seriously erode the Zambian economy. Zambia faces low prices for its mineral exports, a growing burden of foreign debt, the legacy of a series of unbalanced budgets, and increasing corruption. Such problems were not anticipated in the early days of independence, when Zambia experienced the most striking economic growth in Africa.[24] The new difficulties have come about partly because Zambia has paid excessive attention to the needs of higher education and the bureaucracy at the expense of agriculture.

MALAWI

Malawi remains the poorest and least-endowed of the three Central African states. It lacks commercially exploitable minerals. At the time of independence Malawi was heavily independent on the export of manpower and commercial crops. For a brief time, however, Malawi exercised political leadership; African opposition to the Federation of Rhodesia and Nyasaland initially hinged on Malawi. From the start, Banda wielded enormous personal prestige, not only within the ranks of his own Malawi Congress Party but also among liberal European admirers. European liberals apostrophized Banda (in terms familiar to European fascism) as "the national leader, . . . a hero who has arisen from the people, mysterious, confident, certain, decided . . . a man to lead in no uncertain terms . . . as the embodiment of the will and spirit of the people.[25]

After achieving independence, Malawi telescoped the development from parliamentary rule to person autocracy into a few short years. In 1966 Malawi became a one-party state. A constitutional amendment adopted in 1970 appointed Banda president for life. The president acted as both head of state and head of government; he also held a variety of key portfolios (including External Affairs, Justice, Works and Supplies, and Agriculture) and lifetime presidency of the Malawi Congress Party. In his capacity as life president, Banda appointed the chief justice, senior members of the armed forces, and key civil servants. He was empowered to appoint an unlimited number of members of the National Assembly (comprising eighty-seven elected members). He could prorogue or dissolve Parliament; all the ministers were responsible to the president. The president also wielded a great deal of economic power because he had his own personal holding company and could encourage his own supporters — including cabinet ministers and senior civil servants — to invest in agricultural and commercial concerns. The country's armed forces remained too limited to form an effective counterweight.

The Malawi Congress Party formally held the reins of power. It was headed by a National Executive Committee; subordinate organizations consisted of district committees, regional committees, area branches, and local branches. Affiliate organizations included the League of Malawi Women and the League of Malawi Youth. Formally, the party's highest authority was the annual convention, which was attended by the cabinet ministers, members of Parliament, parliamentary secretaries, heads of local government bodies, chiefs, and leading party functionaries down to the level of the leading officials within the district committees. In practice, the annual convention confined itself to debating general issues; complimenting Banda on his presidential performance; praising as Malawi's true foundations the virtues of Unity, Loyalty, Obedience, and Discipline; and condemning perverse practices such as the wearing of miniskirts.[26] For all practical purposes, the Malawi Congress Party remained Banda's personal instrument of power — a means for manipulating public opinion in his government's interest.

In fact, Banda governed Malawi in the manner of a traditional monarch. Kamuzu Day, His Excellency's birthday, became an occasion for compulsory public rejoicing and patriotic sycophancy. Like a conventional colonial governor, however, Banda also took care to work through proper administrative channels. He avoided the mistake made by leaders like Julius Nyerere, who unwisely courted popularity by intervening directly at the lower levels of government, thereby weakening the authority of departmental ministers and heads of department.

When Banda embarked on his presidential career in 1966, he was head of one of the most militant movements in contemporary Africa. Immediately after he became president, however, he dealt the radicals within his party a major blow; he forced six cabinet ministers out of the cabinet and broke with the militant African intelligentsia. Banda instead drew heavily on the less well-educated sections of the populace and, by means of both constitutional and strong-arm methods, crushed all opposition. White expatriates continued to hold a number of key positions (for instance, the post of chief justice). The opposition parties were driven into exile. In the early 1980s the exiled parties included the Congress for the Second Republic (led by Kanyama Chiume, a former minister) and the Malawi Freedom Movement (headed by Orton Chirwa, a former cabinet minister who had been sentenced to death in 1983). Both of these groups centered on Dar es Salaam. A third party, the Socialist League of Malawi (led by Kapote Mwakusula) operated from Harare in Zimbabwe; it claimed support from Cuba and had a military wing — the People's Liberation Army. (The party, known as LESOMA, sustained a serious loss in 1983, when Dr. Ataki Mpakati was assassinated in Harare, reputedly by Banda's agents.) There was also dissension within the ruling party; at one time four leading members, including Secretary General Fick Matenje, were rumored to have been engaged in a plot to kill Banda.

Opposition to the ruling party remained divided however. Dissident groups could not easily make use of ethnic issues of the kind that had divided Bemba from Lozi in Zambia or Ndebele from Shona in Zimbabwe. Malawi had always been composed of many small ethnic communities, most of whom could speak Nyanja (adopted as the national language in addition to English). Overall, Malawians had a stronger sense of common national consciousness than Zimbabweans or Zambians; therefore, the country did not experience the type of interethnic tensions that characterized politics in most other parts of Africa.

Banda's foreign and economic policy also countered the prevailing orthodoxies of Africa. Whereas South Africa's black neighbors were wont to abuse the Pretoria regime in public and trade with it in private, Banda maintained diplomatic relations with South Africa. By doing so, he benefited from South African, as well as Western, aid. At a time when most development economists stressed the merits of central planning, state ownership of (or public participation in) major enterprises, and rapid industrialization, Banda emphasized agriculture. Banda has not seen eye to eye with those theoreticians who looked on the farming industry as a milch cow to provide the required surplus for manufacturing enterprises. Farming and the provision of water supplies have received a substantial share of Malawi's development expenditure.[27] Private consumption has accounted for a higher proportion of the gross domestic product than in the other two Central African states. As a result, the overall increase in Malawi's gross domestic product has exceeded Zambia's and Zimbabwe's, as have the growth rates of the gross national product and domestic saving.[28]

Banda's deliberate goal was a system in which the state would prescribe the general lines of development through public bodies such as the Malawi Development Corporation, the Investment and Development Bank, and the Agricultural and Marketing Corporation, but would entrust the rest of the economy to private enterprise. He permitted export-oriented estates to continue their operations; at the same time he attempted (with some success) to transform subsistence cultivators into small holders integrated into the market economy. By 1980 farming accounted for 42.6 percent of the gross national product: estates contributed 6.4 percent; small holders, 8.8 percent; and subsistence farmers, 27 percent.[29]

This is not to say that all was well with Malawi. In the early 1980s the country remained heavily dependent on a few major cash crops (tobacco, and, to a much lesser extent, sugar and tea). Malawians continued to labor in many parts of sub-Saharan Africa from the Cape to the equator, and, as of old, remittances they sent home indirectly contributed to the national exchequer. The worldwide recession seriously affected Malawi's economy. Malawi had long followed a conservative fiscal policy reminiscent of colonial times. But the 1980–81 budget left the country with a deficit of 10,652 million kwacha (despite a surplus of 11,443 million kwacha in the preceding financial year).[30] Malawians have a lower life average expentancy than Zambians or Zimbabweans (forty-seven years, as compared to forty-nine and fifty-five years, respectively, according to 1979 estimates). Given the paucity of its domestic resources, however, Malawi has performed quite well (certainly much better than Zambia). But much will depend on the country's ability to find a means of assuring a legitimate successor when Banda passes from the political scene.

CONCLUSIONS

During the two decades that followed the breakup of the Federation of Rhodesia and Nyasaland, all three Central African states achieved a considerable success. Whether ruled by whites or blacks, they were all initially able to expand their economies. (In doing so, the black-ruled states of Zambia and Malawi exhibited considerably more success than countries like Zaire and Ghana, which — as indicated in Table 1 — enjoyed a good measure of prosperity at the time of independence.) These early growth rates, however, could not be sustained.

The *étatiste* solutions, advocated with so much fervor during the independence years, failed to work. The new states did not create egalitarian societies; they did not eliminate corruption; they could not sustain the enthusiasm of the independence struggle. On the

Table 1: Average Annual Growth Rate (Percent)

Country	1960–1970	1970–1980
Malawi	4.1%	6.4%
Zambia	6.8	1.5
Ghana	2.0	– 0.1
Zaire	3.5	– 1.3

Source: *World Development Report, 1982*. Published for the World Bank, Oxford University Press, 1982, p. 110.

Note: This report does not break down Zimbabwe's growth rate by decade; it gives only the overall figure of 0.6 percent for the entire period 1960–1980.

contrary, privilege expanded, and the beneficiaries of the anti-colonial revolution became a new privileged class. The new states failed to conform to those democratic standards that critics had used to judge imperial and white settler governments. The new governments did not rest on free elections. They did not respect human rights as understood in the West — or as promised by African activists during the independence struggle. Government by a single party failed to fulfill the expectations it had aroused; party autocracy did not succeed in effectively mobilizing the masses, eliminating internal dissent, or achieving the promised "liberation of the people . . . from poverty, illiteracy, and apathy."[31] Moreover, the mystique of the efficiency of foreign aid was shattered. The amount of foreign assistance received by various African beneficiaries bore no relation whatever to the degree of economic development achieved.

The excessive optimism of the 1960s and early 1970s was not confined to African nationalists or their supporters in the West. This period also witnessed an almost Utopian mood among many intellectuals in the West. The diploma-bearing expert was widely endowed with almost mysterious powers. It was hoped that sociologists could acquire the capacity to formulate precise predictions concerning the future of society; that the insight of political scientists would prove superior to that of the greatest lawgivers of antiquity; and that economists would become alchemists who would discover the formula for global wealth. Together they would construct a new era of universal peace, progress, and prosperity.[32]

By the 1980s these illusions all lay in ruins. Indeed, the failure of social-science prognostications provided new arguments for those academics who had preferred the historical approach and had stressed the continuities between colonial and postcolonial Africa. The new states in Africa all continued to face the manifold problems that had challenged the imperial powers and others. The new states also encountered perils unanticipated either by their founding fathers or by the Western academicians who had backed the cause of independence two generations previously. One of these afflictions was unchecked demographic growth. (In Zambia, the average annual birth rate for 1949–1979 was estimated at 50.0 per thousand; the death rate at 19.0 per thousand. In Zimbabwe, the estimated annual birth rate for 1975–1980 was 47.3 per thousand; the death rate was 13.6 per thousand.) Other difficulties included runaway urban expansion, the failure of national planning to correspond to economic realities, widespread loss of morale, and a pervasive sense of inefficiency — especially in the public sectors of the economy. By 1984 a majority of African states could not feed themselves.

These ills have not been easy to cure. The progressives of the 1960s had assumed that South Africa's white regime would collapse in the foreseeable future. But revolution was clearly not imminent. By 1984 even the Marxist-Leninist regimes of Angola and Mozambique were unashamedly negotiating with Pretoria; South Africa's economic supremacy within the region had become, if anything, even more marked.[33] Instead of sponsoring revolutionary warfare in South Africa, the various black neighbors of the republic (especially Zimbabwe and Mozambique) were dreading the prospect of a South African base for counterrevolutionary subversion. In diplomatic terms, the various African states have continued to adhere to the Lusaka Manifesto (adopted in 1969), which advocated, in conciliatory language, majority rule in South Africa. But the language of ritual diplomacy has increasingly diverged from the realities of policy.[34]

In the realm of socioeconomic policy, the predictions of progressive scholarship in the 1960s also seem to have gone awry. The prescriptions of the 1960s — a rapid expansion of education and foreign aid; deficit financing; the nationalization of key sectors of the economy; accelerated industrialization and relative neglect of agriculture — no longer seem to provide all the answers.

On the contrary, these remedies may have made the patient sicker than before independence. For instance, some of the new afflictions may well have derived from an excessive investment in education — the planners' sacred cow and supreme desideratum throughout the 1960s and 1970s. The new institutions of learning were financed at the expense of local taxpayers, including rural cultivators, who received little direct benefit from the schooling provided to that small minority who managed to graduate from secondary schools and universities. The training provided by schools and universities did not necessarily raise the graduates' economic productivity to the degree that the planners had expected. The postcolonial Central African governments therefore encountered constant pressure to expand the number of available government and party posts and to increase the functions of the state in order to provide more jobs for the diploma-bearing elite. Competition for these positions was apt to exacerbate ethnic tensions, and ethnic affiliation itself became a weapon in the scramble for economic and political advancement. These troubles were not, of course, confined to Central Africa.[35] In none of the new African states had the splendid promises of independence been fulfilled.*

*In elections held in July 1985, Mugabe won 63 out of 79 black National Assembly seats contested at the time. Fifteen seats in Matabeleland went to Joshua Nkomo. Of the twenty white seats, fifteen went to supporters of Ian Smith, and only five to independents willing to cooperate with Mugabe. After these elections — marked by much violence against Mugabe's opponents — Mugabe reiterated his plans for introducing a one-party state within the next five years, and for abrogating those constitutional provisions that stood in the way of this design.

Notes

1. For a history of British imperial penetration into Nyasaland, see A. J. Hanna, *The Beginnings of Nyasaland and North-Eastern Rhodesia, 1849–95* (Oxford: Oxford University Press, Clarendon Press, 1956). For a history of the colonial forces there, see Hubert Moyse-Bartlett, *The King's African Rifles: A Study in the Military History of East and Central Africa, 1890–1945* (Aldershot, England: Gale and Polden, 1956). For social conditions during the early colonial period, see Michael Gelfand, *Lakeside Pioneers: Socio-Medical Study of Nyasaland, 1875–1920* (Oxford: Basil Blackwell, 1964). For subsequent developments, see Griffith B. Jones, *Britain and Nyasaland* (London: Allen and Unwin, 1964). For the rise of African nationalism, see Robert I. Rotberg, *The Rise of Nationalism in Central Africa; the Making of Malawi and Zambia, 1893–1964* (Cambridge, Mass.: Harvard University Press, 1965) and George Shepperson and Thomas Price, *Independent African: John Chilembwe and the Origins, Setting, and Significance of the Nyasaland Native Rising of 1915* (Edinburgh: Edinburgh University Press, 1958).

2. For the history of Southern Rhodesia under colonial governance, see L. H. Gann, *A History of Southern Rhodesia: Early Days to 1933* (London: Chatto and Windus, 1964). For its constitution, see Claire Paley, *The Constitutional History of Southern Rhodesia, 1888–1965: With Special Reference to Imperial Control* (Oxford: Oxford University Press, Clarendon Press, 1966). For an early social

history, see Michael Gelfand, *Tropical Victory: An Account of the Influence of Medicine on the History of Southern Rhodesia, 1890–1923* (Cape Town: Juta, 1953). For Rhodesia's African administration, see J. F. Holleman, *Chief, Council, Commissioner: Some Problems of Governance in Rhodesia* (Assen, Netherlands: Royal Van Gorcum, 1969) and Henry Rolin, *Rolin's Rhodesia* (Bulawayo, Rhodesia: Books of Rhodesia, 1978) [translation of Henri Rolin, *Les lois et l'administration de la Rhodésie* (Brussels: E. Bruyland, 1913]. For white politics, see Colin Leys, *European Politics in Southern Rhodesia* (Oxford: Oxford University Press, Clarendon Press, 1959) and L. H. Gann and Michael Gelfand, *Huggins of Rhodesia: The Man and His Country* (London: Allen and Unwin, 1965). For Zimbabwe's colonial history as seen from the African standpoint, see Stanley Samkange, *Origins of Rhodesia* (New York: Frederick Praeger, 1968); David Changiwa, *The Occupation of Southern Rhodesia: A Study of Economic Imperialism* (Nairobi: East African Publishing House, 1981); T. O. Ranger, *Revolt in Southern Rhodesia, 1896–1897: A Study of African Resistance* (Evanston, Ill.: Northwestern University Press, 1967). For a military history, see John F. Macdonald, *The War History of Southern Rhodesia*, 2 vols. (Salisbury, Rhodesia: Government Printers, 1947–1950).

3. For general histories, see Richard Hall, *Zambia, 1890–1964: The Colonial Period* (London: Longmans, 1976): Andrew Roberts, *A History of Zambia* (New York: Africana Publishing Company, 1979). For its development under British governance, see L. H. Gann, *A History of Northern Rhodesia: Early Days to 1953* (London: Chatto and Windus, 1964). For an early social history, see Michael Gelfand, *Northern Rhodesia in the Days of the Charter: A Medical and Social Study, 1878–1924* (Oxford: Basil Blackwell, 1961). Military history is outlined in William V. Brelsford, *The Story of the Northern Rhodesia Regiment* (Lusaka: Government Printer, 1954). Economic development is covered in Robert E. Baldwin, *Economic Development and Export Growth: A Study of Northern Rhodesia, 1920–1960* (Berkeley and Los Angeles: University of California Press, 1966). The crucial copper industry is covered from a pro-company standpoint in Simon Cunningham, *The Copper Industry in Zambia: Foreign Mining Companies in a Developing Country* (New York: Praeger, 1981); for a critical stance, see Guy Mhone, *The Political Economy of a Dual Labor Market in Africa: The Copper Industry and Dependency in Zambia, 1929–1969* (East Brunswick, N.J.: Farleigh Dickinson University Press, 1982). For an African evaluation, see Henry S. Mbeelo, *Reaching to Colonialism: A Prelude to the Politics of Independence in Northern Zambia, 1893–1939* (Manchester, England: Manchester University Press, 1971).

4. For the federal interlude, see W. V. Brelsford, ed., *A Handbook to the Federation of Rhodesia and Nyasaland* (Salisbury: Government Printer, 1960). For the economic aspects, see William J. Barber, *The Economy of British Central Africa: A Case Study of Economic Development in a Dualistic Society* (Stanford: Stanford University Press, 1961) and Federation of Rhodesia and Nyasaland, *The Breakup: Effects and Consequences on the Two Rhodesias* (Salisbury: Government Printer, 1963). For the politics of the period, see Edward Clegg, *Race and Politics: Partnership in the Federation of Rhodesia and Nyasaland* (London: Oxford University Press, 1960); Robert Blake, *A History of Rhodesia* (New York: Alfred A. Knopf, 1978); Kenneth Kaunda, *Zambia Shall be Free* (London: Heinemann, 1962); David C. Mulford, *Zambia: The Politics of Independence* (London: Oxford University Press, 1967); M. W. K. Chiume, *Kwacha: An Autobiography* (Nairobi: East African Publishing House, 1975); Philip Short, *Banda* (London: Routledge and Kegan Paul, 1974). For a critique of the Federation in general, see Patrick Keatley, *The Politics of Partnership: The Federation of Rhodesia and Nyasaland* (Harmondsworth, England: Penguin Books, 1963); and for a much more friendly account, see L. H. Gann, *Central Africa: The Former British States* (Englewood

Cliffs, N.J.: Prentice-Hall, 1971).

5. Peter Green, "The Furies of Civil War," *Times Literary Supplement*, 20 Jan. 1984, p. 51. See also L. H. Gann, *Guerrillas in History* (Stanford: Hoover Institution Press, 1971).

6. L. H. Gann and Tom Henriksen, *The Struggle for Zimbabwe: Battle in the Bush* (New York: Praeger, 1981), p. 116. For a friendly account of UDI, see Kenneth Young, *Rhodesia and Independence: A Study in British Colonial Policy* (London: J. M. Dent, 1969) and for a critique, see Robert C. Good, *U.D.I.: The International Politics of the Rhodesian Rebellion* (Princeton, N.J.: Princeton University Press, 1973). The war is covered in Gann and Henriksen, *The Struggle for Zimbabwe*; Kees Maxey, *The Fight for Zimbabwe: The Armed Conflict in Southern Rhodesia Since U.D.I.* (London: Rex Collings, 1975); David Smith and Colin Simpson, *Mugabe* (Salisbury: Pioneer Head, 1981); David Caute, *Under the Skin: The Death of White Rhodesia* (Evanston, Ill.: Northwestern University Press, 1983); Dickson A. Mungazi, *The Cross between Rhodesia and Zimbabwe: Racial Conflict in Rhodesia, 1962–1979* . . . (New York: Vantage Press, 1981); and Paul L. Moorcraft, *Chimurenga: The War in Rhodesia: 1965–1980* (Marshalltown, South Africa: Sygma-Collins, 1982). For the economic aspects, see G. M. E. Leistner, *Rhodesia: Economic Structure and Change* (Pretoria: Africa Institute, 1976).

7. International Institute for Strategic Studies, *The Military Balance, 1983–1984* (London, 1983), pp. 75–76.

8. By 1982 there were nine reorganized parties. These included the governing party, officially known as the Zimbabwe African National Union–Patriotic Front (ZANU-FP), headed by Mugabe (with Simon Muzenda as vice president); a splinter group known as the Zimbabwe African National Union-Sithole (ZANU-S), led by the Reverend Ndabaningi Sithole (which held a centrist position); the Patriotic Front (PF), formerly the Zimbabwe African People's Union (Nkomo's organization); the United African National Council (UANC) — Muzorewa's party; the Zimbabwe Democratic Party, a splinter group from the UANC led by James Chikerema; the National Democratic Union, a small conservative group mainly backed by Zezuru people and led by Henry Chihota; the United National Federal Party (UNFP), a conservative body supporting a federal arrangement, led by Chief Kayisa Ndiweni; the Republican Front (formerly the Rhodesian Front), a white party still led by Ian Smith; and a small body, the Zimbabwe National Front, led by Peter Mandaza.

9. *Zimbabwe Project New Bulletin* (Harare, Zimbabwe), Aug.–Sept. 1981, p. 8. For Mugabe's own views, see Robert Mugabe, *Our War of Liberation: Speeches, Articles, Interviews: 1976–1979* (Gweru, Zimbabe: Mambo Press, 1983).

10. *Zimbabwe Project New Bulletin*, Apr.–June, 1982, p. 9.

11. Robert Hodder Williams, *Conflict in Zimbabwe: The Matabeleland Problem*, no. 151 (London: Institute for Conflict Studies, 1983).

12. *Zimbabwe Project New Bulletin*, February 1981, p. 9.

13. ZIMCORD, *Let's Build Zimbabwe Together: Zimbabwe Conference on Reconstruction and Development* (Salisbury, 25–27 March, 1981).

14. In the field of transport, there was the Rhodesia Railways, set up as a statutory body in 1949. In the field of power, there was the Southern Rhodesia Electricity Supply Commission, created in 1936. In the farming industry, there was the Land and Agricultural Bank of Southern Rhodesia, set up in 1924; the Pig Industry Board (1937); the Cold Storage Commission (1938); the Dairy Marketing Board (1938); and various others. World War II witnessed the growth of state intervention in industrial development — for instance, the Industrial Development Board, the Rhodesia Iron and Steel Commission, and various other bodies. For more details, see, for instance, Gann and Gelfand, *Huggins of Rhodesia*, pp. 160–62.

15. For a complete statistical breakdown, see *Africa South of the Sahara*,

1983-84 (London: Europa Publications, 1983), pp. 934-38.

16. For instance, Victor T. Le Vine, *Political Corruption: The Ghana Case* (Stanford: Hoover Institution Press, 1975), an important theoretical as well as empirical study, did not receive publicity comparable to its academic merit.

17. Peter Harries-Jones, *Freedom and Labour: Mobilization and Political Control on the Zambian Copper Belt* (New York: St. Martin's Press, 1975), p. 156.

18. Reported in the *New York Times* 30 January 1970, p. 11.

19. Margaret L. Bates, "Tanganyika", in Gwendolen M. Carter, ed., *African One-Party States* (Ithaca: Cornell University Press, 1962), p. 476.

20. Cited in Gann, *Central Africa*; pp. 15-16.

21. For a detailed discussion, see Andrew A. Beveridge and Anthony R. Oberschall, *African Businessmen and Development in Zambia* (Princeton, N.J.: Princeton University Press, 1979) and Republic of Zambia, *Report of the Committee on Parastatal Bodies* (Lusaka: Government Printer, 1980).

22. Roberts, *A History of Zambia*, pp. 233-34.

23. Republic of Zambia, *The Cause of the People Is the Cause of the Party. Guidelines for the Central Committee* (Lusaka, ca. 1973).

24. For a detailed breakdown of the 1983 budget, see *Africa Research Bulletin*, Jan.-Feb. 14, 1983, pp. 6742-45. The budget provided for a recurrent expenditure of 811.45 million kwacha. This was to be financed by internal loans (84.20 million kwacha), external loans (80.47 million kwacha), and bank borrowing (141.66 million kwacha). Recurrent expenditure on higher education amounted to 65.9 million kwacha, whereas expenditure on agriculture and water development amounted to 86.6 million kwacha (out of a total recurrent expenditure of 811.45 million kwacha).

25. Guy Clutton-Brock, *Dawn in Nyasaland* (London: Hodder and Stoughton, 1959), pp. 55-57.

26. For details of party debates, see Malawi Congress Party Annual Convention, *Resolutions, 1965-1981* (Blantyre: Department of Information and Tourism, 1981).

27. The 1981-82 development plan provided for 39.57 million kwacha to be devoted to agriculture; 12.52 million kwacha for water development and sanitation; 51.19 million kwacha for transport and communications (essential for allowing the cultivators to market their produce); and 25.97 million kwacha for education and social services (out of a total of 155.99 million kwacha). See statistical survey in *Africa South of the Sahara*, p. 542. (In 1983 the kwacha stood at U.S. $1.16, the Zambian kwacha at U.S. $1.22, and the Zimbabwe dollar at U.S. $1.05.)

28. In 1979 private consumption in Malawi accounted for 70 percent of the gross domestic product, as opposed to 63 percent in Zimbabwe and 45 percent in Zambia. Between 1960 and 1979 Malawi's gross domestic product grew (in millions of current U.S. dollars) from $170 to $1,220 — a sevenfold increase. Corresponding figures for Zimbabwe (which for part of the time was stricken by civil war) were $780 and $3,640, and for Zambia, $680 and $3,420. The average growth rate of the gross national product between 1960 and 1979 was 2.9 percent for Malawi and 0.8 percent for both Zimbabwe and Zambia. Gross domestic investment in Malawi in 1979 amounted to 29 percent of the gross domestic product; in Zimbabwe, 15 percent; and in Zambia, 21 percent. *World Bank, Accelerated Development in Sub-Saharan Africa: An Agenda for Action* (Washington, D.C., 1981), pp. 143-47.

29. Gerald Braun, "Malawi Entwicklungsmodell and Perspektiven," *Internationales Afrikaforum* 2, no. 18 (2nd Quarter 1982): 171-79.

30. *African Research Bulletin*, 15 April-14 May 1981, p. 6010.

31. Gwendolen M. Carter, ed., *African One-Party States* (Ithaca, N.Y.: Cornell University Press, 1962), p. 9. For conventional academic views about white settlers during the decolonization era, see, for instance, Boris Gussman, *Out in the Mid-Day Sun: Race Problems in British Central Africa* (London: Allen and Unwin, 1962).

For a different interpretation, see L. H. Gann and Peter Duignan, *White Settlers in Tropical Africa* (Harmondsworth, England: Penguin Books, 1961).

32. For a critique from an economist's viewpoint, see Robert J. Samuelson, "The Failure of Economic Management," *The Atlantic*, February 1984, pp. 98–103.

33. See Institute for Strategic Studies, *The Military Balance, 1983–1984* (London: The Institute, 1983), pp. 71, 73, and 75. Africa's estimated GNP in 1982 (in billions of U.S. dollars) was $71.67; its defense outlay was $2.77. Corresponding figures for Zimbabwe in 1981–82 were $6.24 and $0.39. For Mozambique (1981), the figures were $2.95 and $0.20.

34. The Lusaka Manifesto was signed in 1969 by fourteen East and Central African states in Lusaka at the East and Central Africa Summit Conference; it was adopted in the same year by the Oranization of African Unity heads of states and subsequently approved by the U.N. The Manifesto advocated a transition to majority rule by peaceful means (unless all such means were exhausted). The document specifically rejected black, as well as white, racism and recognized whites in Southern Africa as Africans, regardless of their skin color. Cooperation among all peoples for the benefit of all was to be the ultimate goal, a goal that could not be obtained if white Africans continued to refuse the legitimate aspirations of black Africans.

35. See L. H. Gann, "Neo-Colonialism, Imperialism, and the 'New Class'" (Menlo Park, Calif.: Institute for Humane Studies, 1975), reprinted from *Survey* (London) 19, no. 1 (1973): 165–83.

5 THE STATES OF EAST AFRICA: TANZANIA, UGANDA, AND KENYA

Robert H. Jackson and Carl G. Rosberg

INTRODUCTION

East Africa has generally been thought to consist of Tanzania, Uganda, and Kenya. The concept is British and originated during the colonial era. East Africa was colonized just before the turn of the century. Britain took possession of territories north of Lake Victoria, to which the name Uganda Protectorate was given, as well as the lands between this area and the Indian Ocean, which were first called the East African Protectorate and, after 1920, the Kenya Colony and Protectorate. Germany occupied the largest area, south of Kenya between the lake and the coast, then known as German East Africa and later as the Tanganyika Territory. The islands of Zanzibar, lying off the Tanganyikan coast, were already under British control. Following the defeat of Germany in World War I, Tanganyika became a League of Nations mandate under British administration. The regional identity of East Africa dates from that time.[1]

The three countries occupy almost two million square kilometers: an area slightly smaller than the continental United States west of the Rockies. Tanzania (formerly Tanganyika) is four times and Kenya is three times larger than Uganda. In 1979 the combined population of the region was 46 million (Tanzania, 18 million; Kenya, 15 million; and Uganda, 13 million). The population growth rates of the three countries, at 3 percent or more a year, are among the highest in the world. The World Bank has classified Tanzania and Uganda as low-income countries and Kenya as a middle-income country (by African standards), but Kenya's GNP per capita was under $400 in 1979.[2]

The common heritage of British colonial rule was somewhat different in each country owing to Britain's pragmatic policy of taking African political conditions into account in governing its territories. Consequently, the individual identity that each country possesses today is in part a legacy of colonial rule under a separate government with its own administrative structures and practices (although their identities have been shaped in larger part by events and policies since independence). Uganda and Zanzibar, each with strong, centralized, traditional political systems, were ruled as protectorates; lacking such systems, both Kenya and Tanzania were ruled more directly. Kenya was distinctive in having a vigorous colony of British settlers who exercised considerable influence over the colony's affairs. Tanzania was differentiated from the other two by its international status as a League of Nations mandate and its previous existence as a German colony.

The structure of colonial rule and the shape of African politics were both affected by the distinctive pattern of ethnicity in each territory. In both Uganda and Kenya, ethnic groups have been much more politically significant than in Tanzania. Uganda was split by an ethnic fault line dividing the Bantu kingdoms of the south from the less centralized Nilotic peoples of the north. The kingdoms, particularly Buganda, made possible British overrule, but the British administration also sowed the seeds of separatism in Buganda, which became a state within a state. European settlement was restricted, but Asian traders were allowed to enter the country to facilitate the spread of a cash economy based on African agriculture. Significant Asian communities also existed in Kenya and Tanzania. In Kenya — as in Southern Rhodesia — a substantial settler community developed, which put pressure on some African societies, particularly the Kikuyu of central Kenya, by depriving them of land. The settlers stimulated economic development and made Kenya the wealthiest colony in East Africa. In Tanzania, European settlers and African ethnic groups were less important in determining the country's political history. The African groups were too small and too widely scattered to acquire substantial political weight; the capital, Dar es Salaam, was far removed from the more significant groups — the Chagga around Mount Kilimanjaro and the Bahaya on the Ugandan border. Socioeconomic development also was more extensive and rapid in Kenya and Uganda, with corresponding effects on ethnic identities and distinctions. Kenyan and Ugandan nationalism, as a consequence, was markedly ethnicized, whereas Tanzanian nationalism was practically free of any ethnic overtones. Indeed, in Uganda ethnicity defined the disintegrative pattern of postindependence politics.

Nairobi, the capital of Kenya, became the economic center of East Africa. It could be argued that the British saw East Africa as a hinterland for Nairobi, even though they maintained separate administrative capitals in Uganda (Kampala) and Tanzania (Dar es Salaam). But the development of Kenya probably had more to do with Nairobi's natural growth from its origins as a railway center. The city serviced a productive European settler community that was attracted to this part of East Africa by fertile land and a temperate climate and stayed to build a successful modern economy based on cash-crop agriculture. Most of the region's financial and commercial institutions, transportation and communication networks, manufacturing industries, and so forth, accordingly developed in the city. By the time of independence, Kenya's economic development was noticeably ahead of the other two countries, particularly Tanzania. Without political intervention, Kenya would have continued to receive, more or less automatically, the lion's share of East Africa capital and development.

Unlike the former British territories in West Africa that consumated their independence by severing regional colonial ties, the East African territories attempted to advance regional cooperation by maintaining the linkages that had integrated them during the colonial era. In 1961, with independence in sight, the colonial East African High Commission — which presided over common institutions, services, and infrastructure (including railways, ports, posts and telegraph, an airline, and so forth) — was converted into a new entity, called the East African Common Services Organization (EACSO). This quest for unity was reinforced by an established practice of political consultation among nationalist leaders in the three countries, which aimed at advancing both pan-Africanism and the movements for national independence in each country. (Indeed, in 1960 Nyerere offered to delay Tanzania's independence to enable the three territories to gain sovereignty at the same time and form an East African Federation.) In an attempt to curb disparity in investment between more developed Kenya and less developed Tanzania, the three governments formed the East African Community out of EACSO in 1967. The community administered new rules designed to protect Tanzania's infant industries.[3]

National political-economic disparities eventually proved an insurmountable barrier to East African unity. All three governments were primarily concerned with consolidating their sovereignty by building their own states and national economies. This was at odds with the community ideal that existed to advance the regional economy by means of a common market, institutions, infrastructure, and services. Political intervention by the community to shift resources and opportunities from central Kenya to the periphery was initiated but was not very successful. National economic policies increasingly came into conflict. By the 1970s there was little doubt about the incompatibility of Kenya's market economy and Tanzania's socialist experiment. After Idi Amin's seizure of power in Uganda in 1971, which created an unbridgeable rift with Tanzania, it was impossible for the community's authority — the three heads of state — to meet. In the 1970s the community began to fall apart. The blow that proved fatal came in February 1977, when Kenya set up its own airline after East African Airways had gone into bankruptcy. Tanzania immediately closed its borders with Kenya and kept them closed for six years. By April 1977 it was clear that the East African Community was dead. Ironically, a new building to house the administrative secretariat had just been completed. The possibility of resuscitating the body appears slim.

TANZANIA

Tanzania (then Tanganyika) gained independence on December 9, 1961, under the control of a nationalist party — the Tanganyika African National Union (TANU) — that was without significant rivals and held a de facto political monopoly in the new state. The country was markedly different in this respect from both Uganda and Kenya, where struggles for power between rival, ethnically based parties occurred both before and after independence.

Political monopoly in mainland Tanzania was encouraged by several predisposing conditions. The British colonial postwar policy of developing a multiracial state prompted a reaction among African leaders, who rapidly organized an integrated and territory-wide nationalist movement before competitve general elections were introduced in the late 1950s. This tiny African elite was not large enough to fragment and the country did not contain ethnic groups that were sufficiently populous and cohesive to sustain nationalist parties of their own. Kiswahili, the lingua franca, fostered greater unity and provided a more universal means of political communication than in either of the neighboring countries. Tanzania's economy was extremely underdeveloped and could not sustain substantial class differences among Africans (it could only sustain them between Europeans, Asians, and Africans), even in the fertile

Kilimanjaro and West Lake regions that bordered on Kenya and Uganda, respectively, and were influenced somewhat by political developments across the border. It was this combination of pre-disposing conditions and the skilled leadership of Julius Nyerere that allowed TANU to pre-empt the territory's organizational space and the commanding issues of colonial nationalism.

Julius Nyerere, a young, earnest, and morally uncompromising Catholic schoolteacher who returned to Tanzania in 1952 after completing a master's degree in economics and history at the University of Edinburgh, was a man in the right place at the right time to seize this political opportunity. His intelligence, modesty, and conviction attracted the support of a major following. He became the first president of TANU, which he had been instru-mental in forming, on July 7, 1954. The party grew out of the Tanganyika African Association, which was founded in 1929 and consisted mainly of African clerks and schoolteachers. Nyerere was more a mass politician than a machine or party politician: for him, politics entailed guiding the people rather than politicking with other leaders. Hence his designation as Mwalimu (teacher). He built and led a movement to independence but afterwards sought to confine and control politics within the single-party framework of TANU. Politics thereafter came to consist of ideology and adminis-tration.[4]

The very underdevelopment of Tanzania was a moral and politi-cal imperative for Nyerere, who envisioned a future of prosperity and equality if the necessary plans were made and actions were taken. The first requirement was independence, which entailed the termination of the United Nations trusteeship under which Britain had ruled the former German colony.[5] Then, if suitable principles and techniques of political engineering were adopted and followed, the realization of that future could begin.[6] The fortunes and adversities of Tanzania during the past quarter-century cannot be separated from the ideology, policies, and actions that were authored and authorized by Nyerere, who was perhaps the most authentic philosopher-king among the African rulers. The story of Tanzania since independence is a tale of an earnest and dedicated ruler endeavoring to shape an entire country in accordance with his own design and eventually encountering the rather high, unplanned costs of his rationalist enterprise. Nyerere was also a leader able to secure and maintain unity among his country's party leaders.

The task of state building, as Nyerere saw it, involved the

political problem of building a one-party democracy that could organize the support of Tanzanians in developing the socio-economic conditions of the country. Almost immediately upon achieving the goal of independence, Nyerere resigned the premiership so that he could devote his time and energies to rethinking the role of TANU, which no longer had the task of agitating for independence but was now in a position of rulership. If he was to have any real hope of translating his ideology into political reality, he had to build a state in which the party would be the sole authorizing and directing institution. But could this be reconciled with democracy?

By 1962, according to Cranford Pratt, "Nyerere had come to the firm view that democracy did not require a competitive party system."[7] In January 1963 Nyerere announced that Tanzania would become a legal one-party state and that a commission would design an electoral system for such a state.[8] Evidently the commissioners were prepared to give him most of what he wanted. The result was a system intended to eliminate party competition, enhance national unity, and facilitate political control of the country. District branches of the party were granted modest democratic rights of candidate nomination, subject to the final approval of the national executive of TANU. In 1965, constitutional amendments to implement a one-party state were proposed to Parliament by Nyerere and adopted.[9] The first one-party election occurred in 1965 and resulted in a considerable turnover of parliamentary representatives without changing the government.[10]

Tanzania, like many other former British territories, became independent with a Westminster-style system of parliamentary sovereignty. In December 1962 the country became a republic and Nyerere occupied the new commanding office of president, established in a new republican constitution. The growing strength of TANU and the creation of a de jure one-party state reinforced the presidential position of Nyerere and raised the issue of parliamentary supremacy, which was increasingly anomalous. The dominance of party over Parliament was confirmed in October 1968, when seven TANU MPs were expelled from the party and automatically lost their membership in the National Assembly for claiming that Parliament was still supreme.[11] It was not until 1975, however, that a constitutional amendment recognized the legal supremacy of the party in the state.[12]

In April 1964, Tanganyika joined with newly independent

Zanzibar to form the United Republic of Tanzania, governed by an interim union constitution.[13] In political practice, however, the countries remained separate. The island was under the control of its own leaders and ruling single party, the Afro-Shirazi Party (ASP), which rested its appeal on Zanzibari nationalism. It was not until February 1977 that ASP and TANU merged to form a single ruling party for both territories, Chama cha Mapinduzi (CCM, the Revolutionary Party of Tanzania). Nyerere became chairman and then leader of CCM, and the vice-president of Tanzania, Aboud Jumbe, was elected vice-chairman. In April of the same year, Tanzania's National Assembly replaced the 1964 interim constitution with a permanent one that made provision for ten elected members from Zanzibar. In October 1979, Zanzibar adopted a more "democratic" constitution featuring an elected president and a House of Representatives with both elected and appointed members.

The ambiguous twenty-year relationship has not been an easy one, and the leaders of Zanzibar have persisted in keeping themselves autonomous. In January 1983, the reconstituted National Executive Committee of CCM called for a strengthening of the union and for greater democratization of the instruments of the state.[14] The constitutional proposals were discussed and debated nationally and gave rise to a discussion on the character that the relationship ought to take in the future. The controversy led, in January 1984, to the resignation of Aboud Jumbe as vice-president of the union and president of Zanzibar. Ali Hassan Mwinyi, a former teacher and civil servant, became the new Zanzibari president-designate, charged with the task of finding an acceptable continuing relationship with mainland Tanzania. He was subsequently elected president of Zanzibar and appointed vice-president of Tanzania. The likelihood of a substantially closer union, however, remains uncertain.

Shortly after independence, Nyerere began to give much thought to socioeconomic development. In April 1962, TANU published his seminal pamphlet, "Ujamaa: The Basis of African Socialism." It outlined in clear and simple language Nyerere's basic idea — that traditional African society was constituted on socialist principles, including the absence of class divisions and the sharing of work, land, and tools on a basis of equality and need.[15] Socialism, according to Nyerere, was therefore native to Africa. Capitalism was the alien import of colonialists who made land a commercial commodity and created class distinctions based on the ownership and control of capital: employers versus employees; landholders versus landless laborers. Therefore, the task of socioeconomic development in Tanzania was to restore, in modern form, the African traditions of communal sharing of work and capital. This was where the state entered the picture. The new African state could become, with suitable plans and policies, the traditional African family and community writ large — the *ujamaa*. The TANU government could transform Tanzania from a capitalist dependency into a socialist nation.[16]

In his numerous writings and speeches, Nyerere never wavered in the conviction that socialism is the developmental ideology best suited to Tanzania's circumstances and needs. For him, socialism was the "only rational choice," not only for Tanzania but also for Africa.[17] His career is the record of a single-minded and untiring endeavor to articulate that ideology and translate it into concrete results. In February 1967, TANU published "The Arusha Declaration," based on a draft written by Nyerere, which made explicit many of the practical implications of ujamaa ideology.[18] It became the programmatic framework of one of the most significant attempts yet registered by an African government to get beyond rhetoric and actually begin the construction of a socialist country. The declaration addressed three related problems and offered solutions to each. The first obstacle to socialism, Nyerere wrote, was the growth of a privileged class of party and government leaders. The declaration proposed to meet this difficulty with a leadership code of ethics intended to restrain the acquisitiveness and self-service of leaders and to provide the state with dedicated socialists. A second problem, the predominance of urban wealth over rural poverty, prompted the doctrine of rural development by hard work and simple tools rather than by costly imported machinery and the establishment of collectivized villages. The third impediment, the absence or inadequacy of foreign capital, spurred a resolve to pursue an independent course of national self-reliance that would economize on capital investment and promote nationalization. In the final analysis, development was not the result of money and technology; it was the result of hard work and the proper attitude of mind. Development cannot be done for the people; it can only be done by them. This was the message of Arusha.

An underdeveloped country such as Tanzania is much easier to gain control of politically than it is to manage economically.

Extreme underdevelopment not only presents the state managers with severe material constraints and small margins for error but also provides few real levers of economic power. With almost a million square kilometers of land and a dispersed rural population of 18 million in 1979, Tanzania remains an East African periphery in economic terms. It is still an overwhelmingly agricultural country, which is largely dependent for its livelihood on coffee, cotton, and tea exports. In 1961, per capita GNP was about $50; this figure had grown to $260 in 1979 (without discounting for inflation, which has been substantial in the 1970s and 1980s). The World Bank classified Tanzania as "low income" in a 1981 report.[19] Agriculture accounted for 80 percent of exports and the livelihood of 90 percent of the population in 1981.[20]

At independence the most important growth centers in East Africa were located in central Kenya and southern Uganda, and this continues to be the case today (notwithstanding the severe economic deterioration of Uganda under Idi Amin). The major artery of economic development in East Africa was the railway running from Mombasa to Kampala, which does not pass through Tanzania. Only a rudimentary infrastructure of railways, roads, ports, and other facilities was built during the colonial era to link together this vast country. The infrastructure has been expanded since — most notably by the construction of the Tazara railway with Chinese financial and technical aid. The levers of the Tanzanian economy consisted of tiny rural production units, often family units, spread around the country like pebbles on a beach. In the urban areas they were mainly commercial firms of modest size, sufficient only to service a small cash economy based on a few cash crops. In very brief outline, this is the nature of the economy that Nyerere's state has attempted to control and develop.

The only means available to Nyerere for implementation of his socialist plan, apart from TANU, was to Africanize and enlarge the small state bureaucracy that he had inherited from colonial times. Even here, the pool of Africans qualified to staff state bureaus, especially at the administrative and technical-professional levels, was extremely small at independence, since Africans had been confined almost entirely to clerical grades. There were few experienced African civil servants to fill the places of the expatriates.[21] A pool of qualified African personnel had to be created almost from scratch by building and staffing a new university, institutes, and schools. The task was urgent, as Nyerere said in a 1963 speech inaugurating the University of East Africa: "Our problems will not wait. We must, and do, demand that the University take an active part in the social revolution we are engineering."[22] The university itself had to produce the social engineers. This responsibility was largely in the hands of professors and lecturers, of whom very few had direct, practical experience in government or business. The university and other institutions responded to the demand for government personnel by graduating increasing numbers of Africans who found their way into the government bureaucracy, at first at very senior levels. These same graduates, or later ones, were placed in command when the Tanzanian state took direct control of the national economy in the late 1960s and early 1970s.

Nyerere repeatedly stressed the importance of proper attitudes and skills in the training of managers and workers for a socialist state. He recommended vocational education attuned to national problems: "a university in a developing society must put the emphasis . . . on subjects of immediate moment to the nation."[23] In 1966 he decried and punished university students who had demonstrated against a national service scheme designed to repay the government for some of the expenses of their education; Nyerere repeatedly urged "education for self-reliance."[24] He apparently had no misgivings, however, concerning the wisdom and practicality of statist social engineering conducted by an expanding bureaucracy composed of untested university and school graduates. When the unexpected adversities created by such a development strategy became obvious in the later 1970s, Nyerere responded — like the political moralist he was — by exhorting managers and workers to serve the state with greater effort, diligence, and self-sacrifice.[25]

The difficulties of statism in a large and backward country are perhaps revealed most clearly in the government's rural agricultural policies and their results. Owing to the dispersion of the rural population in small family units, both the colonial and independent governments thought it desirable to relocate people in centers where they could be more readily integrated into the cash economy and provided with public services in a more cost-effective manner. In the immediate postindependence period a program of heavily capitalized settlements was attempted, but it was abandoned after 1966 as too costly. In 1967 Nyerere outlined a new policy in a paper entitled "Socialism and Rural Development," which called for the creation of "ujamaa villages" in which rural people could live more productive and meaningful lives, not only for themselves, but for the national good. Unlike the earlier efforts, this one was to be less capitalized. Nyerere envisioned that villagers would devote some of their efforts to the provision of communal goods.[26] Villagization became a national campaign, with party leaders taking up the president's call. At first persuasion and inducements were used to implement the policy, but later, in 1973–1974, force was increasingly brought to bear. "Operations" were undertaken to move people physically, sometimes by compulsion or threats — rather like the operations of any army fighting a war on many different fronts. Between 1967 and 1977 about 85 percent of the rural population of Tanzania — which then numbered between 11 and 14 million — was moved into villages, a statist action that is without precedent or equal in countemporary African politics.[27]

The process invited enormous state involvement. The new doctrine spawned an elaborate set of bureaucratic criteria for creating and evaluating ujamaa villages, which were required to meet certain standards and to provide specified goods and services. A large number of new roles and organizations were formed, and frequently altered, to administer the agrarian empire. An array of rural agricultural activities was placed under the control of central government agrobureaucrats, who assumed primary responsibility for planning and managing the vast socialist estate. The policy created some 8,600 villages that had to be guided in their development activities. In some areas TANU controlled the villages, whereas in other areas the villages exercised some control. Centralized state bureaucratic management and party politicization led to passivity on the part of the inhabitants: "It is better we wait for them [the bureaucrats] to plan things for us rather than [for us to] plan things they do not want."[28]

In place of the traditional agricultural system and the cooperatives that had been developing, an entirely new system was to be engineered. Of course, in reality the traditional system was not and could not be destroyed, and peasants often retreated into it against the wishes of the agrobureaucrats.[29] But the costs of such a vast state enterprise were great, and the opportunity costs were probably even greater. Although we do not know what these costs were, we have some indication from the adversities that befell Tanzania's agricultural economy during and following the massive project: between 1969–1971 and 1977–1979 agricultural production declined at a rate of 2 percent (food at 1.5 percent and nonfood at 3.9 percent). In the late 1970s Tanzania became a major African recipient of food aid.[30] Although other factors, such as drought, contributed to this decline, it is impossible to overlook the contribution of this enormous experiment.[31] Perhaps the most telling indication of its impact was the 1982 announcement that the government intended to make a retreat from statism in the country-side and to place greater responsibilities on cooperatives and district councils that were to be re-established — having been abolished in the 1970s.[32]

Statism was not confined to agriculture. It pervaded the entire economy, including the commercial and industrial sector, which historically had been formed by the activities of Asian traders and some European estate-owners and firms. The Arusha Declaration called for government ownership of "the major means of production and exchange." Even before the declaration, the Tanzanian state had begun to nationalize the modern sector. Immediately afterward, it took control of banks, food processing, insurance, and trade — creating a large State Trading Corporation. The state also took controlling interests in various other industries: shoe manufacturing, breweries, and tobacco, cement, and sisal production, for instance. The policy eventually led to the creation of approximately 380 parastatal organizations — an astonishingly high figure considering the size and poverty of the country and the capacity of the state. The private economy of small firms managed by their owners eventually became an inflated empire controlled by state officials. Even Asians, who were mainly retailers, were affected by the nationalization of housing in 1971.

Most of the parastatals were formed quickly and at about the same time — in the late 1960s — as a result of Nyerere's declaration. The demand for experienced managers to run them was accordingly sudden and large, but the supply was small. Most of these economic organizations came under the control of general managers who were bureaucrats more than businessmen and consequently ran their domains like civil service bureaucracies. As a result, the working private economy became bureaucratized, and a strong element of personalism and patronage entered into many organizations. It proved difficult to reward efficient managers or to punish incompetent ones and it was equally difficult to promote and dismiss workers in accordance with their job performance. Workers came to regard their jobs as guaranteed by the socialist state. The parastatals were, in fact, politically privileged territory, protected by the official ideology of the state. Without a private sector of any significance, they were untested and could not benefit from competition. Political exhortation to economize and try harder, which was Nyerere's response to the problem of laxity and inefficiency, was no substitute. Instead of investment in productivity, investments went into meeting the political requirements of full employment and workers' welfare. As a result, in the later 1970s the parastatals increasingly reported losses while expansion continued, with the adverse effect of visiting an increasingly heavy burden on the overall economy. The unexpected but almost inevitable opportunity costs of placing the economy in the control of bureaucrats rather than leaving it in the hands of private traders proved eventually to be very high.

Perhaps the most telling indication of the shortcomings of Tanzania's bureaucratized economy was the criticism that Nyerere directed against its managers, workers, and methods of operation in a remarkably candid 1977 speech entitled "The Arusha Declaration Ten Years After." He complained bitterly of the inefficiency, indifference, and laziness of managers and workers in the state-run enterprises. "It is essential that we should tighten up on industrial discipline. Slackness at work, and failure to give a hard day's effort in return for wages paid, is a form of exploitation; it is an exploitation of the other members of the society. And slackness has undoubtedly increased since the Arusha Declaration was passed."[33] When the cost of the nonparastatal government sector, which had grown from nearly 11 percent of national income in 1967 to 16 percent in 1975, was revealed to be 80 percent of recurrent revenue, Nyerere called for more cost-consciousness. "At the root of this whole problem is our failure to understand, and to apply to our own activities, the concept of Self-Reliance . . . We must increase our *discipline*, our *efficiency*, and our *self-reliance*."[34] Unaccounted cash expenditures in the public service increased from 327,000 Tanzanian shillings in 1967–68 to 434,007,000 T.sh. in 1980–81.[35]

In 1979 Tanzania's economy entered a period of substantial deterioration from which it has not recovered by the mid-1980s. Indeed, it may not recover for a long time.[36] Between 1977 and 1982, national output declined by about one-third. In the latter year, manufacturing output was reduced to 20–30 percent of capacity. Agriculture had declined some 10 percent since 1979 and there was a real prospect of continuing deterioration in production and consequently in the terms of trade, which threatened the complete breakdown of the modern economy. Annual inflation was running between 30 and 40 percent; the currency was weak; food dependency was increasing; and black-market activities involving smuggling, illegal foreign-exchange transactions, price gouging, hoarding, and bribery were making major inroads in the economy. Perhaps most serious of all, the high public morale and self-confidence that was so much in evidence in the 1960s and early 1970s had been undermined to the point where many people doubted the ability of the state and the ruling party to cope with the decline. In January 1983, Nyerere's regime uncovered a plot to bring about a coup.

There has been considerable controversy concerning the sources of these adversities. Some were clearly beyond the control of the Tanzanian government, including the breakup of the East Africa Community in 1977 and the resulting replacement costs for services such as airlines and telecommunications; the drought since 1979; high import prices for oil and other commodities, which contributed to deteriorating terms of trade; and the worldwide recession of the early 1980s, accompanied by high interest rates. The huge United States' federal budget deficit, which was at the root of the high interest rates, was another factor. These economic misfortunes were experienced to more or less the same degree, however, by most other African countries — but few were brought so close to the brink of disaster by them. Neighboring Kenya experienced them all but survived in much better shape than Tanzania. The developing crisis in the initial years of the 1980s might have been mitigated if Tanzania had agreed to the terms of the International Monetary Fund.

Moreover, some of Tanzania's difficulties were a direct result of specific government action. The best example is the war with Uganda (1978–1979), which involved an invasion of that country by Tanzanian forces in response to the invasion and occupation of Tanzania's territory by Amin's Uganda. About 40,000 troops were involved at the peak of the campaign — and the occupation continued for some time afterwards at a cost to the Tanzanian treasury of an estimated $500 million. Many commentators regard the war as an external factor beyond the government's control. But Nyerere authorized his troops to invade Uganda against the wishes of the OAU and most other African statesmen. The president of the OAU at the time — President Numeiri of Sudan — tried to dissuade

Nyerere from the action, and most other African governments were alarmed at the prospect, which threatened OAU rules of nonintervention. The military overthrow of Amin was a welcome event for many Ugandans. But it was also a very large additional financial burden for Tanzanians. It certainly was not an inescapable occurrence in the same category as drought or increased oil prices.

By the early 1980s, Tanzania had run up an enormous debt that probably cannot and will not be repaid. Western countries provided large amounts of financial aid at about the same time that the fundamental shortcomings of ujamaa socialism were becoming evident. Tanzania became the largest aid recipient in Africa, $580 million in 1979 alone (of which 94 percent was in outright grants).[37] Major suppliers, in addition to the World Bank, IDA , and other multilateral agencies, were the Scandinavian countries (particularly Sweden), Holland, West Germany, and Canada. Some of these countries have had social-democratic governments that have been strongly in sympathy with Nyerere and his policies. As recently as 1982, disbursement and pledges of aid from the West remained high.[38] But the unprecedented influx of Western aid has been unable to arrest Tanzania's economic decline. It has been argued that many of the funds have been in the form of project aid, and have had little to do with helping to overcome the critical balance-of-payment problem.[39]

In a speech delivered in October 1982 at the ruling party conference, Nyerere admitted that Tanzania had many "very serious and very real" problems, but socialism was not one of them: "We have good policies. We have good plans. We have good leadership." Nyerere seemed to assume that the Tanzanian state was a rational structure of producers, who could and should take command of the economy and contribute to its development. John Hatch reported that, in an interview shortly after the Arusha Declaration, Nyerere had told him that "his object in nationalising industry, trade and finance had been to secure a base from which to move forward to self-reliance."[40] But Nyerere's own criticism ten years later and the deterioration of the economy since the late 1970s suggest that the state apparatus that had been created in Tanzania was actually a layer of bureaucratic consumers weighing down the economy. State managers and workers were taking far more out of the economy than they were returning to it.

After the Arusha Declaration, however, substantial gains were made in the provision of "basic needs," as is evident from

Tanzania's comparatively high literacy, primary school enrollment, and life expectancy. Similar levels have been registered in Kenya and Uganda which suggests that general factors not specific to Tanzania were also contributing to these results. Tanzania, however, started from a lower base.

In conclusion, it is difficult not to believe that the Tanzanian experiment was flawed in its conception and that Nyerere's government was the author of some of the country's misfortunes. Some commentators attribute Tanzania's troubles to international conditions and inept implementation. It would be impossible to deny the significance of both factors. They do not, however, go to the root of the problem, which is the fact that more than most other African political economies, Tanzania's is the result of an ambitious rationalist design. Nyerere and TANU have tried to transform Tanzania into one vast state enterprise in accordance with plans inspired by their Arusha blueprint. The Arusha experiment replaced proven historical sectors of the economy, in particular European and Asian businessmen and progressive African farmers, with a large number of state managers and workers who were not well equipped to take over their functions, much less to improve upon their productivity.

UGANDA

Uganda gained independence on October 9, 1962, ending a period of British overrule that dated from 1893, when the country was originally formed as a protectorate. Until the end of World War II, the British governed the country according to Lord Lugard's famous theory of "indirect rule," which aimed at acknowledging, utilizing, and developing the traditional political systems. Of these, the Kingdom of Buganda in the southern region was the most important.[41] In 1947 British colonial policy virtually abandoned indirect rule and adopted a policy of developing African local government based on the United Kingdom model. In the following decade, steps were taken to constitutionalize and democratize the central government in anticipation of Uganda's emergence as a sovereign state.[42] A fundamental political conflict between centrifugal and centripetal forces and, specifically, between Buganda and Uganda, was thereby inaugurated. The conflict was never satisfactorily resolved before independence and continues to plague the country's political life.

This conflict has assumed a different character in three distinctive periods since independence. Between 1962 and 1971 it was expressed by the increasing alienation of Buganda from the Ugandan government of Milton Obote, the first postindependence ruler, and by the corresponding centralization and radicalism in Obote's public policies.[43] Highly abusive and arbitrary personal rule marked the succeeding regime of Idi Amin, who overthrew Obote's government in a 1971 military coup and retained power largely by force and cunning. Amin, in turn, was displaced in 1979 as a result of an invasion of Uganda by the Tanzanian army and Ugandan exile forces.[44] Since Amin's defeat and, particularly, since 1980 when Obote was again elected president, attempts have been made to restore the civil and socioeconomic well-being of the country, which was very nearly destroyed during Amin's tyranny.[45] Although the economy has recovered to some degree, Ugandan politics continue to be troubled by violence by both government and antigovernment forces and by the alienation of Buganda from the Ugandan state. In short, the political experience of the country since independence has been one of disunity frequently marked by violence.

When the British penetrated the region north and west of Lake Victoria, they encountered several traditional African kingdoms, of which one was particularly well developed: Buganda. In 1862, Speke, the British explorer, was impressed by the development of the kingdom and the power of its ruler, the Kabaka, who dominated surrounding kingdoms and extracted tribute from some. Buganda considered itself in partnership with the British in the conquest and colonization of neighboring peoples and was rewarded with some of their lands. Imperial partnership was reflected in the 1900 agreement with the British, which gave the kingdom political privileges that were denied to other peoples in Uganda.[46] The country takes its name from this kingdom. Under the British Uganda was a protectorate: an imperium that ostensibly safeguarded the traditional political systems within its colonial frontiers. Buganda regarded itself as a state. As one of its spokesmen declared: "We are a nation, not a tribe like the Welsh."[47]

Buganda developed as something of a state within a state. The Ganda embraced Western practices more rapidly and completely than other Ugandans, and some of their members formed the best educated, most economically successful African elite in the protectorate. It was not unusual for them to refer to members of other ethnic groups as "natives" and to consider themselves Europeans.[48] Apter points out that the Ganda did not have to look outside of their traditional society for modern opportunities and experiences because the kingdom became the most modern part of the protectorate and acquired its own modern institutions, such as churches, schools, newspapers, government offices, and so forth.[49] The most developed system of transportation and communications was located within the traditional frontiers of Buganda, and much of the economic development of the protectorate involved Gandans, although in this realm — for example, in the cotton industry — they were subject to the power and control of Europeans and Asians.

The development of Uganda, particularly its political development, could not be perceived as completely separate from Buganda until after World War II. The distinction was never fully accepted by the Ganda, even at independence in 1962. They never wavered in their opposition to the Legislative Council that was established in the 1920s to assist the governor in ruling the protectorate.[50] They opposed postwar steps taken by the British in the 1950s to allow Uganda to develop into an African state, which entailed a loss of sovereignty and independence for Buganda.[51] They were prepared to accept a unitary Uganda, but only under their political leadership and constitutional control.[52] But the other peoples of Uganda were certainly not prepared to accept perpetual Buganda hegemony, not least because the latter constituted some 17 percent of the total population. Perhaps the British excluded the possibility of granting outright independence of Buganda because a Uganda without Buganda would have been very marginal economically. A workable constitutional accommodation had not been found as late as 1960. In that year Buganda declared itself a "separate autonomous state" on the legal grounds that it was reverting to its original sovereignty.[53]

The British rejected Buganda's bid for sovereignty and established an unusual federal-unitary constitution for accommodating Buganda within a Ugandan state. The Kingdom had significant constitutional authority over its territory, including some control of the police and representation on the High Court. The Kabaka was made constitutional head of the new Bugandan state while remaining its monarch. The western kingdoms and Busoga enjoyed a limited quasi-federal relationship with Uganda, and the rest of the country had a unitary form of government. The constitution proved less than expedient. It made possible an alliance of convenience between Buganda's political party in national politics, Kabaka Yekka (KY, King Alone), and Obote's Uganda Peoples Congress (UPC), which enabled Obote to form the first independent government of Uganda in 1962. The historical structure of Ugandan politics, however, ran counter to the alliance. Buganda, including the Kabaka, was jealous of its autonomy, and the head of government, Prime Minister Obote, was desirous of ruling the entire sovereign territory of Uganda, including the extremely important part around the capital city of Kampala, which was occupied by Buganda. For the immediate years after independence, the arrangement was tolerated by both sides, although grudgingly. But the practical questions that ordinarily arise in federal states concerning taxation, social services, planning, budgets, and so forth, and require cooperation between the two levels of government, were not resolved during this time and provoked additional conflict. In the western kingdoms and Busoga, the quasi-federal relationship was quickly undermined by legislation of the Obote regime, "which was in the tradition of unitary administration."[54]

Obote's parliamentary position was strengthened following independence when members of opposition parties crossed the floor of the National Assembly to the government side. As a result, Obote was able to dissolve his alliance with the KY. In reaction to criticism of his conduct and the conduct of some of his ministers, Obote carried out a coup: he arrested his critics, suspended the constitution, and assumed full state powers. Subsequently, he introduced a new constitution that terminated Buganda's (and the other kingdoms') constitutional immunities, fused the head of state and the head of government into a single presidential office, and gave himself authority over the entire country. Buganda ordered the central government out of Kampala, and Obote used the national army, under the command of Idi Amin, to suppress the Kabaka. The institutions and symbols of the Bugandan government were outlawed, some Ganda directly involved in the conflict were killed, and the Kabaka fled into exile in Britain, where he later died. The kingdom was reduced to four local districts under central government control. Obote did not finally resolve the constitutional problem by repressing Buganda. Instead, he planted the seeds of ethnoconspiratorial politics and set the stage for increased abuses and violence. At the same time that he alienated the Ganda, Obote incorporated his own ethnic base of Langi and Acholi into positions of power.

Having imposed a unitary form of government by force, Obote proceeded to build a one-party state that he conceived as a vehicle of both political unity and economic progress. In 1969 he announced a "move to the left" and the adoption of a "Common Man's Charter." The charter addressed the economic inequalities that reinforced regionalism and called for economic independence based on socialism.[55] The model was evidently influenced by Nyerere's socialist experiment in Tanzania. In 1969, Obote was shot while attending the annual UPC conference. He survived, and several Gandans were arrested and apparently confessed to the attempted assassination. Undeterred, Obote's government began in 1970 to implement the charter by, among other things, legislating itself a 60 percent interest in major commercial, banking, and plantation enterprises — many of which were owned either by foreigners, expatriates, or Asians. The UPC's political monopoly was legalized and national elections within the framework of a single-party state were scheduled for April 1971. It was beginning to look as though a more unified Uganda might be in the offing. The elections, however, were never held. While Obote was attending the 1971 Commonwealth Conference in Singapore, his government was overthrown by Amin. Tanzania granted political refuge to Obote and refused to acknowledge the legitimacy of Amin's coup.

Amin's regime was initially well received by the Ganda and by foreign governments, especially Britain. Amin proclaimed an 18-point charter for a free and prosperous Uganda and rescinded Obote's decision to give the state a majority holding in major private enterprises. That action pleased not only the international business community but also the Ugandan commercial elite, including the vital Asian community. Both Britain and Israel announced aid for military training. Political detainees were released, most of them enemies of Obote (including a number of Ganda), and Amin vowed to restore civilian rule within five years. Buganda welcomed Amin and he reciprocated by permitting the Kabaka's remains to be returned to the country and buried in the ancestral tomb. He refused, however, to restore the autonomies and rights that the kingdoms had enjoyed under the 1962 constitution. Amin was not about to turn back the constitutional clock. The coup became, in fact, a revolutionary change in ethnic access to the material goods of government. The Acholi and Langi of Obote's regime were displaced by the Nubians and Kakwa of northwestern Uganda.

The period of post-coup optimism was relatively brief. Amin faced enemies and Obote supporters among the population and even within the army. Most were members of the Langi and Acholi communities, upon whom the UPC government had rested after Obote had alienated the Ganda. Rule by Amin soon became arbitrary. The regime issued decrees that granted extensive powers to deal with political enemies, for example, unlimited powers of arrest and confinement and other deprivations of civil rights. The state used threats and acts of violence to deter and, if necessary, to eliminate anyone believed to be an enemy; in particular, suspect members of the army and police were detained and often murdered. Some who avoided arrest had to flee for their lives. In August 1971 the first major political disappearance occurred (that of the acting director of Uganda television); subsequently, an increasing number of individuals dropped from sight without explanation. In 1972, Obote's supporters launched an unsuccessful invasion from sanctuaries in neighboring Tanzania. Amin reacted by sending extermination squads into army camps to liquidate suspected Obote sympathizers, usually Langi and Acholi soldiers. Assassination and disappearances of civilians began to multiply.[56] These punitive and pre-emptive acts of state violence, prompted by Amin's acute and seemingly irrational fear of rivals, soon created a general climate of apprehension among the population.

In 1972 and 1973, the powers of the violently reconstituted armed forces were extended by decree, removing the military from any remaining legal sanctions or controls. Amin had created, for his protection, a punitive army of undisiplined but very well-equipped mercenaries, who were personally loyal either to him or to one of his loyal Nubian officers. The decrees of legal immunity virtually gave soldiers a license to become small-scale tyrants. They were able to carry out personal vendettas, terrorize civilians, sell government property, and seize private property with impunity. Some soldiers sold or rented weapons (and other goods to which they had privileged access) to thieves, private-enterprises terrorists, and black marketeers. General lawlessness became a feature of Amin's Uganda and acts of *kondoism* — armed robbery and violence — became widespread. Such acts were frequently carried out by soldiers either in their official capacity or as moonlighters. A

1974 study by the International Commission of Jurists concluded that there had been a total breakdown in the rule of law in the country.[57] Civilians in contact with the government were often presented with the dismal choice of either lubricating the Mafia-like regime — for example, by paying protection money to those with power, which people of means could do — or removing themselves from its attention insofar as possible. Many retired into the rural areas, which were not always effective sancturaries; others fled the country altogether. A vicious circle of tyranny was created: "The more people Amin eliminated, the more afraid of revenge he became, and therefore the more ruthless he became."[58]

Amin's tyranny affected adversely both the civil and the socio-economic conditions of the country. The coup was soon followed by a marked deterioration of government operations, especially, but by no means exclusively, at the policy level. Senior officials became vulnerable to Amin's suspicion, jealousy, or enmity and many were removed arbitrarily from their posts. Experienced or talented officials, and particularly those with suspicious Langi or Acholi connections, frequently disappeared or fled the country. Those who were out of suspicion assumed low profiles. Inexperienced and unqualified military officers loyal to the ruler were put in charge of ministries and departments, often with disastrous consequences. Agencies lost their directors and their direction as officials were replaced; extreme caution and inactivity became the norm for survival by those who remained. Unwise policies were sometimes arbitrarily imposed by Amin: "When the Governor of the Bank of Uganda — a dangerous office which changed hands frequently — tried to warn Amin of inflation and currency shortage, he was brusquely ordered to print more money, which began to lose value rapidly."[59] The disappearance and murder of Chief Justice Benedicto Kiwanuka in 1972 and the decrees that placed the military above the law effectively terrorized judges, magistrates, lawyers, and even the police, with the result that the legal system ceased to function in any meaningful sense. In short, the state in its classical meaning as an impersonal institution of public protection and justice ceased to exist and Uganda was reduced to something resembling Hobbes's "state of nature."[60]

The socioeconomic consequences of Amin's rule were markedly adverse and there was a general decline in living standards during his era. The economy registered a negative rate of growth in GDP between 1970 and 1979, following a very substantial rate of increase (5.9 percent) during the previous decade.[61] Two major contributing factors, if we exclude the costs of Obote's belated experiments with socialism, were a dramatic increase in government expenditure on the military and the expulsion of the Asian community. The 1972 defense estimates were 50 percent in excess of the pre-coup budget, and between 1971 and 1974 the military increased from 9,000 to 20,000 men. Soldiers' pay and perquisites also increased, and they became something of a politically privileged class. Of course, military expenditures were increasingly financed by credit expansion in the face of a deteriorating economy, and this quickly led to extremely high rates of inflation.[62] The mass expulsion of 70,000 Asians brought Amin temporary popular support from Africans, particularly from those who were the beneficiaries of the allocation of the property (including buildings, merchandise, bank accounts, homes, cars, furniture, and so forth) that the Asians were forced to leave behind. Amin, his lieutenants, and his closest supporters appropriated the most lucrative property, and the rest was distributed to soldiers as booty. The deportation, however, was purchased at great cost to the economy: productive entrepreneurial, managerial, professional, and technical personnel were lost virtually overnight; efficient industries, such as the Madhvani group of companies, the largest private industrial enterprise in East Africa, were fragmented; the system of trade and distribution was disrupted; employment declined dramatically (over one hundred thousand jobs were lost); and tax revenues fell precipitously.[63]

In important respects, the Ugandan economy under Amin reverted to a traditional mode of subsistence agriculture. Farmers were driven out of cash-crop production by low prices and a highly inflated shilling, which lost more than 90 percent of its value. Production of the major cash crops — coffee and cotton — decreased. A substantial portion of what was produced was undoubtedly smuggled out of the country to fetch a higher price in a sounder currency; the bulk of this production probably ended up in Kenya. Mining (primarily of copper) also declined, as did manufacturing. As export earnings fell, shortages developed in imported goods, some of which were basic commodities such as milk, salt, sugar, soap, and matches. "Hoes and pangas, basic tools used in every household, doubled and tripled in price and were no longer in supply . . . the president's office issued directives that hoes were to be distributed to District Commissioners and then allocated . . .

according to need."[64] The capacity to borrow in foreign capital markets was reduced almost to nil. Many imported goods became virtually unavailable except to black-market dealers, the army (whose canteens were kept well stocked by Amin), and the ruling elite, who appropriated scarce foreign exchange for their own political and even private uses.

Indeed, as the formal economy lost its capacity to perform under the adverse conditions fostered by the regime, the black-market economy (*magendo*) flourished and became the primary mechanism of economic exchange both within the country and internationally. Magendo became the real economy.[65] The cost of living became so high, and salaries for government personnel remained so comparatively low, that officials were driven to find alternative sources of income. Many became magendo enterprisers out of necessity, with the consequence that they neglected their official duties; many were also forced to spend their time raising their own food, which was either unavailable or prohibitively expensive.[66] People who could not survive in the formal economy and were not able to engage in magendo transactions often turned to their own villages and families in the rural areas.

In 1978, Amin's army crossed the border into Tanzania in pursuit of soldiers who had carried out an unsuccessful mutiny. The Ugandans stole property and destroyed the livelihood of many Tanzanians. Many were forced to flee, and some were killed. President Nyerere called on the OAU to censure Amin for this act of aggression, and, when it failed to do so, he ordered his troops to support the forces of anti-Amin exiles in the invasion of Uganda. By the spring of 1979 Amin's forces had been routed, and his regime destroyed. Some of his forces took refuge in neighboring Sudan and Zaire, and Amin sought exile first in Libya and later on in Saudi Arabia. But, in the course of his army's retreat across Uganda, additional property was plundered or destroyed: factories were sabotaged, goods were taken from shops, currency was stolen from banks, and vehicles were hijacked. "Uganda was left not merely bankrupt, but literally bare of much of its infrastructure and physical plant."[67] Immediately after overthrowing Amin's regime, the Tanzanian army, with as many as 40,000 troops, was saddled with the role of maintaining law and order in a country that had been largely without effective government for years and lacked a capable army and police force.[68]

The post-Amin period to date suggests that it is much easier to destroy than to rehabilitate a country. That which Amin had not debased or disorganized during eight tyrannical years often weakened further during the Tanzania-Uganda war and immediately afterwards. A team of Commonwealth economists who were asked to investigate problems of rehabilitation reported that when they arrived in Uganda they found a government staffed by senior officials installed by the liberation forces. These men were inexperienced and were occupying ransacked offices with very few chairs, desks, typewriters, pens, or even sheets of paper. As the economists pointed out, however, the loss of or damage to the physical infrastructure of the country was not the fundamental problem. Restoring the civil and socioeconomic infrastructure was crucial. "The really important need is to reform the institutions and policies the Government has inherited. More fundamentally still, successful rehabilitation depends on political leadership to bridge the rifts in Ugandan society — some long-standing, some of more recent origin — and to create law, order and political stability."[69] The extent to which these conditions have been repaired is a matter of controversy, although the controversy pertains more to civil and political conditions than to economic, since the economy is already showing real signs of recovery.

The initial post-Amin period, from April 1979 until December 1980 (when Obote was re-elected president), was marked by political instability and a perpetuation of lawlessness, violence, and corruption. Magendo continued to be the primary means of economic exchange. Anarchy persisted due to the virtual absence of an organized army and police force in a society in which arms were widely available to warlords, political factions, and thieves. The task of establishing an effective reconstruction government proved more difficult to accomplish than the defeat of Amin, largely owing to the historical ethnopolitical divisions and personal rivalries of the country. Almost as soon as the Uganda National Liberation Front (UNLF) took over the country, rifts began to open within its ranks. The first government installed by the UNLF (that of President Yusufu Lule, a politically unpracticed Ganda academic) lasted scarcely more than two months before it was replaced by an administration led by Godfrey Binaisa. Binaisa was also a Ganda and had been attorney general under Obote. He came to power as a result of a majority vote in the National Consultative Council, which governed the UNLF. Binaisa's regime lasted for almost a year, but was overthrown in a bloodless coup carried out by military officers in the council who were supporters of Obote. In interpreting these events one commentator put her finger on the key problem: "those who sought to restore order to Uganda in 1979 had to engage in the same quest for legitimacy and control that had posed the fundamental dilemma for the former civilian regime before 1971. Their failure was demonstrated by the further intervention of the army in May 1980."[70]

Planning for elections was undertaken and they were eventually scheduled for December 1980. Obote returned to campaign under the UPC banner; the DP was also resuscitated. A new Ganda party, the Conservative Party (CP), and a radical party, the Uganda Peoples Movement (UPM), were formed to contest the elections. Obote's party won an overall majority, and, although the elections were not without instances of violence and allegations of fraud, a team of Commonwealth observers declared them to be a valid expression of electoral choice under the circumstances. Obote was congratulated for being the first African ruler re-elected to office after having been deposed — an assertion that seemed to overlook the fact that an armed invasion of the country was necessary before elections could be held.[71]

Unfortunately, elections themselves did not and could not resolve Uganda's profound political problems, which were deeply rooted in historical ethnoregional divisions. Some of the losers did not accept the results and early in 1981 launched a campaign of terror to discredit Obote. Obote's government initially found it very difficult to suppress the movement owing to the disorganized condition of the army and police. Considerable success was eventually registered in reducing both political and civil violence, and, in late 1982, Obote evidently took some pleasure in reporting that "banditry" had been eliminated in the environs of Kampala and in all but three of Uganda's 33 districts.[72] Of course, the curtailment and even the elimination of violent opposition is not identical to the generation of political legitimacy. There is no clear evidence to date that those who have been deterred from using violence are now reconciled to the government.

The second Obote regime has had somewhat greater success in restoring the economy. One important reason for this has been the fertility and climate of Uganda: given the right circumstances, farmers are able to produce food and cash crops in considerable abundance. But the proper circumstances are not natural — as the Amin regime demonstrated — and have to be created. Obote appears to have succeeded in doing this, primarily by prudently following the advice of the IMF and promoting a free-market economy. Farmers under this system can be sure of receiving a return that is commensurate with their production rather than a sum determined by an officially depressed price (such as those Amin enforced). In other words, a free market was created that could compete with magendo. Coffee, Uganda's most important cash crop, responded with a marked rise in production to levels that had been reached before Amin. Cotton, tea, tobacco, and other crops also responded to the new liberal order.

The Obote government lowered the Ugandan currency from the unrealistically high levels at which it was pegged during the previous regime. As a result, the Uganda shilling began to take on the character of real money, illegal currency transactions declined, inflation came down, and imports again became available on the open market.[73] In conformity with IMF guidelines, however, government salaries and wages were not increased, which made it more difficult for many to purchase imports and other available goods. This undoubtedly brought hardship to some. The government had probably had little choice but to accept this situation for the sake of the overall economy and the need to earn foreign exchange to pay off past debts. Obote had evidently succeeded, at least to 1985 in providing the elementary confidence necessary to regenerate and sustain economic activity.

The liberation of Uganda from tyranny again brought to the fore the critical problem of ethnoregional disaffection, which has subverted the political development of that country since independence. Obote has not yet been able to establish a national authority capable of securing the allegiance of the bulk of Ugandans and enforcing the writ of the central government throughout the country. He has forsaken the temptation to impose the national will arbitrarily, as he tried to do in 1966. His opponents, Gandans in particular, also have not resigned themselves once and for all to the acceptance of a Ugandan state and rule by non-Bugandans. The economy can be re-established and perhaps violence can be suppressed, but, until the leaders of Uganda and Buganda are reconciled to their legitimate existence within one state, the prospects for enduring tranquillity and prosperity will not be great.

KENYA

Kenya became an independent state on December 12, 1963, after some seventy-five years of British colonial rule. Until 1960 British policy aimed at the development not of an indigenous African country — as was the case with west Africa — but, rather, of a multiracial state. Britain hoped that the substantial European settler community that had wielded great power during most of the colonial period would continue to do so under an independent constitution. In this respect, Kenya's development approximated that of Southern Rhodesia (Zimbabwe) more than any other British colony. The working structures of Kenya's colonial government had been fashioned primarily with the European settlers in mind.[74] These structures were not shaped significantly by African institutions and requirements, as was the case in most other British colonies, where European settlers were not present in significant numbers.

Until the latter half of the 1950s, African political participation was largely confined to the local council level of rural government. African electoral politics at that level dated to the 1920s and its early origins reflected the prevailing colonial theory that the proper arena of African political development was rural local government. In 1944 an African was appointed by the governor to the colonial legislature — previously the preserve of Europeans, Asians, and Arabs, whose representations reflected a political calculation by the colonial authorities of their importance to the developing colony. Only in 1957 were Africans granted a very restricted national franchise, which permitted them to elect a small quota of representatives to the colonial legislature.

Post-World War II African nationalism had its origins in the Kenya African Union (KAU), which was founded in 1944 as the Kenya African Study Union. Jomo Kenyatta led the KAU in 1947 after his return to Kenya from England in 1946. The KAU was banned in 1953 following the declaration of an emergency by the colonial authorities in 1952 in reaction to political violence by the so-called Mau Mau movement. The authorities assumed a connection between the two.[75] Thereafter all territory-wide African political organizations were prohibited and the authorities promoted political development based on a multiracial constitution — with weighted representation and voting for designated racial groups — rather than a liberal constitution based on individual representation and one man, one vote. The British, however, faced vigorous and articulate opposition from the small group of elected African representatives in the colonial legislature who demanded majority rule based on a common roll. Carefully aware of the rapid decline of the legitimacy of colonialism as independence movements were occurring in many parts of Africa, Britain in 1960 made a volte-face and declared that Kenya would become an African-governed state. The first common roll election, which was held in February 1961, installed an African-dominated legislature and marked the start of a rapid transition to self-government.[76]

The general election was won overwhelmingly by the Kenya African National Union (KANU), whose presumptive leader, Jomo Kenyatta, was still being detained by the colonial authorities as the alleged leader of the Mau Mau movement. KANU, however, refused to form the government without its leader, and the minority Kenya African Democratic Union (KADU) agreed to form one instead with European and Asian support. KANU thereby temporarily lost its opportunity to shape political events. KADU agreed to a decentralized form of government — the "Majimbo" constitution — that was designed to protect the minority ethnic groups that were the base of its support.[77]

Preindependence elections were held in June 1963. They also were won by KANU, which formed what was to be the first independent African government of Kenya.[78] Kenyatta, who had been released from detention in August 1961 when the colonial authorities realized they could no longer detain the leader of the majority party, became prime minister. The Majimbo constitution was not substantially implemented by Kenyatta's government, whose base of political support was the majority ethnic groups of Kenya, particularly the two largest — the Kikuyu and Luo. With the silent support of many civil servants who did not wish to see the centralized administrative organizations dismantled with a resultant loss of their bureaucratic authority, in December 1964 the emergent state was transformed instead into a unitary republic with Kenyatta as its first president. Kenya became a de facto one-party state at that time, for KADU's leader joined KANU in the knowledge that otherwise they could not participate in the government, protect the interests of their supporters, or provide them with patronage. For most of the time since then, national politics in Kenya has been identified with KANU, which is not a centrally

integrated and organized mass party but, rather, is a loose confederation of leaders with constituency bases in rural and urban
areas. KANU has always been presided over by a personal ruler —
at first Jomo Kenyatta and later Daniel arap Moi — each of whom
has endeavored to stand above all other politicians, not unlike a
"presidential monarch."

The first experiment in one-party government under Kenyatta
was short-lived. It ended in 1966 when Oginga Odinga, the vice-
president of KANU and a prominent leader of the Luo people in
central Nyanza, was skillfully removed from the vice-presidential
position by Tom Mboya — his major Luo rival. Mboya maneuvered successfully, and presumably with Kenyatta's approval, to
have Odinga's post abolished by the party. Odinga had alienated
Kenyatta by assuming leadership of a radical KANU faction that
was beginning to challenge the ruler's paramount political position
and rather capitalist-oriented economic policies. Odinga left
KANU and with 30 MPs formed a new party, the Kenya's People's
Union (KPU), which espoused more socialist-oriented policies that
involved the rejection of Kenya's capitalist inheritance.[79] The MPs
who established KPU were forced to resign their seats in Parliament and seek re-election, and, in a series of by-elections known as
the "little general election," their new party overwhelmingly won
only central Nyanza (Luo) and Machakos (Kamba). KPU MPs
who ran elsewhere were defeated, with one exception.[80] The opposition party was barely tolerated until October 1969, when it was
banned following angry demonstrations by Luos against Kenyatta
when he visited Kisumu, the Luo capital. A primary election in
which only KANU candidates were allowed to contest seats in the
National Assembly was held in December. In effect, the "primary"
was the general election.

The year 1969 marked the beginning of a new era of one-party
democracy in Kenya. In July, Mboya was assassinated on the
streets of Nairobi, and in late October, following the Kisumu
violence, Odinga was arrested and later placed in detention. With
Mboya, the brilliant kingmaker and expected successor, dead, and
Odinga in jail, Luo alienation from the Kenyatta regime became a
reality.[81] Kenyatta was no longer merely primus inter pares but had
become the unrivaled leader of the country with a power base
dominated by his own Kikuyu people.[82] But Kenyatta was astute
enough to permit wide public choice at the constituency level in the
1969 single-party elections. He encouraged numerous candidates to

compete and made it clear that incumbents had no special privileges and would have to win re-election in order to regain their positions. He even allowed two former leaders of the recently banned KPU (who had disowned their party) to stand for election by waiving a rule that required a candidate to be a member of KANU for at least six months. With more than 700 candidates nominated to contest 158 seats in Parliament, KANU's rival leaders were obliged to win popular support before they could enter the regime. Nearly half of the incumbent MPs were defeated, including five ministers and fourteen assistant ministers — an outcome that was repeated in every national election that followed. Of course, no other politician was permitted to compete for the presidency, which was elevated above the democratic process and reserved for Kenyatta. In the public mind, the presidency and Kenyatta became indistinguishable.

Kenyatta therefore did not stage-manage the nomination and election process to create an autocratic regime in which party leaders were dependent on him and isolated from the people, as in many other African one-party states. Instead, he fashioned an authentic but qualified democratic party — little more than an electoral mechanism — that enabled Kenyans to elect representatives of their own choosing and enabled Kenyatta to use the people to do much of his firing for him. Of course, Kenyatta also retained important powers that enabled him to appoint politically loyal or important MPs to cabinet and other posts in his government. Under Kenyatta, KANU therefore became not only a democratic institution but also a crucial instrument of his personal rule. The Kenyan polity under Kenyatta was an unusual, novel, and fairly successful combination of one-party democracy and nonhereditary monarchy.[83]

The president's relations with Kenya's democratically elected Parliament reflected a similar political formula. That assembly has been unusual in contemporary black Africa for its lively and sometimes critical debates on government policies and actions: it has been a legislature in substance as well as name. Kenyatta, however, was clearly above Parliament and was always prepared to intervene in the legislative process — or to circumvent it — when it suited his interests. Rather like a Tudor or Stuart king who had not yet been confronted with the English Bill of Rights, he occasionally detained MPs whose speeches or actions he perceived as challenging his supreme authority regardless of whether they did this inside or outside of Parliament. For example, in 1975 two prominent MPs who made contemptuous remarks about KANU in the National Assembly were promptly arrested and detained under provision of the Preservation of Public Security Act. In 1977 another MP was arrested for making allegations of misconduct against members of Kenyatta's government. But, Kenyatta never entirely muzzled Parliament or reduced it to the subservient status of a rubber stamp, which has often been the fate of national assemblies in other black African countries. In refusing to do this, he parted company with many other personal rulers. Kenyatta astutely recognized the legitimacy that could accrue to himself and his regime from democratic election and a carefully controlled measure of parliamentary freedom.

Kenyatta also was conscious of public relations, as can be seen in his championing of popular issues, such as Africanization of the economy — including the transfer of extensive landholdings from Europeans to African smallholders — and free schooling in the initial elementary grades. He arbitrarily intervened to abolish school fees in these grades. Kenyatta was a personal ruler, but he was also conscious of his public standing, and he stamped his personal approval on policies that he knew were popular.

A central instrument of personal rule was the excolonial provincial administration, which, ironically, had been substantially enlarged in the 1950s in reaction to the Mau Mau movement and the need to increase colonial control in the affected African rural areas. The country had been divided administratively into provincial jurisdictions. African statehood became a reality in rural areas by the rapid Africanization of this former European administration. In each province a commissioner was responsible for law, order, and other activities of government and was directly and personally accountable to the president. Each commissioner, in turn, had a staff of subordinate officers in the districts of the province who were responsible to him. This inherited instrument acquired the earmarks of a kind of royalist administration. Provincial and district commissioners were "the king's men" — authoritative agents who were responsible for all important and routine activities of governance in the countryside. They were courtiers more than barons; servants of the crown who possessed no independent political bases and could be dismissed at will by the ruler.[84]

Kenya's novel one-party democracy was also made to conform to

Kenyatta's political will and was prevented from becoming too anarchical by the provincial administration. The eight provincial commissioners and their subordinates also served as the ruler's political lieutenants. For example, they enabled him to control the political activities of local KANU associations and individual politicians by their authority to issue licenses to hold political meetings and to oversee the nomination of party candidates. Politicians often resented such supervision but had to accept it since the provincial officers had the complete confidence of Kenyatta. These supervisory activities by Kenyatta's provincial servants also had more than an incidental resemblance to the political oversight of colonial governors. Indeed, far from being discarded at independence, the colonial model of a governor and his staff was retained, although with distinctly African trappings and symbols, by both Kenyatta and his successors.

Kenyatta's government also retained continuity with colonialism by retaining the capitalist agricultural export economy originally built by European settlers in the so-called white highlands of southwest Kenya. This prosperous economy had been developed during the colonial era and was the economic backbone of the country. In the 1950s, following the Swynnerton Plan, the colonial government took two important steps to generate African participation in and commitment to a capitalist mode of agricultural production.[85] First, beginning in strategic Central Province — the heart of the Mau Mau area — the so-called tribal land tenure system was replaced by individual ownership. Second, Africans were assisted by rural credit expansion and other means to become producers of coffee and tea, Kenya's most important cash crops. (Previously Africans had been prohibited by colonial regulations from producing those crops.) In 1959 the agrarian color bar that had set aside some 7 million acres of fertile land exclusively for European ownership was ended. Beginning early in the 1960s various African resettlement schemes, entailing the buying out of European farmers at full market prices, were undertaken with financial support from both the Kenyan and British parliaments.[86]

The Africanization of the agricultural export sector was accomplished without any significant sacrifice of productivity as some 70,000 African families took possession of 2 million acres of fertile land. It was a powerful stimulus to petty rural capitalism. The productivity of African smallholdings was often greater than that of larger mixed farms. Indeed, Kenya's primarily agricultural economy grew at the impressive annual rate of more than 6 percent in the first decade following independence, and per capita income increased despite a very high rate of population growth.[87] Moreover, until 1979–80 Kenya remained self-sufficient in food production during most years and provided urban consumers with their food staples at substantially lower prices than in neighboring states. Government policy recognized the centrality of the agricultural export sector, which accounted for about 70 percent of export earning. The government also became firmly wedded to the goal of productivity pursued through market mechanisms, although this did not preclude either modest encouragement of cooperatives and other communal arrangements or the substantial growth of government. Marketing boards have been established, but they have not been used to generate public finance through politically depressed prices — as in Ghana and Nigeria — partly because they have been tied to the marketing and farmers' institutions of the colonial period and partly because Kenya does not have just unorganized small-scale farmers. Each Kenyan sector has a subsector of large, politically influential producers. Moreover, the tax burden on progressive farmers has been kept moderately low and therefore has not discouraged production to the same extent as in many other African countries.[88]

The productive cash-crop export economy has enabled the government to respond positively to local demands for infrastructure and social services as registered in elections and other public expressions. The system of trunk and local roads has been greatly extended since independence, which has facilitated the spread of the cash economy. Education was heavily supported and Kenya today is one of black Africa's highest educational spenders; the goal of free primary schooling was reached in 1979. Four million children were attending primary school in 1980. Health services, primarily in the form of dispensaries, have been extended to rural areas. Government social policies have achieved fairly impressive results in terms of increased life expectancy, lower infant mortality, increased literacy, school attendance, and so forth. Kenya's achievements in these areas have been comparable to those of Tanzania.[89] And, as of 1984, Kenyan accomplishments were being sustained whereas Tanzania's social infrastructure has been deteriorating.

In Kenya the state became directly involved in the creation of an African capitalist class, not only in the agricultural sector but in other modern sectors of the economy, including trade and manufacturing. The government acquired a major role in banking in the 1970s, which it used to provide credit to African businessmen — not infrequently KANU politicians, civil servants, and their relatives or friends. The government also used its authority to encourage private firms, including foreign companies, to Africanize their local operations. Moreover, the state used its powers to license businesses as a lever to increase African participation in smaller-scale trade, which historically was the preserve of the Asian community. Some politicians and civil servants became wealthy silent partners in Asian firms by offering them protection from government regulations and harassment. An African political bourgeoisie that owed its existence and privileges in no small way to the new state and included prominent politicians and civil servants among its members was created as a result of such policies and practices and became a major, conservative force in Kenyan politics. Members of Kenyatta's family and other political or bureaucratic leaders and their relatives were among the most prominent politico-businessmen in the country.

Economic growth and Africanization of the public and private sectors were therefore accompanied by new inequalities and class differences among Africans — between the landed and landless, the more successful and less successful farmers, employers and employees, employed and unemployed, and so forth. A top politico-business elite of very powerful and wealthy "big men" consisting of leading politicians, civil servants, and their families became a marked and controversial feature of Kenya's social structure. In 1974 the top 20 percent of Kenya's households had 60 percent of the national income, whereas the bottom 20 percent had only 2.6 percent, according to the World Bank.[90] These socioeconomic distinctions, and the rapidly increasing and extensive wealth of the ruling class and the circles around Kenyatta in particular, drew criticism from some politicians, journalists, and university lecturers and became the target of a Marxist critique of Kenya's development path.[91] They were also criticized by neighbors, particularly in Tanzania, which considered its socialist approach to be guided far more by a concern for equality. According to the World Bank, however, the degree of income inequality in Tanzania is not markedly lower than Kenya.[92]

Kenyatta's regime can be represented by a series of concentric circles with the ruler at the center. The inner circle consisted of members of his own family as well as old Kikuyu nationalists who stood with him in the early days of the anticolonial movement and came from his own district of Kiambu just outside of Nairobi. Mama Ngina, Peter Mbiyu Koinange (his minister of state and political confidant), as well as some other members of Kenyatta's family were among the most influential members of this circle. The next coterie probably consisted of the provincial commissioners and other very trusted courtiers — such as Attorney-General Charles Njonjo, who was also a Kikuyu and was appointed by Kenyatta not only to the cabinet but also to Parliament. He had no independent political base of his own. Selected cabinet ministers, MPs, and KANU officials probably came next. Kenyatta's patriarchal ruling style was consistent with this image of his regime. For example, he regularly held court at one of the state houses or his country estate at Gatundu in Kiambu District, where he received petitioners, supplicants, emissaries, and various other delegations who sought to curry favor or assistance in matters of some urgency to themselves or their followers and pledged their continued loyalty and support in return.[93]

Since the colonial period, political factionalism has been a prominent facet of Kenyan politics and is tied to patron-client relations between powerful political "barons" and their followers — usually from among rural bases of personal political support.[94] The competition for power has turned primarily on such factions insofar as opposition parties and movements have not usually been permitted. Consequently, competition by party has been impossible. Political factionalism has not always been civil and peaceful and has occasionally been associated with violence. Three prominent politicians have been murdered since the colonial period, including the dynamic and talented Tom Mboya in 1969 and the populist Josiah Mwangi Kariuki in 1975 — each of whom was probably regarded as either a rival or a threat by prominent factions close to Kenyatta. Factional struggles were connected with the question of who would succeed a ruler who was already at an advanced age at the time of independence. Indeed, the first of these struggles — between Mboya and Odinga — predated independence. The departure of Odinga from KANU and the assassination of Mboya put an end to this particular conflict.

Amid increasing uncertainty concerning Kenyatta's health (due to his very advanced age), in the 1970s the succession issue assumed a new urgency and character. In 1976 it surfaced in the efforts of a

Kikuyu-led faction of KANU to prevent Vice-President Moi — not himself a Kikuyu — from succeeding to the presidency as the constitution provided should Kenyatta become incapacitated. Initially, this faction attempted to change the constitutional rules to prevent Moi from succeeding by legal means; later, when this stratagem seemed likely to fail, it sought to dominate KANU's national executive. It did not win Kenyatta's support for constitutional change, however, presumably because a majority of MPs bitterly opposed it. Attorney-General Njonjo issued a public warning that it was a public offense "to imagine" the death of the president, and the controversy was finally squashed by a cabinet statement supporting Njonjo.[95] It was not in Kenyatta's interest to encourage a cabal that was attempting to predetermine the succession at the risk of undermining his own authority. It was in his interest, however, to support a majority of MPs. The struggle then shifted to the KANU national executive elections, which could prove strategic in shaping the succession. The factional conflict became so intense and rancorous in the spring of 1977 that Kenyatta intervened and canceled the elections at the eleventh hour.

Kenyatta died in August 1978 and was succeeded by Moi in accordance with the constitution, which required that a new president be elected within 90 days. With the support of two crucial Kikuyu kingmakers — Charles Njonjo and Kenyatta's finance minister, Mwai Kibaki — Moi was able to secure the leadership of KANU without challenge. This automatically placed the presidency in his hands, owing to the fact that Kenya was a one-party state and no public election had to be held. On October 10, 1978, Moi was inaugurated as Kenya's second president, with Kibaki as vice-president.

Moi's authority initially was heavily dependent on Kenyatta's legacy, and he declared himself to be following in Kenyatta's footsteps — *nyayo*. His immediate position of power depended greatly on the support of Njonjo and Kibaki, who had opposed the "challenge the constitution" faction. He therefore was dependent on others and would eventually have to fashion his own ruling coalition if he hoped to establish his own regime. The 1979 elections presented him with an initial opportunity to begin to create his own political base by using Kenyatta's stratagem of allowing the electorate to defeat many incumbent MPs and some ministers and assistant ministers and to elect new MPs from among whom he could appoint his own ministers. His immediate political task was to reduce his dependence on Kenyatta's old Kikuyu lieutenants. This was assisted, in part, by rivalry between Njonjo and Kibaki over the highest ground from which a possible succession to Moi might be controlled.

Moi came to power toward the end of an era of socioeconomic prosperity that recently had been somewhat artificial, for it rested in part on Kenya's ability to benefit from the serious economic adversities and black market experienced by Uganda during and immediately following the Amin regime. With the beginning of economic recovery in Uganda and a world recession, in 1980 Moi's economic luck changed for the worse. During the period of prosperity opportunities and expectations had been high; fairly extensive state bureaucracies and services were affordable. Government employment and spending continued to grow after revenues began to decline, which resulted in increased public borrowing and debt-servicing costs in an era of very high interest rates. At the same time population growth was unabated in a country that already had one of the highest rates of increase in the world. This kept up the pressure for public spending and services.[96] In July 1982 the government released a report indicating that it could no longer afford to support public services at existing levels and recommending that recipients bear part of the cost; it also called for privatization of some commercial government enterprises and a general reduction in economic regulations and permits.[97] Two years later the government had yet to take action.

Following his succession Moi declared that corruption, mismanagement, and other government malpractices would not be tolerated by his regime. Of course, it is one thing to declare such practices unacceptable and quite another to reduce, much less to eliminate, them. In fact, as the control of government was shifted away from the Kikuyus — who were among the best educated and most experienced public officials — to more marginal groups, it is probable that corruption and mismanagement were not reduced and may have increased. Like Kenyatta before him, Moi allowed his ministers and civil servants to engage in private business, thus blurring the line between private and public and encouraging corruption.

To broaden his base of support, Moi sought to end the alienation of the Luos. In a major move, Moi tried to rehabilitate Odinga after years in the political wilderness; this attempt ultimately failed owing to Odinga's intemperate speech denouncing the late

Kenyatta as a "landgrabber." In May 1982, after advocating the need for a Kenyan party of democratic socialism in a speech delivered in London before members of the British Labour Party, Odinga was expelled from KANU. Moi increasingly came to favor non-Kikuyu ethnic groups, including his own Kalenjin people. Many, ironically, had been the original political base of KADU. By 1982, however, Moi still had not succeeded in establishing his unquestioned personal dominance of ministers and other leading politicians, who were still waiting to see who finally would be Kenyatta's permanent successor.

With a deteriorating economy and increasing criticism of the conduct of some government officials, the regime became apprehensive about losing control. At the same time, opposition politicians, journalists, university teachers, and other critics were emboldened to be more outspoken. The political uncertainty could only be ended by the regime either taking control of the situation and silencing its critics or losing control altogether. Moi indicated in the spring of 1982 that he was prepared to use preventive detention as a last resort. One of the first to be detained was a former MP who had called publicly for the formation of a second party in Kenya. Several University of Nairobi lecturers accused of teaching revolutionary Marxism and of radicalizing students were placed in preventive detention; a leading Nairobi lawyer who had defended some opponents of the regime in court was also detained. One newspaper editorial criticized the government for needlessly provoking public fear by resorting to preventive detention, which, it held, was only justified in wartime and was otherwise against the rule of law; the editor was fired before evening and the newspaper made a public apology to the president the next day. When an MP attempted to secure information about a defense treaty with the United States — the information was publicly available in the United States — he was told that security arrangements could not be discussed openly in Parliament.

On August 1, 1982, an attempted coup was carried out by young, dissident, ground-based air force personnel. The coup appeared to reflect concern about the socioeconomic inequalities of Kenyan society.[98] It was supported only by a small segment of the armed forces, although it was apparently welcomed by demonstrations of some university students. It was suppressed by the army and a police paramilitary force. A considerable number of people were killed. The coup attempt was clearly the most destabilizing episode since independence. At the time it seemed likely that it would weaken and isolate the president further. But in fact it had a different impact: it ushered in a year of transition to a new regime in which Moi secured control of his ministers, the security forces, and all other levels of power. The coup appeared to shock Moi into asserting successfully his personal rule. Reflecting his new strength and confidence, in 1983 he obliquely accused Njonjo, without naming him, of being a traitor, thus signifying his own paramountcy. The consolidation of his authority was provided by the elections of September 1983, which originally were not scheduled to be held until 1984. Although the election did not eliminate all of Moi's opponents, it nevertheless resulted in a sufficiently large turnover of MPs to enable him to construct a cabinet based on a new national coalition. The new cabinet represented not only more diverse segments of the national population but also his own power base, not Kenyatta's.

Since independence Kenyans have enjoyed, largely as a result of deliberate government action and forbearance, democratic rights and socioeconomic goods to a degree that is unusual in contemporary African politics. There has been a clearly discernible, if not always overt, constitutionalism despite the periodic strains of ethnic politics, violations of civil rights, and political violence. It is evident in the role of elections, Parliament, the judiciary, the press, and other institutional spheres. Although "tribal associations have been prohibited and sports clubs may not bear ethnic names, ethnicity has been implicitly acknowledged as an inevitable and positive feature of politics." On the contrary, mechanisms exist to give expression to it in elections, cabinet and ministerial representation, civil service appointments, and so forth. Of course, the results are not always just to every group — as the unfortunate experience of the Luos indicates only too clearly. In the relations between the president and important politicians there has usually been mutual acknowledgment, accommodation, and forebearance, although on occasion such practices have been cast aside by both the president and some politicians. There is evidence of the same practices among politicians and factions contesting for office in Kenya's very lively system of one-party democracy.

But in a new state, such as Kenya, which lacks an established constitutional and civil tradition to fall back on in the moments of serious political conflict that are bound to arise from time to time, stability probably demands that the president err on the side of strength rather than weakness. The succession of Moi is indicative of this. In Kenya civil politics is not yet wholly embodied in and defended by impersonal institutions; it must therefore be defended by politicians. This raises an almost inevitable dilemma: if the president is weak, politics may get out of control, with a resultant threat to stability; if he is too autocratic and forceful, civil and political liberties might be undermined. Both of these possibilities have periodically surfaced and probably will continue to do so in the future. Considering the quite brief experience of Kenyans with modern national government, we are impressed by the overall restraint and civility practised in Kenya as compared to many other tropical African countries. As an index, there have never been more than 25 political detainees or so, and at the end of 1984 there were less than a half-dozen.

Kenya's comparative success to date in providing socioeconomic goods derives from the Kenyatta government's decision to retain the overall structure of the European-built agrarian economy while at the same time transferring land ownership to Africans. The result has been a highly productive system of smallholder cultivation in which hundreds of thousands of Africans have participated. The socioeconomic benefits, not only to Africans but to the entire country, have been considerable. Not all ethnic groups have benefited; the Kikuyu of Central Province and the Rift Valley have benefited the most.

The agrarian economy has enabled the government to finance extensive public services, including schools, clinics, roads, and other benefits in rural districts and localities. Kenyan democracy requires constant attention to the interests and concerns of local supporters: signs of a distinctively "modern," pluralistic polity. There has been a strong continuity in this process of politics since independence, and it is unlikely that any government could abolish it.

Of course, such a polity depends on continued economic growth and there have been disquieting signs of slowdown in recent years. A crucial problem is the limited supply of fixed resources and continuing very high rates of population growth: Kenya illustrates all too clearly the problem of running out of arable land in an agrarian economy. This socioeconomic problem is probably beyond the control of the government and could eventually jeopardize Kenya's hard-won prosperity and stability.

CONCLUSION

The past quarter-century has witnessed the divergence of Tanzania, Uganda, and Kenya and their acquisition of distinctive national personalities. Of course, they continued to exhibit many characteristics in common: comparatively low standards of living, overwhelmingly agrarian and rural economies, rapid urbanization, high birth rates, personalism in government and administration, and predilection for one-party states. But the three territories that once were associated in a regional community have severed their former ties. Their public policies and ideological professions have taken different directions. Indeed, the organization and behavior of the political economies have diverged and their performances, successes, and difficulties have revealed differences that were not so evident at independence. In 1984, as the president of Tanzania said in an interview, it would be rather difficult to re-establish an East African community in the light of the experience each member has had in pursuing its own interests on crucial issues.[99]

The individual character of each country has become more defined since independence. Tanzania, under the personal direction of Nyerere and his ruling party, embarked on a heroic project to become an authentic African socialist state, with very mixed results and some rather large unplanned and probably unanticipated problems. The result to date has been a highly bureaucraticized country and a seriously deteriorating economy weighed down by a large and inefficient state superstructure. A country that had been full of optimism about its future and confidence in its leader and his party — whether justified or not — has become a disillusioned land.

Uganda experienced a rather different problem: not the unexpected consequences of overly optimistic national social engineering but, rather, the difficulties of finding a political covenant between the center and its ethnic constituents, particularly Buganda. Uganda has not been successful but has experienced considerable political turmoil instead: first at the hands of a nationalist who lacked the power or art to create national unity; then at the mercy of a tyrant whose sole preoccupation was to eat well and survive; and next at the hands of a number of unsuccessful interim governments. At present Uganda is once again out of the control of the first nationalist, whose failure the second time around has now been determined.

Kenya alone has achieved considerable postindependence success in both political and economic development by avoiding the destructive ethnopolitical warfare of Uganda and the rationalist utopianism of Tanzania. Kenya managed to establish effective political institutions that contributed to political stability while nevertheless permitting a moderate degree of authentic democracy within a one-party framework. Its governments did not dismantle the economic structures built by the settlers during the colonial era but instead decided to Africanize them and, where possible, to improve them. African smallholders were thereby given a real stake in an economy that had already proved its success. The economy was further developed without being unduly burdened by an expanding state apparatus until the 1980s.

In retrospect, such national divergence does not seem surprising. Before independence the geographical, cultural, historical, and socioeconomic particularisms of East Africa were submerged by the political control of a single sovereign government. Britain treated the region as an entity in some important respects and was responsible for all three colonies. Since independence, the area has been under the control of three sovereign states. The independent rulers and governments of each country have had their own dispositions, abilities, ideas, values, and policies. They have encountered different obstacles and opportunities, problems and solutions, along the way. In short, they have made their own political history just as the numerous other African governments have made theirs. This is not surprising when we recognize that independence involved the acquisition of sovereignty — which is the freedom to create one's own history.

The significance of sovereignty is most evident in the history of Tanzania since independence. But Uganda has endured a war fought on its own soil and has a government not fully accepted by all its peoples. Kenya has perhaps taken fewer liberties with its independence and has prudently sought to build on its colonial inheritance. Under Kenyatta, the presidential role in foreign policy was not evident, but, under Moi, Kenya has begun to project itself more onto the African and world stage. In 1981 the OAU conference was held in Nairobi with Moi as chairman.

Nyerere has used sovereignty not only to remake Tanzania in accordance with his own ideology but also to influence African and world affairs. His platform is small in empirical terms but more than adequate by international law, and Nyerere has used it to remarkable effect, belying the global insignificance of his country. His views on international development, southern Africa, and apartheid, in particular, are widely reported, and he has become one of the most prominent and vocal of all Third World statesmen. In the 1960s, Nyerere sometimes stood on his platform and adopted costly moral stances: he recognized East Germany at the price of a loss of West German aid, and he recognized Biafra against majority African opinion. He later refused to acknowledge the international legitimacy of Amin, with similar effects on African opinion. The war Tanzania waged against Uganda was the action of a sovereign government. Even before the 1970s, when the East African Community began to disintegrate, Tanzania looked southward for more politically compatible allies. Nyerere assumed the leadership of the so-called front-line states, which played a role in Zimbabwe's independence. He permitted his country to become a base of operations for the Mozambique Liberation Front (FRELIMO) against the Portuguese in Mozambique, and he gave sanctuary to other liberation movements. After Mozambique, achieved independence, Nyerere established close fraternal ties and participated in a common market between the two countries. With the support of Chinese aid, which Nyerere sought assiduously, the Tazara railway linking Tanzania and Zambia was built. Tanzania was a founding member of the Southern African Development Co-ordination Conference (SADCC), which hopes to build a southern African common market independent of South Africa. Nyerere has also used his platform to secure unusually large amounts of foreign aid from the West. All of these actions, and many others, are the acts of a sovereign making his way in the world according to his own lights.

In conclusion, independence has had important and often unforeseen consequences for the people of East Africa. In the early 1960s, when Tanzania, Uganda, and Kenya were emerging, many hoped and some expected that independence would have only beneficial consequences. In the mid-1980s it is clear that the results have been mixed. The three states have had inevitably unequal shares of hope and disappointment, fortune and misfortune, success and failure, prosperity and adversity. But these experiences merely reflect those of other Third World and sub-Saharan states during the past quarter-century. They are the ordinary experiences of political freedom, the stuff of which political history is made. The East African states have entered the stage of national and international history.

Notes

1. Roland Oliver and Gervase Matthew, *A History of East Africa*, vol. 1 (Oxford: Oxford University Press, Clarendon Press, 1963); Vincent Harlow and E. M. Chilver, *History of East Africa*, vol. 2 (Oxford: Oxford University Press, Clarendon Press, 1965); Kenneth Ingham, *A History of East Africa* (London: Longmans, 1962); and A. J. Hughes, *East Africa: The Search for Unity; Kenya, Tanganyika, Uganda, and Zanzibar* (Baltimore: Penguin Books, 1963).

2. *Accelerated Development in Sub-Saharan Africa: An Agenda for Action* (Washington: World Bank, 1981), statistical annex, pp. 137–98.

3. Donald Rothchild, ed., *Politics of Integration: An East African Documentary* (Nairobi: East African Publishing House, 1968); Colin Leys and Peter Robson, eds., *Federation in East Africa: Opportunities and Problems* (Nairobi: Oxford University Press, 1965); Joseph S. Nye, Jr., *Pan-Africanism and East African Integration* (Cambridge, Mass.: Harvard University Press, 1965); and Richard Cox, *Pan-Africanism in Practice: An East African Study* PAFMECA 1958–1964 (London: Oxford University Press, for the Institute of Race Relations, 1964).

4. For Nyerere, see William Edgett Smith, *Nyerere of Tanzania* (Nairobi: Transafrica Publishing, 1974); and William R. Duggan and John Civilla, *Tanzania and Nyerere: A Study of Ujamaa and Nationalism* (Maryknoll, N.Y.: Orbis Books, 1976).

5. See Nyerere's speeches and statements to the United Nations Trusteeship Council, which are reprinted in Julius K. Nyerere, *Freedom and Unity/Uhuru na Umoja: A Selection from Writings and Speeches, 1952–65* (Dar es Salaam: Oxford University Press, 1966), chaps. 3–5.

6. The importance of principles was defended by Nyerere in a memorandum to the National Executive of TANU under the title "Principles and Development," reprinted in Julius K. Nyerere, *Freedom and Socialism/Uhuru na Ujama: A Selection from Writings and Speeches, 1956–67* (Dar es Salaam: Oxford University Press, 1968), chap. 21.

7. Cranford Pratt, *The Critical Phase in Tanzania: 1945–1968* (Cambridge: Cambridge University Press, 1976), p. 202.

8. Nyerere, *Freedom and Unity*, chap. 42.

9. See Nyerere, *Freedom and Socialism*, chap. 2.

10. Lionel Cliffe, ed., *One Party Democracy: The Tanzanian General Elections* (Nairobi: East African Publishing House, 1967).

11. Helge Kjekhus, "Parliament in a One-Party State: The Bunge of Tanzania, 1965–70," *The Journal of Modern African Studies* 12, no. 1 (1974): 29–32.

12. See Bismarck U. Mwansasu, "The Changing Role of the Tanganyika African National Union," in Bismarck U. Mwansasu and Cranford Pratt, eds., *Towards Socialism in Tanzania* (Toronto and Buffalo, N.Y.: University of Toronto Press, 1979), pp. 169–92. For an analysis of these formative years in the development of the party-state, see Henry Bienen, *Tanzania: Party Transformation and Economic Development* (Princeton, N.J.: Princeton University Press, 1967); and William Tordoff, *Government and Politics in Tanzania* (Nairobi: East African Publishing House, 1967). A valuable study of an important region is G. Andrew Maguire, *Toward 'Uhuru' in Tanzania: The Politics of Participation* (London: Cambridge University Press, 1969); for the West Lake (Buhaya), see Göran Hyden, *Political Development in Rural Tanzania* (Nairobi: East African Publishing House, 1969); for the Kilimanjaro District, see Joel Samoff, *Tanzania: Local Politics and the Structure of Power* (Madison: University of Wisconsin Press, 1974).

13. Michael F. Lofchie, *Zanzibar: Background to Revolution* (Princeton, N.J.: Princeton University Press, 1965), pp. 257–81.

14. The National Executive Council of CCM also recommended that amendments

to Tanzania's constitution include limitation of presidential tenure to two or three five-year terms and provision for two vice-presidents, one for the mainland and one for Zanzibar.

15. Reprinted in Julius K. Nyerere, *Ujamaa: Essays on Socialism* (London: Oxford University Press, 1968), chap. 1.

16. For a compendium of articles on Tanzania's politics and socialism, see Lionel Cliffe and John Saul, eds., *Socialism in Tanzania: An Interdisciplinary Reader*, 2 vols. (Nairobi: East African Publishing House, 1972). See also Ian C. Parker, "Ideological and Economic Development in Tanzania," *African Studies Review* 15, no. 1 (April 1972): 43–78; and Frances Hill, "Ujamaa: African Socialism in Tanzania," in Helen Desfosses and Jacques Levesque, eds., *Socialism in the Third World* (New York: Praeger Publishers, 1975), pp. 216–51.

17. Julius K. Nyerere, *Freedom and Development: A Selection from Writings and Speeches, 1968–1973* (New York: Oxford University Press, 1972), p. 382.

18. Reprinted in Nyerere, *Ujamaa: Essays on Socialism*, chap. 2.

19. *Accelerated Development in Sub-Saharan Africa: An Agenda for Action*, p. 143.

20. *Africa South of the Sahara, 1982–83* (London: Europa Publications, 1982), p. 832.

21. A. L. Adu, *The Civil Service in New African States* (London: George Allen and Unwin, 1965); and Adebayo Adedeji, "The Tanzania Civil Service a Decade After Independence: Progress, Problems, and Prospects" (Memorandum, 1971).

22. Nyerere, *Freedom and Unity*, p. 219.

23. Nyerere, *Freedom and Socialism*, chap. 20.

24. Ibid., chap. 30.

25. Julius K. Nyerere, *The Arusha Declaration Ten Years After* (Dar es Salaam: Government Printer, 1977). See Jonathan S. Barker, "The Debate on Rural Socialism in Tanzania," in *Towards Socialism in Tanzania*, pp. 95–124; and P. F. Nursey-Bray, "Tanzania: The Development Debate," *African Affairs* 79, no. 314 (January 1980): 55–78.

26. *Freedom and Socialism*, chap. 37.

27. For a comprehensive account, see Dean E. McHenry, Jr., *Tanzania's Ujamaa Villages: The Implementation of a Rural Development Strategy* (Berkeley, Calif.: Institute of International Studies, 1979); for an earlier study, see Clyde R. Ingle, *From Village to State in Tanzania: The Politics of Rural Development* (Ithaca, N.Y., and London: Cornell University Press, 1972).

28. Frank Holmquist, "Correspondent's Report: Tanzania's Retreat from Statism in the Countryside," *Africa Today*, vol. 30, no. 4 (1983): 26.

29. See Goran Hyden, *Beyond Ujamaa in Tanzania: Underdevelopment and an Uncaptured Peasantry* (Berkeley and Los Angeles: University of California Press, 1980).

30. *Accelerated Development in Sub-Saharan Africa*, pp. 166–67.

31. For an early evaluation see Michael F. Lofchie, "Agrarian Socialism in the Third World: the Tanzania Case," *Comparative Politics* 8, no. 3 (April 1976): 479–99.

32. Holmquist, "Correspondent's Report," p. 24. See an interview with President Nyerere, "Tanzania Spotlight," *Africa* 152 (April 1984), p. 69. Speaking of past policy mistakes, Nyerere said "We disbanded the cooperative unions when we should have reformed them. So we are now having to reestablish them on a better basis. We abolished local government, thinking our people would get better service by decentralized central government administration."

33. Nyerere, *The Arusha Declaration Ten Years After*, p. 36.

34. Ibid., pp. 28, 51 (italics in original).

35. Rwekaza Mukandala, "Trends in Civil Service Size and Income in Tanzania,

1967–1982," *Canadian Journal of African Studies* 2, no. 2 (1983): 261.

36. See further details in Colin Legum, ed., *Africa Contemporary Record: Annual Survey and Documents, 1982–1983* (New York: African Publishing Company, 1984), p. B 278–303.

37. *Accelerated Development in Sub-Saharan Africa*, p. 165.

38. "Total Aid is about $440 m. per year, of which 70 percent is in grant form" (*Africa South of the Sahara, 1982–83*, p. 836).

39. See Gelase Mutahaba, "European Aid: Development Effects and Constraints, as Experienced by Tanzania," in Olav Stokke, ed., *European Aid Policies and Performance* (Oslo: Norwegian Institute of International Affairs, forthcoming).

40. John Hatch, *Two African Statesmen: Kaunda of Zambia and Nyerere of Tanzania* (London: Secker and Warburg, 1976), p. 196.

41. See D. A. Low and R. Cranford Pratt, *Buganda and British Overrule, 1900–1955* (London: Oxford University Press, 1960); L. A. Fallers, ed., *The King's Men: Leadership and Status in Buganda on the Eve of Independence* (London, New York, and Nairobi: Oxford University Press, 1964); D. A. Low, *Buganda in Modern History* (Berkeley and Los Angeles: University of California Press, 1971); and D. A. Low, *The Mind of Buganda: Documents of Modern History of an African Kingdom* (Berkeley and Los Angeles: University of California Press, 1971).

42. Cherry Gertzel, "Kingdoms, Districts, and the Unitary States: Uganda, 1945–62," in D. A. Low and Allison Smith, eds., *The Oxford History of East Africa*, vol. 3 (London: Oxford University Press, 1976), chap. 1.

43. G. F. Engholm and Ali A. Mazrui, "Violent Constitutionalism in Uganda," *Government and Opposition* 2, no. 4 (July–October 1967): 585–99; A. G. E. Gingyera-Pinycwa, *Apolo Milton Obote and His Times* (London, New York, and Lagos: NOK Publishers, 1978); Nelson Kasfir, "Cultural Sub-Nationalism in Uganda," in Victor A. Olorunsula, ed., *The Politics of Cultural Sub-Nationalism in Africa* (Garden City, N.J.: Doubleday, 1972); M. S. M. Kiwanuka, "Nationality and Nationalism in Africa: The Uganda Case," *Canadian Journal of African Studies* 9, no. 2 (Spring 1970): 229–47; Colin Leys, *Politicians and Policy: An Essay on Politics in Acholi, Uganda, 1962–65* (Nairobi: East African Publishing House, 1967); J. M. Lee, "Buganda's Position in Federal Uganda," *Journal of Commonwealth Studies*; Michael Lofchie, "The Uganda Coup — Class Action by the Military," *The Journal of Modern African Studies* 10, no. 1 (1972): 19–35; James Mittelman, *Ideology and Politics in Uganda: From Obote to Amin* (Ithaca, N.Y., and London: Cornell University Press, 1975); Edward Mutesa, *Desecration of My Kingdom* (London: Constable, 1967); Ali A. Mazrui, "Leadership in Africa: Obote of Uganda," *International Journal* 25, no. 3 (Summer 1979): 538–64; Akiiki B. Mujaju, "The Role of the UPC as a Party of Government in Uganda," *Canadian Journal of African Studies* 10, no. 3 (1976): 443–67; Apolo Nsibambi, "Political Integration in Uganda: Problems and Prospects," *East Africa Journal*, February 1963, pp. 31–39; Norman W. Provizer, "The National Electoral Process and State Building," *Comparative Politics*, April 1977, pp. 305–25; Selwyn D. Ryan, "Electoral Engineering in Uganda," *Mawazo* 2, no. 4 (December 1970): 3–12; see also "Economic Nationalism and Socialism in Uganda," *Journal of Commonwealth Political Studies* 10, no. 2 (July 1973): 140–58; T. V. Sathyamurthy, "The Social Base of the Uganda Peoples' Congress, 1958–79," *African Affairs* 74, no. 297 (October 1975): 442–46; Michael Twaddle, "The Amin Coup," *Journal of Commonwealth Political Studies* 10, no. 2 (July 1972): 99–112; Peter Willetts, "The Politics of Uganda as a One-Party State, 1969–1970," *African Affairs* 74, no. 296 (July 1975): 278–99; and M. Crawford Young, "The Obote Revolution," *Africa Report* 11, no. 6 (June 1966), pp. 177–87.

44. Garth Glentworth and Ian Hancock, "Obote and Amin: Change and

Continuity in Modern Uganda Politics," *African Affairs* 72, no. 288 (July 1973), pp. 237–55; Henry Kyemba, *A State of Blood: The Inside Story of Idi Amin* (New York: Ace Books, 1977); D. A. Low, "Uganda Unhinged," *International Affairs* 49, no. 2 (April 1973), pp. 219–28; Justin O'Brien, "General Amin and the Uganda Asians: Doing the Unthinkable," *The Round Table* no. 249 (January 1973): 91–104; and Jeffrey T. Strate, *Post-Military Coup in Uganda: Amin's Early Attempts to Consolidate Political Support* (Athens, Ohio: Ohio University Center for International Studies, 1973).

45. Tony Avirgan and Martha Honey, *War in Uganda: The Legacy of Idi Amin* (Wesport, Conn.: Lawrence Hill and Company, 1982); Cherry Gertzel, "Uganda After Amin: The Continuing Search for Leadership and Control," *African Affairs* 79, no. 317 (October 1980): 461–89; Donald Rothchild and John W. Harbeson, "Rehabilitation in Uganda," *Current History* 80, no. 463 (March 1981): 115–19, 134–38.

46. Buganda and the lesser kingdoms of Toro, Ankole, and Bunyoro had treaties with the British and were referred to as treaty states.

47. Quoted in Audrey Richards, *The Multicultural States of East Africa* (Montreal and London: McGill-Queen's University Press, 1969), p. 49.

48. Ibid., p. 45.

49. David E. Apter, *The Political Kingdom in Uganda: A Study in Bureaucratic Nationalism* (Princeton, N.J.: Princeton University Press, 1961), pp. 199–215, 263–300.

50. Ibid., p. 166.

51. John Lonsdale, "Uganda: Recent History Until 1971," *Africa South of the Sahara, 1976–77* (London: Europa Publications, 1976), p. 930.

52. Richards, *Multicultural States of East Africa*, p. 49.

53. The "Termination of British Protection" memorandum is reprinted in Apter, *Political Kingdom in Uganda*, pp. 479–88.

54. Donald Rothchild and Michael Rogin, "Uganda," in Gwendolen M. Carter, ed., *National Unity and Regionalism in Eight African States* (Ithaca, N.Y.: Cornell University Press, 1966), pp. 372–73.

55. Dr. A. Milton Obote, "Proposals for Document No. 1 on 'The Move to the Left'" (Prepared for the Annual Delegates' Conference of the Uganda People's Congress, December 1969).

56. "Extermination squads composed largely of Nilotic and Sudanic personnel purged the various army camps of suspected Obote loyalist officers and soldiers. Langi and Acholi officers were sequestered and individually murdered" (Samuel Decalo, *Coups and Army Rule in Africa: Studies in Military Style* [New Haven, Conn., and London: Yale University Press, 1976], p. 212).

57. The conclusions are summarized in Colin Legum, ed., *Africa Contemporary Record: Annual Survey and Documents, 1974–1975* (New York: Africana Publishing Company, 1975), pp. C 90–91.

58. L. A. Kayiira and E. Kannyo, "Politics and Violence in Uganda," *Africa Report* 23, no. 1 (January–February 1978): 42.

59. Aiden Southall, "Social Disorganization in Uganda: Before, During, and After Amin," *The Journal of Modern African Studies* 18, no. 4 (1980): p. 636.

60. According to one reliable report, perhaps 350,000 Ugandans lost their lives under Amin — many after torture — while thousands of others fled into exile. "Virtually the whole of the modernizing elite was either killed or fled abroad" (Legum, *Africa Contemporary Record, 1982–1983*, p. B 305).

61. See *Accelerated Development in Sub-Saharan Africa: An Agenda for Action*, table 2, p. 144. Under Amin, Uganda joined the list of degenerating African economies, which includes Chad, Upper Volta, Mozambique, Zaire, Ghana, and Angola.

62. "The money supply jumped from Shs. 1.7 bn in December 1970 to Shs. 10.3 bn at the end of March 1979" (Legum, *Africa Contemporary Record, 1980–1981*, p. B 382).

63. See F. J. Ravenhill, "Military Rule in Uganda: The Politics of Survival," *African Studies Review* 17, no. 1 (April 1974): 243–46 and M. J. Schultheis, "The Ugandan Economy and General Amin, 1971–1974," *Studies in Comparative International Development* 10, no. 3 (Fall 1975): 3–34.

64. Schultheis, "The Ugandan Economy and General Amin," pp. 18–19.

65. See the fascinating analaysis by Nelson Kasfir, "State, *Magendo*, and Class Formation in Uganda," *Journal of Commonwealth and Comparative Politics* 21, no. 3 (November 1983): 310–29.

66. Legum, *Africa Contemporary Record, 1980–1981*, p. B 383.

67. Southall, "Social Disorganization in Uganda," p. 645.

68. Legum, *Africa Contemporary Record, 1979–1980*, p. B 350.

69. Dudley Seer et al., *The Rehabilitation of the Economy of Uganda: A Report by a Commonwealth Team of Experts*, June 1979 (London: Commonwealth Secretariat, 1979), 1: 4, quoted in *Uganda: Country Memorandum* (Washington, D.C.: World Bank, 1982), p. 9.

70. Cherry Gertzel, "Uganda After Amin: The Continuing Search for Leadership and Control," *African Affairs* 79, no. 317 (October 1980): 462.

71. "Uganda Elections, December 1980: The Report of the Commonwealth Observer Group" (London: Commonwealth Secretariat, 1980).

72. Achieng Owino, "Uganda at Crisis Point," *New Africa*, no. 183 (December 1982): 13. In July 1982, Amnesty International reported that human rights were still being violated with impunity, mainly by the army. But a British human-rights investigator and member of Parliament reported in November that Obote's government was openly acknowledging the problem of human-rights violations by soldiers and was cooperating with external investigators to an unusual degree (Legum, *Africa Contemporary Record, 1982–1983*, p. B 311).

73. See Colin Legum, "After the Amin Nightmare," *Africa Report* 28, no. 1 (January–February 1983): 17.

74. George Bennett, *Kenya: A Political History* (London: Oxford University Press, 1963); Ruth Dilley, *British Policy in Kenya Colony* (New York: Thomas Nelson and Sons, 1937); Elspeth Huxley, *White Man's Country: Lord Delamere and the Making of Kenya*, 2 vols. (London Chatto and Windus, 1935); and Elspeth Huxley and Margery Perham, *Race and Politics in Kenya* (London: Faber and Faber, 1956).

75. Carl G. Rosberg and John Nottingham, *The Myth of "Mau Mau": Nationalism in Kenya* (New York: Frederick A. Praeger, 1966).

76. George Bennett and Carl G. Rosberg, *The Kenyatta Election: Kenya 1960–1961* (London: Oxford University Press, 1961), pp. 3–45.

77. *Majimbo* is a Swahili term denoting regions; hence, a regionally based not a centralized government.

78. See Clyde Sanger and John Nottingham, "The Kenya General Election of 1963," *The Journal of Modern African Studies* 2, no. 1 (1964): 1–40.

79. See Oginga Odinga, *Not Yet Uhuru: An Autobiography* (London: Heinemann, 1967).

80. Cherry Gertzel, *The Politics of Independent Kenya, 1963–8* (Evanston, Ill.: Northwestern University Press, 1970), pp. 73–124; and David Koff, "Kenya's Little General Election," *Africa Report* 11, no. 7 (October 1966): 57–60.

81. For an outstanding study of a major Kenyan leader, see David Goldsworthy, *Tom Mboya: The Man Kenya Wanted to Forget* (New York: Africana Publishing Company, 1982); for Mboya's political views on the eve of independence see Tom Mboya, *Freedom And After* (London: Andre Deutsch, 1963).

82. For a historical account of Kenyatta as a nationalist leader see Jeremy Murray-Brown, *Kenyatta* (New York: E. P. Dutton, 1973); also see Donald C. Savage, "Kenyatta and the Development of African Nationalism in Kenya," *International Journal* 25, no. 3 (Summer 1970): 518–37.

83. For a study of Kenya's politics and governance in the first decade see Henry Bienen, *Kenya: The Politics and Participation and Control* (Princeton, N.J.: Princeton University Press, 1974).

84. Cherry Gertzel, "The Provincial Administration in Kenya," *Journal of Commonwealth Political Studies* 4, no. 3 (1966): 201–15.

85. M. P. K. Sorrenson, *Land Reform in the Kikuyu Country* (London: Oxford University Press, 1967).

86. For a study of the politics of farm settlement schemes see John W. Harbison, *Nation-Building in Kenya: The Role of Land Reform* (Evanston, Ill.: Northwestern University Press, 1973).

87. For an excellent study see Arthur Hazelwood, *The Economy of Kenya: The Kenyatta Era* (New York: Oxford University Press, 1979); also see Judith Heyer, "Agricultural Development Policy in Kenya from the Colonial Period to 1975," Judith Heyer, Pepe Roberts, and Gavin Williams, eds., *Rural Development in Tropical Africa* (New York: St. Martin's Press, 1981), p. 52.

88. Robert H. Bates, *Markets and States in Tropical Africa: The Political Basis of Agricultural Policies* (Berkeley, Los Angeles, and London: University of California Press, 1981).

89. See *World Development Report 1983* (Washington: World Bank and Oxford University Press, 1983), pp. 192–98.

90. *World Development Report 1983* (Washington: World Bank and Oxford University Press, 1983), p. 200; see also Hazelwood, *Economy of Kenya*, pp. 175–204.

91. See Colin Leys, *Underdevelopment in Kenya: The Political Economy of Neo-Colonialism* (Berkeley and Los Angeles: University of California Press, 1974); and Nicola Swainson, *The Development of Corporate Capitalism in Kenya, 1918–1977* (Berkeley and Los Angeles: University of California Press, 1980).

92. *World Development Report 1983*, p. 200.

93. Leys, *Underdevelopment in Kenya*, pp. 246–49.

94. Joel D. Barkhan and John J. Okumu, "Linkage Without Parties: Legislator and Constituents in Kenya," in Kay Lawson, eds., *Political Parties and Linkages: A Comparative Perspective* (New Haven and London: Yale University Press, 1980), pp. 289–324; Joel D. Barkhan, "Legislators, Elections, and Political Linkage" in Joel D. Barkan and John J. Okumu, eds., *Politics and Public Policy in Kenya and Tanzania* (New York: Praeger Publishers, 1979), pp. 64–92; for studies of factions see Cherry Gertzel, "Factions in Kenyan Politics: An Overview" (School of Social Sciences, The Flinders University of South Australia, n.d.). Richard Stren, "Factional Politics and Central Control in Mombasa, 1960–1969," *Canadian Journal of African Studies* 4, no. 1 (Winter 1970): 33–56; Gideon Cyrus Mutiso, *Kenya, Politics and Society* (Nairobi: East African Literature Bureau, 1975), pp. 209–48; Geoff Lamb, *Peasant Politics: Conflict and Development in Muranga* (New York: St. Martin's Press, 1974); and Richard Sandbrook, *Proletarians and African Capitalism: The Kenyan Case, 1960–1972* (London and New York: Cambridge University Press, 1975), pp. 123–43.

95. Legum, *Africa Contemporary Record, 1976–1977*, p. B 219.

96. The World Bank projection for the period 1980–2000 gives Kenya the highest rate in the world at 4.5 percent (*World Development Report 1982*, pp. 184–85).

97. Legum, *Africa Contemporary Record, 1982–1983*, pp. B 187–90; *Report and Recommendations of the Working Party, Appointed by His Excellency the President*, Chairman Philip Ndegwa (Nairobi: Republic of Kenya, 1982).

98. Legum, *African Contemporary Record, 1982–1983*, pp. B-172–183.
99. *Africa*, no. 152 (April 1984): 72.

6 THE HORN OF AFRICA

Christopher Clapham

INTRODUCTION

The Horn of Africa is a region of peculiar character; its incorporation in a survey of black Africa since independence presents distinctive problems of comparative perspective. In a sense, much that has
taken place in this region during the past quarter-century seems
familiar enough; the problems caused by the imposition of artificial
boundaries, ethnic conflicts, the decay of civilian political institutions, and subsequent military takeovers have been quite as intense
in the Horn as in other parts of the continent. The region shares
with the Third World as a whole the difficulties resulting from
economic and (particularly in this region) military dependence on
the industrial states. But the setting is nevertheless different.
Central to an understanding of the Horn is the premise that the
political evolution of the region is driven by an indigenous, and not
an imported, dynamic of statehood. Three striking facts serve to
illustrate this dynamic. First, of the five territories that made up the
region during the main part of the classic colonial period from 1890
to 1950, only one (the insignificant microstate of Djibouti) has
followed the postcolonial pattern prevalent in other parts of Africa
and attained independence as a separate state; the others —
Ethiopia, Eritrea, former British Somaliland and Italian Somalia
— have been incorporated into larger units whose boundaries ultimately derive from the late nineteenth-century partition but whose
ethos go back to precolonial identities. Second, the region has
experienced a level of political violence both within and between
states that even exceeds the violence produced by settler colonialism
and failed decolonization in the southern part of the continent and
that derives directly from the conflicting structures of statehood in
Ethiopia and the Somali Republic. Third, the two main states in the
region have both experienced real revolutions (not simply military
coups); Ethiopia in particular has provided the most unequivocal
example of revolution anywhere in Africa. This chapter will
explore the implications of this peculiar dynamic of statehood and
its effects on the range of issues dealt with in this volume.

In terms of size, centrality of position, and historic dominance, the core state of the region is the ancient empire of Ethiopia. Ethiopia was the sole indigenous black African state to survive as an independent unit throughout almost the whole of the colonial period. For many centuries its social and economic strength was derived from the comparatively densely populated communities of the central Ethiopian plateau. It had a broadly feudal political structure headed by an Emperor (or King of Kings). Its religious self-identity was derived from the practice of Coptic Orthodox Christianity; this sharply demarcated its peoples from those of surrounding regions where Islam and animistic religions prevailed. Moreover, Ethiopia has long been an empire — and not simply because of its domestic form of government. The imperial ethos has also been tied to an intensely held belief in Ethiopia's manifest destiny to rule over its peripheries. This belief derived ideological justification from an assumption that non-Christian peoples were inferior, economic incentive from the wealth acquired by the extraction of resources from (and trade through) these peripheral areas, and political impetus from the fact that (unlike the produce of the core areas, which was easily appropriated by local lords) much of this surplus could be monopolized by the emperor and used to strengthen the central government. As happened in France after 1789 and Russia after 1917, the ancient dynamic of empire has been adapted for, and intensified by, the new revolutionary regime; the ideology of a Marxist-Leninist republic has simply replaced that of a Coptic empire as a legitimating formula for central dominance and national integration.

Although its population is no more multiethnic than many African states, Ethiopia is a state formed of a core and a periphery. A state thus formed stands in much greater danger of being rejected by its components than one formed (like Zaire or Nigeria) by the fortuitous combination of colonized peoples. The two most overt challenges to the Ethiopian state have come from its Somali population (who are understandably attracted to the neighboring Somali Republic) and from the Eritreans (who, although themselves ethnically divided, have sought to create a new nationalism on the basis of the old Italian colonial territory). A more fundamental threat may yet come from the Oromo or Galla peoples. These groups never constituted a common political unit, and to some extent they have been incorporated into the national political structure. But together they form the largest single ethnic group in Ethiopia — more numerous than even the historically dominant Amhara of the central plateau.

The dynamic of Somali nationhood differs from both the multi-ethnic imperialism of Ethiopia and the inherited colonial statism of most of the rest of Africa. Alone among African states, the Somali Republic is derived from the sense of self-identity of a single people who possess a common history, culture, religion, and language (but who have never been governed by common political institutions). The Somali nation is composed of people who — because of language, culture, and descent — consider themselves to be Somali. For other African states, boundaries have been as given, and the national mission has been to construct some sense of identity among those peoples who chanced to find themselves within them. For the Somalis, the sense of nationhood has been taken as given, and the national mission has been to expand the formal boundaries of the state to encompass all those peoples who already identified themselves as Somali. At independence in 1960, this attempt initially resulted in the successful integration of the former British and Italian Somalilands into a single state. It has subsequently resulted in conflict with Ethiopia, and — more generally — with the African conception of statehood, which is based on respect for the boundaries inherited from colonialism and is entrenched in the principles of the Organization of African Unity (OAU).

The tragedy of both states in the Horn has been that the civilian political institutions they inherited (in the one instance, from decolonization, and in the other, from the imperial tradition) have proved quite inadequate to achieve their national goals — goals that, moreover, have been particularly ingrained in the thinking of their armies. Because of this, in both cases military intervention did not simply result in a guardian regime pledged to an eventual restoration of a liberal democratic political order, but in an avowedly Marxist-Leninist government pledged to a comprehensive plan for national transformation.

In each case, therefore, revolution may be interpreted as a response to the failure of existing institutions to achieve the objectives implicit in the national dynamic of statehood. The objective of the revolutionary regimes has been the achievement of what their predecessors sought, but failed, to accomplish; the means selected has in each case consisted of an intensification of the power of the state. The role of political institutions has not been entirely neglected, but it has been very strictly subordinated to that of state institutions backed by military force. This emphasis has in turn engendered a high level of dependence on external military patrons. Not surprisingly, this intensification of state power has provoked a corresponding level of opposition. The opposition has been most marked in Ethiopia, where the basis for nationhood has always rested on an inherent discrimination against peripheral ethnic groups (if not necessarily against individuals from peripheral areas). In both Ethiopia and the Somali Republic, the capacity of the revolutionary regimes to achieve their ambitious goals has remained very much open to question.

IMPERIAL ETHIOPIA

This volume's baseline date of "independence" is a delightfully inapposite one for a state that has been independent in recognizable form for some two thousand years; an equivalent date for Ethiopia, however, would be 1941, when Haile-Selassie was restored to his throne following Italy's five-year occupation. Haile-Selassie had been emperor since 1930 (and regent in 1916 under the name Ras Tafari, by which he was well known to the black people of the Americas), but his restoration marked one of the clearest junctures in a process of monarchical evolution that had been under way in Ethiopia since 1855. Over that period two major changes in the nature of the monarchy had been taking place. First, a previously well-established system of succession by descent had been replaced by a struggle for power, in which the title of King of Kings had become the prize for whichever regional warlord could impose his authority on the others and (from about 1900) gain control of the capital at Addis Ababa. (Haile-Selassie gained power in 1916 in the same way that he lost it nearly sixty years later — by coup d'etat.) Second, a feudal monarchy, in which political power was derived from the control of land and the peasantry who worked it, was progressively replaced by a centralizing autocracy, in which power derived from the control of a state apparatus. The main trends in this process of monarchical modernization were the development of a central standing army controlled by the emperor (in place of levies controlled by local governors), the development of a central administrative machinery, and the creation of a cash economy to sustain the army and bureaucracy. Because of the need for arms, skills, and markets, all these developments resulted in increased interaction with the industrial world and helped to create a state that was in some ways analogous to those simultaneously being forged by colonial administrations in other parts of Africa.

By the time of the liberation from Italian occupation in 1941, this process was well advanced. The provincial nobility had been so weakened by the occupation that it was possible to replace the pre-war patchwork of governance by a hierarchical system in which the emperor — although he paid some attention to local susceptibilities — had a much greater control over appointments. The army, the central bureaucracy, and the taxation system were reorganized with the help of British advisers. (In order to counter the dominance of the United Kingdom in the region at this time, Haile-Selassie actively pursued relations with the United States.) The period after 1941 was, in a sense, one of rapid institutional development. But it was a development of governmental capability — not of political organization or popular participation. The key institution was still the monarchy, and to this Haile-Selassie brought an acute political mind and a relentless concern for administrative detail.

From liberation until 1955 (and to some degree until the overthrow of the monarchy in 1974) the emperor — and the court institutions surrounding him — continued to constitute the linchpin of the administration. Haile-Selassie was never an autocrat, as defined in *Personal Rule in Black Africa*.[1] He was, rather, the ideal type of the prince, concerned not so much with laying down policy himself as with guiding and manipulating a group of courtier-politicians, whom he kept dancing attendance on the throne. (This technique is made easier in a monarchy, since every member of the political class is ascriptively excluded from the top position in the state. In Ethiopia, the one person not so excluded — Crown Prince Asfa-Wassen — was kept at arm's length and was allowed only a minor role in the government.)

The principal decision-making mechanism was a formalized system of weekly appointments, called *aqabe saat*, in which individual ministers and some other notables brought matters for decision to the emperor; the resulting imperial orders were issued through an official known, appropriately, as the Minister of the Pen, who thereby became the emperor's chief of staff. Walda-Giyorgis, who held this office from 1941 to 1955, was the dominant figure in the government at that time. His power easily outranked that of the figurehead prime minister, Makonnen Endalkachew. Like other key officials — including the ministers of finance, commerce, and foreign affairs — Walda-Giyorgis was a commoner of humble background. His maneuvers within the introverted politics of the palace reflected the characteristic conflict in court administrations between imperial protégés (like himself) and noblemen (like the prime minister) who enjoyed some independent status. The commoners tended to predominate in areas of government that required a higher level of education and technical expertise; the noblemen predominated in fields like defense and provincial administration. The leaders of the resistance to the Italian occupation of 1936–1941, known as the Patriots, were generally associated with the noble faction. Having fought their own battles for Ethiopia at a time when the emperor and his entourage had retired to safety in England, these former leaders enjoyed both prestige and a measure of local political support independent of the throne. Although they were considered incapable of seriously challenging the concentration of power in Haile-Selassie's hands, they bore close watching, they were responsible for a number of plots and provincial revolts in the postliberation period.

Recruitment to political office was carried out by means of the classic processes of patronage appropriate to a patrimonial administration. The emperor's role as provider of benefits was symbolized by his purely formal tenure as head of the Ministry of Education and by his practice of receiving Ethiopians leaving for or returning from education abroad. Supplicants for office were expected to submit to a period of formal waiting on the emperor, known as *dej tenat*. Those who achieved political, rather than career, administrative posts almost invariably had patrons or relatives at court. Ministers generally held office for many years at a stretch, except for occasional reshuffles among an established group of courtier-politicians. (During the period 1955–1960, however, rapid upheavals reflecting factional instability followed the dismissal of the previously dominant Walda-Giyorgis.) Considerable maneuvering over office reflected a rivalry between factions and followings that was manipulated by the emperor in order to maximize his own freedom of action.

These factions, however, were based on personal connections and social origins rather than on ideological orientations, policy prescriptions, or bases for political support. Most importantly, they did not reflect regional or ethnic differences. In the quarter-century following liberation over 60 percent of high officials came from the central province of Shoa, including Addis Ababa. These people benefited both from the heavy concentration of educational opportunities in the capital and from the preferential access to patronage available to the followers of what was an essentially Shoan monarchy.[2] For example, quite a number of officials were associated with the group of Shoan administrators who had worked under Haile-Selassie's father — and later Haile-Selassie himself — in Harar in southeast Ethiopia in the late nineteenth and early twentieth centuries.

This Shoan bias of the imperial government was much more evident than any ethnically exclusive Amharan domination. Shoa lies at the southern edge of the Amhara area (Addis Ababa is on the borderline between Amhara and Oromo), and many Shoans — including Haile-Selassie — are a mixture of the two ethnic groups. The important point was that this Shoan ruling elite inherited the statist tradition of imperial Ethiopia. Its primary goal was the maintenance of effective central government — not simply the domination of a particular ethnic or religious group.

The next most numerous contingent in the central government came from Eritrea. In the same twenty-five year period, Eritreans accounted for 14 percent of high officials; Tigre, Gojjam, Bagemder, and the Oromo province of Wallega provided 5 percent each. The rest of the country (especially the southern provinces, with the exception of Wallega) was almost entirely excluded. Moreover, even those ministers who came from outlying areas of the country, did not represent these areas in any real sense. They did not regularly visit their regions of origin, had no political organizations to provide ties with their constituencies, and, by the act of accepting central government office, largely cut themselves off from their homelands. At most, they might show favor to protégés from the region by building patronage networks in the central government (as did Yilma Deressa, a long-serving minister of finance and a Wallega Oromo).

At sub-court levels, some institutionalization of the state machinery took place because of the need for technical expertise, the sheer expansion of the administration, and (from the mid-1960s onwards) the aged emperor's progressively failing stamina. In the late 1940s and early 1950s technical responsibilities — such as those required by the national airline, highways, and telecommunications systems — were assigned to specialized parastatal organizations. The intent was to provide an appropriate institutional mechanism to accommodate foreign management and external fund-raising. At first, some of these organizations — like Ethiopian Airlines and the Imperial Highway Authority — were managed by seconded personnel from foreign corporations; most were Ethiopianized in the early and mid-1960s. (It was a matter of some pride to the country that Ethiopian pilots began to fly commercial jets at a time when other African airlines were still relying on Europeans.)

Foreigners never attained executive positions in the regular bureaucracy, but advisers of many nationalities provided professional expertise in fields such as accounting, legislative drafting, and negotiation with multinational corporations. Foreign training was both essential and especially delicate in the armed forces. At liberation, the British took the responsibility of forming the new professional Ethiopian army, but their position was always uneasy. They controlled almost all of the surrounding territory, did little to encourage the Ethiopian government's determination to absorb the former Italian colony of Eritrea (which they administered), and — by means of their brief sponsorship of the Bevin Plan for Somali unification — threatened the territorial integrity of Ethiopia itself. The British military mission was withdrawn in 1951 and replaced by a U.S. mission that remained until after the revolution. In order to ensure that no single foreign state could gain a monopoly, however, Swedes and Norwegians were brought in to train the air force and the navy, respectively.

The expansion of bureaucracy resulted in an increase in the powers of the second prime minister, Alilu Habtewald, who absorbed the Ministry of the Pen after Walda-Giyorgis' dismissal and, from 1961 onwards, turned the Prime Ministry into the co-ordinating center for the civil administration. The aqabe saat remained, but it was supplemented by regular meetings of the Council of Ministers. Beginning in 1966 the prime minister formally gained the power to appoint his own ministers — a power that he did not use in any way that challenged the pre-eminence of the throne. The constitutional model implicit in this gradual process of devolution was an English one — a long-drawn-out shift in power from the court to central institutions that in some distant future, would become politically accountable to an elected parliament. The problem was that those to whom power was being transferred had no political base from which to exercise it. The construction of specifically political institutions had scarcely begun. Indeed, the leitmotif of the emperor's reign had been the dismantling of such institutions as existed — to the advantage of a bureaucratic state run by himself.

The techniques used with such success against the provincial nobility were called into play after 1952 to disarm the threat presented by the autonomous Eritrean administration. This administration was federated with Ethiopia under the terms of a U.N. General Assembly resolution and derived its authority from elections conducted on a political party basis. Over the ten-year period from 1952 to 1962, Eritrea was converted from a multiparty autonomous region to a no-party province incorporated within the ordinary administrative hierarchy of the empire. (This process echoes the similar fate shared by liberal-democratic institutional arrangements elsewhere in postcolonial Africa, in which neither multiparty nor federal systems have enjoyed much success; it is not necessary to postulate any peculiarly Ethiopian antipathy to inconvenient political institutions.)

Ethiopia's differences from almost all other African states lay partly in the core-periphery configuration already discussed and (with the exception of Eritrea) partly in the total absence of a period of permitted political mobilization like that produced by decolonization elsewhere on the continent. The most obvious explanation why this mobilization did not take place is that there was no need for it; an already-independent state required no nationalist movement. But a more basic explanation — and one that accounts for the central government's special hostility to parties in Eritrea — is that mobilization carried with it the inherent risk of articulating and intensifying the latent tension that existed between periphery and core. The suppression of participation did not, of course, avert the danger; it produced in Eritrea a guerrilla liberation movement in many ways more dangerous than a simple opposition party would have been. But whether the central government sought to prevent participation or to channel and control it, the growth of participation necessarily threatened the survival of a state historically dependent on a high level of central control. It is a problem that the revolutionary regime has found it equally difficult to resolve.

The one attempt made by the imperial regime — however halfheartedly and inadequately — to meet the requirements of political participation was to create the revised constitution of 1955. This constitution provided that beginning in 1957, one chamber of the bicameral parliament was to be directly elected by universal adult suffrage and the other was to be appointed by the emperor. Although political parties were never formally banned, no one had the temerity to start one, and candidates stood for election on the strength of their local connections. The House of Representatives was chiefly composed of rural notables (along with a few ambitious persons like small-town school teachers anxious to move to Addis Ababa). In the southern provinces, elections were sometimes rigged to favor settlers or officials from the north.

In the capital Parliament had some influence on legislation but virtually no control over the executive. Members of Parliament sometimes challenged the government on matters that affected their interests (such as a proposed agricultural income tax) but managed to establish no authority remotely sufficient to enable them to withstand (let alone profit from) the upheavals that were to come. Other channels for political organization were rigorously controlled. One instructive example of such control was an Oromo-Galla cultural and self-help association, Metcha Tulama, set up in 1966. This association encompassed a large group of people and therefore carried dangerous implications. It was immediately suppressed (although associations catering to much smaller population groups and areas were permitted to exist). Other permissible channels for making political demands were personalist in nature and extremely limited in scope; the main one consisted of the right to make a humble petition to the Emperor. The government's response likewise took the form of imperial benevolence. (Its inadequacy was never more sharply exposed than in its way of dealing with the catastrophic famine in eastern Ethiopia in 1973–1974.)

This nonpolitical system, although highly adept at dealing with factional rivalries within the setting of the court, was virtually incapable of handling demands made by any substantial, mobilized section of the population. There were two constituencies from which demands of this sort might be expected to arise: the urban educated elites and the unrepresented rural dwellers. Of the two, the first constituency was the more immediate and articulate; the second, ultimately the more dangerous. The urban elites were, of course, the essential instruments of Haile-Selassie's centralization goals. They constituted the armed forces (especially the officer corps) and the civil bureaucracy and were recruited from a student population heavily concentrated in Addis Ababa. The earliest generation of bureaucrats and officers looked to the throne as an ally and protector, and the postwar graduates who made it to the top benefited from imperial patronage. For subsequent generations, however, the monarchy was, at best, an irrelevance, and for many it provoked feelings of deep and violent disgust, which in 1960 (and again in 1974) were expressed in the gratuitous massacre of courtier-politicians.

By Samuel Huntington's criteria in *Political Order in Changing Societies*, Ethiopia was ripe for a "breakthrough coup," which would transfer control of the government to the urban elites on which it already effectively relied.[3] Something of this kind was attempted in December 1960, when the commander of the imperial bodyguard and his brother (a radical graduate of an American university) launched a coup that drew on the modernizing rhetoric of nationalist leaders elsewhere in the continent. Apart from university students in Addis Ababa, the attempt gained little overt support, and it was crushed by loyalist forces within a few days. Sporadic student demonstrations throughout the 1960s and early 1970s nevertheless served as a touchstone for latent urban opposition to the regime, and the danger of further intervention enabled the armed forces to exact a series of pay rises from the government. The regime sought to insure the loyalty of individual officers by means of traditional measures such as providing them grants of land in the southern provinces.

Land alienation was a potential trigger for rural opposition — capable in Huntington's terms, of leading not to "urban breakthrough" but to "green uprising." It was often assumed that the countryside constituted a reservoir of traditionalist support for the monarchy, which the emperor could call upon if he needed to suppress opposition in the towns. In fact, Haile-Selassie's life's work had consisted of a deliberate reduction of the power of the countryside so that it would not pose a threat to his own centralized urban administration. As is usual in the Third World, however, the countryside provided most of the economic resources on which this administration relied. Ethiopia had an almost entirely agricultural economy; like other African states, it was dependent on the sale of cash crops on the international market. By far the most important of these was coffee, which accounted for over half of Ethiopia's export earnings.

The two most important characteristics of Ethiopian cash crop agriculture were first, its location, and second, the mechanism for its exploitation. Cash crops were not grown in the central Ethiopian plateau that stretched from Addis Ababa north to Tigre. Here, an unincorporated peasantry held its land under traditional tenure systems and was able to retain control over production. Agriculture in this region was therefore heavily oriented toward subsistence. Cash agriculture was restricted almost entirely to peripheral areas — partly because of ecological considerations, but also because in these areas the central government could alienate land and control the labor force in a way that was not possible in the core area. Some of this land was owned by local notables and small holders, but large tracts had been taken over by central government nominees — including members of the imperial family. Land grants were the standard method of rewarding government service, and local governors could get land for themselves by fair means or foul. (Coffee land in the southwest was especially sought after.) Agricultural development schemes — like one that was implemented with Swedish aid in Arusi Province south of Addis Ababa — led to the expulsion of peasants so that landlords could benefit from more efficient and mechanized means of exploiting their holdings.[4]

Although this system of agriculture was dependent on state power, the state itself undertook virtually no direct productive activity. National coffee and grain boards served as buying and marketing agencies, and, in the area southeast of Addis Ababa, the Awash Valley Authority regulated relations with multinationals that were chiefly engaged in sugar and cotton production. Multinational penetration into the economy was not great, however, and this was the only major area of agricultural production not in Ethiopian hands. (Mineral production was almost nonexistent; other multinationals were restricted to import-export trade, services, and low-level import-substitute industrialization.)

Rural opposition movements could therefore cite a combination of economic exploitation and political alienation. The regime was in no position to address these grievances because of its own revenue requirements and its centralizing ethos — not to mention the interests of the landowning class both at the center and in the peripheral regions themselves. The only mechanisms employed to deal with rural opposition were the cooptation of local notables (by appointing them to minor government office or, more often, by simply granting them honorific titles) and the imposition of force. Even in the Amhara heartland, the government had very little ability to deal with revolts — such as the one in Gojjam, which was induced by the imposition of an agricultural income tax in 1968.

(The regime had similar problems with a number of local insurgencies that broke out, notably in Bale province, in the emperor's later years.) By far the most important revolts, however, took place in Eritrea and the Somali-inhabited areas; the experience of political mobilization and autonomy (in the first area) and the common heritage of Somali nationalism (in the second) provided a focus for an alternative political identity.

By early 1974 a number of unrelated factors combined to bring about the empire's collapse. The most dramatic of these was a devastating drought and resulting famine in eastern Ethiopia that caused thousands of deaths. The government's efforts to hush up the extent of this tragedy did much to destroy the emperor's carefully nurtured image as the protector of his people. A mutiny in a distant southern garrison demonstrated the depths of discontent in the lower ranks of the army. A strike by Addis Ababa taxi drivers (in protest of higher petrol prices produced by the OPEC price increase) triggered a series of riots, strikes, and demonstrations in the towns. Attempts to stave off disaster with hasty governmental and constitutional changes ended in failure. On 12 September 1974 the monarch was deposed, and an anonymous committee of the armed forces — the Derg — took control of the government.

REVOLUTIONARY ETHIOPIA

The collapse of the empire in 1974 did not simply lead to a new regime; it also critically challenged the survival of the Ethiopian state. Ethiopia had hitherto survived as a political unit only by way of the centralized control exercised by the monarch; a wealth of experience and popular lore associated imperial weakness with central government collapse. Haile-Selassie's deposition introduced a sense of profound uncertainty and resulted in an immediate weakening of the links between the periphery and the government in Addis Ababa. The empire fell because it had been unable to create any effective political institutions through which demands for participation could be channeled. Such institutions were lacking in the urban area but also (and more basically) in the national periphery and the countryside as a whole. The fall of the empire therefore sharply pointed up the question of whether any such institutions could be created, and if so, on what basis. This was a problem that required solutions at both the urban and the national level and, ultimately, at the international level. In the decade that followed the collapse of the empire, it became clear that Ethiopia was no Habsburg state, dependent on its dynasty for survival, but that it had reserves of nationhood that would be set against equally intense pressures for fragmentation. The problem of institution-building, however, has remained unresolved.

The urban situation appeared to be the most straightforward, since the main problem in this area seemed to be the monarchy itself. Much of the impetus for the creeping revolution of 1974 had stemmed from a disgust with the narrow self-centeredness of the old regime (an attitude that was most cruelly revealed during the famine by the contrast between the conditions of the emperor's pampered lapdogs and the thousands of people dying in Wallo). This disgust was shared by the army, the intelligentsia, and city dwellers in general. It was gruesomely expressed in the massacre of some sixty of the ex-emperor's leading supporters in November 1974 — an action by which the new regime also indicated that they were set on on a course from which there would be no turning back.

Nevertheless, urban unity proved difficult to achieve. The formal ruling institution after September 1974 — the Provisional Military Administrative Council (PMAC, which directed the Provisional Military Government of Socialist Ethiopia, or PMGSE) — derived its origin from the Derg, a shadowy body composed of three representatives from each of the forty-two principal military units. The Derg had proved extremely effective in maintaining the unity of the armed forces during the long-drawn-out takeover of power, but it was far too cumbersome to serve as an instrument of government. Its representative basis was swiftly eroded (since units could not recall and replace the delegates they had appointed), the views of its members were varied and often uncertain, and it was riven by personal political rivalries. The first chairman of the PMAC, General Aman Andon (who was not a member of the Derg), was killed during the massacre of government officials in November 1974, in large measure because he advocated reconciliation with the rebels in Eritrea. The execution of his two leading supporters within the Derg ushered in a period during which the penalty for failure was death. A ruling triumvirate then emerged, in which Brigadier Tafari Bante assumed chairmanship of the PMAC, with two junior officers — Mengistu Haile-Maryam and Atnafu Abate — as his deputies. Mengistu killed Tafari in February 1977 and Atnafu the following November. With his rivals out of the way, he emerged at the head of a rump of the original Derg, from which position he consolidated his leadership over the next few years.

The achievement of control over urban civilian groups was equally violent. Far from being a conventional military coup, the overthrow of Haile-Selassie had involved sustained participation by the people of Addis Ababa in strikes and demonstrations throughout much of 1974. These people (and especially their leaders) were reluctant to see this process culminate in a military government in which they would have no say. The first attempts to organize the urban population were made by political factions (it would be a misnomer to call them parties) that had arisen among radical Ethiopian students both at home and abroad in the late 1960s and early 1970s. The two main groups — Meison (an Amharic acronym for the All Ethiopia Socialist Party) and the Ethiopian Peoples' Revolutionary Party (EPRP) — differed in strategy, tactics, and composition. Although both were Marxist in ideology, Meison had a higher proportion of southerners (especially Oromo) in its leadership, was more committed to Ethiopian national unity, and was prepared to work in tactical alliance with the PMAC to seek an ultimate transfer of power to a socialist ruling party (itself). In the early years of the revolution it was extremely successful in persuading the military leadership to adopt the measures that were to push Ethiopia in an irrevocably revolutionary direction. EPRP included a higher proportion of northerners (especially Tigreans and Eritreans), was more open to the possibility of secession, and regarded the army not as a potential ally, but as a repressive force inherently opposed to the liberation of the masses.

The clash between Meison and EPRP, and between EPRP and the Derg, got under way only gradually. Initially, all these organizations were very small, many of their leaders were still abroad, and their positions were ill-defined. Meison operated in collaboration with the more radical wing of the Derg and became the leading force in an umbrella organization — the Provisional Office of Mass Organizational Affairs (POMOA) — that was intended to be the nucleus of an eventual mass party. Meison founded an ideological training school and moved its adherents into the *kebelles*, or urban associations, the base units of urban administration that were the first revolutionary grassroots organizations formed by the regime. The EPRP was much better established among the student body and had links with trade unionists and other opponents of the Derg. When it was cornered by the regime in September 1976, it resorted to a policy of urban terrorism that was directed as much against Meison as against the Derg. The EPRP was crushed in the pitiless "red terror" of 1977, in which several thousand militants were killed. Meison did not long survive it. After the death of Tafari Bante early in 1977, Meison lost much of its influence over the military leadership. Tafari had been prepared to envisage a mass party built up from the base, but the new strongman Mengistu was only interested in a loyal party built from the top downwards. Meison was no longer needed as a counterweight to the EPRP. In the atmosphere of wartime crisis that followed the Somali invasion of July 1977, Meison's attitude on the national question was suspect. Additionally, by this time the regime had been strengthened by the promise of massive Soviet military aid. When Meison went underground in August 1977, PMAC's control of the cities became complete, but, by the same token, the country was left with no institutional structure through which civilian participation in the regime could be channeled and consolidated.

The attempt to create institutions to link the new regime to the countryside ran into similar (but more serious) difficulties. In 1974 it was easy to postulate that the basic problem (in the countryside, as in the cities) had been the structure of the old regime and that once this was altered, all groups would be able to coalesce around a common national interest expressed by a socialist ideology. For example, the Eritrean insurgency could be seen not as a war of national liberation, but as a class struggle against Ethiopian feudalism that had been forced into a secessionist policy by the nature of the central regime. But just as it had in the cities, the destruction of the old regime starkly illuminated issues associated with political power in the countryside that could not be resolved even by a shared ideological framework.

Nevertheless, a genuine attempt was made. The new regime immediately set about a program to demystify and destroy the institutions through which the cultural supremacy of the core had been expressed. This included the elimination of the special status given to the Orthodox Church and (to some degree) to the Amharic language. Thousands of students were despatched to the countryside in a campaign (called the *zemecha*) to educate the peasantry and create the type of urban-rural linkages that the previous imperial government had so totally neglected. Most importantly, the abolition of private landholding in March 1975 removed the economic basis of core denomination and destroyed the landowning class by which this domination had been maintained.

At the same time, the PMAC continued its rigid insistence on the doctrine entrenched in the ethos of the Ethiopian army — that the unity of the national territory was sacred. This stand prompted the regime's first major internal crisis. In November 1974 the PMAC's chairman — the liberal Eritrean Aman Andom — was killed for advocating reconciliation with the secessionists in Eritrea. For their part, the Eritrean liberation movements were reluctant to submit themselves to a regime based on their old enemy the Ethiopian army, regardless of how ideologically enlightened it had become. Similar problems arose in other areas. *Zemecha* students — enthusiastically involved in implementing the land reform — found themselves confronting a local administration that was run by settlers from the core areas and that had historically served as a political adjunct to the exploitative landowning economy. The land nationalization scheme, which was greeted with great enthusiasm in the south, aroused deep suspicions in areas of the north where peasants controlled their own means of production. Caught in the contradictions inherent in a centralizing socialism, many of the *zemecha* students fled or went into opposition.

From the central government's point of view, the old land tenure system served two essential functions. It extracted a food surplus from the peasantry that could be used to feed the cities, and it produced the cash crops for export that sustained the central government apparatus. Once this system was demolished, the flow of food to the cities decreased. This decrease was partly a result of the upheavals caused by land reform, but it was also partly caused by low buying prices and the fact that the peasants simply consumed more food themselves. The food shortage problems of the cities, combined with the effects of famine and civil war in the northern and eastern regions converted Ethiopia into a country that was chronically food-deficient and heavily reliant on western relief agencies.

The peasants associations, which along with the urban associations, or *kebelles*, formed the basic low-level institutions of the new order, were vital foci of local conflicts (especially between richer and poorer peasants); despite the existence of an All-Ethiopian Peasant Association, however, these groups had few effective links with the towns. By September 1978 Mengistu Haile-Maryam was calling for the creation of more state farms — as a means both of consolidating political control over the countryside and of extracting a greater surplus from it. Six years later, however, no more than 4 percent of arable land was under state farms (and a further 1 percent under co-operatives), and the state farms in particular absorbed a very high proportion of agricultural investment without any commensurate increase in yield. The government's main agricultural emphasis was placed on the production of cash crops for export. Revenue from these crops was essential to meet the debts incurred from the purchase of Russian arms. Ethiopia was able to fill its quota under the International Coffee Agreement and have something left over in good years for barter deals with Eastern European states. But coffee production nevertheless appears to have declined, and by the mid-1980s the quota could only be achieved by squeezing the domestic market.

The record elsewhere was even more patchy. Forced labor from the towns was used to cultivate the Humera region in the northwest, which in the last years of the imperial regime had been the boom area of Ethiopian agriculture. By 1984, however, the land area under cultivation had fallen dramatically. Overall, per capita food production declined fairly steadily, leaving the countryside in no condition to withstand the effects of the catastrophic drought of 1983–84, and the parastatal organizations set up to manage the urban economic enterprises nationalized in 1974–1975 suffered from inefficiency.

Upheaval in the countryside engendered a greatly increased level of political mobilization and awareness, but there was no effective mechanism through which this awareness could be institutionalized beyond the local level. For a while, this fragmentation served everyone's interests. The peasants had quite enough to handle in the countryside, and the Derg, which had its hands full in the cities, did not want competition from any rural political organization that might threaten its own autonomy. The danger of fragmentation, however, was brought home by armed rebellion in those regions — Eritrea, Tigre, and some parts of the south — where there was a political leadership capable of mounting a direct challenge to central authority. The Derg also needed both to create peasant armies to counter these insurgencies and extract an economic surplus, which pointed up the necessity for political institutions — and, especially, for an effective party system.

The international element eventually assumed critical importance. Since the later nineteenth century, all Ethiopian regimes have required external support (chiefly arms supplies) to retain central control over the periphery. From 1954 on Haile-Selassie's support came mainly from the United States; this support was balanced, overtly or covertly, by Soviet support for the regime's opponents in the Somali Republic and Eritrea. Although American military support was maintained at an increased level during the first few years after the revolution, declining central government effectiveness facilitated a sharp increase in the power of the Eritrean separatists. By the end of 1977 the separatists had gained control of the whole province of Eritrea (with the exception of four surrounded garrisons). The apparent weakness of the new regime, together with the uncertainty of continued U.S. protection, ultimately induced the Somali invasion of July 1977. The same socialist ideology that the Derg had employed in its efforts to seek allies in both the cities and the countryside was similarly used to obtain Soviet and Cuban military aid. After the rupture of their alliances with the Somalis and Eritreans, the Soviets and Cubans supplied this aid to the Derg in decisive quantities.

Like the socialist alliances in city and countryside, however, these foreign alliances posed critical questions of institutionalization and control. In northwest Africa the Soviet Union had had a long and dispiriting history of supporting regimes led by radical nationalist army officers who abandoned the Soviet connection as soon as it presented any threat to their own freedom of action. Variations on this pattern had been repeated in Egypt, Sudan, and the Somali Republic; in Ethiopia the Soviet Union's first concern must have been that Mengistu might go the same way as Sadat, Nimairi, and Siyad once the urgent need for weaponry had receded.

There were, however, grounds for the Soviets to regard Ethiopia as a better prospect than the other three countries had been. For one thing, the situation in Ethiopia had parallels in the history of the Soviet Union. The decaying autocracy, the upheavals in the cities, the landlord problem, and the peripheral rebellions supported by reactionary powers all provided ready points of reference for the Soviets and encouraged them to think that a Soviet-Ethiopian alliance might be based on a lasting sense of similar revolutionary experience rather than on the tactical needs of an unpredictable dictator. Only one (but, for the Russians, important) thing was missing in Ethiopia: there was no communist party. Various political factions had claimed to be Marxist-

Leninist, but these had been suppressed by the Derg, which claimed the same label itself. The formation of a communist party that would serve not only as a symbol of revolutionary respectability but also as a mechanism for Soviet penetration below the level of the top military leadership became the first priority of Russian policy.

Ethiopia's need to create a communist party in order to institutionalize her revolution had been acknowledged by every political faction since 1974. Each faction, however, considered that an Ethiopian communist party could be made to serve its own interests. For the civilian ideologues, it would be a means of controlling the military; for the military, a means of controlling the civilians; for the periphery, a means of influencing the center; for the center, a means of imposing itself on the periphery; for nationalists within the Derg, a means of creating a powerful and independent Ethiopia; and for the Soviet Union, a means of ensuring socialist solidarity. The suppression of Meison and EPRP insured that the party would not constitute a federation of existing factions but would be made up of individual members; it would be built, not from the bottom up, but from the top down. The Commission for Organizing the Party of the Working People of Ethiopia (COPWE) was established in 1979; over the next five years it constructed an embryo party, which Mengistu formally launched as the Ethiopian Workers' Party (EWP) on the tenth anniversary of the revolution in September 1984.

All the indications are that this party is more than a simple facade for a military government. The time taken to construct it, the careful creation of branches and study groups at the regional level and within organizations (including the army), and the vetting and occasional purges of its members, all provide evidence that it is worth serious consideration. Thousands of party cadres have been trained in the Soviet Union and other East European states. It is equally clear, however, that loyalty to its leader, Mengistu Haile-Maryam, is the most important membership criterion of all. In this chapter, written at the very moment of the party's formal establishment, it is much too early to speculate on whether or not the new Ethiopian communist party will be able to institutionalize the contradictory aspirations of the Ethiopian revolution.

THE SOMALI REPUBLIC

The experience of the Somali Republic fits more easily into a general African pattern of postindependence state formation than does that of Ethiopia. The nationalist movement, the postindependence decay of political institutions, the eventual coup, and the subsequent attempt at reconstruction under military leadership are all variations on common themes. The Somali experience, however, has many peculiarities that derive from the distinctive nature of Somali society and state formation.

At base, these peculiarities reside in the structure of a nomadic society, in which shared identities of culture, language, and religion nevertheless coexist with intense factional conflict resulting from perennial competition for very scarce resources. This dichotomy is symbolized in the Somali national genealogy, which, on the one hand, traces the descent of all Somalis from a common ancestor (Somal) and on the other, divides them into clans that provide a natural base for political factions. Following independence in July 1960, there was an immediate push to unify the two Somali colonies; Somali leaders have nevertheless found it necessary to make constant attacks on "tribalism" ever since.

The 1960 independence date was imposed on Italian Somalia by the ten-year limit set up by the United Nations for the Italian trustee administration in 1950; independence was rushed through on very short notice in British Somaliland in order to permit immediate unification with the south. At independence, therefore, the administration of the country was not only rudimentary; it also had to be conducted in two different languages — Italian and English. Somali, the only language shared by all administration members, had no generally accepted written form.

Clan divisions formed natural dividing lines for political parties, and these parties rapidly began to reflect clan rivalries. The largest party, the Somali Youth League (SYL), owed its main support to the Darod group of clans. These clans were based mainly in former Italian Somalia but also lapped over into the north and into Ethiopia and Kenya. This broad geographical base gave the SYL a particular commitment to Somali unification. In contrast, the Somali National League (SNL) was largely restricted to the Isaq clans in the north, and the Hizbia Digil-Mirifle Somali (HDMS), to the sedentary people of the southern river valleys. Divisions within parties, however, were just as important as divisions between them. This was because each member of the national assembly directly represented the interests of his own clan, and at the local level individual clans were constantly at odds with their neighbors.

This endemic fragmentation was intensified by a number of factors. First, since the underlying unity of the nation could be taken for granted, the pressure to impose a facade of unity was not as intense in the Somali Republic as it was in more artificial states. Because of this, and also because of the democratic ethos of Somali nomadism, Somali nationalism had no single dominant leader — a situation that was almost unique in Africa. The first prime minister under the Italian trustee administration, Abdillahi Ise, came from the minority Hawiye clan group; he was replaced at independence by Abd ar-Rashid Ali Shirmarke from the Darod clan, and former HDMS leader Aden Abdillah Osman became president. As leader of the SNL, Muhammad Haji Ibrahim Igal was the principal northern leader, but he represented a minority group within the country as a whole. Shirmarke was not even in control of the Darod clans; after the 1964 elections he was replaced as prime minister by fellow Darod Abdi-Razak Haji Hussein. Shirmarke was unexpectedly elected to the presidency in 1967, and Abdi-Razak was ousted as prime minister (since the conventions of coalition-building dictated that members of the same clan group could not hold both of the top state offices at the same time) and replaced by Igal. The Somali Republic set a record unequalled anywhere in Africa by removing and replacing both its president and its prime minister in a peaceful and constitutional manner.

The common pattern in African states has been for the president — by means of his control of the administrative apparatus — to impose control over the party. In the Somali case almost the opposite occured. Here, the bureaucracy was weak, and the parties were almost uncontrollable. Opposition parties were able to form and maintain themselves with anarchic freedom throughout the period of civilian government. Attempts to create a united opposition by the formation of the Somali Democratic Union in 1962 and the Somali National Congress in 1963, however, fell prey to normal Somali factionalism, and the pre-eminence of the SYL eventually produced a dominant-party state. The SYL, however, functioned primarily as a device for seeking patronage within the National Assembly (where any control was rendered virtually impossible by the practice of a secret ballot). At election time even the semblance of unity disappeared; candidates sought to project themselves as defenders of their own clans, and opportunistic parties sprang up like the proverbial flowers after a desert rain. The 1969 elections were contested by sixty-two parties. Seventy-three seats went to SYL candidates; fifty were won by their opponents, and all but one of these instantly joined the SYL in the quest for patronage.[5]

It is not surprising that this system did not result in a particularly effective government. For instance, the various factions found themselves quite unable to agree on a script for writing Somali. The three alternatives — Roman, Arabic, and an indigenous Somali script called Osmaniyya — each had their dedicated supporters, but it was left to the postcoup military regime to resolve the issue in favour of the Roman. With the exception of the nomadic subsistence sector, the economy was heavily dependent on external aid and on protected foreign markets (notably the Italian market). The Somali Republic's per capita GNP rated among the lowest in the world, and her per capita aid, among the highest. The country thus provided a classic case of the ineffectiveness of foreign aid as a stimulus for economic transformation. Her gross domestic product rose by only 1 percent per annum during the 1960s — a record exceeded by every country in the world with the exception of Chad and Haiti. (During the same period she experienced a 2.8 percent growth in population.)[6]

The Republic did succeed in attracting aid from a wide variety of sources — mostly Western. The Soviets also provided assistance for a port at Berbera in the north (which later gained brief prominence as a Russian naval base), and the Chinese built a road to link the northern and southern parts of the country (regions that had formerly been almost cut off from each other by the great wedge of the Ethiopian Ogaden).

It was not possible, however, to maintain a balance between aid donors in the military sphere. The cherished goal of Somali unification required a much larger army than the country either needed or could afford for purely internal and defensive purposes. This goal also brought the Republic into confrontation not only with those countries whose territory it was seeking (Ethiopia, Kenya and Djibouti) but also with their external military protectors (the United States, Britain and France). Soviet military aid was therefore the logical choice. This was agreed upon in 1963; it led to the formation of a disproportionately large, Soviet-trained army with an ethos very different from that of postcolonial militaries in other newly independent African states. This army seized power in October 1969 in the wake of a chaotic general election and the assassination of President Shirmarke. A plausible case has been made for Soviet complicity in this coup; indeed, given the role of Soviet military advisers in the Somali army at the time, it could scarcely have taken place without their knowledge and tacit assistance.[7] The circumstances surrounding it were so similar to those that have produced coups in other parts of Africa, however, that it can easily be accounted for on domestic grounds alone.

Unlike the situation in Ethiopia, the military takeover in the Somali Republic (subsequently renamed the Somali Democratic Republic) initially constituted a coup rather than a revolution. Although the new government called itself the Supreme Revolutionary Council (SRC), its leader, General Siyad, was middle-aged, cautious, and uninspiring. He was astute enough, however, to establish himself in unchallenged control after alleged plots by his successive vice-presidents were exposed in 1970 and 1971. Nevertheless, on the first anniversary of the coup, the military government announced its adherence to scientific socialism; thereafter it promoted itself (not entirely fraudulently) as a Marxist-Leninist revolutionary regime.

This move was partly motivated by the Somali military's need to curry favor with its patron. The military's institutional goal of Somali unification could only be achieved with a high level of Soviet support. This support would be much more readily supplied to an ideologically acceptable regime than to one that was simply a partner of convenience. Portraits of the great revolutionary leaders (Marx, Lenin, and Siyad), accordingly made their appearance in the Republic, and Soviet military aid began a climb that reached its apex in the mid-1970s.

But there were also domestic reasons for the move to Marxism-Leninism. The failure of liberal democracy constituted more than just an indictment of a particular system of government. It also demanded a transformation of the society on which that system of government was based. The principal target of the new revolutionary regime was "tribalism." In the Somali context this concept referred to the clans that had provided the main basis for political identity and factionalism. The new regime also resolved the vexing issue of the Somali script and undertook vigorous campaigns to promote literacy and sedentarization. In 1976 the SRC formally gave way to the Somali Democratic Socialist Party

(SDSP), and the Republic became a one-party state. Unlike the Ethiopian Workers' Party, however, the SDSP appeared to be largely a cosmetic device designed to secure the approval of the Soviet Union.

Although by Ethiopian standards the Somali revolution was peaceful (only a small number of opponents were publicly executed), it changed the tenor of life in both the towns and the countryside. The free-for-all of party politics was replaced by a leadership cult of General Siyad, and civilian freedom of expression gave way to a climate of repression policed by the National Security Service and the green-uniformed Victory Pioneers. A heavy emphasis on political re-education encouraged many Somalis (especially the educated) to seek employment in the Gulf states. Islam was accepted as the national religion, but some measures (particularly those promoting sexual equality) aroused traditionalist opposition; a group of conservative religious leaders were executed. In contrast to the situation in Ethiopia, there was no great issue — like land reform — around which to rally support for a socialist economy. Nevertheless, the import-export trade and other existing industries were brought under closer state control. A literacy campaign, initially launched in the towns, was extended to the countryside in 1975. That same year a drought devastated the nomadic population. Unlike the imperial government in Ethiopia, the Somali regime responded actively to this disaster; it sought foreign aid and used the catastrophe to further promote its sedentarization policies. The rural development campaign was converted into a drought relief organization, and a number of imaginative farming and fishing schemes were devised to provide alternative sources of livelihood. Adult literacy (according to the government) increased from 2 percent to 60 percent between 1960 and 1980. At the same time, however, substantial numbers of Somalis began to gather in refugee camps, and over the next ten years became a depressing, and seemingly permanent, feature of the country.

These traumas culminated in the Ethiopian-Somali war of 1977–1978 — to date, the major international conflict involving independent black African states. In the most basic sense, the war represented the clash of two competing regional concepts of nationhood: the Ethiopian, based on central hegemony, and the Somali, based on cultural identity. It was precipitated by the apparent collapse of the Ethiopian central government after 1974 and the deterioration of the United States–Ethiopian alliance at a time when increasing Soviet military aid was providing the Somalis a temporary military advantage. The window of opportunity was potentially short-lived, however, because increasing Soviet interest in Ethiopia presaged a possible switch in alliances. Opinion differs as to whether or not the July 1977 attack on Ethiopian forces in the Ogaden was launched by Western Somalia Liberation Front guerrillas independent of the Somali government. At all events, the regular Somali army was quickly committed to the invasion, and it rapidly occupied the entire Somali-inhabited area of Ethiopia. The outcome of the war from this point on was almost entirely dependent on the direction and level of Soviet response.

Any rational calculation of Soviet interest favored Ethiopia. Ethiopia was a larger, richer, and, for the most part, more well-situated state — hence, a more desirable client. Although both contestants claimed to be Marxist-Leninist, the close parallels noted above between the Russian and Ethiopian revolutions appeared to make the Derg a more reliable ally than a personalist Somali regime bent on international adventurism. Additionally, the Ethiopians were squarely on the side of the OAU consensus, which was pledged to uphold the existing African boundaries that the Somalis were fighting to overturn. The Western states, which the Somalis subsequently approached for support, had no interest in alienating the great majority of African governments — particularly at the behest of a state that had previously been the USSR's closest ally on the continent. Just as in every other case in which Africa's inherited frontiers have been threatened, the international system came down heavily on the side of the status quo.[8]

In the aftermath of defeat, ethnic Somalis who were normally resident in Ethiopia flooded across into the Republic. The number of these refugees is a contentious political issue; the Somali government has an interest in inflating the total in order to strengthen its case against Ethiopia and to qualify itself for more relief aid. The official figure of ca. 700,000 in 1983 was arrived at by negotiation rather than count. But even the commonly estimated figure of 250,000 constitutes a major burden for a country whose total population numbers under five million.

Politically, the defeat threw the process of institution-building into sharp reverse. The unity engendered by the national struggle gave way to factional conflict, and opposition movements re-emerged. Hostility to the regime was especially great in the northern part of the country, which had experienced the worst of the war and had the fewest connections with the government in Mogadishu. An attempted coup was crushed in April 1978, resulting in some five hundred deaths. Opponents of the Siyad regime attempted a counterinvasion from Ethiopia in 1982. The regime did not formally abandon its Marxist revolutionary pretensions, but it was forced to revert to the same sort of dependence on clan loyalties and factional maneuvering that it had earlier set out to eradicate. Although the Siyad government has made dramatic changes in Somali life during its fifteen years in power, from the perspective of 1984 it now seems fair to conclude that the attempt to construct new and revolutionary political institutions has failed.

CONCLUSION

Even by the standards of postindependence Africa, the experience of the Horn since 1960 has been particularly traumatic. At the time of Somali independence, the area as a whole was the least politically mobilized of any major region on the continent. Ethiopia seemed to have avoided the upheavals then sweeping the rest of Africa. In the Somali Republic, nationalism was tied to an indigenous Somali nationhood and was readily incorporated within the existing structures of clan and nomadism. Within a couple of decades, however, both countries had governments that claimed to be Marxist-Leninist, and they have provided two of Africa's most convincing examples of the attempt to use revolution as a means of overcoming the multiple problems of social, economic, and political change. Moreover, the major upheavals occurred during the shattering five-year period between 1973 and 1978. The most critical immediate precipitant was the drought, but this natural disaster merely served to expose the existing fragility of both Ethiopia's ancient polity and the Somali Republic's nomadic economy. From then on, millions of people in each country were to become the pawns of circumstances beyond their control — as famine victims, relief aid recipients and political refugees. Additional millions were to be caught up in political actions of a kind that would previously have been unthinkable. In both cases, the ruling regime's response to ecological disaster was sharply to increase the power of the state. In Somalia, the military government had the chance to take its revolutionary pretensions seriously. The drought resulted in a sudden increase in the dependence of the people on the government; this gave the government a much greater capacity to organize the people and to effect relief and sedentarization programs. The startling increase in literacy provides the clearest example of its success. In Ethiopia, the ramshackle empire gave way to a regime that was, on the one hand, vastly more ruthless, and, on the other, so riven by internal rivalries that it temporarily lost its grip over much of the country. The land reform movement, the *zemecha* campaign, and the setting up of urban and peasants associations changed the structure of rural and urban life beyond recall. Soviet and Cuban aid and the mobilization of mass peasant armies numbering some 300,000 enormously increased the coercive power of the state.

This increase in state power, however, produced mixed results for Ethiopians and Somalis. Some — like literacy and land reform — were clearly positive. But increased state power also led to violent conflicts both within the two states and between them. The Ethiopian-Somali war of 1977–1978 destroyed hopes for Somali unification, vastly increased the region's external military dependence, and turned the Somali regime into an international mendicant whose main goal was survival. The Eritrean insurgency — initially encouraged by the decline in central government effectiveness and later stopped in its tracks by the Ethiopian counterattack in 1978 — eventually became bogged down in a bloody stalemate with the central government forces. In other regions (as in France after 1789 and Russia after 1917) the mobilization fostered by the revolution of 1974 induced a countermobilization from the national periphery. It is likely that these insurgencies will eventually be brought under central control with the help of external military aid — and at a cost in human suffering that is yet to be reckoned.

One way in which the cost can already be assessed is in the number of refugees. In 1979 these numbered over a million — the highest total of any region in Africa — made up some 9 percent of the world's refugees (in an area that accounted for only some 0.8 percent of world population).[9] Another indicator is the region's decline into chronic food dependence. In 1974 — a famine year — Ethiopia and Somalia together imported 160,000 metric tons of cereals and received a further 169,000 tons in food aid; by 1981 these figures had increased to 639,000 tons and 558,000 tons respectively. Per capita food production was at an index level of 100 for 1969–1971; by 1977–1981 it had dropped to eighty-five in Ethiopia and sixty-five in the Somali Republic.[10] If a state's first priority is to fulfill its people's basic needs for food and security, both of the main states in the Horn have failed lamentably. Moreover, despite definite achievements, their revolutions (at least during the period we have covered) have made the situation worse rather than better.

An analysis of a state's performance is an exercise to be conducted with great caution, and this caution must be all the greater in the case of revolutionary regimes. Comparative statistics, which in Africa are unreliable or misleading, are even less trustworthy (or virtually nonexistent) after revolutionary upheaval. Conflict and disruption are the immediate aftermath of any revolution, and things are likely to get worse before they get better. The period of fifteen years since the Somali revolution (and ten since the Ethiopian) is all too short a timespan in which to reach any reliable conclusions — particularly because (especially in the rural areas) there is an inevitable lag before adequate information about what is actually going on becomes available for assessment. Both the Ethiopian and the Somali regimes have had to struggle with the effects of environmental disaster. Nevertheless, the lesson of the Horn is that the question of whether an increase of power in an African state does or does not lead to any increased welfare for its people is one that must be no less critically asked of revolutionary states than of their nonrevolutionary predecessors and contemporaries.

Notes

1. Robert H. Jackson and Carl G. Rosberg, *Personal Rule in Black Africa* (Berkeley: University of California Press, 1982), pp. 77–79.

2. Christopher Clapham, *Haile-Selassie's Government* (London: Longman, 1969), p. 77.

3. Samuel P. Huntington, *Political Order in Changing Societies* (London: Yale University Press, 1968), chap. 4.

4. Michael Stahl, *Ethiopia: Political Contradictions in Agricultural Development* (Stockholm: Raben & Sjoren, 1974).

5. I. M. Lewis, *A Modern History of Somalia* (London: Longman, 1980), p. 204.

6. World Bank, *World Development Report 1983* (New York: Oxford University Press, 1983), Tables 2 and 19.

7. Gary D. Payton, "The Somali Coup of 1969: The Case for Soviet Complicity," *Journal of Modern African Studies* 18 (1980): 493–508.

8. Robert H. Jackson and Carl G. Rosberg, "Why Africa's Weak States Persist," *World Politics* 35 (1982):

9. See Aderanti Adepoju, "The Dimension of the Refugee Problem in Africa," *African Affairs* 81 (1982): 21–35.

10. World Bank, *World Development Report 1983*, Table 6. Among sources not specifically cited should be noted Rene Lefort, *Ethiopia: An Heretical Revolution?* (London: Zed Press, 1983) and John Markakis, *Ethiopia: Anatomy of a Traditional Polity* (Oxford: Clarendon Press, 1974).

7 SOUTH AFRICA

Peter Duignan and L. H. Gann

South Africa both resembles and differs from the black states of modern Africa. South Africa faces many of the same economic, social, and political problems that confront the black states and has also chosen many of the same solutions to them (including a heavy reliance on the state, the use of parastatals in the economy, and an authoritarian and undemocratic form of governance). But the differences between South Africa and black-ruled Africa are equally striking. Whereas black Africa belongs to the Third and the Fourth World, in South Africa, the First World is superimposed on the Third World. In black Africa, the state is often ineffective; it is run by what Johnson Asiegbu, a modern Nigerian historian, terms "predatory elites."[1] In South Africa, the state machinery works. South Africa may be a racist society that denies democratic rights to the great majority of its population, but the state effectively enforces its laws. The state can provide goods and services. The economy continues to expand. The bulk of the officials are capable and responsible. The condition of all ethnic communities (in terms of life expectancy, consumption of goods, the provision of educational — and other — services, and so forth) has improved, albeit at strikingly different rates. South Africa has not experienced civil wars like those that occurred in Sudan or Nigeria, ethnic massacres of the type that befell the Hutu in Burundi, mass terror of the variety enforced by African dictators like Sekou Touré or Idi Amin.

South Africa is the only modern, capable state in sub-Saharan Africa. Its capacity for effective rule is not equaled by any black-ruled state on the continent. In contrast, many black states, possess sovereignty in name only; they are colonial territories writ large. These states endowed by the international community with sovereignty, but, on the whole, this sovereignty is not comparable to that of older states. If it were not for Western aid, loans, and grants, many of the newly sovereign African states would be in an even more parlous condition than they are at present. South Africa, however, has always managed without foreign assistance of the humanitarian kind. For all its internal tensions, South Africa's

283

economy continues to expand; in contrast, the majority of African states find themselves in economic disarray. (Most black African states can no longer feed their own peoples, and many village cultivators have returned to substinence farming.)

According to the academic orthodoxy of the 1960s and 1970s, exactly the opposite should have occurred. Black Africa was expected to have a successful future characterized by nation building and evolving prosperity; South Africa was expected to succumb to inevitable breakdown and revolution. Our essay attempts to show why the facts have so far belied the predictions.

There Are No South Africans proclaimed the title of a well-known study published just after World War II.[2] In the author's opinion, South Africans were too ethnically and racially diverse to consider themselves a single nation; they also possessed no common view of their own past. These strictures remain as true today as they were forty years ago. For instance, English and Afrikaners, Colored and Zulu, Tswana and Sotho would not readily agree on the date that their country became independent of British imperial control. The formation of the Union of South Africa in 1910 created a sovereign and independent state within the British Commonwealth, but — according to the most militant of Afrikaner nationalists — the Union remained, in fact, an imperial dependency. Another break occurred in 1948, when the National party secured office (the party that has succeeded in holding on to power to this day). The Nationalists' victory gave to Afrikaners a sense of having at last come into their own. To African nationalists, however, the switch merely represented a change of masters; true independence was yet to be secured. South Africa underwent a significant change on the legal plane in 1961, however, when it became a republic and (in the same year) withdrew from the Commonwealth — a move that coincided with the accelerated pace of decolonization in the rest of Africa. The year 1961 therefore forms a convenient point of departure for a consideration of the country's most recent history.

A quarter of a century ago South Africa was in many ways quite different from what it is at present. Compared to the rest of Africa, which was just becoming free of colonial tutelage, South Africa was an economic giant. Its gross domestic product, however, was one a fraction of what it is today. (Between 1960 and 1983 the gross domestic product rose from 4,983 million rand, at factor cost, to 81,347 million rand.)[3] During this period the economy became greatly diversified. Gross domestic investment rose from 4,101 million rand to 21,376 million rand. The population increased from 15,994,000 in 1960 to 23,772,000 in 1980.[4] The cities changed in size and appearance. Many more students of all colors were enrolled in schools, technical colleges, and universities. (See Table 1.) The literary scene underwent a transformation, especially after the arrival of the *sestigers* (the men of the 1960s) on the Afrikaner literary scene. At first glance, the list of changes seems endless.

Yet in many other respects, the country had apparently stood still. According to critics, the constitutional changes of 1982 had left the white power base in tact and provided no advancement for the country's black majority. The threat of revolution, which had been taken very seriously in the international community at the time of the Sharpeville affray in 1960, had not come to fruition. On the contrary, by early 1984 even Marxist-Leninist states like Angola and Mozambique were ready to negotiate with Pretoria. Academicians abroad, although still committed to the assumption that time was running out for South Africa, had muted early predictions that revolution was an immediate possibility.[5] The continuities and discontinuities in South Africa's most recent development remain complex and therefore merit more detailed examination.

POLITICS

The Formal Structure

The republican constitution adopted in 1961 followed the Westminster model used by the framers of the South African constitution in 1910. Unlike their counterparts in Canada and Australia, the founders of the South African Union resolved to set up a unitary state. (In contrast to the Canadian provinces, the four South African provinces were granted only local powers, and their provincial councils concerned themselves with parochial issues only.) In South Africa, however, the Westminster model had always operated as the constitutional instrument of a white ethnocracy. Parliamentary franchise and eligibility for office in the central government had remained confined to white citizens over the age of 18. Ceremonial power was vested in the state president, who is elected for a period of seven years by the House of Assembly. The House consisted of 165 directly elected white members; additional members were nominated in proportion to the position of the parties in the Assembly. The head of state picked the prime minister from such members of parliament as could command a majority in the legislature.

In South Africa, the prime minister had traditionally been the most powerful man in politics, wielding far more influence than any U.S. President (or even a British prime minister). Individual members of parliament have always counted for far less in South African politics than have legislators in Washington, D.C. There is nothing comparable in the South African government to the congressional staff that provides U.S. senators and congressmen with facts, figures, and critical analyses. The prime minister, in contrast, could draw on a substantial body of information from bureaucratic sources. He selected his own ministerial colleagues (nineteen in 1983), each of whom headed a major government department. The prime minister supervises the running of the country. In doing so, he received assistance from the Prime Minister's Department, a major agency whose power within the administrative structure had tended to increase. The prime minister served as chairman of the State Security Council (set up in 1972 to coordinate defense). The prime minister also ran his own party in a manner inconceivable to any American president. In some intangible sense the prime minister was widely accepted — by virtue of his office — as the leader of the Afrikaner nation and, as such, possessed powers that transcend his purely political role. Nevertheless, within the context of white politics, South Africa operated almost like a presidential democracy. Although in some respects it resembles the one-party states in Africa that are led by charismatic leaders, its government is much more efficient and less corrupt than almost all African states.

In South Africa the central executive remains subject to a variety of restrictions that do not apply in most of the black states of Africa. These derive from the constitution, from dissensions within the ruling party itself, from pressures exerted by opposition groups, from a vigorous and relatively independent press, from the churches (including the three Dutch Reformed Churches, to which most Afrikaners belong), from trade unions, and — last but not least — from a judicature proud of its integrity and its traditions derived from Roman-Dutch law.

In response to increasing pressure to widen its political base by at least making some concessions to Indians and Coloreds, in 1983 the government pushed through parliament a new constitution designed to strengthen the executive and reform parliament. This proved to be a difficult task because white (especially Afrikaner) public opinion set strict limits on the kind of concessions the government could make to non-Europeans. The voting in parliament, however, marked a watershed, P. W. Botha's National party, supported by the conservative, mainly English-speaking New Republic party, mustered 119 votes (as compared to thirty-five votes mobilized by their adversaries), an outcome that would have been inconceivable twenty years earlier. The opposition rested on an ill-assorted alliance between the liberal wing of the white community (represented by the Progressive Federal party) and the right wing (represented by the Conservative party). There was a similar split among the ranks of the disenfranchised. Subject to reservations, the Colored Labor party agreed to collaborate with the new constitution; all black political organizations opposed the project. Later in 1983 the government consolidated its victory by means of a referendum, gaining close to a two-thirds majority among the white electors (1,360,223 of these voted for the scheme, and 691,557 voted against it). This landslide victory signaled the end of the monolithic Afrikaner party; a majority of English speakers voted for the government, but many Afrikaners voted against Prime Minister P. W. ("Piet") Botha.

The new constitution — which may undergo further changes in the future — essentially embodies a set of guidelines adopted by the government in 1982. For the time being, blacks remain excluded from all power on the central level. Nevertheless, the new proposals represent a striking departure from the principles of racial apartheid on which the National party originally attained office. Under the reformed dispensation, the central legislature consists of the president, a parliament consisting of three chambers (one for whites, one for Coloreds, and one the Asians), and a President's Council that advises the president at his request on matters of national importance and legislation. The president appoints his own cabinet, the members of which need not necessarily be members of any legislature. The president also has a decisive say in the composition of the President's Council, which consists of twenty whites, ten Coloreds, five Indians elected by the chambers, and twenty-five members appointed by the President. Once elected, the president does not sit in any of the chambers.

In the event of a conflict among the chambers over matters of mutual interest, the decision of the President's Council will be binding on the president. Each chamber will decide on matters of concern to its own community. Using the relevant provisions of the constitution as guidelines, the president will in each instance determine whether the matter under discussion is of national interest or of community interest only. Legislation on matters of mutual interest may be passed by majority vote of all chambers separately. Executive power is vested in the president, in whom the offices of the existing state president and the prime minister have been united; the President's Council has become part of the legislature. The president is chosen by an electoral college consisting of fifty whites, twenty-five Coloreds and thirteen Indians elected by the chambers from their own members.

At the time this essay went to press (June 1985), P. W. Botha had assumed the state presidency and formed the country's first racially mixed cabinet. But no expert could be certain how the new scheme would work in practice, how much it would be modified, or if the tricameral legislature would prove as transient as the three separate Houses of the Estates General established by Louis XVI on the eve of the French Revolution.

Despite the concessions made, the new constitution pleased neither Indians nor Coloreds. Something like 70 percent of the registered Colored, and 80 percent of the registered Indian, voters refused to go to the polls; the abstention rate was especially high among the well educated and the town dwellers. (Allan Hendrickse's Labor party won all but four of the Colored seats; the adherents of Armichand Rajbansi and J. N. Reddy obtained all but five seats in the forty-member Indian chamber.)

According to Botha's critics, the new arrangement is simply the old one in disguise. In other words, the dominant party (that is, the Nationalists) in the white chamber will always prevail in the choice of the president. If the Indian and Colored chambers try to contradict the majority in the white chamber, the quarrel will be settled by the new President's Council, which has a National party majority. There is no provision for joint sessions among the three chambers. The President's Council merely acts as the state president's alter ego. The constitution itself rests on discriminatory laws. Even with the greatest possible good will on all sides, the new constitution — with its elaborate system of committees and its intricate network of checks and balances — will be difficult to make function. It will probably entail delays and deadlocks, create all manner of anomalies, and weaken the existing powers of Parliament.

The new constitution definitely strengthens the central executive, however. Under the new dispensation, the state president holds a position even more powerful than that of the former prime minister. According to a new combination of ministerial portfolios announced in September 1984, the state president supervises (in addition to his own office) the National Intelligence Services (including the Secretariat of the State Security Council) the Commission for Administration, and the transport services. (It is a constitution that would have pleased General de Gaulle; it is not for nothing that satirists have referred to Piet Botha as *le grand Pierre*.)

The White Parties

The country's ruling party is the National party. It is composed mainly (although by no means exclusively) of Afrikaners. The party began its career as a rural party — one that primarily represented the interests of farmers, white working people, and Afrikaans-speaking professionals. It was these professions — especially clergymen, school teachers, and attorneys — who provided most of the party leadership; they saw themselves as spokesmen for an underprivileged white community that was excluded from most positions of power in both the state government and the economy.

During the years following World War II, however, the Afrikaners became a mainly urban people. They made rapid advances in the ranks of business, banking, and the professions. Henceforth, the character of the National party changed. Anti-Semitism disappeared as part of its dormant ideology, and its antiurban and anti-industrial romanticism became muted. The party began to attract a minority of English speakers. (By 1975 83.3 percent of Afrikaans-speaking whites and 23.4 percent of English-speaking whites expressed a preference for the Nationalists.) In its social composition, and to some extent in its political orientation, the National party therefore became more similar to the (by then defunct) United party that it had displaced in 1948. The difference was that the United party had drawn its main strength from English speakers, whereas the National party was dominated by Afrikaners, who had become the new *Staatsvolk* (the dominant ethnic group in the state). (This type of ethnic domination resembles that in some black African states — for example, Rwanda, Burundi, and Ethiopia.) By 1984 the National party represented a coalition of middle-class people, government employees, technicians, skilled artisans, white-collar workers, and farmers. It derived its main support from city dwellers. During this time the Nationalists also expanded their parliamentary strength. (In 1953 the Nationalists held ninety-four seats, as compared to fifty-seven held by the United party and six by the white Labor party. By 1983 the National party commanded 126 seats, as compared to twenty-seven held by the Progressive Federal party, seventeen by the Conservative party, and eight by the New Republic party.)

From the standpoint of doctrine, class composition, or structure, the National party is by no means a homogeneous body. It is founded on the federal principle and is composed of four provincial parties held together by a thirty-member Federal Council. Council members include the leaders of the party's parliamentary caucus, seven delegates from each provincial congress, and one representative from the Youth League. All decisions of the Federal Council concerning policy and organization must be approved by the four provincial congresses (in the Cape, the Transvaal, the Orange Free State, and Natal) before they become binding on the provincial national parties. The provincial parties are in turn headed by a provincial leader and provincial congresses, which have subordinate constituency divisional councils, district councils, and branches. (None of these subcouncils may have more than 500 members.) Membership is restricted to whites who are at least seventeen years of age.

The party's strength is not confined to its parliamentary organization. It also derives from a great variety of allied organizations, such as the Jeugbond (Youth League). The party maintains informal links to a broad range of voluntary religious, cultural, professional, educational, and athletic organizations, all of which place emphasis on their Afrikaner heritage. All of these organizations are of relatively recent origin; they were developed at a time when the traditional organizations of Afrikaner society — the extended family, the church, and the *kommando* (a military organization based on the universal militia principle) — were no longer able to cope with the demands of a new society. Besides the Jeugbond, other organizations include the Voortrekkers, an Afrikaans Scout movement (35,000 members), and the Afrikaanse

Studentebond (about 50,000 members). A particularly powerful organization is the Federasie van Afrikaanse Kultuurvereninge (FAK), set up in 1929. The FAK has traditionally performed a wide variety of tasks to promote Afrikaans culture. In the economic sphere, it has set up a number of organizations designed to promote Afrikaners in industry, commerce, and finance. The most important of these is the Ekonomiese Instituut, followed by the Afrikaanse Handelinstituut, which represents businessmen.

Some believe that the National party is secretly governed by the Broederbond — an organization of about 10,000 members drawn from the Afrikaner elite. Although the Broederbond is important, it is not able to impose its policies on the entire National party. The Broederbond's membership is strictly confidential; entry is by invitation only. According to its critics, the Broederbond uses conspiratorial tactics and serves as a bastion of reactionary attitudes. In fact, its overall importance has probably declined over the last thirty years. Along with the teachers, academics, clergymen, and civil servants who are heavily represented in its ranks, the Broederbond has become increasingly reformist over the years.

Today the National party, constitutes the most important national institution of the Afrikaner people. The party's character, however, has recently undergone some subtle changes. Although the present-day National party includes both a *verlig* (reformist) and a *verkramp* (reactionary) wing, the average member of parliament is more likely to describe himself as *behoudend* (conservative). Far more than in the past; there is wide disagreement on a great variety of issues.

The party has, moreover, lost the intense ideological commitment of olden days, when apartheid seemed a workable program for the future. Its activists have become middle aged, and it can no longer mobilize as many enthusiastic volunteers to ring bells and distribute literature as before. The party bureaucrat has assumed more importance than previously. Whereas, traditionally, clergymen, academics, or lawyers guided the party, Piet Botha rose from the ranks of the party bureaucracy (and is the first leader to have done so). At a more subtle level, Afrikaners (although still respectful) have lost some of their old deference to the dedacticism of pastors and traditional politicians. The values of the big city have begun to seep into politics as well as into every other aspect of life. Additionally, the National party no longer has a monopoly on

Afrikaner voters; two major splits have divided the Afrikaner nation.

Compared to the National party, the other white political organizations in South Africa wield only limited power. The official opposition party is the Progressive Federal party, led by Dr. F. van Zyl Slabbert. It follows a mildly liberal course and mainly derives its strength from the well-to-do English-speaking suburbs of Johannesburg and Cape Town. It attracts support from professional people, academics, and liberal bankers and businessmen. It is strongly backed by the English-language press and the English-language universities, and it therefore receives a degree of international publicity unwarranted by its electoral strength in South Africa itself. After much soul-searching, the Progressive Federal party has recently advocated a universal franchise within a federal system (subject to various restraints).

The extreme right wing is splintered. At present, the Herstigte Nasionale party (HNP), led by Jaap Marais, stands for the undiluted Afrikaner nationalism of the past, but it has ceased to be of electoral significance. The Conservative party, led by former Nationalist Party leader Dr. Andries Treurnicht, is considerably more influential, but it will probably not be able to acquire a dominating position. Both groups were formed by right-wing Nationalists who had been expelled from the parent party; their departure has enabled the National party to commit itself to its present centrist course — one that would have been inconceivable at the time the Nationalists first gained power in 1948.[6]

The Extraparliamentary Opposition

White South Africans pioneered the creation of political parties in South Africa. Educated Indians, Coloreds, and Africans learned from their white neighbors' example and created a network of organizations whose diversity mirrors South Africa's ethnic and social diversity. Brown or black nationalists could never quite agree on how far they should cooperate with their white sympathizers. African politicians in particular were divided into those who envisioned a multiracial South Africa — to be set up in cooperation with white allies — and those who advocated a black South Africa in which whites and Indians would only be tolerated as minorities.

South Africa's oldest nationwide black party is the African

National Congress (ANC), founded in 1912 on a liberal program that advocated the inclusion of blacks in a nonracial South Africa. In the beginning, the ANC represented black clerks, contractors, shopkeepers, pastors, elementary school teachers, and educated chiefs. As African educational standards rose, leadership (almost always drawn from the Xhosa, an African people residing in the Cape Province) passed into the hands of professionals. The Congress extended its influence among city-born blacks and its political approach changed from moderation to militance. During the 1950s the ANC began to call for an end to white domination and embarked on passive resistance campaigns against the pass laws, the Group Areas Act, the Suppression of Communism Act, and other features of apartheid.

In 1955 the ANC and other black congresses joined together to issue the Freedom Charter, a milestone in the history of South African opposition. The Freedom Charter went beyond the ANC's traditional demand for constitutional reforms and called for public ownership of "the mineral wealth . . . the banks and monopoly industry" and also a division of land among the tillers. The rhetoric of Marxism replaced the moderate and social democratic idiom. The ANC became, in effect, a front for the South African Communist party (SACP). (At present, however, there are several factions within the ANC that are critical of SACP control of the movement.)

After the Sharpeville riots in 1960, black opposition became less overt in character. But it gradually increased, concomitant with the rapidly increasing number of educated black men and women. By 1978 there were more black than white students in South African secondary schools. Although whites still commanded a leading position in technical schools and universities, South Africa could by then also draw on the skills of a substantial number of black graduates — as shown in Table 1. There was also an appreciable rise in nonwhite incomes. (Between 1960 and 1980 the real personal incomes of Asians rose by 339.5 percent; of Coloreds, by 246.6 percent; of blacks, by 220.0 percent; and of whites, by 122.1 percent.)

In 1969 there was a new political development; blacks broke away from the multiracial, English-dominated National Union of South Africa Students. The black dissidents formed their own South African Students' Organization (SASO). In 1972 SASO helped establish the Black Peoples' Convention (BPC) as a political movement for all nonwhites. The Black Consciousness Movement

Table 1: Education in South Africa 1960–1979

Primary & Secondary (ordinary):	1960	1970	1975	1978	1979
Teachers:					
Total	70,402	110,502	140,119	145,434	153,624
Asians	3,963	6,057	6,871	7,617	8,195
Blacks	25,644	45,953	67,841	66,146[1]	71,380
Coloreds	9,656	16,483	20,842	24,438	25,410
Whites	31,139	42,009	44,565	47,233	48,639
Students: Primary					
Total	2,301,477	3,738,696	4,635,315	4,141,797	4,268,090
Asians	111,197	123,443	135,955	147,779	150,119
Blacks	1,452,246	2,614,961	3,378,873	2,784,941[1]	2,899,000
Coloreds	276,245	456,481	546,593	602,944	613,752
Whites	461,789	543,811	573,894	606,127	606,219
Students: Secondary					
Total	338,671	532,200	786,867	970,206	1,037,367
Asians	16,841	40,082	48,485	60,226	16,362
Blacks	47,598	122,489	318,568	443,385	495,100
Coloreds	28,585	59,027	89,831	119,107	129,698
Whites	245,647	310,602	329,983	347,627	348,207
Universities and Teachers' training colleges:					
Lecturers	4,039	7,879	10,626	9,772	10,677[2]
Students:					
Total	56,666	101,526	148,125	171,022	178,461
Asians	2,156	4,303	6,744	10,039	11,085
Blacks	6,186	12,035	24,744	26,661	29,092
Coloreds	2,584	4,411	8,833	10,563	12,438
Whites	45,740	80,777	107,804	123,759	125,846
Technical and related institutions:					
Lecturers	2,603	3,272	3,434	3,827	4,075
Students:					
Total	53,992	66,578	80,233	92,036	97,088
Asians	4,569	6,642	5,605	3,094	3,214
Blacks	1,734	3,652	4,607	3,245[1]	3,300
Coloreds	2,274	3,705	4,268	6,647	6,574
Whites	45,415	52,579	65,753	79,050	84,000

Notes:

1. Republic of Transkei excluded as from 1977; and the Republic of Bophuthatswana excluded as from 1978.

2. From 1977, certain personnel at white residential universities were no longer regarded as lecturing personnel; Lecturers at black teachers' training colleges included as of 1979, previously among teachers at ordinary schools.

Source: Census Department, Pretoria.

evolved from these groups. The government suppressed SASO and the BPC in 1977. (Both movements had been popular among students, and in 1976 there had been widespread disturbances in Soweto and other townships.) Subsequent arrests and flight once again destroyed black opposition groups, although in 1978 the Black Consciousness Movement was reconstituted as the Azania Peoples Organization (AZAPO) for nonwhites. AZAPO was committed to nonviolence and an end to apartheid.

It should be noted that in 1959 the ANC split into two wings: the Pan Africanist Congress, dedicated to black supremacy (now led by John Nyati Pokela), and the African National Congress (now headed by Oliver Tambo, as president, and Alfred Nzo, as secretary general). Both organizations were banned in 1960, and many of their leaders were imprisoned. The ANC had been closely linked to the South African Communist Party (which had also been outlawed in the 1950s).

After the SACP was banned, its dominance of the ANC increased. The two organizations are linked by a common doctrine and by a socialist version of interlocking directorates.[7] The ANC regards itself as part of a wider "revolutionary alliance in which each organization has a distinct and vital role to play."[8] The ANC never materially diverges from the SACP line. Like the SACP, the ANC believes in armed resistance to achieve the ultimate goal of a socialist and nonracist South Africa. (The militant wing of the ANC, Umkonto we Sizwe, gained membership after the Soweto riots; thousands of educated youths fled to Lesotho, Swaziland, and Botswana, from whence they were sent to Angola for training.)

The ANC is enmeshed in a complex international network that includes both pro-Soviet front organizations and non-Communist bodies that simply oppose apartheid. Examples are the Anti-Apartheid Movement in Great Britain and the World Peace Council, a Soviet-backed body. The ANC's journal, *Sechaba*, is published in London. In addition, the ANC maintains offices as far afield as New York, East Berlin, Stockholm, Lusaka, and Dar es Salaam. ANC broadcasts to South Africa from radio stations in Luanda, Lusaka, Madagascar, and Dar es Salaam. It attempts to maintain underground cells in South Africa and to mobilize mass opinion in the major cities on occasions like the public funerals of ANC members killed in action.

The extent of ANC support in the cities is hard to assess. A German research team found that 21.7 percent of urban respondents expressed support for ANC leaders (as compared to 7.4 percent for leaders of the Pan Africanist Congress). Like its militant rivals, the ANC draws most of its support from the educated and prosperous classes rather than from the ill-educated and poor sections of the population.[9] In the 1980s the ANC's campaign of active sabotage has enjoyed a good measure of passive support simply because it has been the only group actively resisting the apartheid system. But since the ANC has apparently suffered a good deal from penetration by security agents, its effectiveness has remained strictly limited.

The South African Communist Party (founded in 1921) is South Africa's oldest multiracial political organization and the oldest Marxist-Leninist party in Africa. The SACP operates in exile and is presently headed by Moses Mabhida, an African. The party advocates a "national democratic revolution," to be achieved by means of a broad coalition (or front) composed of the workers, the petty bourgeoisie, and the "national bourgeoisie." Victory is to be gained by means of an armed struggle. Once it accomplishes its objectives, the national democratic revolution will rapidly evolve into a socialist revolution.[10] The SACP follows a rigidly pro-Soviet course and faithfully echoes every Soviet demand in world affairs. The party is, however, an army of officers without soldiers; its leadership is dominated by whites. Its appeal in South Africa is mainly to radical intellectuals, especially those of British, Jewish and Indian extraction.

The SACP compensates for its lack of numbers by its discipline, its extensive backing from the Soviet bloc, and its intellectual sophistication (which is reflected in its organ, the *African Communist* — published in London but printed in East Berlin). The party reaches out to other African socialist and radical parties. Like the Spanish communists during the Spanish Civil War, the SACP has shown an exceptional ability to mobilize support among men and women who haven't the slightest inclination toward communism. The Ruth First Foundation, set up in Great Britain as a charitable trust, serves to commemorate the name of a hard-line South African activist and former SACP Central Committee member who was murdered in Maputo in 1982. The foundation is supported by Olaf Palme, prime minister of Sweden; Archbishop Trevor Huddleston; Sir Hugh Casson, president of the Royal Academy of Arts; Lord Soper, former president of the British Methodist Conference; Andre Deutsch, the publisher; and other equally distinguished personages.[11]

The extraparliamentary opposition within South Africa has many facets. Orginally, the trade union movement was a largely white preserve. By the early 1980s however, South Africa contained both nonracial and black unions. Some of these have remained unregistered and are therefore devoid of those privileges that go with registration. Since 1979, however, even unregistered unions are no longer illegal, and some of them have become active in the political field. The churches have been equally important as opposition organizations, including a great variety of black congregations that adhered either to traditional churches (such as the Anglican Communion or the Evangelical Lutheran Church) or to dissident African sects. Ecclesiastical politics have today often become allied with national politics and therefore frequently cut across purely racial lines.

The South African Council of Churches (SACC) evolved from overseas-based mission societies. It has traditionally opposed racial segregation and advocated a unified nonracial South Africa. It has also been a principal educator of black people and has trained almost all of the leaders of African nationalism. The SACC has been a firm supporter of African nationalism and Black Consciousness. Because of this, it is strongly opposed by the government. It is under constant attack — for instance by the Eloff Commission, which investigated possible SACC misuse of its monies. The former secretary-general of the SACC was arrested in 1982.

Church opposition to apartheid has increased since 1982. One of the Dutch Reformed Churches (N. G. Sendingkerk) declared apartheid a heresy and joined the SACC. The World Alliance of Reformed Churches (WARC) suspended two South African members for supporting apartheid and appointed Dr. Alan Boesak, a Colored opponent of the government, president of the WARC. (The WARC is made up of the Calvinist churches of the world; for this group to call apartheid a heresy is a threat to the moral basis of South African government policy.)

An even more important source of opposition comes from the Homelands. The Homelands were established partly to divert African politics into safe channels, that is, into a concern with local, rather than national, affairs. (By 1984 the Transkei, Bophuthatswana, Venda, and Ciskei had attained formal independence, comprising a total of 57,933 square miles and about 8,000,000 people. Lebowa, Gazankulu, Qwaqwa, Kwazulu, and Kangwane were exercising self-government, and KwaNdebele was scheduled for independence in 1984.) Although they were poverty-stricken territories, the Bantu Homelands did provide legally recognized bases for African political action. Influential Homeland leaders began to involve themselves in those national South African issues that the architects of apartheid had hoped to keep out of Homeland politics.

The most influential Homeland leader is Gatsha Buthelezi. In the early 1970s Buthelezi reactivated the Inkatha Ye-Nkululeko yeSizwe (the national cultural liberation movement), a Zulu nationalist organization originally founded by King Dinizulu in 1928. In the same year the South African Black Alliance (SABA) came into being, an umbrella organization (also headed by Buthelezi) that comprised Inkatha, the Indian Reform party, the Linkoanketla party (mainly supported by the South Sotho of Qwaqwa), and — for a time — the Labor Party of South Africa (a Colored body). SABA's influence is hard to assess. Its one-time claim to have enjoyed the support of 8,000,000 people seems unrealistic. Nevertheless, the previously cited inquiry by Hanf and others found that Buthelezi was regarded as the most popular African leader; he was rated first by 48.8 percent of all informants. SABA's membership is disparate and fluctuates a great deal. Its formal organization leaves much to be desired. Nevertheless, Buthelezi's personal influence is considerable, not only among the Zulu, but also among many Africans of other ethnic origins — including educated urban Africans who approve of Buthelezi's call for a peaceful end to apartheid and a national convention to draw up a constitution for a nonracial South Africa.

Politics in the Homelands has come to mirror those in independent African states characterized by one-party rule, pervasive corruption, and expanding bureaucracies.[12] The opposition has generally fared badly, even though the total number of political prisoners in the Homelands (estimated at 215 at the end of 1983) has remained small (as compared to those in countries such as Angola, Mozambique, Uganda under Amin, or Guinea under Sekou Touré).

At the time of writing, the various black organizations remained relatively powerless — subject to all manner of financial and organizational weaknesses and beset by internal dissensions. Nevertheless, they can draw on universal opposition to apartheid and a widespread sense of long-term optimism. (According to the investigation carried out by Hanf's team, more than 60 percent of all blacks expect to be "happy" in the next ten years, whereas whites are much more inclined to believe that their condition will change for the worse during the next decade.)[13] The ready availabity of foreign broadcasts (accessible even in remote villages by means of cheap and affordable transistor radios), the impact of South Africa's extensive and variegated press, the spread of education among black people and their gradual progress into skilled and even managerial professions, and the enormous growth of the economy has caused blacks to believe that time is on their side.

Whites, moreover, are declining as a total proportion of the population. (According to current estimates, the European population is likely to decrease from 16.2 percent of the total population in 1980 to 13.7 percent by the year 2000.) These changes are certain to bring about a fundamental shift in South Africa's power equation and render unrealistic any expectation that constitutional concessions could be confided only to Asians and Coloreds and to the Homelands.

At the present time (1984), the various African opposition movements continue to be splintered and relatively powerless — limited to occasional symbolic acts of terrorism and assassination or outbreaks of violence in townships over local issues.[14] The black opposition is too dependent on intellectuals; it is organizationally weak and lacks soldiers and arms. It has failed to create effective underground movements or a revolutionary counterstate. To date, the police and informers have suppressed all political opposition in South Africa.

Nevertheless, the number of political prisoners and banned people is quite small by the standards of African one-party states or Marxist regimes. Similarly, the number of political prisoners who have died in prison (fifty-six) is small when compared to those killed by the bloody regimes of African and Arab dictators.

By 1985 political opponents were restricted to four types:

1. Convicted political prisoners in state prisons like Robben Island. These number 451, of which forty-four are Namibians.
2. Political detainees held without charge or trial are of three types: those held under Section 6 of the Terrorism Act; those detained as political state witnesses under the Internal Security Act; and those held in preventive detention under the Internal Security Act. It is difficult to establish the number of political

detainees, since the authorities do not publish their names or inform their families. The Christian Institute and the South African Institute of Race Relations estimates that 700 people were detained after the Soweto riots. From 1974 to 1976 217 people were detained.

3. Banned people at present number about twelve. In all, more than 1,300 people have been under banning orders since the Suppression of Communism Act was passed in 1950. Forty people were banned in 1976. (Banned people live at home.)

4. The category of banished people is no longer used. More than 140 were banished from their homes to internal exile in the 1940s and the 1960s.[15]

Early in 1984 the ANC had to rethink its strategy of national liberation (having apparently lost the use of all its privileged sanctuaries in adjacent countries. (By this time the ANC had been shut out of Mozambique, Swaziland, and Lesotho. Botswana and Zimbabwe had never sanctioned military action against South Africa from their territories.) In 1984 the ANC's ally the South West African People's Organization (SWAPO) lost the use of its bases in southern Angola because of a new agreement between Angola and South Africa (see the article in this volume by L. H. Gann and Peter Duignan on Namibia and the BLS states — Botswana, Lesotho, and Swaziland). In all probability, South Africa's military and diplomatic successes will strengthen the Black Consciousness Movement, discourage militant Maxist-Leninist groups, and persuade the masses that military action is at present futile.

By 1984 legal opposition derived from many sources. These included most of the South African churches. The churches were coordinated by the South African Council of Churches under the guidance of Bishop Desmond Tutu, a leading critic of apartheid, and a Nobel Peace Prize laureate. A most vocal political group is the Azanian Peoples Organization (AZAPO). But the most important opposition force was the United Democratic Front (set up in 1983), led by Allan Boesak — a young Colored preacher who reminded many South Africans of Martin Luther King. The Front operated as a loose alliance of trade unions and civic organizations that generally supported the ANC's Freedom Charter and attempted to secure the support of all races in its opposition to the new constitution. Blacks — especially the educated, the youthful, and the town bred — supported the Front in large numbers.

Widespread demonstrations and violence broke out in 1985, with the result that, for the first time, South African authorities made army units available to support the police in Soweto. Militants encouraged widespread rioting that resulted in numerous deaths from police fusillades. So-called collaborators were murdered, militants attempted to render nugatory the work of the elected city councils set up in the black townships. Black militants also succeeded in assuring an extremely low voters' turnout for municipal elections. (For instance, only 10.9 percent of the voters participated in the Soweto poll for 1983.) (Municipal services in the black townships were originally provided by white municipal councils. Far-reaching changes began in the 1970s; these were extended in 1982 by the Black Local Authorities Act, which provided for the establishment of black municipal authorities outside the Homelands with powers comparable to those of the white local authorities.)

Black unions (a potentially strong political force) have been legally recognized since 1979 as a result of the recommendations of the Wiehahn Commission. (Unofficial black unions had developed between 1973 and 1979 and had had an estimated membership of over 50,000.) The unions movement has since grown rapidly; by 1984 over 300,000 black workers belonged to unions. Black unions are split on two major issues: should they be organized on non-racial or black consciousness lines; should they be political or non-political? As a result of police harassment and numerous arrests, by 1984 union leaders had become more concerned with questions of wages and hours and less with political issues. (This changed early in 1985 as a result of police violence in the Eastern Cape.)

THE STATE MACHINERY

In 1948 the South African system was officially called apartheid; subsequently, it advocated separate development; since 1981 it has aimed at a constellation of states — or confederalism. But no matter what it has been called, the system has been racially discriminatory. Personal freedom, freedom of movement and residence, and freedom of speech have always been drastically curtailed. Although various apartheid restrictions have lessened since the 1970s (for example, racial separation and segregation), the basic legal system and the state machinery imposes racial segregation and discrimination and suppresses opposition to the system.

There is an unequal allocation of civil rights on the basis of color or race; there is less discrimination against people on grounds of race in respect to services, facilities, and employment; there is separation of people by race, and there were laws prohibiting marriage or sexual relations across racial lines until 1983. Separation leads to a feeling of inferiority for blacks, Indians, and Coloreds. Services for non-whites are generally inferior to those provided for whites. Severe legal restrictions on people's freedoms drive opposition underground and make peaceful change difficult. The two most drastic laws are the Terrorism Act, No. 83 of 1967 and the Internal Security Act, No. 44 of 1950. Although there has been much reform and improvement, as of 1985 the apartheid system is still discriminatory and repressive.[16] South Africa resembles most African one-party states in having an oppressive state machinery, but it differs from them in its legalism. There is rule by law, but the law is unjust.

The Civil Service

The public services are a bastion of the South African establishment. Originally, they were largely a preserve of English-speaking South Africans — as were the officer corps and the major corporations. After the Nationalist victory in 1948, the public service sector began to expand rapidly. (Between 1950 and 1965 it expanded from 106,956 to 198,496 members; these included all ranks, from the administrative class to the great army of typists and semi-skilled workers.) Afrikaners began to occupy an ever-increasing share of the positions within the service sector and a sound knowledge of Afrikaans became an almost indispensable qualification for promotion.

After 1965 the service continued to expand at the rate of about three percent a year. There was none of the administrative elephantiasis that troubled independent black states like Nigeria and Zambia. There was expansion, but it primarily affected the parastatals, the complex network of agencies set up to develop the Homelands, and the regional, provincial, and local administrations. Total expenditures for the public sector — including those for provincial and local governments, but excluding public corporations — increased each year. (These accounted for 25 percent of the gross national product in 1960 and 33 percent in 1975.) (See Table 2.)

Table 2: Civil Service Establishment

	1965	1977
Administrative Division	7,773	5,985
Professional	7,230	8,897
Technical	9,766	8,125
Clerical	20,897	14,063
General A	2,859	2,008
General B	42,792	28,083

Source: *State of South Africa Yearbook*, 1968, p. 36; J. N. Cloete, "The Bureaucracy," in Anthony de Crespigny and Robert Schire, eds., *The Government and Politics of South Africa* (Cape Town: July, 1978), p. 60.

In the South African Republic (RSA) in 1960, an estimated 30 percent of the economically active whites worked in the public sector; by 1966 the number had increased to 35 percent. Between 1960 and 1979 the public sector (excluding the public corporations) augmented at an annual rate of 3 percent. The private sector grew at a rate of 2.4 percent, but a large portion of that growth was in the public corporations. (See Table 3.)

For all its addiction to bureaucratic routine, the civil service was small enough to permit rapid decisions, and, in contrast to that of most African states, it generally performed in a reasonably efficient manner. Despite a few scandals (including the so-called Muldergate affair), it remained largely free from corruption. This gave South Africa an immense — and little appreciated — advantage over most black African states in which the civil service and state corporations often became part of a nationwide system of patronage and extortion. There are a number of explanations for this phenomenon. In South Africa, private enterprise remained powerful, as did the press, the Parliament, and white public opinion. Moreover, the public service sector was never politicized in the way that it was in African one-party regimes; this constitutes a crucial difference between South Africa and the black states. The public service was never regarded as the executive arm of the ruling party.

Politically, the public service is by no means homogeneous. It reflects all the divisions that beset white society as a whole. The technical departments, the administrations of the large municipalities (which have their own separate administrative machines), the higher ranks of the armed services, and the departments concerned with economic development tend to be reformist on the all-pervasive issue of white-black relations. In contrast, the police,

Table 3: Employment in the Public and Private Sectors, 1974, and Cumulative Growth Rates, 1960–1974

	Persons employed in 1974 (thousands)	Cumulative annual rate of growth, 1960–1974[b] (percent)
Private Sector		
Agriculture	1,505	nil
Mining	664	0.50
Industry	1,316	5.33
Construction	405	8.83
Commerce	494	3.64
Banks and building societies	70	5.80
Total: private sector	4,454	2.36
Public Sector		
Electricity	52	4.11
South African railways	232	0.47
Communications	64	3.22
Central government	371	5.39
Provincial administration	209	2.97
Local governments	203	2.13
Universities	22	7.60
Total: public sector[c]	1,153	2.99

Notes:
   a. Given to provide relative proportions.
   b. Growth rate in number of persons employed.
   c. Not all categories of public servants are included in the table, and therefore the totals should not be accepted as comprehensive. The annual rates of growth are nevertheless representative for purposes of comparison.

Source: A. D. Wassenaar, *Assault on Private Enterprise* (Cape Town: Tafelberg Publishers, 1977), p. 73.

the strictly administrative departments, and the lower ranks of the military and civil service tend to be conservative on this issue.

Structurally, the civil service mirrors a white society in which there are no rigidly separate status groups. Just as an able white private in the army can work his way up to be a general, an ambitious white clerk can work his way up to the rank of under secretary in the civil service. The bureaucracy does not form part of a privileged social caste. Although they enjoy social respect, civil servants rank no higher than bankers or business people; the snobbish contempt for trade that commonly characterizes senior bureaucrats in Great Britain and many Third World countries is nonexistent. Members of the higher levels of the civil service are well educated; most of them spend their careers in one particular department, which results in a considerable degree of administrative conservatism, experience, and stability.

The civil service is run by the Public Services Commission. The Commission oversees most departments (with the exception of those concerned with the coercive powers of the state: the Bureau of State Security, the Department of Defense, the South African Police, and the prison service). The Public Services Commission supervises recruitment, promotion, and general conditions of service. It also attempts to raise general efficiency. To further this end, in 1979 the Public Services Commission drew up a "rationalization plan" designed to reduce the number of government departments, restructure the personnel system, and modernize existing legislation.

Within the service, the power elite comprises the members of the Administrative Division, who make the basic policy decisions. The Professional Division is composed of the specialists; below them rank the officers in the clerical and technical divisions; these are followed by a great army of semiskilled and unskilled employees. In the past, one of the most powerful fiefs was the Department of Cooperation and Development. This formed almost a state within a state and was concerned with a broad range of administrative services and economic functions having to do with the black population.

Beginning in the early 1980s, however, the government began to dismantle this vast administrative empire in a major attempt at administrative reform. Labor relations moved to the Department for Manpower, relations with the Homelands to Foreign Affairs, numerous legal functions to the Ministry of Justice, population registration for blacks to Home Affairs, a variety of educational tasks to the Department of Education, economic development to the Development Bank, and so forth. In what constituted a major bureaucratic power shift, the once mighty Department of Cooperation and Development (once known as the Department of Bantu Administration and Development) was transformed into a mere coordinating agency. (In contrast, the Department of Constitutional Development and Planning assumed a key role in mapping out future policy.)

The Department of Cooperation and Development has originally also operated a number of major statutory bodies that together constituted a great administrative and economic empire of their own. One of these bodies was the Corporation for Economic Development, set up in 1959 to, among other things, provide financial help to black business people, make loans and technical assistance available to them, and act as a savings bank. Another was the Mining Corporation, set up to develop mineral industries. These and other agencies administered the world's largest aid program in terms of the taxpayer's per capita contribution. (The amount increased from R 27 million in 1959 to R 108.8 million in 1979; the 1979 amount represented 10.8 percent of that year's national budget.)[17]

In other words, by the early 1980s South Africa had become a strange combination of a coercive society and a welfare state — of state socialism and free enterprise. Within its confines, the bureaucracy had come to wield an immense amount of political and economic influence, which, in many ways, exceeded that of Parliament. Both at the national and the municipal level, South African bureaucrats operated an immensely complicated and expensive system of state control and regulation. Transfer payments and subsidies were designed to control opposition groups and to benefit special groups, including African business people and laborers and the recipients of protected markets and subsidized rents. These groups, along with many other special interest groups who were similarly subsidized, consequently acquired a limited stake in the existing order.

The South African authorities have tried to silence criticism of their constitutional reforms by making changes in the laws governing urban blacks. The Riekert Commission called for a review of all legislation controlling urban blacks and of the local government authorities controlling black communities. The Black Local Authorities Act (1982) established town and village councils. The Black Communities Development Bill (1984) changed administrative boards into development boards. The third of the Koornhof Bills — the Orderly Movement and Settlement of Black Persons Bill — was passed in mid-1984. These three bills have shown that Botha's government accepts the fact that urban blacks form communities of their own in South Africa that have needs different from those of Homeland blacks. The new legislation gives both groups new and wider opportunities for decisionmaking and for development of their areas.

Nevertheless, problems abound under this new dispensation.

What, for instance, is to be the source of financing? Black townships are not economically viable; in recent years they have depended on government grants and loans to upgrade their infrastructures and services. In order to make further improvements in these areas, black communities will need outside aid. The Croeser Working Group is looking into the question of financing for local authorities. In March of 1984 black taxpayers gained tax parity with other racial groups in South Africa. About 80 percent of blacks will now pay less than they did under the discriminatory Black Taxation Act.

By 1984 twenty-six black town councils were in operation, but they faced a variety of difficult problems. The councils were unpopular among black militants. The councils found themselves under pressure to increase services at a time when their deficits were increasing. They had to cope with all manner of administrative anomalies because the division of responsibility between the black local authorities and the development boards was ill defined with regard to housing, influx control, and so forth. There were also wider political questions that emerged after the passage of the Koornhof Bills. Would the granting of political rights to permanently urbanized blacks in the third tier (the municipal level of government) be a step toward giving blacks political rights in the first tier (the national government)? Or would blacks continue to have political rights only in the Homelands? The grant of ninety-nine year leases to blacks in the white cities was an improvement, but the question of permanent landownership remained unresolved. A much more serious issue was the relocation of Africans by the government in order to put into practice official theories about separate development. The scale of this relocation program was staggering; something like three-and-a-half million people are estimated to have been moved in a series of expensive and disruptive operations. Africans were shifted for a variety of reasons: to remove black enclaves in white areas, to strengthen influx control, to eliminate urban slums, to get rid of black squatters on white farms, and to promote the growth of villages and townships in the Homelands.[18]

On January 25, 1985, the state president made a major policy statement in Parliament. He called for "cooperative coexistence" between the races and accepted the "permanence" of the many black communities outside the "national states" in the Republic of South Africa. His government would be prepared to negotiate with blacks concerning the grant of property rights within the Republic of South Africa and the "national states." There would also be negotiations for the creation of new political "structures" that would enable blacks outside the national state to share power and participate at the highest level in the government of their own affairs. The "credibility" of black local authorities would be increased by allowing them to rule themselves (councils, police, tax power). "Clarity" would have to be attained on the citizenship question. The government would set up an "informal, nonstatutory forum." It will meet on an ad hoc basis; membership will be by invitation. It will enable "interest groups" and government representatives to create the basis for negotiations in the constitutional field. Botha also promised to change influx control measures (that is, control black travel and access to jobs) and to change resettlement policies.

The direct and indirect costs of these measures, and the expense and extent of new services provided, were not made clear to the taxpayer; in fact, the government concealed their full extent so as not to create difficulties for itself with a white electorate that was disenchanted with the growing tax burden and reluctant to support the Bantustans or Homelands.

Without quite being aware of the mechanism involved, South Africa has become both an oppressively interventionist state and by far the most extensive and comprehensive welfare state in Africa. In these characteristics, South Africa is essentially modern and comparable, not to black states, but to the United States and European states. South Africa operates a more efficient security system, and regulates its peoples lives more extensively and effectively than the most Marxist-Leninist African states.

The Parastatals

In South Africa the state has intervened in economic life since the inception of the Union in 1910. The government subsidized European agriculture and intervened in the mining industry and in the business of transport and production. The South African Railway and Harbors (formed in 1910) dominated the country's entire transport system. In 1922 the Electric Supply Commission (ESCOM) supplied a portion of the electrical power; by 1949 ESCOM provided the major portion of it. In 1928 the government established the Iron and Steel Corporations (ISCOR); by World

War II ISCOR extended its operations into manufacturing. ISCOR became a vast steel empire by means of controlling interests in a great variety of corporations. In 1940 South Africa established the Industrial Development Corporation (IDC), designed to promote the country's industrial development by assisting private industries. Thereafter, the IDC's economic power expanded enormously. (Between 1940 and 1979 its authorized capital rose from R 10 million to R 350 million.) It set up a great manufacturing complex with interests in scores of companies. It even collaborated with foreign concerns, both in South Africa and in Namibia (for example, Rio Tinto). In 1960 the corporation launched an export finance scheme to promote trade and development north of the Limpopo River. (In Malawi and Lesotho the IDC pattern was copied by the Malawi and Lesotho Development Corporations.) The IDC and ESCOM also played a significant part in the Cunene Project in Namibia and in financing the Cabora Bassa hydro-electric complex in Mozambique.

Most importantly, the IDC encouraged the creation of other state enterprises. In 1947 the IDC launched the South African Coal, Oil, and Gas Corporation (SASOL). Like the Southern Oil Exploration Corporation (SOECDR), it was originally designed to increase South Africa's fuel independence; later it was used to protect South Africa against an international oil boycott. SASOL now operates the world's only viable oil-from-coal plant and at present is greatly expanding its operations. The Armaments Development and Production Corporation (ARMSCOR) develops and manufactures weapons; the National Defense Research Institute of the Council for Scientific and Industrial Research (CSIR) conducts military research in conjunction with the research departments run by ARMSCOR's subsidiaries. In South Africa (as elsewhere), the Atomic Energy Board (founded in 1949) is a state corporation; so is the Nuclear Fuels Corporation. The state owns the Phosphate Development Corporation (FOSCOR — set up by the IDC in 1955), and the Aluminium Corporation of South Africa (ALUSAF), among others.

The Homelands development plans were also largely dependent on state enterprise. Beginning in 1959 the IDC began setting up new parastatal bodies to deal with the nonwhite population, such as the Bantu Investment Corporation, the Xhosa Development Corporation, the Bantu Mining Corporation, the Colored Development Corporation, and the Rehoboth Development Corporation.

Table 4: Gross Domestic Fixed Investment by Type of Oranization, 1960–1978

(R million)

	1960	1970	1978
Public authorities	370	1,038	2,840
Public corporation	67	342	2,362
Private business	624	1,769	4,692
Total	1,061	3,149	9,894

Source: *Official Yearbook of the Republic of South Africa, 1980–81* (Johannesburg: Van Rensburg Publication, 1981), p. 879.

This growth of government enterprise revolutionized South African investment policy. In 1950 private investment far exceeded that of public authorities and public corporations. By 1971 public investments almost equalled those made by private corporations, and by 1976 private investment formed less than half of total investments. (See Table 4.)

In sociological terms, the parastatal bodies served several distinct purposes. They helped to strengthen South Africa in the military sphere. They provided an outlet for the energies of public-spirited people, especially Afrikaners. The state controlled broadcasting and television (as in Sweden), and programs were designed not merely to entertain but also to provide what planners regarded as instruction in morality. (Not that the planners escaped attack. They incurred censure from many critics, including Afrikaner businessmen such as Andreas Wassenaar — an Afrikaner nationalist who accused the parastatals of conducting a public assault on private enterprise.)

From the early 1980s the Botha government (as part of its wider policy of administrative decentralization) began a variety of reforms regarding parastatals that were designed to favor at least a limited degree of reprivatization. Nevertheless, the public sector remains of crucial importance and will continue to play a major part in South Africa's future.

The parastatal organizations have played their part in weakening the hegemony of English-speaking South Africans in the financial sector — a major aim of the Nationalist government elected in 1948. Parastatal bodies helped independent Afrikaner businessmen to rise by means of state patronage; they also served as instruments of separate development, thereby perpetuating the tradition of state enterprise in the Homelands. Additionally, parastatal bodies drew on South Africa's tradition of supporting private enterprise with public expenditure in the field of African administration. For instance, white taxpayers had traditionally made substantial contributions to provide subsidized housing for Africans in urban areas. Employers in commerce and industry were able to reduce their wage rates because their workers were accommodated partly at public expense. Parastatal bodies also used public funds for black development in South Africa — an enterprise that might have been carried out with greater success by the private sector.

Taken together, the major state corporations became a great power in the land. Between 1946 and 1975 the share of gross fixed investment of these bodies rose from about 3 percent to an estimated 17 percent of the nation's total investment. Their growth has recently shown some sign of diminishing, however (ISCOR's estimated expansion program for 1975–1984 cost about 3,240 million rand). The state corporations have been important in what might be called the bureaucratization of South Africa and the growth of state capitalism.

The work force of the central government grew by 276 percent between 1937 and 1966, as compared to a total population growth of 87 percent. By the early 1970s something like 30 percent of all economically active whites were employed in the public sector, including 44 percent of all whites with university qualifications. By the early 1980s about 40 percent of working whites worked in the public sector.

South African parastatals face problems identical to those encountered by their opposite numbers in many other parts of the world. (For instance, ISCOR — a major concern — incurred a massive 244 million rand loss in 1982–83.) But the South African parastatals are not inefficient. (ISCOR, to give just one example, managed to cut its losses in the operating year 1983–84 by means of a substantial rationalization program.)

The South African parastatals compare favorably to those in black countries like Zambia, Angola, and Mozambique. In Kenya, for instance, a Committee in Review of Statutory Boards concluded in 1979 that "there is clear evidence of prolonged inefficiency, financial mismanagement, waste, and malpractices in many parastatals." The Board also charged that Kenyan parastatals resisted efforts to make them accountable to the state and engaged in corruption and nepotism.[19] Most of these charges dealt with mismanagement; they did not attack the underlying cause of failure of most parastatals — monopoly control and lack of market accountability. In contrast, South African parastatals have, on the whole, been competently managed by some of the country's ablest industrialists. In general, the large state corporations have been profitable and appear to have been run as efficiently as private corporations. Nevertheless, the move to privatize these concerns in South Africa has grown stronger in the 1980s. The state's need to attract capital to expand its services appears to be the driving force behind the selling off of state corporations to private citizens who can provide equity capital. (A few other African states appear to be doing the same thing.)

This demand for capital from the South African government has escalated with the need to provide defense and to expand state enterprises such as schools, housing for blacks, grants for Homelands, and so forth. By shifting some of the state corporations to the private sector, the government can borrow money for its other demands. In 1979 the government began the process by selling 70 percent of its control in SASOL enterprises concerned with converting oil from coal. Possible other targets for privatization are ESCOM and the Post Office Telecommunications. ISCOR has said it could be ready to go public by 1985. Although the government does not have a timetable for privatization, it has continually carried on talks on this subject with business leaders.

The cost to the public of these corporations is not easy to establish. Whereas private companies charge depreciation of existing assets as an expense before deriving profit figures, the state corporations charge the estimated value of replacing their assets. Allowing for inflation, these estimates are much higher than depreciation costs. The true worth of state corporations is therefore masked by accounting procedures and inflation. For the period 1978–1983, ESCOM sales increased at 15.7 percent per year, and operation profits at 18.5 percent per year. Similarly, ISCOR has had a 14 percent growth and an 18.5 percent profit per year — but shows a R 6.7 million loss for 1978–1983. Between 1978–1982 state corporations had a net investment of R 12.4 billion (compared with R 17.6 billion for all private concerns.) These figures will probably be reversed in the coming years as South Africa moves away from state corporations with state involvement.

State corporations that do not make a profit, or that involve security or defense matters, will obviously not be privatized.

The Armaments Corporation of South Africa (ARMSCOR) is such a corporation. ARMSCOR is one of the country's largest industries. From 1974 to 1981 ARMSCOR's assets increased from R 200 million to R 1,200 million, and the number of its employees increased from 12,000 to 29,000. Another 60,000 are employed by associated companies in the private sector. Today the South African armament industry is the tenth largest in the world. ARMSCOR has had to expand in order to circumvent the UN arms embargo of 1977. South Africa is now self-sufficient in almost all types of arms, equipment, and ammunition. Only the most advanced aircraft, bombers, naval ships, and computers are currently beyond ARMSCOR's capabilities. ARMSCOR produces 30 percent of the country's arms; ARMSCOR subsidiaries produce another 15 percent; the private sector produces the remainder. Up to now, ARMSCOR has been able to supply the South African Defense Force with all the weapons it has needed; this makes an arms embargo (like other embargos against South Africa) ineffectual.

In the past four years, the South Africa government has been trying to strengthen the free enterprise system. State corporations are being sold (although over 300 are still in operation). Deregulation has been marked, but many restrictions remain. There are restrictions on labor, especially by the labor bureau, which controls mobility and recruitment. Influx control prevents qualified blacks and Indians from using their skills in all geographical locations. Until recently, land tenure laws prohibited freehold tenure for blacks in the urban areas, and it remains limited to this day. Land tenure laws prevent whites from helping to develop the Homelands. Housing regulations slow up the number of low-cost housing that can be built. Security laws interfere with the operation of black trade unions. Restrictive licensing interferes with the efficient operation of black and white businesses and limits operations to racial areas.

Defense and Police Forces

From its beginnings, South Africa relied for its defense on small professional cadres, which were expanded in wartime by white conscripts. (By the end of the 1970s the career posts in the Permanent Force made up only 7 percent of the entire military establishment and less than 3 percent of the land forces, resulting in an Israeli-type defense force.) This system enabled South Africa rapidly to expand its forces in wartime. During World War II the Union raised a total of 345,049 men who distinguished themselves as far afield as East Africa, North Africa, and Italy. After the end of the hostilities, this force was rapidly demobilized. The subsequent rise of African nationalism led to some expansion, but as late as 1962 the South African armed forces remain limited, exceeded in strength by the South African police force. (In 1963 the total armed forces numbered 25,000 men, as compared to 28,325 in the police force.)

After this, however, the armed forces expanded at a rapid rate, as did the arms industry. After 1977 and the UN arms boycott, the South African arms industry became capable of producing a whole new range of quality weapons. These included armored cars, missiles, and arms like the new G.5 — a 155 mm howitzer mounted on an extremely mobile self-propelled six-wheeled chassis, which ARMSCOR claims is superior to any gun produced by either NATO or the Warsaw Pact. (An unintended consequence of the South African arms was that it forced South Africa to expand its capacity; this, in turn, increased its power over its neighbors.)

South Africa's enlargement and modernization of its armed forces owed a major debt to P. W. Botha, who served as minister of defense until 1978. Not for nothing was he known within his party as "Piet Wapen" (Pete the Weapon). By 1983 the armed forces were officially reckoned at 82,400 men (incluing 53,100 conscripts). (The true number of mobilized men may have been higher however.) This force was composed of one armored brigade, one mechanized brigade, four motorized brigades, one parachute brigade, one special reconnaissance regiment, twenty artillery regiments, supporting specialist forces, a balanced air force, and a small navy organized for coastal defence. Overall, South Africa's total strength was assessed at 404,500 men.[20]

The defense forces as a whole were organized with an eye toward integrating the three services (army, air force, and navy) — particularly at their apexes. The armed forces were designed to perform a dual mission — to counter all forms of insurgency, and to maintain a conventional force capable of defending the country and of making retaliatory strikes if necessary. The counterinsurgency force was decentralized into nine territorial commands. These were staffed by personnel from the Permanent Force (who controlled training, logistics, and other administrative functions within their areas), a few specifically selected Citizens Force units, and the Commandos (who specialized in local defense).

The army was linked with the air force, navy, and medical services in a single command structure under the chief of the South African Defense Force (who was, in turn, accountable to the minister of defense). Overall, this establishment cost a good deal of money. (Between fiscal years 1963–64 and 1983–84, the defense budget rose from U.S. $219.8 million to $3.092 billion.) This increase, however, was paralleled by a striking growth in the GNP; hence South Africa experienced no excessive difficulty in shouldering its new defense burden (4.1 percent of the GNP in 1983–84). Although during the 1970s the South Africans lost the outer defense perimeter formerly made up of Rhodesia and the Portuguese colonies, they have become immeasurably superior in military strength to all their African neighbors combined.

The burden of maintaining this armed strength fell mainly on the whites, who, alone, among South Africa's various ethnic communities, were subject to conscription.[21] By partially enfranchising the Indians and Coloreds, the proposed parliamentary reforms raised the question of extending the draft to brown citizens as well as to citizens of European descent. The South African defense establishment, moreover, ceased to be lily white. Indians, Coloreds, and blacks, became eligible to serve as volunteers and even to attain commissioned rank. (By 1982 the army comprised 5,400 black and Colored professionals.) Conscription was administered fairly. (The South Africans did not make the same mistake the Americans did in the Vietnam War, when they designed a system of exemption that placed an unduly heavy burden on blue-collar workers.) A number of (mainly English-speaking) whites left the country to escape conscription and the hostilities in Namibia, but, overall, morale remained high (as exemplified by the low number of soldiers tried for desertion or other serious disciplinary offenses).

South Africa also has regional defense plans that included the use of the Homeland armies. Starting in 1975, the South African Defense Force began organizing and training armed forces for the independent Homelands of Transkei, Bophuthatswana, Venda, and Ciskei forces in battalion strength (250–300 men). These soldiers are used in the army, in the police, and in antiterrorist forces, and, since several occupy strategic border areas, South Africa clearly intends for them to provide a *cordon sanitaire* and to act as antiguerrilla units.[22]

The South African Defense Force reflects both the strengths and weaknesses of the country's white society at large. It contains a high proportion of men with developed technical skills. South Africans can therefore more easily maintain and deploy sophisticated technical equipment than can black African forces, whose privates are drawn mainly from the villages. Since the army is essentially representative of the white electorate, the country has not and does not face the danger of military coups of the black African and Latin American variety. Unlike the Rhodesian army during the latter part of the Zimbabwean civil war, the South African army has a strong sense of bureaucratic hierarchy; the generals defer to their civilian superiors and, although they have influence, cannot aspire to political power.

In recent years, the army's technical performance has improved greatly, owing to the creation of battle schools with realistic and efficient training procedures and the development of operational intelligence. The army is highly motivated and is skilled in both counterinsurgency warfare and in conventional mechanized operations (as evidenced in the 1984 maneuvers — Operation Thunder Chariot — that provided training for 11,000 troops in blitzkrieg type warfare). The conscripts have a sense of having to defend their own country rather than some remote dependency beyond the ocean. The armed forces are nonpolitical in the sense that their members are not expected to belong to any particular party. In so far as they have any political leanings, they tend to be more pragmatic than the police. The army's leadership is apt to be *verlig* (enlightened) for functional rather than ideological reasons. The officers would like to attract recruits of all colors, they believe in technological efficiency, and they would much prefer to fight a foreign rather than a domestic enemy. Overall, the armed forces regard themselves as an instrument of reform rather than repression. In this capacity, their influence will surely increase in the future.[23]

For white South Africans, the police force, rather than the army, has traditionally represented the country's first line of defense. The army has rarely been used for purposes of maintaining internal order; the police force has always served as the "mailed fist of apartheid." (It also maintains paramilitary units for use against guerrillas.) According to its critics, South Africa is a police state; a brutal and overpowering force keeps the country in an iron grip. In fact, the proportion of police officers to citizens is less than it is in the United States. In 1980 the South African Police (SAP) numbered 32,095 men (including 887 Indians, 1,845 Coloreds, 12,939 blacks, and 16,425 whites); that is, 1.4 police officers per thousand people. (Since then, the police force has expanded to a total of 47,000 men. In October 1984 the authorities announced that in response to recent unrest, they would expand the police force to a total of 68,000 men.) Despite numerous cases of police brutality against real or suspected revolutionaries, the South African police do not conform to the image presented of them by many white South African liberals — as a collection of semiliterate toughs. The police force has a good record on crime-solving. (In 1977–78 the police solved 92.7 percent of cases involving the safety of the state and 47.0 percent of cases involving offenses against property.)[24] The police are widely feared by urban black Africans, but the fear of criminals among urban blacks is even greater.[25]

Not that all is well with the police. They are ill paid. They must perform a very large number of ordinary administrative functions. These include inquiries on behalf of other government departments in centers where the volume of work does not merit the maintenance of separate offices by the agencies concerned. In rural areas the police have to institute criminal prosecutions and act as excise officers, immigrations officers, census takers, postal agents, meteorological observers, inspectors of vehicles and licenses, and so forth. Much of their work deals with the enforcement of apartheid laws, especially the hated pass laws. These are the activities that result in a greater degree of unpopularity for the police than for the armed forces. Additionally, the major South African cities face a serious crime problem — one that is likely to get worse rather than better.

Nevertheless, the police should not be underestimated. On the average, life and property are safer in South African cities than in most urban African or American communities of similar size. Armed with the support of an extensive intelligence network, and with the supervisory power embodied in the various pass laws and antiterrorist and anti-Communist legislation, the police function as a vital force in the defense of the existing power structure. The police are trained to act in cooperation with the armed forces and the civil administration and are well equipped for the task of counterinsurgency. The South Africans are now operating on the principle that, as far as possible, each major population group should be policed by its own members. Indians, Coloreds, and black African officers have become eligible for promotion to senior ranks. No revolution could occur unless it was preceded by an effective disruption of the police establishment.

The Bureau of State Security (BOSS) was formed in 1969. It performed internal and external secret police activities and gathered intelligence information on a worldwide basis. BOSS was much feared and hated, and it was blamed for assassinations and infiltration work both inside and outside South Africa. BOSS was reorganized in 1981 and now appears to have lost its dominant position to the military.[26]

The ultimate responsibility for defense lies with the cabinet. In its decisionmaking capacity, the cabinet is advised by the State Security Council (SSC), a major cabinet committee set up in 1972 to coordinate all agencies concerned with national security. The State Security Council consists of the president, the four ministers of defence, the chief of the South African Defense Force, the secretary for foreign affairs, the secretary for justice, the commissioner of police, and other officials who may be coopted by the council. The president serves as the SSC's chairman, a position that adds to his already extensive powers. The SSC has its own secretariat and is subdivided into separate branches (National Intelligence, Interpretation, Strategy, Strategic Communications, and an administrative branch). The SSC's functions include the formulation of plans, the coordination of strategies, and the utilization of intelligence. Intelligence is gathered by the National Intelligence Service (NIS, formerly BOSS) and the Military Intelligence Service (MIS).

The SSC maintains a working committee composed of about eleven department heads and the chairmen of the working groups of other cabinet committees. The SSC also draws on fifteen Interdepartmental Committees. (Together, these IDCs cover a remarkably wide spectrum; they include, among others, a Political Action Committee, a Coordinating Economic Committee, the Committee for Science and Technology, and the South African Telecommunications and Electrical Power Supply Committee.) The final component of the SSC network consists of a series of Joint Management Centers (Gesamtlike Bestuursentrums, GBSs). Each of these serves a different geographical area corresponding to areal commands of the Defense Force.[27]

Reorganization was designed not only to coordinate all aspects of defense but also to close the Boer-Brit fissure that has always divided the South African establishment. This object has not been wholly achieved. By 1985 the president was still heavily reliant on an inner ring of Afrikaners, including Magnus Malan, minister of defense; Constant Viljoen, chief of the South African Defense Force; Jan Geldenhuys, senior army command officer; R. F. ("Pik") Botha, foreign minister (whose Foreign Ministry Policy Planning Section became closely integrated into the new structure); and Lukas Barnard, head of the NIS (whose organization compared favorably with the former Bureau of State Security under its *eminence grise*, General Hendrik van den Bergh ("Lang Hendrik"). The president, however, also found in the Anglo-Afrikaner business community a keen ally, on which he could draw for advice and managerial talent. In an unprecedented manner, the president also began to take advantage of the South African academic community. Former government officials began to be hired by universities and institutes; increasing numbers of academics moved into government positions.[28]

According to its architects, the new structure is designed to turn back what South African policy makers regard as a "total onslaught" on their country from abroad. The "total onslaught" concept, developed by Deon Fourie (a South African soldier-scholar) under the influence of General André Beaufre's "total strategy" doctrine, has widely become a journalistic slogan. In its original form, the concept did not attest that South Africa was about to be assaulted from every side, but that the country would have to plan its defense on many levels — military, diplomatic, economic, and so forth. South African grand strategy incorporates three aspects. It seeks to expand the country's military and industrial base. It emphasizes the political aspects of internal war, as taught in British and French military academies. (It is instructive that many South African strategists admire the French colonial school of thought — especially the Galliéni-Lyautey concept of the army as an instrument of enlightened sociopolitical development — but find little to admire in the American experience in Vietnam.) In addition, it is outward-looking, that is, it seeks to establish South Africa's credibility and status so as to be an acceptable partner for other African (including even Marxist) governments on the continent.

How efficient is this sytem? All indications are that it operates well (a theme to which we will return in the section on "The

Inevitable Revolution"). The SSC apparently manages to achieve coordination; the bureaucratic structure is not overly complex. (The Secretariat, for instance, only comprises forty-five members.) The South Africans appear to have built up an extensive intelligence network, whose tentacles extend not only into their own country but also into the so-called African Front Line States and Western and Eastern Europe. The ANC's failure to achieve more than a limited success to date could be partly attributable to infiltration by agents of South African intelligence into the ranks of the ANC and its supporting organizations. Above all, the South Africans have developed what the African Front Line States lack — a unified command and a central direction of resources. This is a formidable combination that is in marked contrast to the dissensions and dispersion of effort that characterizes South Africa's many opponents.

THE ECONOMY

When the Union of South Africa came into being in 1910, the country corresponded in every respect to the modern image of a neocolonial dependency — a backward country locked into a cycle of poverty allowing of no easy escape. South Africa relied heavily on the export of raw materials, especially gold; its industries remained in the infant stage; its main trade partner was Great Britain, and this country also supplied much of the Union's capital. Deprivation was rife, not only among black Africans and Colored, but also among Afrikaners; as late as 1931 a Carnegie study commission classified half of South Africa's white population as poor, and no less than 17.5 percent were described as living "in dire poverty" or as unable to live except by means of charity.[29]

This situation prompted many gifted academic experts to vie with each other in making pessimistic prognoses. For instance, in 1941 C. W. de Kiewiet, a leading U.S. scholar, published a seminal work on South Africa's economic history. His book remains a classic. For all his analytical skill, however, he mistakenly predicted that manufacturing would develop only slowly in South Africa. (This prediction was made at the very moment that the country was poised for startling advances.) His pessimism was shared by other experts, who assumed that the operation of the industrial color bar, the persistence of the migrant labor system among black Africans, the small size of South Africa's domestic market, and the relative lack of domestic capital would all act to inhibit any rapid industrialization of the country.[30]

South Africa had many economic assets, however. The gold industry provided the country with a ready export that could be easily taxed to provide indirect support for agriculture and other industries. South Africa possessed a stable system of government and administration, a substantial reservoir of technical skills, a solid infrastructure of banking and commercial undertakings, and efficient railways and ports. There was a relatively productive farming industry, mainly dependent on white entrepreneurs. (By 1957 white agrigulture was based on some 100,000 farms; of these, 75,000 were worked by their owners, 3 percent by managers, and the remainder rented or leased to sharecroppers.) Standards of farming varied greatly — from very poor to excellent. Generally, however, the less efficient farmers were squeezed out by rising costs and tough competition. (Between 1960 and 1976 the value of South Africa's farm output increased more than threefold — from 802 million to 2,938 million rand — whereas the number of farming units fell by one quarter.) This agricultural productivity sharply contrasted with the failure of agriculture in most of black Africa. (In 1984 twenty-one African states could not feed their populations and had to import food.)

Industrial development expanded tremendously during World War II and its aftermath, when South Africa was forced to manufacture all manner of weaponry and civilian equipment that could no longer be imported from Great Britain. When the guns stopped firing in 1945, South Africa was therefore set for an African *Wirtschaftswunder*. (Already by 1945 manufacturing accounted for a larger portion of the GNP than any other economic pursuit; twenty years later, the share of manufacturing was larger than that of agriculture, forestry, fishing, mining, and quarrying combined.) Unlike the rest of Africa, South Africa became capable of supplying the bulk of its investments from its domestic savings. Foreign investment, although important, provided no more than a minor share of South Africa's total domestic capital. By 1979 foreigners had a total of 22.9 billion rand (about U.S. $22 billion) invested in South Africa and their Homelands. In this year the EEC countries accounted for 56 percent of the total and the United States for 23 percent (as compared to 65 percent and 17 percent, respectively, in 1973). Gross domestic savings for the year 1978 amounted to over 11 billion rand. This evolution, along with the indigenous development of South African technology, were widely ignored abroad. Advocates of disinvestment remained wedded to an archaic interpretation of South African economic realities — one that was modeled on her situation in the late nineteenth century and that assumed that South Africa was still a backward country.[31]

South Africa's sustained economic expansion, although contrasting sharply with the economic situation in most black-ruled states, remained subject to severe cyclical fluctuations. Foreign critics continually expected these setbacks to presage the inevitable breakdown of South Africa's apartheid regime. For instance, after the bloody rioting at Sharpeville in 1960, capital began to flee the country; many experts expected a rapid collapse of South Africa's existing order, which was not thought to be able to survive the inevitable tide of decolonization in Africa. According to analysts like Pierre van den Berghe, a sociologist of international reputation, the internal contradictions of South African capitalism (and more especially, those of the apartheid system) had created — and would continue to create — so many "dysfunctions" that the country was headed for a rapid breakdown.[32]

But, once again, South Africa defied the prophets. Its economy recovered and continued to expand at a rapid pace. The annual growth rate of the gross domestic product was 12.5 percent between 1965 and 1970; between 1971 and 1977 it was 15.7 percent.) South African factories turned out an increasing number of capital goods characteristic of a highly developed economy — for instance, mining and agricultural machinery, cranes, ships, and electrical equipment. In doing so, South Africa solidified its position as Africa's economic giant. (By 1970, with only 6 percent of Africa's total population, South Africa generated close to 24 percent of the continent's total income.) Instead of remaining inefficient and half-starved, the South African black labor force became better educated and better paid. (Between 1970 and 1975 the disposable income of black Africans doubled; business therefore increasingly looked to black and brown, as well as white, customers for profits.)

This is not to say that South Africa solved all of its deep-seated problems; far from it! Overall, disparities remained between white and black incomes. The apartheid system continued to impose innumerable hardships; a maze of laws and regulations interfered with the citizens' rights to reside and work wherever — and marry whomever — they pleased. Although they made some progress,

Table 5: Per Capita Gross Domestic Product at Market Prices for
Selected Countries, 1974, in U.S. Dollars

United States of America	$6,670
France	5,440
White South Africans	4,936
Colored South Africans	998
Chile	920
Black South Africans (Soweto)	575
Black South Africans (average)	451
Ghana	451
Nigeria	330
Black South African Homelands	255
Kenya	200
Tanzania	160

Source: Art Spandau, *Economic Boycott Against South Africa: Normative and Factual Issues* (Johannesburg: University of the Witwatersrand, Labor Research Program, 1978), p. 83.

the Homelands remained backward islands, incapable of solving any of their difficulties unaided; they were essentially backward Third World countries like most of those in Africa. Nevertheless, in comparative terms, brown and black South Africans did make considerable advances. Contrary to what many (although not all) of South Africa's critics abroad asserted, South African blacks were far from being the world's most poverty-stricken people. (See Table 5.)

From the mid-1970s to the mid-1980s, the South African economy once again experienced severe fluctuations. The country became enmeshed in a worldwide recession, whose full effects were only delayed by the cushioning effects of gold exports, massive borrowing abroad, and heavy public expenditure. The long years of cheap oil came to an end; South Africa, like other importers, was forced to pay more for its fuel. Recession was followed by recovery. Between 1980 and 1982 the GDP rose from 57,765 million rand to 72,777 million rand. In 1982 the primary sector (including agriculture and mining) provided 20.5 percent; the secondary sector (manufacturing, electricity, construction, and so forth) furnished 32.10 percent; the tertiary sector (trade, finance, government services, and so forth) supplied 35.0 percent; the rest was accounted for by miscellaneous pursuits. After 1982 prosperity receded once again. By 1983 the country found itself in the throes of a severe depression that was made worse by a devastating drought and by the government's inability to end inflation (12.4 percent by the middle of the year).

South Africa continued to face a great variety of social and economic problems. Unemployment heavily affected the black community. It is not precisely known how many blacks found themselves without jobs; unemployment estimates for the late 1970s varied from 800,000 to 2,000,000 people. Despite the government's efforts to improve their agricultural productivity, the rural areas remained poverty-striken. More and more African workers continued to pour into the labor market, a process that none of the government's urban influx controls were able to prevent.

South Africa's export earnings remained heavily dependent on gold — an exhaustible resource. (In 1983 gold still accounted for about 46 percent of the country's export earnings.) By an ironic twist, the inflationary policies long adopted by welfare states in many parts of the world raised world gold prices, thereby providing an unintentional subsidy to South Africa. The public sector (discussed in the section on parastatals) suffered from a broad range of disabilities. There were also far-reaching changes within the economic power structure; control over the private economy became increasingly concentrated in the hands of a few major conglomerates. (By 1983 seven companies — Anglo-American, Barlow Rand, Rembrandt Group, Anglovaal, Old Mutual, Sanlam, and Liberty Life — together controlled an estimated 80 percent of the value of stock listed on the Johannesburg Stock Exchange. Anglo-American and its subsidiaries alone made up no less than 56 percent of the exchange's total value of R 90 billion.)[33]

South Africa remained a country within which the First World was superimposed on the Third World. South Africa therefore shared the problems common to both — rapid urbanization, a high rate of demographic expansion, crime, pollution, and traffic snarls — besides all the inequities derived from the country's ethnocratic power structure. The country's unwillingness to do away with residential segregation, for example, continued to inhibit the mobility of labor. Skilled labor remained in short supply. In fact, a shortage of skilled white labor continued to run parallel to a surplus of unskilled black labor (an endemic feature of the South African economy that tardy reforms proved unable to eliminate.)[34]

Despite many difficulties, by the mid-1980s the South African economy again displayed a remarkable resilience that had no parallel in any other African country. The government made a number of concessions to African workers. It finally permitted black trade unions; it permitted a far-reaching relaxation of the color bar that had reserved certain jobs for whites; and it made at least some effort to reduce the wage gap between employees of European and non-European origin.[35] Africans all found new job opportunities, and there was more occupational mobility for brown and black workers than had existed in the past. The average income of South Africans of all races increased. (Between 1970 and 1980 average monthly earnings for whites rose from R 298 to R 768; for blacks, from R 43 to R 189; for Coloreds, from R 88 to R 245; and for Asians, from R 101 to R 336.)

South Africa also enjoyed other advantages. The country became a major producer of base minerals — including metals (such as chrome) and fuels (such as uranium and coal). (By 1982 South Africa had become the world's sixth largest producer of coal — ahead of both India and Great Britain.) Major new capital-expansion projects came to fruition (including the new harbors at Richards Bay and Saldanha Bay, nuclear power stations, and great enterprises designed to turn coal into oil). South Africa also exported food to its black neighbors.

The Labor Movement

The black labor movement in South Africa has a long history. The movement only began to achieve prominence in the 1970s, however — especially after 1979, when black unions were legalized and membership increased. Unions were organized on a plant-to-plant basis. They appear to be politically significant, since the union movement constituted the only way in which blacks could exert influence. (By 1982 300,000 blacks belonged to unions, and black unions now represent about 10.6 percent of the black industrial work force.) They currently face many obstacles, however. They are weak; they are not united; factionalism abounds; and they have suffered arrests and harassment from the police.

The primary legal unions for blacks are: The Trade Union Council of South Africa (TUCSA), affiliated black trade unions, the Council of Unions of South Africa (CUSA), the Federation of South African Trade Unions (FOSATU), and independent trade unions.[36]

It is important also to mention the illegal nonfederated unions, since they form the bulk of the organized unions in the eastern and western Cape. The illegal unions are: Motor and Component Workers Union of South Africa (MAWUSA/GWUSA), the General Workers Union (GWU) and the combined African Food and Cannery Workers Union/Food and Cannery Workers Union (AFCWU/FCWU) for Coloreds.[37]

Since 1979 TUCSA has increased its efforts to create parallel black trade unions so as to have some control over them and prevent them from becoming political. The largest TUCSA-affiliated union is the National Union of Clothing Workers (NUCW), which has over 16,000 members. It has its own secretary-general — Lucy Mvubelo, a black woman. NUCW scorns political activism and is primarily concerned with jobs and wages.

CUSA was formed in 1980 and has about 45,000 black members. FOSATU, established in 1978, has over 50,000 members, is open to all races, and is organized on a countrywide basis. There are about seven important independent trade unions, which together have about 80,000 members. Some of the more important unions are the Commercial, the Catering and Allied Workers Union, the Food and Beverage Workers, and the Media Workers Association of South Africa (MWASA).

The South African Allied Workers Union (SAAWU) was at one time a fast-growing political union organized in the Ciskei in the eastern Cape. It has now lost many leaders and followers, however. SAAWU opposed independence for the Ciskei and was harassed by the authorities.

The National Union of Mineworkers (NUM) was recognized by the Chamber of Mines in 1983 and, for the first time, was allowed to organize black miners — an important victory for black trade unionism in South Africa. By the end of 1984, the union claimed 110,000 members and was engaged in an active campaign to do away with the last remnants of the industrial color bar in the mining industry.

The black union movement in South Africa is split on several issues: whether to follow a nonracial or a black consciousness line; whether unions should be political or nonpolitical; whether they should or should not have links with the government (for example, should or should they not register with the Department of Manpower).

FOSATU and CUSA have not registered with the government. (Since they are federations, they have allowed their affiliates to register if they wish.) They have avoided political stands and have stressed wage improvement. The two unions have not escaped government repression; they have suffered arrests, detentions, and, in 1981, banning. The more militant union leaders have nevertheless criticized their moderation, claiming that black workers will become disillusioned with the moderates.

Realistically, one must assume that the government will not tolerate black political unions. To date, scores of militant unionists have been jailed, detained, and banned. For example, all of the leaders of MWASA were banned in the early 1980s and three militants of the Motor Assembly and Component Workers Union of South Africa were banned in 1982. By 1984 union leaders appeared to have learned the harsh lesson that the security police will not allow political activism, and that the police may not leave unions alone even if they are only concerned with issues of wages and hours.

Labour unrest and strikes have been common since 1979. Unions have concentrated on building industry-wide representation and bargaining in three key industries — automobiles, steel, and textiles. Unions have continued to avoid populist political issues in order to avoid arrests and banning. But black unions are beginning to feel their power and to make more significant demands. Early organizational problems and original inexperience seem to have been overcome.

The Economic Embrace: Homelands and SADCC

According to their critics, the Bantu Homelands are purely exploitative institutions. They serve as instruments for stabilizing South Africa's African labor reservoirs, for depriving their denizens of South African citizenship, and for providing an ideological excuse for white supremacy. The Homelands, however, remain too small in size and too lacking in natural wealth to respond to development — let alone to be turned into genuinely independent states. They are impoverished rural ghettos, fated to remain stagnant in both an economic and a political sense.[38]

These generalizations are far from true. A number of Homelands are situated in well-watered areas. For instance, three quarters of the Transkei enjoys a rainfall of more than 30 inches per annum and could, in theory, be turned into a South African breadbasket.

It is also incorrect to say that there are no mineral riches in any of the Homelands; the available wealth (promoted by the Mining Corporation set up in 1969) is considerable and includes a variety of metals from anthracite to platinum. The size of the area included in the Homelands is not neglible. Lebowa is as large as Israel; the Transkei is bigger than Belgium and has a per capita income estimated to be greater than that of twenty members of the United Nations. The Transkei's territory is much more extensive than that of the West Bank, which is widely regarded as a fit homeland for the Palestinians. The population density of the Homelands is relatively low — a mere fraction of the population density of Western Europe or India.

Homeland economies are not stagnant. The states that are nominally outside of South Africa (Transkei, Bophuthatswana, Venda, Ciskei) have grown economically. So have the black national states that, according to South African legal theory, at present remain legally part of South Africa. (Between 1975 and 1980 the increase in the external states' gross national income, in millions of rand, was as follows: Kwazulu, 743.5 to 2,001.0; Qwaqwa, 34.3 to 138.2; Lebowa, 298.5 to 730.2; Gazankulu, 70.0 to 187.0; KaNgwane, 57.8 to 226.4. Total: 1,195.4 to 3,283.0.) The Homelands do rely heavily on the export of labor to South Africa, but in this respect they are not unique; independent African states like Lesotho and Mozambique also export labor to South Africa. (By 1982 at least 1,282,272 foreign workers from countries as far afield as Botswana, Angola, Lesotho, Malawi, Mozambique, Swaziland, Zambia and Zimbabwe had found employment in South Africa.) Undoubtedly, the Homelands' economic base remains slender, but it is nevertheless superior to that of many independent African states. (By 1982 Bophuthatswana had a per capita gross national income superior even to Nigeria's; KwaZulu and the Transkei were both considerably better off than countries as varied as Chad, Ethiopia, Gambia, Guinea, Sudan, Tanzania, Togo, Uganda, Zaire, and many others.)

Nevertheless, the Homelands have serious disadvantages. Whereas the Transkei is a relatively large and compact territory, others are fragmented. (Bophuthatswana, for instance, has seven parts.) By their very existence, the Homelands create serious citizenship and residential problems for black South Africans. (For instance, according to the Transkei's constitution, both persons born in the Transkei and those born to Transkei fathers outside the

Transkei are considered Transkei citizens.) The Homelands have been found to accept vast numbers of Africans whom the government (in its ill-advised and cruel policy of enforcing apartheid) has shipped back to the rural areas. The Homelands do provide islands exempt from the operation of apartheid.[39] But, like the independent African states, the Homelands have appreciably failed to improve the lot of the village cultivator. The main benefits — such as they are — go to chiefs and their families, politicians and their clientele, government employees, and a small class of African entrepreneurs (especially those who are recipients of the government aid extended to the Homelands by public bodies like the Xhosa Development Corporation). On its own, the most enlightened Homeland policy cannot solve South Africa's black problems.

The Homelands are heavily subsidized by the South African treasury. (According to a statement made by Zyl Slabbert in the South African Parliament, the South African taxpayers provided 2.2 billion rand to the Homelands between 1983 and 1984.[40] (The full extent of the subsidy may exceed official statistics, since the South African government has a stake in concealing the full cost of this foreign-aid bill from the white electorate.) The South African Homeland policy would certainly be unfeasible without a heavy infusion of South African funds and without South African planning, financial, and technological expertise. This subsidization of the Homelands (what South Africans call "multinational development") continues despite South Africa's own financial difficulties.

In November 1982 P. W. Botha met with four Homeland leaders to plan for regional development. A southern African development bank was established in September 1983; it is to be the linchpin in the government's economic development program. Multinational development activities are planned in the fields of agriculture, economics, education, health, conservation, tourism, transport, and veterinary services. Other development activities may also include labor, environment, water, and forestry.

The 1982 meeting set up a development bank to stimulate regional development; a multinational development council and economic financial committee to cooperate with various South African government bodies; regular meetings on agricultural problems; and programs to develop commerce, forestry, agriculture, and mining industries in the various countries. Yet by 1980 the Homelands contained an estimated 1.43 million people without visible means of support — without jobs, land, cattle, or remittances. (By this time the population of the Homelands had increased to about 11 million people.)

In spite of all these problems, by the early 1980s South Africa was the only country on the African continent that had an economy sufficiently diversified, complex, and well run to adequately cope with the worldwide recession. In the economic as well as in the military sphere, South Africa continued to overshadow other African countries. These countries' attempts to fortify their positions by the formation of the Southern African Development Coordination Conference (SADCC) made only a marginal difference. South Africa remained the cornerstone of a wider system of South African states. South African railways, harbors, and airports played a key role in the commerce of Namibia, Zimbabwe, Botswana, Swaziland, Lesotho, and Mozambique. South Africa's neighbors came to rely considerably on South African capital, know-how, technical services, and skilled and managerial personnel. In addition, about 300,000 temporary workers came to South Africa from the BLS countries. Since the BLS states are land locked, they must import and export goods through South Africa. (South Africa also collects customs revenues for them.) South Africa's external power therefore continues to be strongly tied to the Republic's diplomatic influence. South Africa has had (and, for the forseeable future, will continue to have) an immense impact on political and economic development in neighboring African states — no matter who rules in Harare, Maputo, or Lusaka.

The SADCC was founded in July 1979 at Arusha (and formalized by the Lusaka Declaration in April 1980) for the purpose of promoting the economic liberation of its black-ruled member states: Botswana, Angola, Lesotho, Malawi, Mozambique, Swaziland, Tanzania, Zimbabwe, and Zambia. The SADCC is designed to counter South Africa's economic dominance of the region, which it accomplishes in concert with a constellation of states bordering, and included within, South Africa. The SADCC seeks to promote economic development and regional cooperation. It comprises both Front Line States and nonparticipants like Lesotho, Malawi, and Swaziland (which are all much more conservative than the Marxist or semi-Marxist members). Each member state selects a major sector of the economy — like transport or food — for which it will assume special responsibility. Participation in the SADCC does not, however, interfere with other bilateral relationships.

In 1981 SADCC members set up a Preferential Trade Area for East and Southern Africa. This arrangement poses particular difficulties for Botswana, Lesotho, and Swaziland, which remain members of the South African Customs Union (SACU). SADCC's member states have divergent policies, which they seek to resolve by low-key pragmatic programs. They attempt to avoid an excessively bureacratic machinery and to persuade foreign powers and banks to provide aid. Foreigners usually prefer bilateral relationships, however. Zimbabwe's Conference on Reconstruction and Development (ZIMCORD) raised U.S. $1.4 billion in 1981. The EEC insists that aid recipients should belong to the Lomé Convention. The United States does not recognize Angola and SADCC states are too politically, economically, and administratively varied to allow effective cooperation. (The SADCC states tend to agree, however, on political issues such as Namibian independence.)

We deem South Africa's past policy of hostility toward SADCC unwise. SADCC's fusion of militant goals and pragmatic methods will probably allow the Conference to achieve small, but tangible and substantive, gains. By the mid-1980s, drought, recession, and a period of peace will probably weaken SADCC and confirm South Africa's dominance in the region.

THE INEVITABLE REVOLUTION?

In 1947 Arthur Keppel Jones, a South African historian who later chose exile, published what was to become a well-known book of that time — *When Smuts Goes*. His futuristic account predicted South Africa's impending breakdown and even provided a detailed scenario. Many other writers — including both academics and journalists — have since made similar forecasts. According to these writers, revolution was to result from South Africa's supposedly irreconcilable internal contradictions; in other words, from the inability of the white minority to permanently suppress a great black majority. These problems would be added to the impact of foreign opinion, the support given to South African blacks by their African neighbors, the gnawing effects of strikes, riots, and passive resistance, and the internal demonstration effect of the liberation struggles in the former Portuguese colonies and Zimbabwe. Three metaphors frequently recurred in the literature on the subject: the clock externally poised at five minutes to midnight; the overheated boiler without a safety valve, ready to explode; and the irresistible tide of history (that would sweep away the hated regime).

Revolutionary victories are not inevitable, however. They occur only under certain well-defined conditions. The incumbent's administration should be inefficient or corrupt (as it was in Cuba and South Vietnam). The government forces should be demoralized by either prior defeat in war or internal dissensions. Even if government forces are efficient, they should suffer from overstretched resources (as happened in Rhodesia). Rebel guerrillas should preferably be able to rely on inviolate sanctuaries abroad, and they should be sustained by conventional forces. Also, it is much more favorable if the guerrillas can (by promises, propaganda, or well-designed political concessions), win over a substantial segment of those who support the incumbent power.

By the mid 1980s none of these conditions fully applied to the situation in South Africa. The opposition had managed to expand its power — not only by means of the ANC, but also by means of the United Democratic Front. There was widespread discontent. But the revolutionaries had failed to penetrate the (as yet, mainly white) power structure. (In theory, Marxist-Leninists should not find this problem insuperable, since the bulk of the whites do not own the means of production.)

Among non-Europeans, there was plenty of discontent. This discontent, however, was not sufficient to find expression in effective underground organization. Also, there was not enough disenchantment to result in that uniformly reliable symptom of alienation — widespread emigration. Whereas close to 10 percent of Cuba's entire population chose to leave their country after Castro's revolution, only an insignificant portion of South Africa's population — white, Indian, Colored, or black — chose to depart.[41] On the whole, South Africa's administrative and coercive machine was neither inefficient nor corrupt; its economy — for all its problems — was more vibrant than any other in Africa.

The Outward Sanctuaries

The experience gained by guerrillas in Zimbabwe should certainly have been of use to partisans operating in South Africa. Nevertheless, given the vast disparity in military and industrial resources existing between Ian Smith's Rhodesia and South Africa, it was possible to overestimate the relevance of these past campaigns. (In 1978–79, at the apex of the white Rhodesian defense effort, Rhodesia's estimated GNP (in U.S. dollars) amounted to $3.1 billion, and its defense expenditure, to $242 million; another $60 million was spent on the police force. The corresponding figures for South Africa for the same year were $43.8 billion and $2.62 billion, respectively.) The armies of Zambia and Zimbabwe and/or Mozambique did not pose a serious menace to South Africa. (For the defense establishments of the first two countries, see the article by L. H. Gann on Malawi, Zambia, and Zimbabwe in this volume.) Also, South African partisans could not rely on inviolate sanctuaries in adjacent countries.

The point bears repeating that South Africa has been able to retain its position of undisputed economic supremacy — dwarfing its neighbors in, among other things, gross national product, energy production, transport moved, goods produced, research and development, and food production. (To give just one example, South Africa's per capita income of U.S. $2,290 in 1980 was eight times that of Mozambique, four times that of Zambia, and three-and-a-half times that of Zimbabwe.) In 1981 South Africa employed 301,700 foreign blacks, most of them from adjacent countries. South Africa dominated African trade. The South African Customs Union and the Rand Monetary Area have carried South Africa's financial influence beyond its borders. Although the disruption of these institutional bonds would be injurious to South Africa, it would wreak even greater havoc among her neighbors.

Within the wider contest of economic dependency, by far the strongest of South Africa's neighbours was Zimbabwe. By the early 1980s Zimbabwe enjoyed the advantage of geographical proximity to the Pretoria Witwatersrand-Vereeniging complex, which is strategically and economically the heartland of modern South Africa and accounts for almost half of South Africa's industrial output. Zimbabwe, however, remained heavily dependent on South Africa. Along with Zambia, the country continued to rely substantially on South Africa for foreign capital, mining technology, managerial skills, and, above all, transport services. The port facilities at Dar es Salaam on the Indian Ocean were not sufficient for Zambia's needs. Beira and Maputo in Mozambique could not service the majority of Zimbabwe's exports. (The Beira harbor suffered from heavy silting; the Maputo harbor had only a limited capacity, and by 1980 75 percent of the port's activities were linked to South Africa.) As a result, Zimbabwe continued to use Durban and — to a lesser extent — Port Elizabeth, despite high freight costs and periodic congestion on South African rail routes.[42] Despite all the SADCC's efforts, Zimbabwe was unable to disengage from its South African connections. Troubled by ethnic problems of its own, and fearful of antagonizing South Africa into support for Ndebele dissidents, the Zimbabweans had no choice but to deny the use of their territory to the South African dissidents — in spite of ZAPU's former alliance with the ANC.

Lesotho, Swaziland, and Basutoland are in much worse shape; they have remained almost totally reliant on South African communications. Namibia is not capable of surviving as an independent state without the South African connection. Its infrastructure is largely sustained by South African aid for transport facilities, hydroelectric power, and irrigation projects. Namibia depends heavily on South African transport facilities and profits from the services provided by South African research institutes and universities. Also, Namibia is part of a common monetary sphere that uses the rand as currency and enjoys a free flow of funds.

At first sight, Mozambique would appear to be in a somewhat stronger position. Its armed forces and security services draw on support from the Soviet bloc. Mozambique has its own ports, but, as we have pointed out before, it continues to use South African facilities. The country also relies on South Africa as a customer for its railways and hydroelectric power. Additionally, Mozambique is vulnerable from an internal standpoint; the government has to contend with widespread resistance in parts of the countryside that are supported by South African arms and cash. Although Mozambique gave shelter to small ANC detachments, the South Africans struck back repeatedly, and the Mozambique forces were in no position to retaliate.

In March 1984 Mozambique signed a nonagression agreement (the Accord of Nkomati) with South Africa — the first to be concluded between South Africa and its postcolonial neighbors. Under its terms, South Africa ceased support for the Mozambique National Resistance Movement (MNR) and Mozambique no longer allowed the ANC to make use of its territory. At the time of writing, the precise implications of the treaty still remain to be elucidated. As far as Mozambique's Marxists are concerned, did the treaty imply coexistence between contrasting social systems, or did the treaty merely entail peaceful coexistence between differing state systems (the Soviet doctrinal interpretation)? Was the treaty an African equivalent of the Nazi-Societ pact of 1939? How will FRELIMO militants regard the arrangement? Will the signatories violate the treaty terms in a clandestine fashion?

South Africa's counterstrikes against Mozambique reflected South Africa's priorities in combatting rural insurgency. According to its doctrine, the most cost-effective method of striking against guerrillas is to attack their bases; the second and third most effective countermeasures are, respectively, good intelligence and plenty of foot-slogging. Purely defensive operations, such as the protection of key points and administrative posts, and the safeguarding of important people like headmen, come at the bottom of the list; these operations are regarded as no more than necessary evils.[43] The South African successes in Mozambique and Angola have seemed to confirm Pretoria's correct apportionment of these priorities.

On the face of it, however, the South Africans had achieved a major victory. An avowedly Marxist-Leninist regime made a commitment to end effective support of its revolutionary comrades. Even more embarrasingly, the South Africans subsequently stepped in to arrange a ceasefire between Mozambique government forces and anti-FRELIMO partisans. At the request of both parties, South African soldiers were to patrol in the bush in Mozambique to monitor the peace agreement.

If these arrangements are observed, they will vindicate South Africa's outward strategy. The arrangement may conceivably be considered a milestone, with implications for the future evolution of relations between Marxist-Leninist and Western countries in general. The new compact certainly seems to bode ill for the ANC and for those of its foreign supporters who hope to intensify the armed struggle against South Africa. The revolutionary solidarity that the ANC previously established with FRELIMO appears to have ended.

Angola — unlike Mozambique, Zimbabwe, and Zambia — was economically independent of South Africa. At the time of writing, its government derived support from an estimated 30,000 Cuban troops stationed on Angolan soil. For many years Angola provided sanctuary for SWAPO guerrillas operating against Namibia. The Angolan economy remained in a shambles, however. Moreover, Angola suffered from a guerrilla struggle of its own — one that

pitted UNITA forces against those of the Marxist-Leninist government. The South Africans (like the Israelis, but unlike the former
Portuguese colonial forces in Mozambique) recognized no
privileged sanctuaries. By 1985 close to 30,000 South African
troops were deployed on Namibia's northern border. South Africa
land and air units continually struck at southern Angola. The
Cuban forces were in no position to aid their allies.

The South Africans compelled the SWAPO guerrillas to withdraw their staging points, camps, and supply depots to a distance
of 200 miles from the Namibian border. This forced the guerrillas
to cover great distances in order to reach their targets. The necessity
to traverse great stretches of arid bush on foot entailed bitter hardships. The guerrillas could not rely on trucks or helicopters to bring
food, medical supplies, or ammunition or to carry out the
wounded. A badly wounded guerrilla is a man condemned to die —
a serious problem for guerrilla morale. Moreover, the guerrillas
could not easily carry heavy weapons; in fact, they were constantly
tempted to drop those they had on the long weary trek to the South.
By the end of 1984 SWAPO had suffered heavy losses and was
almost out of the picture as a force to be reckoned with.

Not surprisingly, the Angolans also entered into negotiations
with South Africa in 1984. The last word has not been written on
Namibia's future, however. South Africa's military power has
failed to match its political skill in Namibia. SWAPO certainly has
more influence in the country now than it did five years ago, when
the South Africans failed to hand effective power to a moderate
movement (the Turnhalle Democratic Alliance, formed in 1977).
But even if Angola and South Africa were to arrive at an agreement
in which South African military forces would leave Namibia in
return for a simultaneous Cuban withdrawal from Angola (or even
if SWAPO were to duplicate ZANU's 1980 electoral success in
Zimbabwe), Namibia would not constitute a secure base for the
ANC. Namibia's poverty, its economic reliance on South Africa,
its distant location, and the harsh nature of the countryside in its
border regions would militate against any effective use of the
country by the ANC. Namibia's open countryside, its poverty, its
lack of resources, and its scanty population (which exceeds one
million people) would make the implementation of a militant anti-
South African policy a virtual impossibility.

Operations Within South Africa

What of ANC's operations in South Africa itself? By 1984 about 6,000 black Africans were supposedly receiving training in countries as far afield as Angola, Ethiopia, Tanzania, Mozambique, and Warsaw Pact member states. Seventy-five percent of these trainees were said to be members of the ANC; the rest belonged to the Pan Africanist Congress (PAC). Fighters were equipped with small arms, antipersonnel devices, and explosives provided by Eastern Europe and the Soviet Union. They were staging scattered assaults on police stations and on industrial and military establishments (including the Koeberg nuclear power facility, in 1982, and, in 1983, the South African air force headquarters at Pretoria). The ANC slogan *amandla* (Zulu for "power") was becoming a widespread expression of defiance. Large demonstrations erupted at funerals of ANC guerrillas. Overall, the scale and skill of ANC operations has improved. But compared to South Africa's massive military and industrial strength, these affrays are as yet mere pinpricks. They have no impact on South Africa's economic production, which, as we have seen, has actually expanded. The severity of the pass laws, the efficiency of the police and its widespread network of informers, the difficulties of infiltration, and the excellence of South Africa's communications and telecommunication network all make the partisans' task one of extraordinary difficulty.

Given the extent of the training and financial assistance provided to the ANC by its backers, its performance has been disappointing. Between 1980 and 1984 the ANC engaged in a series of operations that it thought would be spectacular and would receive wide media coverage. There were sabotage attempts on industrial installations (such as those at the Koeberg and SASOL plants) attacks on military and government targets, assaults on police stations, and a number of incidents in which bombs were set off in urban areas (including one outside the South African Air Force offices in Pretoria). The propaganda value of these operations was not wholly positive for the ANC, however. The average television viewer or newspaper reader does not readily approve of assaults that may kill civilian bystanders (like himself or herself or one's family members). The high success rate of police investigations benefited the authorities. So did efforts to computerize intelligence data, which provided the security forces with new ways of evaluating information and assessing long-term trends.

The ANC, for its part, has also made some gains. It has achieved a measure of international legitimacy abroad. It is well-financed by the Soviet bloc and has managed to establish an effective political presence overseas, complete with a network of publications and allied organizations. In the future the ANC may make more effective use of selective bombings, land mines, and/or surface-to-air missiles (SAMs) directed against South African civilian planes. They may also engage in raids against South African embassies overseas or targeted assassinations of African police officers. By themselves, however, these operations stand no chance of overthrowing the South African power structure.

In the long term, South Africa would find itself in a much more dangerous situation if ANC operations (or excessively hasty reforms) were to provoke a guerrilla response among militant white workers. The white workers have military training; they are familiar with the strengths and weaknesses of the industrial economy; they are mainly skilled people. The whites possess what the ANC lacks — good contacts within the South African police force and military. The Rand Rising of 1922 (the only serious armed urban rising ever experienced in Africa) demonstrated the military potential of the white workers. If, in some hypothetical future, white workers were again driven to desperation, a reformist South African government might find itself caught in a crossfire between the extreme left and the extreme right. Fortunately for the South African establishment, the extreme right — organizations like the Afrikaanse Weerstandsbewging (AWB) — now consists only of crackpots without effective organization or mass support. As long as the Afrikaner people remain aloof from armed resistance — whether inspired by the left or the right — an armed revolution in South Africa seems unlikely to gain success.

Guerrilla activities are, of course, more effective when they are backed by strikes, riots, and passive resistance. South Africa has had a full share of all of these activities. But again, their scale has remained inadequate to effect a revolutionary upheaval. Industrial strikes of partial political inspiration are almost certain to increase in number. But only a small proportion of black African workers are unionized (9.9 percent of unskilled workers, 11.3 percent of semiskilled workers, and 15.2 percent of skilled workers). Overall, 10.6 percent of all black workers are unionized. Widespread unemployment among blacks reduces the unions' bargaining power, and their scanty financial resources make extended political strikes difficult. Internal divisions within the unions make it hard to maintain concerted action. In any case, the experience of British workers in the General Strike of 1926, and of Polish workers in the Solidarity movement of the early 1980s does not lend support to the belief that a well-entrenched government can be overthrown by industrial action alone.

The Soweto riots of 1976 and 1977 publicized black grievances for the entire nation. These included the pass laws, control of free entry into the cities, the operation of the color bar, discriminatory forms of education, police actions, and the existence of a multitude of other restrictions, great and small. The massive participation of high-school and college students in the riots strikingly illustrated the expansion in African education over the previous two decades; there was a new and powerful constituency of well-schooled Africans.[44] (See Table 1.) The riots also revealed the severe internal cleavages existing within the African urban community — between the employed and the unemployed, between workers and students, and between young people (mainly high-school and university students) and their elders.

An expert analysis undertaken by the South African Communist Party provided a detailed assessment of the riots. The riots failed to break the government's administrative or military machine; they did not involve the mass of rural people, revealing "the very low level of rural liberation organization." The people lacked arms, and this fact alone reduced the possibility of transforming the demonstration into an effective assault on state power.[45] The guerrillas faced a defense establishment that had the advantage of a unified command and reasonably effective coordination between civilian and military agencies. By the early 1980s the South African top military brass was confident, youthful, and well educated — a formidable combination for any would-be revolutionary, to face. (The South African generals in key positions had all reached these positions while in their forties. A B. Mil. degree from the Military Academy at Saldanha Bay had become obligatory for higher military office.)[46] Still, the structure of white supremacy has developed major cracks. The government is no longer able to control African education in many cities. There are numerous school children who have not gone to school for as much as two years. These youngsters have become politicized. They will turn, in many cases, to crime, or they might go into the bush. Rioting has become endemic. The black influx into the Eastern Cape has become uncontrollable. The government's writ now only partially runs in some parts of the country.

The gap between the business community and the government has widened. The U.S. disinvestment campaign will further widen the gap. Revolution is not around the corner, but the National Party will further weaken when Piet Botha goes. The two most likely contenders for power are Viljoen and de Klerk. De Klerk will probably win. In all likelihood, he will seek to conciliate the right wingers — especially the Conservative Party. This may bring about a secession of the reformists within the National Party. These secessionists may or may not join the progressives — depending on an agreement concerning the future allocation of party posts.

The UDF has become the most powerful African force. It differs from its predecessors because of its widespread support. The UDF is organizationally decentralized, unlike the ANC, but it maintains links with the ANC. The UDF's grass-roots support is such that it cannot be effectively broken.

In March 1985, the United States joined the members of the Security Council of the U.N. to condemn South Africa for "killing defenseless people," and arbitrarily arresting leaders of the United Democratic Front. The United States lobbied against the resolution but then voted for it. This was the most severe criticism to date by the Reagan administration. Divestment groups became active in major universities and numerous anti-South African bills were introduced into Congress.

Then in June 1985, South Africa raided into Angola and Botswana and transferred authority to an unelected Namibian government. These acts coming at a time of congressional consideration of further sanctions against South Africa for the violence in the Eastern Cape forced the Reagan administration to reconsider its policies. Both the Senate and House called for a severe package of sanctions against Pretoria. Constructive engagement, if not dead, was severely damaged.

Whatever the future may hold, in the mid-1980s the long-heralded South African revolution still appears to be only a distant possibility. Shall South Africa therefore be condemned to a state of eternal *immobilisme*. Our answer remains necessarily speculative, but educated guesses are both possible and legitimate. It is at least possible that important changes can be effected from within. Now that parliamentary representation has been granted to Coloreds and Asians, it can scarcely be permantly withheld from black Africans. Once the present constitutional reforms begin to work, South Africans will probably have to extend representational rights to urban Africans that go beyond local councils. A regime committed (at least in theory) to free enterprise will be under continual pressure to create (for the first time in South African history) a genuinely free economy — complete with freedom of labor, freedom of movement, freedom of interracial association and marriage, and freedom to settle and purchase land. These freedoms would revolutionize South Africa far more effectively than any guerrilla combat squad. Prophets have perennially predicted breakdown and disaster for South Africa. The future may continue to belie these prophecies of doom.

Notes

1. J. U. S. Asiegbu, *Nigeria and Its British Invaders, 1851–1920* (New York: Nok Publishers International, 1984), p. xxlx.

2. G. H. Calpin, *There are No South Africans* (London: T. Nelson, 1946).

3. Unlike most other countries, South Africa does not measure its own economic performance by gross national product (GNP), but by gross domestic product (GDP). This is because the extremely wide fluctuations in the price of gold cause major fluctuations in real GNP from year to year. In 1981 the GNP amounted to 67,465 million rand, whereas the GDP amounted to 70,529 rand.

4. This figure actually underestimates the total increase because the population census of 1980 excluded Transkei, Boputhatswana, and Venda (including Ciskei). Ethnically, in 1980 the population broke down as follows: blacks, 15,970,000; whites, 4,453,000; Coloreds, 2,554,000; Asians, 795,000.

5. For differing interpretations, see L. H. Gann and Peter Duignan, *Why South Africa Will Survive* (New York: St. Martin's Press, 1981); Report of the Study Commission on U.S. Policy Toward Southern Africa, *South Africa: Time Running Out* (Berkeley: University of California Press, 1981); and R. W. Johnson, *How Long Will South Africa Survive?* (New York: Oxford University Press, 1977).

6. The literature on South African politics is extensive. Studies critical of the existing white establishment include Leonard Thompson and Andrew Prior, *South African Politics* (New Haven: Yale University Press, 1982) and Ian Robertson and Phillip Whitten, eds., *Race and Politics in South Africa* (New Brunswick, N.J.: Transaction Books, 1978). Howard Brotz, *The Politics of South Africa: Democracy and Racial Diversity* (Oxford: Oxford University Press, 1977) takes white anxieties somewhat more into account in addition to black grievances. The standard work on the National party is O. Geyser and A.H. Marais, *Die Nasionale Party* (Pretoria: Academica, 1975). For a detailed account of the party in English see W. Kleynhans, "White Political Parties," in Anthony de Crespigny and Robert Schire, eds., *The Government and Politics of South Africa* (Cape Town: Juta, 1978), pp. 94–116.

7. For details about ANC-SACP links, see Gann and Duignan, *Why South Africa Will Survive*, pp. 127–28.

8. *Sechaba*, September 1981, pp. 4–5.

9. Theodor Hanf, Heribert Weiland, Gerda Viertag, *Südafrika: Friedlicher Wandel? Möglichkeiten demokratischer Konfliktregelung* (Mainz: Matthias Grünewald Verlag, 1979), pp. 371–74. For the ANC's history, see Peter Walshe, *The Rise of African Nationalism in South Africa: The African National Congress, 1912–1952* (Berkeley: University of California Press, 1971), and Thomas Karis, Gwendolen Carter, et. al., *From Protest to Challenge: A Documentary History of African Politics in South Africa, 1882–1964*, 4 vols. (Stanford: Hoover Institution Press, 1972–1977) and Gail Gerhardt, *Black Politics in South Africa* (Berkeley: University of California Press, 1982). See also the chapter by Thomas G. Karis entitled "Black Challenge" in Report of the Study Commission on U.S. Policy Toward Southern Africa, *South Africa: Time Running Out* (Berkeley: University of California Press, 1984), pp. 168–205 and Karis's article "The Resurgent African National Congress: Competing for the Hearts and Minds in Southern Africa," in Thomas M. Callaghy, ed., *South Africa: The Intensifying Vortex of Violence* (New York: Preager Special Studies, 1983), pp. 191–236.

10. Sheridan Johns, "South Africa," *Yearbook on International Communist Affairs, 1983* (Stanford: Hoover Institution Press, 1983), pp. 41–44.

11. See Ronald Segal, "Ruth First Memorial," Letter to the editor asking for support, *New York Review of Books*, 2 February 1984, p. 49.

12. See, for example, Nicholas Haysom, *Ruling with the Whip: A Report on the Violations of Human Rights in the Ciskei* (Johannesburg: DSG ISARS Publication, 1983).

13. Hanf et al., *Südafrika: Friedlicher Wandel?* pp. 371–72, 441.

14. In 1980 the ANC was involved in thirty actions and in 1981, sixty-two actions. In 1982 there were ninety-eight incidents in six months. See *Special Report: South Africa: Political Violence and Sabotage* (Capetown: Terrorism Research Center, 1982).

15. See Gann and Duignan, *Why South Africa Will Survive,*, chap. 4; Gail M. Gerhart, *Black Power in South Africa: The Evolution of an Ideology* (Berkeley: University of California Press, 1978); and Tom Lodge, *Black Politics in South Africa Since 1945* (London: Longmans, 1983).

16. *Race Relations as Regulated by Law in South Africa, 1948–1979*. Compiled by Muriel Horrell. (Johannesburg: South African Institute of Race Relations, 1982) and Sheila T. Van Der Horst, ed., *Race Discrimination in South Africa: A Review* (Cape Town: David Philip, 1981). In 1973 the government desegregated all elevators in public buildings and railway and airline offices; in 1973–74 the major cities desegregated their parks, libraries, museums, and so forth. In 1975 hotels were permitted to become multiracial if they wished; in 1978 restaurants, theaters, and private hospitals were allowed to become multiracial.

17. *South Africa, 1980–81: Official Yearbook of the Republic of South Africa* (Johannesburg: Chrys van Rensburg, 1981), p. 185.

18. See Richard Humphries' analysis in *The South African Foundation News*, March 1984, p. 1. For the most extensive extant study on removal, see *The Surplus People Project Report: Forced Removals in South Africa*, 5 vols. (Cape Town and Pietermaritzburg: The Project, 1983).

19. Republic of Kenya, Review of Statutory Boards and Recommendations of the Committee Appointed by His Excellency the President, 1979 (Nairobi: Government Printing Office, 1979), p. 3.

20. For detailed figures, see *Institute for Strategic Studies: The Military Balance, 1983–1984* (London: The Institute, 1983), pp. 75–76.

21. Military service lasted twenty-four months, followed by a reserve commitment. Reservists were required to serve twelve years in the Citizen Force, and subsequently, five years in the Citizens Reserve Force.

22. See Kenneth W. Grundy, "South Africa's Regional Defense Plans: The

Homeland Armies," in Thomas M. Callaghy, ed., *South Africa in Southern Africa*, chap. 6 and Kenneth W. Grundy, *Soldiers without Politics: Blacks in the South African Armed Forces* (Berkeley: University of California Press, 1983).

23. For a detailed assessment, see Gann and Duignan, *Why South Africa Will Survive*, pp. 187–217.

24. *South Africa Official Yearbook, 1980–81*, p. 237.

25. Among urban Africans in Durban, 25 percent of Africans with less than a high-school education and 37 percent of high-school-educated Africans stated that they "feared and disliked most" the police. Corresponding figures for criminals were 49 percent and 46 percent. Only 18 percent and 21 percent, respectively, expressed resentment of government and administration in general. Four percent and 15 percent, respectively, listed the helping professions, ministers of religion, teachers, and social workers among the people "feared and disliked most," and only 1 percent of both dreaded witches most of all. See Lawrence Schlemmer, *Black Attitudes: Reaction and Adaptation* (University of Natal: Institute for Social Research, Durban, 1975), pp. 9 and 11.

26. See Gordon Winter, *Inside BOSS: South Africa's Secret Police* (London: Allen Lane, Penguin Books, 1981).

27. General A. J. van Deventer, "The State Security Council — The Official View," *South Africa Foundation News*, November 1983, p. 3, and October 1983, p. 2.

28. James M. Roherty, "Beyond Limpopo and Zambezi: South Africa's Strategic Horizons," *South Africa International* 14, no. 1 (July 1983): 320–39.

29. Floyd Dotson and Lillian O. Dotson, "The Economic Role of Non-Indigenous Ethnic Minorities in Colonial Africa," in Peter Duignan and L. H. Gann, eds., *The Economic of Colonialism* (Cambridge: Cambridge University Press, 1975), p. 574.

30. See C. W. de Kiewiet, *A History of South Africa: Social and Economic* (Oxford: Clarendon Press, 1941), especially the last chapter, and S. H. Frankel, "An Analysis of the Growth of National Income of the Union in the Period of Prosperity Before the War," *South African Journal of Economics* (June 1955): pp. 1–28.

31. For detailed figures, see Gann and Duignan, *Why South African Will Survive*, p. 161, and *South Africa Official Yearbook, 1980–1981*, p. 329.

32. Pierre van den Berghe, *South Africa: A Study in Conflict* (Berkely: University of California Press, 1967), especially p. 263.

33. *Africa Research Bulletin* (August 15–September 14, 1983): 6974–76.

34. Racial Distribution of Occupational Categories, 1980
(percent)

	Management	Skilled	Semi-skilled	Unskilled
Whites	21.5%	56.2%	21.0%	1.3%
Coloreds	0.8	24.2	43.2	31.8
Asians	2.6	25.5	56.9	15.0
Blacks	0.2	3.0	38.9	57.9

35. By 1980, average monthly pay in rand for Asians, blacks, Colored, and whites, respectively was as follows: Management: 722, 563, 625, 1,193. Skilled: 542, 389, 499, 744. Unskilled: 231, 173, 186, 281. Of the portion of workers employed by the labor force, the following percentages were members of the trade unions: Asians, 25; Blacks, 10.6; Coloreds, 32.7; White, 35.0. See D. W. F. Bendix and S. M. Swart, "A Survey of Employment Conditions in the Repubic of South Africa,

1980'' Unpublished paper made available to the authors.

36. See Jess Harlov, *Labor Regulation and Black Workers' Struggle in South Africa* Research Report, no. 68 (Uppsala: Scandinavian Institute of African Studies, 1983).

37. Richard F. Weisfelder, "The Southern African Development Coordination Conference (SADCC)" in *South Africa International* 13, no.12 (Oct. 1982): 74–96.

38. Richard Gibson, *African Liberation Movements: Contemporary Struggles Against White Minority Rule* (London: Oxford University Press, 1972), p. 20.

39. See, for instance, Newell M. Stultz, *Transkei's Half Loaf: Race Separation in South Africa* (New Haven: Yale University Press, 1979).

40. Between 1982 and 1983 the six Nonindependent national states received 197 million rand in statutory grants and 500 million rand from additional grants by Parliament. Between 1981 and 1982 funding from South Africa constituted 77 percent of their total incomes. See "Homeland Development Failing," *South Africa Foundation News*, July 1984, p. 3. See also *South African Hansard*, 26 June 1984, cols. g827–40.

41. The total number of emigrants in 1979 was 20,078. Of these, 4.8 percent left for other countries in Africa; 10.4 percent, for the Americas; 22.2 percent, for the European continent; 46.4 percent, for Great Britain; and the remainder for, other destination. *South Africa Official Yearbook, 1980–81*, p. 255.

42. Hermann Giliomee, *Zimbabwe: The Short and Long-Term Socio-Political Prospects of a New State* (University of Stellenbosch: Bureau for Economic Research, 1980), pp. 11–12. For a general discussion, see Economist Intelligence Unit, *Interdependence in Southern Africa: Trade and Transport Links in South, Central, and East Africa* (London: The Economist, 1976). See also Gwendolen M. Carter and Patrick O'Meara, *International Politics in South Africa* (Bloomington, Ind.: Indiana University Press, 1982).

43. Lt. General J. J. Geldenhuys, Chief of the South African Army, "Rural Insurgency and Counter-Measures," in M. Hough, ed., *Revolutionary Warfare and Counter-Insurgency* (University of Pretoria: Institute for Strategic Studies, March 1984), pp. 40–45. See also Gen. P. J. Coetzee, Commissioner of the South African Police, "Urban Terror and Counter Measures," in Hough, *Revolutionary Warfare and Counter-Insurgency*, pp. 32–39.

44. Between 1960 and 1979 the number of African secondary students increased from 47,598 to 495,100; college and technical college students increased from 7,920 to 32,392. *South Africa Official Yearbook, 1980–81*, p. 876.

45. *African Communist* 70 (Third Quarter, 1977): 31–32.

46. For this point (and also for a general critique), see Kenneth W. Grundy, *The Rise of the South African Military Establishment: An Essay on the Changing Locus of State Power* (Cape Town: South Africa Institute of International Affairs, 1983).

8 NAMIBIA, BOTSWANA, LESOTHO, AND SWAZILAND

L. H. Gann and Peter Duignan

Namibia and Botswana, Lesotho, and Swaziland (termed the BLS states) differ greatly from one another. Their inhabitants speak a variety of languages; their geographical habitats, population densities, and local cultures vary considerably. But they all have one thing in common — they form part of the South African system. Like Zimbabwe, each has in the past barely missed incorporation into the old Union of South Africa. But for a series of historical accidents, South Africa today might form a huge territorial bloc, bound in the north by the Zambezi River.

Namibia owes its creation as a modern territorial entity to German conquest, which tenuously unified its disparate indigenous communities under Hohenzollern rule. After World War I, Germany lost is *Kolonialreich*, and, for all practical purposes, South Africa annexed the former German Protectorate of South-West Africa under the guise of a Class C mandate, bestowed by the League of Nations on the South African conquerors. Botswana (formerly Bechuanaland), Lesotho (formerly Basutoland), and Swaziland, by contrast, are unusual in black Africa in that — like Ethiopia, Rwanda, and Burundi — they trace their origins as modern political units to precolonial African kingdoms. Whereas Namibia and also Zimbabwe are European colonial creations that have been subjected to large-scale white settlement, Lesotho, Botswana, and Swaziland managed to preserve their status and resisted the domination of South African whites by accepting — after many vicissitudes — permanent protection from the British crown (in 1884, 1885, and 1902, respectively). Thereafter the British consistently opposed South African attempts to annex what were then known as the High Commission territories, and these countries were among the last African states to achieve independence (Botswana and Lesotho in 1966, Swaziland in 1968). Namibia is the last colony remaining on the continent, subject still to South Africa's sway. Nevertheless, Namibia's inclusion in a book concerned with Africa since independence seems justified, because of its political importance within the Southern African context and the likelihood that the territory will attain sovereign status before long.

Suzerain or not, all four territories share a common reliance on South Africa. The BLS states and Namibia form part of a South African Customs Union, which apportions revenue from a common pool and makes some provision for the protection of infant industries in the BLS states. Except for Botswana, these states belong to the Rand Monetary Area; this means that they have free access to South African capital and money markets, with harmonized exchange control and transferability of funds, subject to certain restrictions designed to benefit the less-developed members of the union. Historically, the BLS states and, to a much lesser extent, Namibia have served as labor reservoirs for South Africa, and its railways, harbors, and airports have played a key role in the commerce of them all. Except for Namibia, all are landlocked countries that must wholly rely on the South African communications network. Namibia alone has access to the coast, but Walvis Bay, its main port, belongs to South Africa. All drew to a considerable extent on South African capital, know-how, and technical services; they cannot do without South African imports and markets. In the past, the South African impact was also powerful in the field of education. The creation of the University of Botswana, Lesotho, and Swaziland (1964), followed by its later disaggregation into three national universities, reduced but did not eliminate South African academic influence. Together with Great Britain, South Africa plays a role in scientific research. South African influence is felt in the news media and in many other fields. All four countries have small domestic markets, vulnerable to great fluctuations in demand; all heavily depend on the production of primary commodities. In an economic sense, they have many of the problems confronting South Africa's Bantu homelands; they remain dependent on South Africa's economic fortunes to an extraordinary degree.

On the map, the territories of Botswana and Namibia look grand in size — as compared to Lesotho and Swaziland.[1] But the former two states comprise enormous waste regions, desert, semiarid steppe, and dry bushland. Whether large or small in terms of acreage, the four states are what the Germans call *Zwergstaaten*, dwarf states; each has fewer people than a single medium-sized U.S. city such as Houston, Texas (with 1,594, 086 inhabitants in 1980). In 1980 Botswana had an estimated population of 819,000;

Lesotho, 1,341,000; Namibia (in 1981), 1,009,000; and Swaziland, 634,678). The four states have low per capita incomes, especially the BLS states, which lack Namibia's extensive mining wealth. (Lesotho's GNP per capita in 1979 stood at $340, Swaziland's at £650, and Botswana's at £720.) In the BLS states, a high percentage of the labor force is engaged in agriculture (87 percent in Lesotho in 1979, 55 percent in Lesotho, and 52 percent in Swaziland.) Many of their citizens can neither read nor write. The estimated rate of adult literacy in 1976 amounted to 65 percent in Swaziland, 52 percent in Lesotho, and 35 percent in Botswana. They have high rates of natural increase. Between 1970 and 1979, the annual population growth in Lesotho stood at 2.3 percent; Swaziland, 2.6 percent; and Botswana, 2.2 percent.[2]

This state of dependency is not likely to diminish in the near future. South African wage rates (including wages in the mining industry) have greatly increased over the last decade. The average migrant laborer can therefore make a great deal more money by working in a South African mine or factory than by tilling his plot at home. South African agriculture, moreover, is highly efficient. The greater part of the white-owned farms and agrobusiness enterprises in South Africa are well run and well capitalized; they enjoy the advantages of direct and indirect governmental assistance. Cultivators in countries such as Lesotho or the Transkei thus have great difficulties in competing with inexpensive imported food — an added incentive for working in the city.

All four territories must make do with a small domestic product. All their African peoples have a relatively low life expectancy compared to neighboring South Africa (although their averages are higher than the rate for Africa as a whole 47 years). The estimated life expectancy in 1983 stood at 40 years in Botswana, 52 in Lesotho, 52 in Namibia, and 61 in South Africa. Namibia and the BLS states all face difficult economic problems that defy easy solutions. But, except for Namibia, they are relatively homogeneous ethnically; therefore they lack the bitter internecine struggles between competing black ethnic communities that have endangered the internal stability of many postcolonial states in Africa, from Zimbabwe all the way to Ethiopia.

NAMIBIA

Namibia is a huge and half-empty land, covering an area larger than Great Britain, West Germany, Italy, and the Low Countries combined, with a population (1,009,000) smaller than that of metropolitan Cape Town. Much of the land is not arable; water is so sparse that in over 70 percent of Namibia even dry-land cropping is out of the question. Except in part of the better-watered north, grazing is the major form of agriculture, but in this drought-ridden land most pastures have a low carrying capacity. Namibia's mineral resources are immense; only a fraction has been exploited. Namibia's sheer size and scanty population make it expensive to build and operate services such as water supplies, railways, electrical undertakings, and so forth.

Ethnic breakdown

Namibia's greatest asset is its variegated and youthful population, a high proportion of which is of working age. The territory contains more than a dozen ethnolinguistic groups, many of them subdivided. Blacks (including such people as the Bushmen or San, who do not speak Bantu languages) represent about 78 percent of the population, whites about 12 percent, and most of the remainder are people of mixed origin.

After 1962, the South African government embarked on a policy — since abandoned — of assigning the various ethnic groups their own homelands. From the European perspective, such a policy had great advantages. If Ovamboland were split from the rest of the country, whites would form about one-fourth of the population, and Europeans and Euro-Africans together would approach nearly two-fifths of the population. A homelands policy does not, however, square with the demographic facts. Most members of the main northern groups — Caprivi, Kavango, and Kaokolanders — do indeed live on their accustomed soil; about 80 percent of the Ovambo reside in what was called their homeland. The majority of Herero, Damara, and Nama, however, dwell in what were once known as white areas. Even in the cities, the whites are outnumbered; to quote J. H. P. Serfontein, an Afrikaner journalist, "there is no white area. There is a black northern area, and a common area in the central and southern parts."[3]

The various ethnic communities, moreover, lack homogeneity. The Ovambo, the most numerous group, embrace seven major ethnic groups — Kuanyama, Ndonga, Kuambi, Ngondjera, Kualuthi, Mbalantu, and Ndolorkati-Lunda. They make their living largely from arable farming and herding cattle, using a wide variety of agricultural methods. In the past, distance and topography protected the Ovambo against European penetration. Today, however, the market economy has made considerable inroads into the traditional culture. Most Ovambo now belong to some Christian church; the Lutherans have the largest following. More than half the people are literate; many are politically active, and SWAPO (the South West African People's Organization) derives the bulk of its following from the Ovambo — a subject to which we shall return in the section on politics.

Ovamboland suffers from a great many disadvantages. It is distant from profitable urban markets; it is the only part of Namibia to have suffered seriously from guerrilla and counter insurgency operations; and Ovambo farmers cannot easily export their surplus. Something like one-fifth of the population, mostly young men, are away from their homes at any particular time working for employers in the south, usually on temporary labor contracts.

Next in political importance among Africans come the Herero. The Herero, originally a cattle-keeping people, suffered heavily in wars against the Nama, a non-Bantu-speaking people whose way of life had been strongly influenced by the culture of Afrikaans-speaking white frontiersmen. Later German conquerors inflicted catastrophic losses on the Herero and the Nama in the kaiser's wars of conquest. The Herero, like many of their neighbors, lost many of their accustomed grazing grounds. Today, most Herero dwell outside of what used to be called their homeland, and many make their living in the cash economy as laborers, clerks, and teachers. The Herero wield a political influence disproportionate to their numbers; many of the leaders of SWANU (South West African National Union), and some of SWAPO's leaders, are Herero. Namibia's ethnic palette is further enriched by numerous other black and Euro-African communities. The following table provides an appropriate breakdown, but does not give a full picture of the country's ethnic complexity.

Table 1: Population Groups and Ethnic Groups in Namibia

Group	1970 Census	1981 Census
Ovambo	352,640	505,744
Kavango	49,512	94,840
Herero (including Kaokoveld)	57,156	78,213
Damara	66,291	76,169
White	90,683	76,946
Nama	32,935	48,539
Colored	28,512	42,241
East-Caprivi	25,580	38,594
Bushman (San)	22,830	29,441
Rehoboth-Baster	16,649	25,181
Tswana	4,407	6,700
Other	15,089	12,403
Total	762,284	1,035,011

Source: 1970 and 1981 census figures, as provided by Southwest Africa/Namibia Information Service, Windhoek, Namibia.

Colonial status

After the end of World War I, South-West Africa was, for all practical purposes, annexed to the Union of South Africa. So-called Class C mandate gave the Union of South Africa plenary administrative and legislative powers over the territory, which could be administered as though it were an integral part of South Africa, subject to certain safeguards. The humanitarian standards of the nineteenth century shaped the terms of the mandate. The framers of the mandate thought in terms of a trusteeship, designed to protect the indigenous people, but the treaty makers did not envisage African political independence for the Class C mandates. The mandate therefore made no provision for self-government, and it imposed no effective restrictions on the manner in which the laws of the mandatory power could be applied. The post war years saw a steady diminution of German influence as an increasing number of South African immigrants, mainly Afrikaners, came to Namibia. By 1925 German-speaking registered voters in the territory were outvoted by their new South African compatriots, most of whom — though Afrikaners — sympathized with General Smuts.

After World War II, the South African delegation to the U.N.

General Assembly informed the newly formed body that, in Pretoria's opinion, the League of Nations mandate had lapsed, and the territory of South-West Africa should be incorporated into the Union. The U.N. General Assembly refused to sanction South Africa's request, but South Africans continued to extend their country's administrative hold over Namibia. The U.N. General Assembly, by contrast, sided with SWAPO, and in 1966 it declared the South African mandate at an end. (In the following year, the U.N. set up its own Council for Namibia.)

The U.N., however, failed to make any effective headway in the matter. In 1973 the General Assembly agreed to recognize SWAPO as the sole authentic representative of what had become known, as yet quite inaccurately, as the Namibian nation. The South Africans responded by sanctioning the so-called Turnhalle Constitutional Conference (1975–1977) which sought an internal settlement based on local parties. At the same time, the South Africans, under a new administrator-general, began to dismantle the structure of apartheid as it had hitherto functioned in the country. In 1978 the South Africans announced plans for an election to the National Assembly, resulting in a decisive victory for the Democratic Turnhalle Alliance (DTA).

The South African initiative again failed to secure a favorable international response. The Western powers refused to acknowledge the validity of the elections. The U.N. persisted in an even harder line, calling for effective reprisals against South Africa. President Reagan's election and his new administration's commitment to "constructive engagement" gave a new lease of life to the previous efforts at conciliation by the Contact Group, composed of five Western powers (the U.S., Canada, Britain, France, and West Germany). But, in the end, no agreement was reached. The South Africans since 1981 have intensified raids against SWAPO bases in southern Angola, while at the same time providing support for UNITA (União Nacional para a Independência Total de Angola) guerrillas operating in Angola. After Ronald Reagan became president, Pretoria and Washington established a new principle: a Cuban withdrawal from Angola should be a precondition for internationally acceptable election and South African withdrawal from Namibia.

As of 1985, the South Africans have attained a position of complete military predominance. Angola and South Africa have agreed to a cease-fire; they set up a joint Angolan-South African commission to monitor the disengagement of South African forces from southern Angola; no members of SWAPO or UNITA and no Cubans were allowed to operate in the border region.[4] France left the Western Contact Group, declaring that this body should "be left dormant in the absence of any ability to exercise honestly the mandate confided to it."[5]

The South African-Angolan arrangement matched a nonaggression treaty between South Africa and Mozambique made in 1984; for the time being, at any rate, Pretoria had consolidated its position, and the political initiative remained with South Africa.

But it remains to be seen whether the peace will hold. SWAPO cannot function as a military force without bases in Angola. The African National Congress (ANC) is certain to be hamstrung without sanctuaries in countries such as Mozambique. If these two movements abstain from military action, they will likely lose much of their international standing; moreover, they may face serious challenges from militants within their own ranks. The government of the Movimento Popular de Libertação de Angola (MPLA) is not in a position to survive in its existing form without help from Cubans, East Germans, and Soviets. If these foreigners depart — an unlikely prospect — the MPLA will have to seek reconciliation with UNITA; such an arrangement had already failed in 1975, when the Portuguese, UNITA, MPLA, and the Frenta de Libertação de Angola (FLNA) concluded a short-lived agreement for a tripartite provisional government.

Civil and Military Administration

South African policy originally intended to absorb Namibia. From 1950 to 1974, some elected members from South-West Africa represented the territory in South Africa's all-white Parliament. At the same time, the South Africans attempted to duplicate their homelands policy in South-West Africa, albeit with scant success. (For instance, an Ovambo Legislative Assembly came into being in 1968, a Kavango Legislative Assembly in 1970, a Damaraland Advisory Council in 1971, a Caprivi Legislative Assembly in 1972, and a Nama Council in 1976.) The South Africans attempted to sustain this policy economically through bodies such as the Bantu Investment Corporation, which made considerable investments in the homelands.

As a result of both external and internal opposition to the South African connection with Namibia, the South Africans thereafter reversed their policy. In 1977 they appointed an administrator-general with far-reaching executive powers, and in 1978 elections were held for a National Assembly (dissolved in 1983). The administrator-general was assisted by a twelve-member Ministerial Council (increased to fifteen members in 1981), set up in 1980 with authority over a large variety of administrative functions, but excluding such key areas as constitutional, security, and foreign affairs. The Ministerial Council was dissolved in 1983 after the resignation of the chairman of the DTA, Dirk Mudge, and Pretoria had to reimpose direct rule.

Earlier, the South Africans had begun to take steps to reorganize the administration and to provide for the transfer of all administrative functions to a future Namibian government. To this end, planners made provisions for ten central directorates (Foreign Affairs; Civic Affairs and Manpower; Economic Affairs, Finance; Justice; Agriculture and Forestry; National Health and Welfare; Education; Post and Telecommunications; Water; and Constitutional Development.) To run these and other agencies, Namibia, like most independent African states, developed an extensive bureaucracy. (By 1970, 15.7 percent of the labor force was engaged in government and related services, as compared 8.3 percent in commerce and finance, 7.4 percent in mining; 4.1 percent in transport; 13.3 percent in manufacturing, power and construction; and 51.2 percent in agriculture, forestry, and fishing.)[6] Out of a total budget of 1,038.8 million rand for 1983–84, 777.8 million rand went to government expenditure, including central government departments and eleven ethnic, second-tier governments. Within a space of five years, state expenditure in Namibia had risen from 32.2 percent of the GDP (gross domestic product) to 62 percent. Namibia thus had become a highly bureaucratized state.

As in South Africa and most independent African states, parastatals came to play a major role in the Namibian economy. As the planners in Namibia saw it, Namibia could not easily develop its agriculture and industries for many reasons. Its domestic market was small, and many raw materials needed for processing or refining were deficient or altogether absent (especially coal and iron). The country suffered from a scarcity in managerial and technological skills and an inadequate supply of local capital. The sheer size of the territory and the geographical characteristics of the terrain rendered extremely costly the development of services such as water, power, transport, education, and medical services. Furthermore, Namibia's own middle classes were small in size and economic power. All these characteristics Namibia shared to a greater or lesser extent with other African states.

State agencies stepped in, as they had in South Africa, to fill the gap. The South African railways supplied a broad range of services, including rail and road transportation, many tourist traveling facilities, harbor services in the main port, and extensive technical training. Namib Air in 1982 operated under the control of the state (the Namabian interim government having acquired 51 percent of its holdings in 1982). The state became responsible for setting up more than two hundred domestic water-supply schemes and conducting constant research into the technique of supplying and storing water in a dry country. The Industrial Development Corporation of South Africa set up the South West Africa Water and Electricity Corporation to supply power. The South-West African administration financed a variety of urban housing schemes. The Bantu Investment Corporation, with some success, promoted a variety of enterprises in African areas for the purpose of integrating these areas into the market economy and creating an independent black middle class.

The state also took far-reaching steps to promote industrial development. The First National Development Corporation of South West Africa (FNDC) derived its funds from the state, but had a board of directors derived from the private sector. The FNDC aimed at stimulating private enterprise and encouraging investments from outside. The corporation itself acted as a private entrepreneur in areas where private initiative seemed deficient. It did so by providing training; giving loans to private concerns; taking responsibility for meat processing and canning factories, wholesale and retail shops, butcheries, and dairies in backward rural areas; and by acting in partnership with private undertakings (for instance, in establishing an oil press at Omaruru).

The parastatals in Namibia, as in South Africa, operated in an economy in which enterprises (especially in mining and farming) were left to private ownership and private entrepreneurs held a powerful position in economic planning. The parastatals, moreover, were able to draw on South African technical and administrative expertise, which enabled them to operate with reasonable efficiency. Nevertheless, Namibia's heavy state expenditure was made possible only by South Africa's willingness to subsidize Namibia's heavy foreign debt and massive budgetary deficits. South Africa guaranteed commercial loans, mainly advanced by South African banks, to cover Windhoek's administrative deficits (valued at $184.7 million for the 1983–84 budget). Overall, South Africa's direct and indirect expenditure on Namibia stood at an estimated total ot $453.6 million for the year 1984–85, in addition to a projected defense expenditure of $324 million to $405 million.) Were Namibia to attain complete independence, the resultant financial burden would form a crippling charge on a country beset by heavy costs for drought relief, large debts, and falling prices for its raw material exports.[7]

Namibia's dependent status, moreover, unwittingly contributed to extensive and expensive administrative growth. Already by the latter part of the 1970s, Namibia's scanty population helped to sustain its own Namibian administration, separate administrations for the homelands, and a substantial defense effort. South African departments continued to exercise important functions in Namibia. South African ownership of the country's railroad network and its rolling stock provided South Africa with an additional instrument of control; so did South African possession of Namibia's principal port, Walvis Bay, a deep-water harbor with modern facilities and good railroad connections.[8] By the latter part of the 1970s, over 20,000 Namibians (including about 9,000 whites) were working for government agencies or semiprivate bodies. Administration, as in so many other African countries, had become a major industry. Namibia remained not merely a dependent but also — like South Africa — a much overgoverned country, run along bureaucratic procedures and principles developed in South Africa. The central administration, as distinct from the local second-tier administrations, was reasonably competent and generally free from corruption, a major asset in the ongoing modernization and counter insurgency campaign.

Administrative dependence went hand in hand with military dependence. The South Africans soon found that the South African Police (SAP) stationed in Namibia could not on their own cope with guerrilla incursions and internal unrest. From 1972 the South African Defense Force began to deploy along the northern border, and the South Africans built a massive military infrastructure, complete with bases, roads, and air fields. The army not only engaged in military tasks but also attempted to win the confidence of the people through civic-action programs that sometimes cut across the functions exercised by the second-tier governments. The South African army officers, by this time, had become indifferent to apartheid as a system; they saw nothing wrong with deploying black as well as white soldiers against SWAPO's People's Liberation Army of Namibia (PLAN). The military had been persuaded that the war could not be won without gaining the confidence of the civilian population. Thus military effort itself became an unintentional solvent of apartheid.

In tune with the new policy of military and social reformism, the South Africans in 1977 began to build both a local Namibian police and a Namibian defense force (SWAFT, the South West Africa Territory Force.) The new force, for all practical purposes, remained firmly integrated into the South African defense structure. It was organized on South African lines and shared the military ethos of the South African forces. By 1980, SWAFT had an official establishment of 10,100 men, organized into both ethnic battalions (with separate units for Ovambo, Herero, Coloreds, Tswana, Nama, and others) and multiethnic units (including a battalion containing whites and soldiers of other ethnic origins.) SWAFT, like the South African Defense Force, consisted of both long-term professional soldiers (the permanent force) and conscripts. In 1981, the authorities attempted to extend the draft to Africans, but this decision led to widespread protests from both political parties and churches, so that the draft remained selective in nature. Operationally, SWAFT was divided into a command infrastructure, a permanent-force infantry component, a citizen force (most of whom formed part of a conventional motorized-infantry brigade), a "commando" network for local defense, logistic and administrative units, and a training wing. By the early 1980s, SWAFT had made considerable progress. But, despite a professed desire to create an all-Namibian national defense force, SWAFT was organized mainly on ethnic lines. The overall structure of the military reflected the South Africas' uncertainty regarding the political order they meant to create. With its organizational confusion, the diverse composition of its units, and the apparent uncertainty of its command structure, SWAFT for the time being was in no condition to shoulder the burden of defending Namibia without South African help.[9]

Economic Development

Sixty years ago, South-West Africa was one of the most under-developed regions in southern Africa. Its population scarcely exceeded 200,000 (including 177,462 Africans, 30,845 people of mixed birth, and 19,432 whites in 1921.) Windhoek, the capital, had less than 10,000 inhabitants; the remaining centers (Luderitz, Keetmanshoop, and Swakopmund) were no more than overgrown villages. By the early 1980s, the country's economy had been transformed. Nevertheless, Namibia remained essentially a raw-material producer, and most of its black population lived on the land. But the "traditional areas," once designated as homelands, contributed less than 5 percent to the GDP, not much less than the tiny commercial and industrial sectors.

The primary sector was dominated by mining, (which accounted for 40 percent of the GDP). Namibia's economy as a whole strikingly resembled South Africa's sixty years ago, in that the territory exported close to 80 percent of what its people produced and imported about the same proportion of their consumption needs — mostly from South Africa. By 1967, South Africa had invested 29 million rand in the mining sector (of a total investment of 59 million rand). Outside companies provided Namibia with its mining capital, technological expertise, and marketing skills. Local capitalists played a negligible part. Namibia was company country par excellence. Three large companies, Consolidated Diamond Mines (CDM, with a capital investment of 750 million rand), Rössling (linked to Rio Tinto South Africa, with an investment of 900 million rand), and Tsumeb (with a capital investment of 500 million rand) dominated the economy by their sheer size.[10]

Within the mining sector, diamonds provided the most important individual product; but the importance of this particular industry within the country's economy is likely to diminish. From 1977 onward, output has declined as a result of falling world prices, outside competition, and the growing menace of artificial gems. South-West Africa's resources are not inexhaustible, even though experts disagree on the extent of the industry's potential resources. In the early 1980s diamonds remained trumps, and diamond-mining taxes accounted for the largest single source of government revenue (180 million rand out of a total of 460 million rand for 1980–1981). In addition, Namibia contains a wealth of other minerals — uranium, copper, lead, zinc, vanadium, and lithium.

About one-third of the country is covered by mining concessions, and the government has tried to encourage additional foreign participation. But falling prices have seriously affected all sectors of the mining economy, with grave consequences for Namibia's fragile prosperity.

The fishing industry, once insignificant, stood second to mining as an export industry. The fisheries in turn sparked the creation of new processing plants, but the whole industry has been endangered by overfishing on the part of the fishing fleets of the USSR, various East-bloc countries, Japan, the Republic of Korea, and others. In an attempt to protect their fishing grounds, the Namibian authorities extended their territorial waters to 200 nautical miles, but overfishing unfortunately has continued.

Agriculture in Namibia has also seen considerable expansion, despite the problems occasioned by droughts, fluctuating world prices, and the difficulties in marketing occasioned in part by the enormous size of the territory. Over the last fifty years, the growth of motor transport and a road network has diminished the accustomed isolation of backwoods farms, and new goods — bicycles, transistor radios, sewing machines, soap, low-priced textiles, and such — have made their appearance even in remote black communities. The government, through the Bantu Investment Corporation (BIC), has attempted to promote African agriculture. Since 1974, several major projects have got under way — the Kavango Cattle Ranch, the Ovambo Meat Factory, and the Mukwe Irrigation project, among others. BIC officials believe that the Kavango regions could one day become Namibia's breadbasket, but such projects will only come to fruition in the remote future.

Namibian agriculture today is dominated by Europeans. White farmers helped to introduce new techniques (dry farming and the use of artificial fertilizers), new machine-made devices (barbed wire fences and agricultural machinery), dams, boreholes, cattle dips, and such. The territory has thus developed into an important beef and wool supplier for the South African market. By 1981 there were about 1,700,000 head of cattle in the country as compared to an estimated 200,000 in 1913. Sheep (especially Karakul) during the same period increased from an estimated 22,000 to something like 4,500,000. Farming, mainly the livestock sector, by the early 1980s accounted for 12 percent of Namibia's GDP.

Despite these successes, by the early 1980s Namibia's economic prospects were grim. The country faced the threat of low or falling prices for most of its raw materials; uncertainty about its political future; high inflation rates; massive unemployment, especially among blacks; widespread corruption in the second-tier governments; heavy administrative expenditures (making up about three-quarters of the 1983–84 budget); difficult social problems derived from black labor migration from the north to the central and southern parts of Namibia; periodic droughts; and the probable exhaustion of Namibia's fishing resources. White, as well as black, Namibians had cause to criticize the extent of government regulation and interference in all sectors of the economy. There were complaints concerning South African competition in manufacturing. Namibian producers argued that they could purchase raw materials and machinery more cheaply abroad were it not for South Africa's protection of its own products. South African incentives for industrial decentralization did not apply to Namibia, thereby helping South African producers to undercut Namibian firms. But, for better or worse, the Namibian economy remained inextricably linked to South Africa's — any immediate and radical attempt to break the link would lead to disaster.

Politics

In 1977 Namibia embarked on what might have been a promising political departure. Dirk Mudge, an Afrikaner and, in our opinion, probably the ablest white politician to have emerged in Namibia, resigned from the National Party and formed a new political party. This party, made up of a multiethnic coalition including whites as well as Coloreds and Africans, took the name Democratic Turnhalle Alliance (DTA). It was based on the principles of free enterprise and multiracial cooperation. In elections held during the following year, the DTA gained 41 of 50 seats in the newly established National Assembly.[11] At the same time, Justice Martinus Steyn, the new administrator-general in Windhoek, took steps to amend or dismantle existing apartheid legislation. The contract labor system administered by the South West Africa Native Labor Agency (SWANLA) vanished; influx control into the cities disappeared, as did Group Area-type regulations forbidding blacks to own land in urban or rural areas.

The DTA, however, failed to receive effective powers. As the DTA politicians saw it, Pretoria sabotaged the party's attempt to run a functioning central government in Namibia and to rally public opinion behind the DTA. The South African government feared alienating the right wing within the ruling National Party. The majority of Namibian whites, especially the Afrikaners, became fearful of both the *swart gevaar* and the *rooi gevaar* (the black and the red peril, respectively); they turned, accordingly, to conservative groups such as the HNP. The DTA itself failed to keep its cohesion and had to compete with an array of local ethnic parties, such as Justus Garoeb's Damara Council, the Kavango Namibia Christian Democratic Party, and Moses Katjivonga's South West Africa National Union (SWANU), which is a Herero association.

In 1983, the administrator-general dissolved the National Assembly and continued to run what was, in effect, a colonial state. South Africa, the equivalent of the metropolitan power, held the key portfolios of defense and foreign affairs. The administrator-general remained in charge of Namibian central government and legislative powers. The second-tier administrations continued to operate with separate departments for functions such as education, welfare, roads, and so forth. Third-tier (or municipal) administrations ran the towns. Overall, government in Namibia remained fragmented in both a political and an administrative sense, and it was wholly dependent on Pretoria.

Pretoria, in turn, faced a dilemma. The South Africans wanted a moderate government in Namibia, a government of the kind agreeable to the *verlig* ("enlightened"' or reform-minded) element within the National Party. Yet the South Africans had failed to sustain the DTA. Pretoria dreaded a further long-term commitment, lest such involvement should turn into an electoral liability. Yet the South Africans equally dreaded any agreement that might lead to a SWAPO takeover, lest a Marxist seizure of power should occasion an exodus of Namibia's Afrikaners to South Africa, where the exiles would surely strengthen the right-wing opposition to Botha's government.

The main Namibian opposition derived from SWAPO (South West Africa People's Organization of Namibia). SWAPO operated in exile, with offices in Lusaka, Luanda, London, New York, and other cities. It maintained training camps abroad and recruited many refugees who had sought refuge in Angola. The party was headed by Sam Nujoma, its president; Brendan Simbwaye was vice-president and David Meroro was national chairman. An internal branch of SWAPO operated by peaceful means and has so far not been banned.

SWAPO should be distinguished from SWAPO-Democrats, a breakaway group formed in 1978 and headed by a former SWAPO leader, Andreas Shipanga. This organization operated legally on Namibian soil. In accordance with its constitution, SWAPO's national congress elected an 11-member national executive and a 35-member central committee whose secretariat attended to SWAPO's day-to-day actions. The national executive also supervised particular departments concerned with subjects such as defense, education, and transport. It likewise maintained links with allied organizations, a Women's League, a Youth League, and a Council of Elders.

Politically and ideologically, SWAPO did not describe itself as a Marxist-Leninist party but rather — as the MPLA and the Frente de Libertação de Moçambique (FRELIMO) had done in Angola and Mozambique, respectively — as a "popular movement." Its constitution called for the creation of a national economy on the principles of "scientific socialism," but with considerable concessions for the so-called national bourgeoisie. In foreign policy, SWAPO, having formed alliances with MPLA, FELIMO, the ANC in South Africa and, formerly, with ZAPU in Zimbabwe, unreservedly backed the Soviet Union. Like other liberation movements supported and partially financed by the Soviet Union, the MPLA looks to a "national democratic revolution" in alliance with "progressive elements" from the petty bourgeoisie and the "national bourgeoisie," as well as with workers and peasants. The national democratic revolution, Marxist-Leninists hope, will later merge into a full-fledged socialist revolution. But, depending on the character of its audience, SWAPO spoke with different voices. As the *African Communist*, organ of the South African Communist Party, sympathetically commented:

SWAPO is faced with a strategic problem similar to that facing the Zimbabwean liberation movement: to resist the ideological and financial pressure from the West, while exploiting to the full the Western powers' desire to accommodate to some degree, and for their own reactionary motives, the force for change in Southern Africa. And both these tasks have to be fulfilled while at the same time advancing the armed struggle . . . the only path to liberation.[12]

SWAPO statements did not, however, suffer from ambiguity with regard to the measures that the party proposed to take against its opponents once it had achieved power. All those deemed guilty of "counter-revolutionary acts," taking part in the establishment of "a cabal or any organized group with an aim of committing crime [sic] against the Namibian People's Revolution," engaging in "excessive exploitation or exportation of Namibian natural resources of animal, vegetable, mineral or any other origin," or "perfidious and disguised impairment of the means of 'production' would be treated as felons, to be executed or jailed for as long as 20 years."[13]

By 1984, SWAPO's immediate tasks were fourfold: to intensify the armed struggle, to widen the basis of its support in Namibia, to enlarge its international backing, and to strengthen its administrative ability so that it might more easily shift from a party in exile to a governing party.

Late in 1984, SWAPO's immediate military prospects looked gloomy. South Africa's agreements with Angola and Mozambique, enforced by superior South African strength, apparently occasioned dismay in Moscow, where the Soviet press warned both Luanda and Maputo that South African efforts at peace were no more than a trick.[14] But SWAPO was by no means out for the count. The South African army's military performance on the northern border had admittedly improved a great deal since the early 1970s; the South African army had gained much experience and had been hardened by life in the bush. Namibia's own territorial defense force had likewise bettered its training; particularly noteworthy were the performances of Herero and San (Bushman) units against the perceived Ovambo enemy. But PLAN, the SWAPO forces, had likewise gained in competence. Cuban trainers were replaced by highly efficient cadres from East Germany. By 1982, plans were afoot to provide each SWAPO company with an East German commander and four platoon commanders. Six of these companies made up one battalion, each of which was trained or commanded by a Soviet or East German citizen.[15] At the time, the Soviet Union began to upgrade the range of equipment supplied to SWAPO, whose armory began to comprise some weapons of considerable sophistication.

SWAPO also has extended its political influence among the Ovambo people. (According to estimates cited by Hans Germani, a West German journalist and an expert on African political affairs, had a U.N.-supervised election been held in 1982, it would have given SWAPO 90 percent of the Ovambo votes, 2–3 percent of the Damara and Hottentot votes, no votes among the Kavango, and 20 percent among the Caprivi.[16] SWAPO gained such political successes not merely by intimidation but also de-emphasizing the Marxist-Leninist part of its program, taking a relatively moderate stance, and partially camouflaging its communist linkages.[17] This tactic was bound to pay dividends in Namibia, a country where something like 90 percent of the population professed Christianty, especially the Lutheran and — to a secondary degree — Catholic faiths. SWAPO was somewhat successful in overcoming the deleterious effects of past splits and breakaways.

The South Africans, by May 1984, had agreed to participate with SWAPO and the main Namibian parties in negotiations to extend the cease-fire to the SWAPO forces. The South Africans, however, still faced the difficult task of finding an acceptable substitute for the DTA as a governing party to pit against SWAPO in the political arena. They had given their blessing to an alliance formed in 1983 in Windhoek, known as the Multi-Party Conference (MPC) and led by Andreas Shipanga. (This coalition consisted of SWANU, the DTA parties, the SWAPO Democrats, the Rehoboth Liberation Front [representing Rehoboth Basters], the Namibian Christian Democratic Party [Coloreds], and some others.) By 1984, however, the Multi-Party Conference, remained too loosely organized to form an effective governing party. SWAPO, on the one hand, condemned the alliance on the grounds that its members were puppets; on the other hand, critics to the right of the Multi-Party Conference argued that its immediate future would be no more auspicious than that of Bishop Muzorewa's short-lived ruling party in Zimbabwe.

In March 1984, "the father of liberation" in Namibia, Herman Toivo ja Toivo, was released from prison after sixteen years. South African officials probably thought his release would cause a split in SWAPO; this hope proved unrealistic since the men in the bush lead SWAPO, not those in Windhoek. In addition, Toivo ja Toivo denounced South Africa and the MPC.

SWAPO's Achilles' heel, aside from the military, was the paucity of its cadres. The Germans had made deliberate attempts to train civilian as well as military experts capable of taking over Namibia. But, by the mid-1980s, neither their numbers nor their technological expertise were sufficient to run a socialist state of the kind initiated earlier, with such disastrous consequences, by the MPLA in Angola and Frelimo in Mozambique.

In 1985, Namibia's future therefore seemed uncertain. The Reagan administration was determined to link a South African withdrawal to a Cuban withdrawal from Angola. This policy, however, ignored the growing importance of the East Germans and the Soviets in Angolan and SWAPO military power. In our view a settlement should therefore be linked to a withdrawal of all Soviet-bloc military experts from Angola and the disbandment of SWAPO's military formations. It seems unreasonable to hold elections when one of the political parties among the various contestants commands its own private army, a well-trained force resolved to liquidate its political opponents upon the achievement of victory. However, unpopular the South African connection might be among Namibians of all colors, the South African link remains — for the time being — Namibia's life belt. As matters now stand, Namibia is much more effectively run than its northern neighbors. This state of affairs will continue as long as the whites remain. Should they depart under a new settlement, of whatever kind, Namibia will undoubtedly descend to the condition of Angola or Mozambique.

THE BLS STATES

Botswana

In terms of physical size and political influence, Botswana is the most important of the three BLS states. At first, Botswana seems a land destined for failure. It covers 236,000 square miles — a little smaller than Texas. Much of the land is desert, semiarid steppe, or bush, fit only for cattle farming; only about 5 percent of Botswana enjoys adequate rainfall and suitable soil for the cultivation of crops, and even these areas are subject to drought. About four-fifths of the country's scanty population (819,000 people in 1980), including seven of the eight major Tswana ethnic communities and most of the European and Asian residents, live in the country's eastern strip. Admittedly, the country's potential is considerable; the Okavango-Chobe swamps in the north, for instance, could sustain a much larger population if the land was drained and properly developed. In addition, Botswana contains substantial deposits of diamonds, coal, manganese, asbestos, copper, nickel, salt, and other riches. Development, however, requires a great deal of money and a great deal of skill — at a time when both these assets are in short supply and the population keeps growing at an astounding rate (an annual birth rate of 50.7 per 1,000 for 1975–1980, and a death rate of 17.5 per 1,000).

Botswana faces other troubles. It is a landlocked country, almost totally dependent on the Republic of South Africa for the joint collection of customs revenue, most of its rail and air communications, and most of its imports (467,659,000 rand of a toal import bill of 537,593,000 rand.) South Africa provides not only machinery and a broad range of manufactured goods but also the bulk of the grain consumed by the Tswana. The Tswana resent Pretoria's racial policies but dare not offend their overly powerful neighbor. Militants at the university in Gaborone may prefer to turn Botswana into a staunch member of an anti-South African coalition in concert with Zimbabwe, Angola, and Mozambique. But most radicals — unlike their elders in the civil service and the government (commonly trained in South Africa) — do not fully grasp the power of South Africa's stranglehold over Botswana's supplies. Indeed, Botswana remains one of South Africa's "political hostages" — together with the other BLS states.[18] Botswana's external position was not improved by periodic friction with Zimbabwe, a giant by Botswana standards and a country that resented real or supposed support given to ZAPU from Botswana territory. Moreover, Botswana has had to cope with an influx of refugees from countries as far afield as Angola, Zimbabwe, South Africa, and Namibia, an influx that puts additional pressure on the country's scanty resources.

Botswana suffers from great inequality of income, not only between whites and nonwhites but also within the black rural community, where a relatively small proportion of prosperous cattle owners command a large share of the wealth. These prosperous cattle owners benefit most from government programs (such as free veterinary and disease-control services, or the provision of low-cost feed for livestock). They frequently have personal links to senior civil servants, many of whom invest their wealth in cattle, the accepted means of saving. Agriculture cannot, however, provide an acceptable living to all the rural people. An estimated 12 percent of Botswana's laborers continue to travel to South Africa every year in search of jobs.

Botswana also must cope with inflation, an unfavorable trade balance, and a great deal of unemployment. In terms of political economy, Botswana's position is scarcely better than that of a South African homeland; yet Botswana does not enjoy the massive subsidies that South Africa has granted to its homelands and to Namibia. Capital for Botswana's development remains scarce; so are technical skills and markets for Botswana's exports — this during a period of falling world prices for many of Botswana's raw materials.

Given these daunting circumstances, Botswana has achieved a remarkable degree of political and economic success. Botswana deservedly maintained a high rating from Freedom House (a U.S. civil-rights organization) for the high regard its leadership holds for civic liberties. Relations between whites and blacks remained acceptable; elections were noteworthy for the generally high standards of integrity with which they were conducted. From its beginnings, independent Botswana has been fortunate in the quality of its leadership. Sir Seretse Khama, the country's first president, outshone all other political men within the BLS states and carefully balanced his country's interests between east and west, South Africa and black Africa. Botswana has also profited from continuity of leadership. Quett Ketumile Masire served as Sir Seretse's vice president before succeeding him in 1980. Botswana remains a country of limited resources and limited political influence in South Africa and in the international world. But it has developed a moderate, conservative internal order that has brought stability and economic development and the rewards of foreign aid and loans.

Botswana, though a constitutional state, shares with most independent African countries a strong commitment to presidential power. All executive power lies with the president (whose election to office is linked to the election of members of the National Assembly). When more than two candidates compete for office, the candidate commanding more than half the votes of the elected members is declared president. Incumbent president Masire also served as president of the ruling Botswana Democratic Party (BDP), which, in the general elections of 1979, secured 29 of 32 elected seats. The BDP mainly rested on ethnic support from the Bamangwato people and stood for a policy of moderation and support for private enterprise. Opposition derived from the Botswana National Front (BNF), a Marxist-inclined body headed by chief Bathoen II. Bathoen resigned his chieftainship of the Bangwaketse group to run for the lower house of Parliament. Other opposition groups included the Botswana People's Party, the Botswana Liberal Party, and several minor bodies. The opposition, however, remained divided, and, for all practical purposes, Botswana was run as a one-party state.

Botswana's government was not, however, a dictatorship. It profited from a number of advantages. Botswana, by comparison with most other African states, was relatively homogeneous in an ethnic sense. There were, indeed, some divisions, for instance, the landless Bakalaka tribe, once an appendage to the ruling Bamangwato, was strongly entrenched in the civil service, to the displeasure of many of their countrymen of other ethnic backgrounds. But Botswana faced nothing like the conflict that divides, for example, Shona and Ndebele in neighboring Zimbabwe. The bulk of the land, moreover, was held by Africans, unlike the situation in Namibia.

Botswana has other unusual features. A visitor to the capital, Gaborone, was struck by the frugality of government — unusual in late twentieth-century Africa. The Tswana have labored hard to balance their national budget. (Revenue for fiscal year 1982–83, a year of almost universal budget deficits, stood at 293.40 million pula; expenditures were 293.95 million pula. At the time the U.S. dollar was valued at 1.08 pula.) The country generally ran its affairs in a spirit of fiscal responsibility reminiscent of those Scottish missionaries who first preached the Gospel in Botswana during Queen Victoria's reign. Government offices were modest, ministries were modest, even ministerial cars were modest. Senior civil servants worked late hours; department heads punctiliously met important appointments on schedule. In Botswana, as in most other countries, there was some graft, especially at the lower levels of government, but the senior civil servants' scrupulous integrity, noticed in the past by such veteran administrators as Anthony Sillery, a historian of Botswana, commonly came as a surprise to those businessmen used to the way of Zambia, Zaire, or Nigeria. The armed forces accounted for only a negligible share of the country's expenditure. (The Defense Force, set up in 1977, amounted to 3,000 men, in addition to a paramilitary police force of 1,260 men.)[19]

Botswana's economy also benefited from other advantages. Its GNP demonstrated striking economic growth. (From 1960 to 1969, the average annual growth rate had amounted to 5.7 percent, and it rose to 13.6 percent between 1970 and 1979.) Botswana's economic expansion was sustained by a high rate of gross domestic investment (with an average annual rate of 25.3 percent for 1960–1970 and 5.6 percent for 1979–1980, as compared to the respective figures for Tanzania of 9.8 percent and 3.0 percent.)[20] A substantial part of the National Development Plan (1979–80 through 1984–85) went to projects that benefited rural people. (Of a total projected expenditure of 704.3 million pula, 213.0 million were earmarked for works and communications; 127.9 million for local government and land; 83.2 million for agriculture; and 39.9 million for mineral resources, water development, and drought relief — as compared to 63.2 million for defense; 51.7 million for education; and 18.9 million for the office of the president.)[21]

At the time of independence Botswana was poor; it had no national economy and could not even provide for its own budget. There was only a cattle industry operating and a low-level agricultural sector. The infrastructure was very limited and development prospects appeared dim.[22]

Yet with the help of foreign capital and a modest government organization economic development has been good since independence. Mineral discoveries sparked growth and investment and a partnership between mineral corporations and government. Taxes gave government sufficient funds for a balanced budget, and new investments came readily to Botswana. An effective national state developed as did a good system of schools, health services, and roads.

Class formation has proceeded slowly and steadily. The government has legitimacy, which few other African governments have retained. The farmers, workers, the governing elite, and others cooperate to build a modern state. All classes and groups feel they have benefited, so the state is stable at the present time.

One major reason for this stability, lacking in so much of Africa, is the continuity in the peasants' relationships on the land. The economy has steadily expanded and this growth has satisfied most of the people. Future developments may not be so secure. The peasant sector may not remain content especially if land erosion and over-grazing continue; dependency may not be ended. The elite may start to quarrel over the distribution of the resources of the state. The loss of political unity and consensus and the slowing down of economic growth may threaten the continued stability of

Botswana, but for now it is one of the success stories of African self-rule. Things are better in Botswana today than they were at independence.

How much has been achieved overall since independence? For all the progress made, Botswana by the 1980s remained an overwhelmingly agricultural country. (By 1979, 83 percent of its working population was employed in farming, 5 percent in industry, and 12 percent in services.) During the first fifteen years of independence, the country's economic progress had indeed been among the most astounding in Africa. This minor *Wirtschaftswunder* derived partly from increased beef exports and partly from encouragement of agricultural improvements in general. This policy accompanied reforms designed to change accustomed systems of land ownership, to introduce provisions for 99-year leases, and to encourage commercial ranching. The Tswana, at the same time, strengthened their agricultural processing industries and improved their veterinary services. For instance, a new Foot-and-Mouth Vaccine Institute coped with domestic outbreaks, and the government initiated a national plan to deal with overgrazing and to encourage arable farming.

Botswana's success, however, did not come cost-free. The bureaucracy has become increasingly powerful in the country. For instance, the Botswana Meat Commission (BMC), a public corporation, occupied a key economic and political position by acting as a monopoly buyer of cattle for slaughter. Bureaucratic agencies have greatly expanded their influence over the last decade. They were aided in this endeavor by foreign aid, supplied in the past by Western donors with such generosity that state agencies in Botswana have become even more isolated from their respective societies than they might otherwise have been.[23]

Botswana's second source of wealth derived from mining, especially the new diamond industry, in which the Botswana government and De Beers in South Africa held equal shares. Diamond prices by the end of 1983 showed some signs of improving; but the production of metals such as nickel and copper had fallen on hard times, despite a heavy infusion of government funds. Manufacturing remained of limited importance and heavily subject to government intervention. Industry was dominated by the Botswana Meat Commission, a public-sector meat-processing enterprise run on lines familiar in South Africa and what was formerly Rhodesia. The government attempted to provide additional enterprises through public agencies such as the Botswana Development Corporation. This policy went hand in hand with official attempts to institute wage-and-price controls that were based on the unfortunate principle that salaries in the private sector should not exceed those for comparable grades in the public sector. Botswana, moreover, continued to rely heavily on foreign loans and grants to finance its development budget — a course of action that strikingly differentiated Rhodesia under past settler rule. (Such aid by 1983 accounted for more than one-quarter of Botswana's development expenditure.) Masire faces many problems: drought, rapid urbanization, unemployment, and pressure from Pretoria to sign a nonaggression pact, especially to exclude formally the ANC from setting up military bases. Only the future can show whether this particular formula for a mixed economy sustained by foreign assistance will continue to work.

The Two Mountain Kingdoms

Lesotho and Swaziland remain the only monarchies in sub-Saharan Africa. Economically, both depend wholly on South Africa; both have proved as inhospitable to parliamentary democracy as most other African countries. Nevertheless, there were considerable differences between the two. By 1984 Lesotho was a one-party state in which the monarch exercised only formal functions. Real power rested with the Basotho National Party (BNP), formed in 1959 and headed by the prime minister, chief Leabua Jonathan. The BNP claimed a total of 150,000 members. It dominated the National Assembly and governed in an extraconstitutional fashion — Jonathan having suspended the constitution in 1973. Under pressure from both his own party and the opposition, Jonathan in 1973 set up an interim National Assembly in which 34 seats went to the BNP, 22 to the principal chiefs, 11 for nominees appointed for "distinguished service," and 26 to the opposition parties. Jonathan represented the traditional elements in Lesotho society; he derived support from the Catholic Church within the country. He sought to steer a semi-independent course by supporting the Southern Africa Development Coordination Conference (SADCC), publicly criticizing apartheid, giving some covert assistance to the ANC, introducing his own currency in 1980, and promoting an agricultural development program designed to reduce Lesotho's dependency on imported food. Militarily, Jonathan relied on a small para-military force drawn from his own supporters, a force that he meant to expand into a national army.

The main opposition derived from the Basotho Congress Party (BCP), formed in 1952.[24] The BCP adhered to the ideas of pan-Africanism; it divided into an internal wing, opposed to political violence and willing to accept some ministerial positions, and an external wing. The latter operated in exile; it maintained an armed formation, the Lesotho Liberation Army (LLA), headed by Ntsu Mokhele, a militant in exile. Jonathan repeatedly accused South Africa of harboring LLA personnel and permitting them to raid Lesotho as punishment for his relatively independent foreign policy, which had sought closer ties with Yugoslavia and the People's Republic of China, as well as with Mozambique, Zimbabwe, and other African countries. South African security forces, moreover, carried out raids of their own, designed to stamp out ANC exiles operating in Lesotho. Given Lesotho's total economic dependence on South Africa, Jonathan's position in 1984 was precarious and he was overthrown by the army in 1986.

In Swaziland, by contrast, executive power was vested in the monarch, whose position was confirmed by a new constitution promulgated in 1978.[25] The constitution was based on traditional tribal communities and provided for a bicameral parliament (Libandla) comprising a House of Assembly with 50 deputies and a Senate with 20 members. Parliament exercised no more than advisory functions; no political parties were permitted to operate. On the death in 1982 of King Sobhuza II, the architect of Swaziland's postindependence regime, the regency was entrusted to Queen Indlovukazi Dweliwe. She was assisted by Prince Sozisa Dlamini, who also served as chairman of the Liqoqo, the Supreme Council of State, which consisted of 15 members appointed by the monarch. The regency was intended to last until Sobhuza's successor, Prince Makhosetive, came of age. The office of the prime minister fell in 1983 to Prince Bhekimpi Dlamini, a strict traditionalist. The royal regime derived support from the Imbokovu National Movement (formed in 1964). A number of political organizations resisted it, including the Ngwane National Liberatory Congress (NNLC), whose leader, Dr. Ambrose P. Zwane, for a time went into preventive detention.

The opposition stressed the grievances of Swazi labor migrants in South Africa, complained of the real or alleged misconduct of

South African residents in Swaziland, and censured what it considered South African exploitation of Swazi resources. The opposition also clashed with the regime over a projected arrangement with South Africa, whereby Swaziland would acquire the so-called KaNgwane homeland, as well as portions of the KwaZulu homeland lying between Swaziland and the Indian Ocean — a deal bitterly opposed by Chief Gatsha Buthelezi, the most powerful of South African homeland leaders.

Like Lesotho, Swaziland also had to cope with the problem of the ANC. In his lifetime, King Sobhuza II had protected the ANC; after his demise, the Swazi increasingly turned against ANC refugees on Swazi soil. Having been turned out of Mozambique as a result of the 1984 agreement between Maputo and Pretoria, many more ANC activists sought refuge in Swaziland. The Swazi put on more pressure, and a number of armed frays occurred between the ANC and the Swazi police. At the same time, the Swazi authorities cooperated with South African police against the ANC, reputedly to the extent of cooperating in the kidnapping of ANC members from a Swazi police station.

Given their economic reliance on South Africa, the political deference paid by the two mountain kingdoms to Pretoria with regard to the ANC should occasion no surprise. Lesotho and Swaziland are both members of SADCC, but SADCC, by 1984, had not done much for them. Both kingdoms are rich in scenery but poor in wealth. In Lesotho, only 13 percent of the surface is cultivable. Most of the country's fertile western portion is overpopulated in relation to existing resources, and the land consequently suffers from overgrazing, soil erosion, land shortages, and a high rate of labor migration to South Africa. Swaziland, by contrast, is rich in minerals (coal, asbestos, iron, and others); Swaziland's perennial rivers also provide opportunities for irrigation and hydroelectric development.[26]

Improvements in traditional farming methods are not easy to make — not because village cultivators are necessarily unprogressive, but because they are poor. Poor people are naturally reluctant to take the considerable risks and contribute the additional labor widely entailed in changing their methods. Traditional farming systems offer a form of social insurance to their beneficiaries; such methods are hard to abandon unless the reformers can create a new kind of security. Nevertheless, both Lesotho and Swaziland need to reform traditional systems of land tenure that permit unlimited grazing rights for every community member in good standing. The Sotho and Swazi alike must change customary land rights so as to encourage land improvements through fencing, the use of fertilizers, the investments of private capital, and the use of land as security for agricultural credit. By the early 1980s, some rural development work had got under way in Lesotho. In Swaziland, individual tenure farms, together with rural industries, had expanded and accounted for just over 40 percent of the GDP. In addition, some progress had been achieved in manufacturing (mainly through agricultural and wood-processing plants).

Despite the poor reputation they acquired among African progressives, and despite the extraordinary obstacles that the two countries faced in the economic field, the two states had actually done quite well during the 1960s and 1970s. According to World Bank information, both kingdoms were able to boast of high rates of gross domestic investment and respectable growth rates in their GDPs. Between 1960 and 1970, Swaziland's average annual growth rate amounted to 8.6 percent; during the 1970s it grew at 4.6 percent. Corresponding figures for Lesotho were 4.6 percent and 7.0 percent. The average annual growth rate of domestic investment for Swaziland stood at 10.6 percent for 1960 1970 and at 13.3 percent for 1970–1979. Corresponding figures or Lesotho amounted to 18.5 percent for 1960 to 1970 and an asto..ishing 24.4 percent for 1970–1979, one of the highest figures in Arrica.[27]

Nevertheless, the two mountain kingdoms continued to face enormous difficulties. Both territories remained backward islands within the context of a rapidly expanding South African economy. The two kingdoms are situated away from the main lines of communication linking the Republic of South Africa's economic heartland with the main ports. The republic remained the only significant market for the two territories' exports of labor and crops. Many of the most enterprising Sotho and Swazi — teachers, artisans, nurses, and businessmen — were permanently lost through emigration to South Africa. Black workers returning from South Africa's mining and industrial complexes were confirmed in their aversion to farm work. At the same time, the two territories remained politically separate from South Africa and thereby failed to benefit from the financial largess extended by the South African taxpayer to Namibia or South African homelands such as the Ciskei (whose industrial investment rose from 40 million rand to

150 million rand between 1981 and 1984). Both kingdoms devoted too little of their national expenditure to agriculture. (In Lesotho, the proportion of total expenditure devoted to farming actually dropped after the territory attained independence, from 7.3 percent in 1935–1936 to 5.4 percent three decades later.)[28]

From 1980 on, the Lesotho National Development Corporation (LNDC), formed in 1969 increased its industrial development program. In 1980, in order to create job opportunities more than twenty new manufacturing and commercial projects were set up by combining foreign aid incentives, government planning, and private enterprise. Lesotho has done reasonably well in the past four years. First developed were import-substitution industries in beer-brewing, soft-drink bottling, maize milling, wool and mohair processing, clothing, and footwear. Exports to Western Europe and South Africa have increased.

Tax incentives, the building of industrial parks and plants, and the training of labor have brought some South African industries to Lesotho: for example, a bag factory, a clothing factory, a shoe factory, a furniture industry, and a tire retreading unit. Cooperation with SADCC has continued, and Lesotho hopes to develop salt production, the manufacture of farm implements, and wood-processing plants.[29]

The South African Customs Union (SACU), founded in 1969, embraces the BLS states and South Africa. Tension has developed in SACU because of the way its revenue is doled out and because of differing development policies within the region. South Africa collects customs and excise duties on all imports coming into the area and distributes the revenue by a negotiated formula. South Africa keeps about 50 percent of the revenue. In 1982 Botswana received 37 percent of its government revenue from SACU; Swaziland received 60 percent, and Lesotho received 71 percent.

SACU has been efficient and cost-effective, but BLS states are still unhappy. They claim that they subsidize South African industrial development by buying nine-tenths of their quotas from South Africa, whose high import quotas protect South African manufacturers and allow them to charge high prices. Also, BLS states complain that it takes two or three years to get full payment of the revenues due to them. Inflation and loss of interest causes further losses. Finally, BLS states feel that the large development incentives offered in South Africa and the homelands attract investors away from the BLS states.

The world slump of the early 1980s created a host of new difficulties for the two kingdoms, as for all their neighbors. None of these troubles will soon be solved. Whatever the future may hold, all the minor states will find their fates ties to the political and economic fortunes of their South African neighbor.*

*In June 1985 South Africa issued a proclamation establishing a new government for Namibia, but South Africa retained responsibility for the key functions of defense, foreign relations, and negotiations for independence.

Notes

1. Namibia covers 318,261 square miles; Botswana, 222,000 square miles; Lesotho, 11,720 square miles; and Swaziland, 6,704 square miles.
2. Comparative figures are from the World Bank, *Accelerated Development in Sub-Saharan Africa: An Agenda for Action* (Washington, D.C.: The World Bank, 1981), 143 ff.
3. J. H. P. Serfontein, *Namibia* (Randburg, South Africa: Focus Suid Publishers, 1976), p. 18.
4. *Africa Research Bulletin: Political, Social, and Cultural Series*, February 1–29, 1984, pp. 7150–7155.
5. *Africa Research Bulletin: Economic, Financial, and Technical Series*, December 1–31, 1983, pp. 707–77.
6. Erich Leistner, Peter Esterhuysen, and Theo Malan, *Namibia/SWA Prospectus* (Pretoria: Africa Institute, 1980), p. 6.
7. *Africa Research Bulletin: Economic, Financial, and Technical Series*, February 15–March 15, 1984, p. 7184.
8. See, for instance, Richard Moorsom, *Walvis Bay: Namibia's Port* (London: International Defence and Aid Fund, 1977).
9. International Defence and Aid Fund for Southern Africa, *Apartheid's Army in Namibia* (London, 1982); and Kenneth W. Grundy, *Soldiers Without Politics: Blacks in the South African Armed Forces* (Berkeley: University of California Press, 1983), pp. 249–72.
10. "Namibia," Supplement to *Financial Mail* [Johannesburg], July 22, 1983, p. 21.
11. The DTA gained 41 seats; AKTUR (Action Front for the Retention of Turnhalle Principles), formed by the National Party of South West Africa, a white party linked to the National Party in South Africa, received 6 seats; and the Namibia Christian Democratic Party, the Rehoboth Liberation Front, and the Herstigte Nasionale Party, (a right-wing party) secured 1 seat each. The DTA consisted of the Caprivi Alliance Group, the Kavango Alliance Group, the Namibia Turnhalle Party, the Namibia People's Liberation Front, the National United Democratic Organization, the Rehoboth Baster Vereniging, the Republic Party, the Seopoesengwe Party, the South West Africa People's Democratic United Front, and the Tsumkwe Front.
12. *African Communist* [London], no. 68 (1977): 12.
13. SWAPO, *Laws Governing the Namibian People's Revolution Adopted by the Central Committee of SWAPO on September 24, 1977* (Lusaka: SWAPO Publicity and Information Department, 1977).
14. *Africa Research Bulletin: Political, Social, and Cultural Series*, March 1–31, 1984, p. 7196.

15. Hans Germani, *Retter Südwest* (Munich: F. A. Herbig, 1982), 143, 152.

16. Germani, *Rettet Südwest*, p. 169.

17. Sam Nujoma, "Where SWAPO Stands," in "Namibia," Supplement to *Financial Mail* [Johannesburg], July 22, 1983, pp. 12–13.

18. The phrase derives from Jack Halpern, *South Africa's Hostages: Basutoland, Bechuanaland, and Swaziland* (Harmondsworth, England: Penguin Books, 1965).

19. See Richard Dale, "The Botswana Defense Force," in *Round Table* [London], April 1983, pp. 1–18.

20. For details on the economy, see, for instance, *Botswana: A Review of Commerce and Industry* (Gaborone, Botswana: T. Directories, 1981); Charles M. . Harvey, ed., *Papers on the Economy of Botswana* (London: Heinemann, 1981); and Christopher Colclough and Stephen McCarthy, *The Political Economy of Botswana: A Study of Growth and Distribution* (London: Oxford University Press, 1980). For Botswana's history, see Anthony Sillery, *Founding a Protectorate: History of Bechuanaland Botswana, 1885–1895* (The Hague: Mouton, 1965); and Jack Parson, *Botswana: Liberal Democracy and the Labor Reserve in Southern Africa* (Boulder, Colo.: Westview Press, 1984). See also Calvin A. Woodward, *Prospects for Political Stability in Botswana, Lesotho, and Swaziland* (Pretoria: Africa Institute, 1984).

21. Figures from *Africa South of the Sahara 1983–1984* (London: Europa Publications, 1983), p. 228.

22. See Parson, *Botswana: Liberal Democracy and the Labor Reserve in Southern Africa*, pp. 111–18.

23. We are indebted to John D. Holm, who permitted us to read, before publication, his important article "The State, Social Class, and Rural Development in Botswana," a study that especially emphasizes the role of the state in development.

24. The other two opposition parties are the Marema Tlou Freedom Party, formed in 1962 (made up of both traditionalists and modernizers) and the much smaller Lesotho United Democratic Party. B. M. Khoketla and M. S. Lephoma, respectively, serve as secretaries-general of the parties.

25. See Alan R. Booth, *Swaziland: Tradition and Change in a Southern African Kingdom* (Boulder, Colo.: Westview Press, 1983).

26. For the economic development of these territories, see G. M. E. Leistner and P. Smit, *Swaziland: Resources and Development* (Pretoria: Africa Institute, 1969); G. M. E. Leistner, *Lesotho: Economic Structure and Growth* (Pretoria: Africa Institute, 1966); and Percy Selwyn, *Industries in the Southern African Periphery: A Study of Industrial Development in Botswana, Lesotho, and Swaziland* (London: Croom Helm, 1977). For a critique of the labor migration system, see Colin Murray, *Families Divided: The Impact of Migrant Labour in Lesotho* (London: Cambridge University Press, 1981).

27. World Bank, *Accelerated Development in Sub-Saharan Africa*, pp. 146–47.

28. Leistner, *Lesotho: Economic Structure and Growth*, pp. 13, 50.

29. See *Newsletter: Lesotho National Development Corporation* (Maseru, Lesotho: 1981–): The newsletter appears quarterly.

9 LUSOPHONE AFRICA: ANGOLA, MOZAMBIQUE, AND GUINEA-BISSAU

Thomas H. Henriksen

Angola, Mozambique, and Guinea-Bissau constitute Lusophone Africa in the sense that Portuguese serves as the language of law, administration, politics, and scholarship. Although the people of these three states are ethnically diverse and speak a variety of African tongues, the Portuguese influence — derived from a common colonial experience — remains powerful. All three territories have a number of important features in common. They were the last African countries to gain independence from direct overseas control. The People's Republics of Angola, Mozambique, and Guinea-Bissau were the first African states to be expressly founded on the principles of Marxism-Leninism. They are all subject to one-party rule, and all derive their legitimacy from what they consider to be a common revolutionary experience. Although their economic potentials vary strikingly all three countries remain undeveloped in that they continue to rely mainly on the production of primary materials for their livelihoods. Although their populations are fairly sparse in relation to the size of their territories, all are experiencing rapid population increases. (In 1981 Angola's population density was 5.8 persons per square mile; Mozambique's was 15.8 persons per square mile. From 1975 to 1980 Angola's average annual birth rate was 47.6 per thousand, and its death rate was 23.1 per thousand. Respective figures for Mozambique were 44.8 and 19.0.) Guinea-Bissau's population density in 1983 was 39.43 per square mile.

The three states differ strikingly in size, population, and potential resources. Of the three, Angola is by far the most economically significant. It is blessed with many natural resources (including oil, iron, and diamonds), and has an area of 481,345 square miles and an estimated population (in 1981) of 7,262,000. Mozambique covers 308,641 square miles, and in 1981 had an estimated population of 12,130,000. In contrast, Guinea-Bissau is a small country; it has an area of 13,948 square miles and a population (in 1979) of only 767,739.

With the notable exception of Zimbabwe, Angola, Mozambique,

and Guinea-Bissau underwent far more sweeping and violent transitions from colonial to independent status than all other European-dominated states in sub-Saharan Africa. The Portuguese fought long and hard to hold on to their empire. Although the guerrilla wars were protracted (lasting for more than a decade), the insurgent forces in all three territories nevertheless came to power unexpectedly, without adequate preparation for governing.

The revolutionary histories of the three states are diverse. In Mozambique and Guinea-Bissau the revolutionary forces were split by serious factional quarrels. Nevertheless, they fought under a single banner, and, long before the Portuguese decided to pull out, rebel units had managed to secure effective control over large portions of the disputed territories. In Angola Portuguese power was far more firmly entrenched. The anticolonial forces were divided (and to this day continue to be divided) into three separate guerrilla parties, none of which ever managed to seize power over extensive liberated zones of their own. All three battled among each other as well as against the Portuguese. From the beginning of independence, all three territories faced a prolonged crisis, but it was worse in Angola than in Mozambique or Guinea-Bissau.

THE COLONIAL LEGACY

The Economic Infrastructure

According to the anticolonial orthodoxy of the 1960s, Portugal had been doubly guilty. By means of a series of unprovoked aggressive acts, she had appropriated a large share of Africa. Subsequently, she had failed to develop her colonial legacy and had allowed her possessions to continue in a state of economic backwardness as well as political dependence. In fact, the outbreak of anticolonial guerrilla warfare during the 1960s coincided with a remarkable burst of economic development. Having profited from increased economic prosperity at home, Portugal began to invest more funds in her overseas possessions. At the same time she vastly expanded the size of her armed forces in Angola, Mozambique, and Portuguese Guinea. This created a military market, which gave an additional stimulus to economic growth. The launching of partisan operations also had the unintended effect of easing relations between the metropolis and the white settlers, who suddenly realized that they could not stand on their own and that they needed Portugal; *separatismo* (separatism) ceased to be a living creed among the colonists. The metropolis was no longer hampered in its development policy by the fear (widely held in those days of Salazar) that a powerful white settler community might one day seek to set up an Angolan state on Rhodesian lines.

At this time, the Portuguese colonial governments also began to open their doors to foreign lenders whom they had previously viewed with mistrust. Foreign capitalists were granted a number of privileges denied to smaller domestic entrepreneurs. For instance, large-scale investors were able to repatriate their earnings with much less difficulty than ordinary settlers. Foreign investors, technicians, and businessmen achieved a position of prominence within the Portuguese colonies. By 1966 private foreign investment already accounted for nearly 25 percent of the gross fixed capital formation in the overseas territories (compared to less than 15 percent during the early 1960s). In addition, Portuguese policy-makers deliberately set out to develop the colonies to legitimate their rule in Africa in the face of mounting criticism at home and abroad.

Despite the impact of war, Angola experienced an extraordinary economic boom. Between 1953 and 1973 the country's European population increased from something like 100,000 to about half-a-million. Land-settlement schemes for whites did not prove particularly successful because the colonists encountered many technical difficulties. Also, both urbanization in Portugal and emigration of Western Europe diminished the supply of farmers willing to make their homes in Africa. But cities like Luanda, Nova Lisboa, and Benguela grew remarkably. The Angolan economy, originally largely dependent on coffee, became more and more diversified. Between 1963 and 1973 the value of Angola's exports increased nearly fourfold, and by then the territory had also become an important supplier of oil, diamonds, and iron ore to the world market.

The growth of exports was structurally linked to the emergence of local industries designed to process agricultural products, to repair plants and equipment, and to produce import substitutes at a time when the territory was facing considerable balance-of-payment difficulties. Between 1969 and 1973 the index of industrial production doubled (a notable achievement under conditions of widespread internal strife) and light industries began to attain a position of some importance within the Angolan economy. The development of manufacturing was also significant in structural terms. Although the funds placed in the mining industry were largely derived from foreign (especially American, British, Belgian, West German, and South African) and metropolitan sources, most of the capital invested in secondary industry was generated locally.

By the early 1970s Angola began to benefit from a fundamental improvement in her balance-of-payments position. (In the late 1960s the territory had run up an adverse trade balance — occasioned in large part by heavy expenditures on capital goods and equipment for the Cassinga iron mines and the Cabinda oil fields.) By 1974 a sizable proportion of her debt to Portugal had been extinguished.

In contrast, Mozambique's economy during the same period remained relatively backward. The country continued to face severe structural problems with respect to her foreign payments because of her heavy dependence on agriculture and services. In the fifteen years before the end of colonialism, the agricultural sector expanded considerably and accounted for about 50 percent of the Mozambican cash economy. Services included earnings derived from railways, airports, and seaports that provided facilities for South Africa, Rhodesia, Zambia, and Malawi; wages paid to some 200,000 migrant African workers in South Africa and Rhodesia; and cash disbursed by South African and Rhodesian visitors. The colony's visible exports were mainly agricultural products. The so-called traditional sector — composed of 1.7 million African cultivators (often mistakenly referred to as subsistence farmers) — accounted for a substantial proportion of the agricultural output. African villagers produced mainly cashew nuts, groundnuts, and cotton. Europeans primarily grew sugar (initiated by British entrepreneurs before World War I), sisal (initiated by German immigrants), and tea (dominated by the Portuguese). Nevertheless, during this period the Portuguese succeeded in creating the beginnings of a modern infrastructure, complete with modern roads, railways, seaports, telegraphs, some manufacturing plants, and substantial hydroelectrical development (made possible by the internationally financed Cabora Bassa dam).[1]

Governance

The Portuguese were the first European colonizers to establish an empire in Africa and the last to leave. For centuries, however, Portuguese colonial governance had been confined to a few coastal enclaves and a handful of trading stations in the interior. Effective governance over the bulk of Angola and Mozambique dates from around the turn of the present century; in some parts of the empire, pacification was not completed until the 1930s. From the start, the Portuguese believed in centralized rule (a model imitated to some extent by their postcolonial successors). Lisbon at first ruled by means of military officers, but she gradually replaced these uniformed administrators with civilians. In the early twentieth century the Portuguese government introduced the *circumscrição* (circumscription), the fundamental rural administrative unit of Portugal. Headed by a European administrador, the *circumscrição* predominately had jurisdiction over black African affairs. The *circumscrição* was, in turn, split into two to six *postos* (posts), which were placed under the control of a *chefe de posto* (the Portuguese official most closely involved with the African population). By the 1960s, the *postos* typically encompassed ca. 40,000 inhabitants. Therefore, Portugal's direct control was minimal in rural areas.[2] The *chefe de posto* supervised tax collection, presided over disputes, dispensed punishment, and, when events warranted, oversaw village agriculture and small government projects. Depending on his temperament, he might be sympathetic to his charges, or he might abuse his authority for purposes of spite, profit, or lust. Especially in the early colonial period, the tyranny of some of these officials was responsible for a bitter and cruel chapter in Portuguese Africa. In some cases the *chefe de posto* worked through an African administrator-chief, ultimately known as a *regedor*. This (sometimes uniformed) African official had responsibility for a *regedoria*, or group of villages. As late as 1965, about 90 percent of the *regedores* in Mozambique were still traditional chiefs. (Considered collaborators with an exploitative colonial state, the *regedores* incurred the enmity of the revolutionaries both during the guerrilla war and after independence.)

The local administrative apparatus was different for Europeans in urban areas or settlements. Modeled on metropolitan municipalities, the *concelhos* (councils), or townships, enjoyed some limited self-government. But keeping with the tradition in

Portugal, however, municipal government was never strong. African *circumscrição* and European townships made up the colonial districts, and the district governors, whether military or civilian, reported to the governor-general of each colony. As the highest official in each of the colonies, he answered to Lisbon and implemented her policies. The legislative councils in Angola and Mozambique were mainly consultative bodies, and they never held any meaningful legislative powers. The selection of delegates — whether by election or by designation — was not carried out in a manner likely to encourage the principle of parliamentary accountability. Lisbon thus maintained a pyramid of power in which there was no room for political parties or democratic values — a state of affairs that mirrored conditions under the Salazar dictatorship in Portugal itself. It was only at the very end of the colonial era that the Portuguese cautiously began to change their course. But last-minute attempts at political reform came too late; the Portuguese retreat from power was so precipitous that all opportunities to install parliamentary measures were lost.

Decolonization was accomplished most rapidly in Portuguese Guinea, in which Portugal's economic stake was negligible, and in which the morale of the army had been severely shaken. Mozambique, home of the huge Cabora Bassa project and a substantial white population, presented a more difficult problem. The guerrillas' popular support was far from universal. Numerous ethnic communities — notably the Makua — held aloof. Lisbon at first insisted that the guerrillas lay down their arms before elections would be held. Subsequently, however, the Portuguese changed their line and agreed to the formation of a provisional government in which the guerrillas would supply six of nine ministers — pending full independence in 1975. At this point, white militants, feebly supported by a number of Africans hostile to FRELIMO, attempted to improve their bargaining position by a short-lived, but abortive, coup in Lourenço Marques. The rising quickly collapsed, however, and the new alliance between the Portuguese army and the guerrillas remained unshaken; Portuguese soldiers joined with their erstwhile enemies to maintain a tenuous degree of order in the strife-torn city. Many whites fled the country, and a number of the revolutionaries' opponents lost their lives. The guerrilla organization emerged from the encounter stronger than before and ready to head a sovereign Mozambique — politically independent, but economically in a state of disarray.

In Angola, the Portuguese and the three liberation movements concluded an agreement in January 1975 that provided for the election of a constituent assembly, the setting up of a provisional government, and the subsequent independence of the country. The new accord recognized Angola as an indivisible entity and the three revolutionary movements as "the sole and legitimate representatives of the Angolan people" — thereby excluding rival groups, including a number of short-lived white political associations. The agreement also called for the integration of the armed forces of the three liberation movements on terms of parity; each was to supply 8,000 soldiers (and the Portuguese army was to furnish 24,000 soldiers for Angolan defense). This accord, although sensible in theory, broke down in practice. There was bitter and prolonged fighting, which was resolved finally in favor of the MPLA (see below) by joint Soviet-Cuban intervention (an intervention one can assume had been long-planned by the Soviets).[3] In the end, sustained by a substantial garrison of Cubans and reinforced by Soviet and East German specialists, the MPLA managed to establish its rule over the greater part of Angola.

THE ANTICOLONIAL WARS

Angola and Mozambique both continue to carry the legacy of the liberation wars that helped to shape the postcolonial societies. The violence of the Angolan rebellion in 1961, which began the anticolonial wars, at first caught Lisbon off guard. Some 400 settlers, and perhaps as many as 50,000 Africans, died as a result of the revolt and the Portuguese reprisals.[4] The 1961 Bakongo revolt in northwestern Angola managed to shake Lisbon's complacency, but it failed to expel Portugal from Angola. This poorly planned uprising was initiated by what ultimately became the Frente Nacional de Libertação de Angola (FNLA). Guerrilla attacks continued fitfully after this revolt; the FNLA restricted most of its hit-and-run raids to the nearly inaccessible Dembos hill country or to territory abutting its sanctuaries in neighboring Zaire.

In 1966 two rival nationalist parties started guerrilla campaigns in eastern Angola. The Movimento Popular de Libertação de Angola (MPLA) — Marxist-oriented and *mestiço*-led — launched raids in the remote borderlands of east-central Angola and scattered and less-fruitful attacks in Cabinda (Cabinda was an oil-rich enclave surrounded by Zaire and Congo-Brazzaville. Although geographically separate from Angola proper, it was administered by the Portuguese as part of this colony.) Formed in 1956 with the help of former members of the Portuguese Communist Party, the MPLA depended on the urban and educated *mestiço* population of the capital city of Luanda for leaders and on the Mbundu people of the north-central region for followers. Its relations with the other two rival movements consisted of fire fights in the bush. Soon after Portuguese forces staged a military coup in Lisbon, the MPLA received massive amounts of Soviet weaponry and thousands of Cuban regular troops to crush its rivals. Despite its support from the Soviet Union in the precoup conflict with Portugal, the MPLA succeeded only in carving out base areas in the eastern frontier region contiguous to Zambia. Its factionalism and poor military progress prompted the Soviets to suspend assistance in 1973. After the Lisbon coup, however, Moscow switched its policy and resumed aid on an enormous scale, making possible the MPLA's complete victory over its rivals.

The third major national movement was formed as the result of a personality clash and an ethnic squabble within the FNLA. Jonas Savimbi, who had been foreign minister in the FNLA, left the Bakongo-dominated organization in 1964. Two years later, he formed the largely Ovimbundu-controlled Uniao Nacional para e Independência Total de Angola (UNITA) in the southeastern district of Moxico. Until the Portuguese coup, this fledgling movement experienced serious difficulties. It was outgunned by the MPLA, which attacked its patrols. Nevertheless, under Savimbi's charismatic leadership, UNITA enjoyed widespread support in many regions of the country. In the months preceding the coup, UNITA began to surface from relative obscurity to become the front-runner among the Angolan parties. But the massive Soviet and Cuban expeditionary forces aborted its campaign for national prominence.

In Mozambique and Guinea-Bissau the national causes did not suffer as severely from fragmentation as in Angola. But these countries, too, experienced the blood-letting caused by political assassinations, splinter groups, and internecine quarrels. Fighting erupted in Maryland-sized Guinea-Bissau in 1963, when, after three years of political organizing, the Partido Africano de Independéncia de Guine e Cabo Verde (PAIGC) unleashed raids in the southeastern region. Launching its guerrilla forays first from sanctuaries in the Republic of Guinea and then in Senegal, the PAIGC systematically expanded the war zones. The impoverished, colony, which produced little besides rice and peanuts, was nevertheless the hottest combat zone in the late 1960s and early 1970s. Assignments to its swamplands often reduced battle-hardened Portuguese NCOs to tears. (Although late in the independence wars, Mozambique was to surpass Guinea-Bissau as a killing ground for Portuguese troops, Guinea-Bissau's reputation as a grueling, snake-infested swamp of death endures to this day.)

Guerrilla raids broke out in northern Mozambique on September 25, 1964. From staging areas across the Rovuma River in Tanzania, insurgents from the Frente de Libertação de Moçambique (FRELIMO) spread southward until 1968, when tough Portuguese countermeasures and ethnic animosities forced the guerrillas to redirect their efforts to the northwestern district of Tete. This second front took the Portuguese military establishment by surprise. The colonial forces were spread too thinly to contain the guerrillas in their new theater. The insurgents steadily advanced into the central region of the country. By the early 1970s, FRELIMO had penetrated deep into the central waist, a region in which there were white farm settlements and important communications lines from Rhodesia to the seaport of Beira. This posed crucial problems for a hard-pressed and psychologically exhausted Portuguese officer corps.

The Lisbon officers' coup and the subsequent political collapse in Africa took both sides by surprise. Nationalist leaders and Portuguese politicians had predicted a continuing state of war through the 1970s. The guerrillas came to power with unanticipated suddenness, unaccustomed to rule, and untrained to manage modern economies. In Angola and Mozambique they took over countries that (by the standards of previous generations) had acquired a modest degree of prosperity and that had taken tentative steps on the road to racial integration. (Much to the surprise of their white Rhodesian neighbors, the Portuguese had, for example, begun to integrate white and black soldiers into mixed army units.) The outbreak of the liberation wars, combined with the influx of foreign capital and the expansion of their own domestic economy during the prosperous 1960s, had acted as a powerful inducement for the Portuguese to develop their long-neglected colonies.

Following a standard pattern, Portugal waged a hearts and minds campaign, together with a far-reaching economic development effort and a military counterinsurgency, to defeat the guerrilla forces. Even in the political realm, Lisbon had begun (however haltingly and reluctantly) to move toward a form of autonomy for its African territories. She had also terminated the worst form of colonial abuse — forced labor. Additionally, Lisbon's programs made solid commitments to the economic infrastructures of the territories. For example, Cabora Bassa, the giant hydroelectric project on Mozambique's stretch of the Zambezi River, constituted the cornerstone of the territory's economic development.

Guerrilla attacks dealt no body blows to the Angolan and Mozambican economic infrastructures. Raids on railway tracks or roads were quickly repaired without lasting harm to transportation or communications. The tight Portuguese defenses of such vital targets as Cabora Bassa went a long way toward assuring that the subsequent Marxist regimes inherited factories, roads, railways, and plantations capable of sustaining and improving growth. It is a myth that Portugal left her colonial economies in a shambles. In Angola, the civil war between the three guerrilla movements after the Portuguese defeat disrupted the economic well-being of the country far more than the anticolonial war. Similarly, the ongoing fighting betwen the MPLA regime and its chief opposition, UNITA, has done more to ruin the agricultural output of the southern coffee and cotton plantations and vegetable farms than the war ıor independence did.

MOZAMBIQUE

Governance and Economy

From its beginnings, independent Mozambique was committed to socialism. The Mozambique constitution (adopted in 1975, revised in 1978) specifically proclaimed FRELIMO the leading force of the state and society. The republic vowed to eliminate the colonial and traditional structures, to build a people's democracy, and to construct the material and ideological base for a socialist society. The constitution placed far-reaching powers in the hands of the head of state; Samora Moises Machel was president of FRELIMO, president of the Republic, commander in chief, and had overall responsibility for the Ministry of Defense. He presided over the Council Ministers, the People's Assembly (composed of approximately

215 members), and the Central Committee of FRELIMO. From its ranks, the People's Assembly elected a Permanent Commission along the lines of FRELIMO's Central Committee (which was also chaired by the president). Together, these organs were intended to express the will of the people and to realize the aims of the republic as defined by FRELIMO.

Mozambique's formal structure resembled Angola's in many ways. But the Mozambican road to socialism was by no means parallel to that of Angola. Unlike the MPLA, FRELIMO had attained power not by foreign bayonets but by its own efforts. FRELIMO's foreign support during the revolutionary struggle had been more varied than the MPLA's; it had received aid from the People's Republic of China as well as from the Soviet Union and its allies. Unlike the MPLA, FRELIMO had taken over extensive parts of the country before the Portuguese withdrew. FRELIMO had therefore acquired some practical experience in governing before coming to power and subsequently attempted to apply the lessons of the revolutionary war to the task of building socialism in the country at large. For instance, it continued to invoke the war-time slogan *a luta continua* (the struggle continues) to mobilize support for its development efforts. From its guerrilla war experiences, FRELIMO looked to the liberated zones for direction in the building of a socialist economy and society. It was these liberated zones — or regions dominated by insurgents — in the remote northern areas of the country that FRELIMO had envisioned as models for a future collectivist, egalitarian society. By providing the most basic services to a small number of scattered groupings, FRELIMO attempted to administer a revolutionary state in embryo. (FRELIMO nostalgically continues to view village clearings in the bush as forerunners of a modern state organization. Current party literature is replete with references to guerrilla cadres organizing village political committees, crop production, people's shops, judicial systems, rudimentary schools, and health care.) Yet FRELIMO showed much less willingness to acknowledge the far more elaborate cooperative institutions in its sanctuary bases across the northern border in Tanzania.

During the war, FRELIMO established large refugee camps across the Rovuma River in southern Tanzania where they were safe from Portuguese reprisals. The sanctuary camps grew crops and manufactured soap. This helped sustain the refugees and guerrilla forces to the south. The camps also sold items on the

Tanzanian market, which provided currency for the rebels. These camps had systems of cooperative farming and administration that served as models of collectivized life (much in the way that North Korean bases in Manchuria during World War II served as models for the system that was extended to Korea after 1945).[5] In its post-independence rhetoric, FRELIMO did not stress the significant role that these camps had played in shaping its convictions about the way Mozambican society should be restructured. Yet it is obvious that the wartime experience in Tanzania played a vital role in shaping FRELIMO's immediate postwar policies.

Unfortunately, however, wartime experience in running remote rural settlements proved inadequate to the task of running a country. FRELIMO's commitment to the rapid destruction of colonialism and the construction of a collectivist society was counterproductive. Once in power, the revolutionaries strove to reduce the influence of the Catholic church, moved against private property by confiscating factories and plants, and leveled criticism against what they considered the bourgeois values of the colonialists. Individualism, alcoholism, and prostitution were designated colonial vices incompatible with a socialist society. The new government demoted chiefs and village headmen, tried to eradicate tribal initiation rites, bride price, and traditional religious practices, and raised women's subordinate status in some areas of society. Socialist values were instilled by means of extensive literacy programs for young and old. Mass organizations for youth, women, and members of some professions provided another vehicle for the inculcation of the new values. In short, FRELIMO tried — albeit unsuccessfully — to create a "new person." Unfortunately for FRELIMO, the growing sense of personal insecurity among whites (along with the partial confiscation of their property) convinced most Europeans to flee, taking their skills and capital with them. Besides their homes, they left behind a substantial infrastructure consisting of schools, hospitals, factories, railways, and hydroelectrical plants — all of which needed the services of a trained staff that FRELIMO was ill-equipped to provide. (Of the 80,000 to 100,000 whites who remained in Mozambique after independence, only 25,000 were left by the end of 1975.)

FRELIMO tried to deal with its problems by placing about 5,000 of its members in the government and provincial administrations. Whites were re-engaged on contracts. The Eastern European countries and the white South Africans provided a great deal of technical expertise. South Africans helped to run the railways, serviced the port of Maputo, and assisted in the great Cabora Bassa hydroelectric project that provided power to South Africa from Mozambique. Despite these efforts, FRELIMO could not prevent a general economic collapse. Its leaders, and the handful of senior civil servants who staffed the ministries and planning councils, were able and well-educated. But the lower echelons of men and women — often chosen on the basis of their revolutionary loyalties or personal connections — constituted the profiteers of the revolution. They took advantage of inflated salaries in the minor posts which had been left vacant (particularly in the public service); frequently, they were barely competent to fill them; FRELIMO, was also criticized by African opponents of the grounds that Goanese from the former Portuguese colony in India and Portuguese-speaking mulattos wielded excessive influence within the ranks of the ruling party. All expatriates did not prove satisfactory either. Many were ignorant of local conditions. Their salaries (which were higher than those of the Portuguese colonialists) imposed a severe drain on hard currency reserves. In fact, President Machel himseli was disagreeably surprised by the exacting conditions and salaries required by Soviet technicians. Many of the doctors supplied by North Korea and Bulgaria were unaccustomed to tropical medicine. Cuban advisors were unable to avoid a near disastrous drop in the 1976 sugar harvest.[6]

In the first flush of revolutionary enthusiasm, FRELIMO nationalized a wide variety of enterprises (including the great conglomerate Companhia União Fabril), along with schools, apartment buildings, church properties, and even the services of doctors, lawyers, and morticians. The party sought to fill the vacuum with government officials and committees. It founded committees and worker production councils to operate the railways, the plantations, and the factories. Workers' control over manufacturing was viewed as the basis for increased production. At the Third Congress, the party articulated a program "making the building of heavy industry the decisive factor in breaking with misery and imperialist domination."[7]

Unfortunately, the quality of management did not match such revolutionary aspirations. (By the early 1980s, industrial output is estimated to have fallen to less than 50 percent of its prewar level.)[8] Signs of neglect and deterioration soon appeared everywhere. Elevators stopped (or became too unsafe to ride). Finding a telephone that worked became a hit-or-miss proposition. Vehicles broke down for lack of proper maintenance or available spare parts. Sewerage lines ruptured beneath the capital's streets. Industrial investment almost ceased after the Portuguese — with their propensity to save — departed. Beset by high inflation, graft on every level of government, and an unwillingness or inability to provide adequate incentives, the Mozambique economy rapidly contracted. Many citizens turned to the growing private underground economy, thereby becoming guilty in FRELIMO's eyes of profiteering or economic sabotage (offenses that were punished with draconian methods).

FRELIMO's agricultural policy derived its original inspiration from the same revolutionary romanticism that had shaped FRELIMO's industrial policy. While fighting in the bush, FRELIMO leaders had extolled the virtues of rural life over urban decadence and of collectivized agriculture over traditional, scattered farming and livestock tending. Communal villages (so the argument ran) would increase cash crop production and thereby feed the city dwellers and raise rural living standards. In order to modernize the countryside, FRELIMO sought to bring together about 1,250 families (or ca. 7,000 inhabitants) to form planned villages. In these model villages, the planners envisioned the centralization of facilities for education, health, and social services. By improving the amenities of country living, the party hoped to stem the population flow to the urban centers that was straining the social and sanitation services and depriving the rural regions of labor. (This policy, in fact, continued efforts at rural resettlement made by the Portuguese during the revolutionary war, when *aldeamentos*, or protected villages, were formed with the intention of both modernizing village life and isolating villages from the guerrillas.) These rural policies, however, did not work for FRELIMO any more than they had for the Portuguese. FRELIMO opted for communal village agriculture rather than for mechanized state farms of the Soviet type. But agricultural output declined so drastically that the Third Congress endorsed a Central Committee report that set a four-year goal to duplicate preindependence 1973 crop production levels by 1980. Cashew, cotton, and sugar output eventually improved, but only tea production managed to surpass the peak year of 1973 by the target year of 1980. The declining harvests and the need to import foodstuffs contributed to a balance-of-payments deficit of $200 million in 1980. FRELIMO's attempts at social engineering ran up against both societal obstacles and climatic reversals. First, heavy rains caused devastating floods in the southern regions of the country. Droughts followed, causing crops to wither and livestock to perish. The worst period of desiccation in decades gripped southern Africa, raising havoc with the region's economies. Mozambicans sarcastically complained that "when the Portuguese left, they took the rains."

By the end of the 1970s, "guerrilla socialism," as it might be called, had come to be widely recognized as a failure, even among some of FRELIMO's leading cadres. Despite the constant infusion of foreign aid, the country's debt burden had greatly increased. The majority of the country's state-owned enterprises continually ran up deficits. Private loans from abroad became difficult to secure, especially after 1978, when the government nationalized all but one of the country's banks and credit institutions. There was widespread popular discontent over government interference, and the emergence of a newly privileged class of party functionaries made the grand slogans of the revolution begin to sound stale.

Therefore, beginning in 1979 President Machel turned to a more conciliatory policy — one that might perhaps be likened to Lenin's New Economic Policy (NEP), instituted in 1921. By late 1979 high FRELIMO officials were publicly denouncing inefficiency, spoilage, maladministration, and corruption. Machel made unannounced visits to stores, warehouses, and dockyards. Before a huge crowd in Maputo's Independence Square in March 1980, he told his listeners, "We found organized red tape; bureaucracy transformed into a system to paralyze our economy." He then declared "war on the enemy within."[9] The president denounced what he called corruption and parasitism in the bureaucracy, incompetent planning practices, and general disregard for discipline. He denationalized retail trade and replaced the almost worthless *escudo* by a new currency, the *metical* (whose value in turn declined — from 50.06 *meticais* per U.S. dollar in 1980 to 79.47 *meticais* per U.S. dollar in 1982). At the same time, the government began to reintroduce wage incentives for many public enterprises. Additionally, in 1981 the government formulated a new ten-year development plan, giving first priority to agriculture and second priority to heavy industry.

To implement this new policy, Machel reshuffled the cabinet, or Council of Ministers. He assigned Marcelino dos Santos, Minister of Economic Planning, and Jorge Rebelo, Minister of Information, the task of strengthening the party and the economic war effort. Machel thus sought to emphasize the role of the party in the reactivation of the economy. FRELIMO was to mobilize the population's understanding and their commitment to the battle against sagging production. In addition to calls for discipline in national life, the president created ministries to streamline operations. He formed an Office of Control and Discipline to hear cases of sabotage and incompetence. Despite these — and other — reforms, however, peace and prosperity for Mozambique have proved elusive.

A Revolutionary Foreign Policy

From the outset, FRELIMO regarded itself as part of a worldwide revolutionary movement; not for FRELIMO, the old Stalinist slogan of "socialism in one country." FRELIMO operated as part of a revolutionary alliance that included the MPLA, the ANC (in South Africa), and ZAPU (in what used to be Rhodesia) — an alliance that received both material and ideological support from the Soviet Union and its allies. Committed from the beginning to sustaining the Patriotic Front in Rhodesia, FRELIMO gravely miscalculated the consequences of involving Mozambique in the operations designed to end settler rule in Salisbury. In 1976 the Mozambique government closed its borders to traffic with the white-ruled state. This stoppage of transit resulted in the loss of fees from Rhodesian use of Mozambique's railways and the port of Beira. The shortage of transit revenue accounted for an estimated $175 to $200 million of Mozambique's $300 million yearly balance-of-trade deficit during the war. The cessation of rail and ship traffic turned the seaport of Beira into a virtual ghost town; stevedores, railmen, and truck drivers either moved to Maputo or idled away their days waiting for better times.

The FRELIMO government also allowed Zimbabwean guerrillas to stage raids into Rhodesia from Mozambique. This decision involved Mozambique in the war itself, for (unlike the Portuguese, who almost entirely abstained from retaliatory raids on transborder sanctuary camps) the Rhodesians adopted an aggressive preemptive and counterstrike strategy. The white settler regime of Prime Minister Ian Smith not only hit back hard at the insurgent bases on Mozambique soil but also struck at the Mozambican economic infrastructure. These Rhodesian air assaults and commando raids destroyed Mozambique's communication routes, warehouses, fuel tanks, freight cars, and trucks in the central section of the country (which bordered the settler state).

The retaliatory raids peaked in 1979, causing damages estimated at $26 million in that year. The Rhodesians also timed a series of destructive blows to coincide with the 1980 Lancaster House negotiations in London, which brought about the transfer of power to Robert Mugabe and his party (the Zimbabwe African National Union, or ZANU) after a British-supervised election. Salisbury aimed its military strikes at Mozambique's "breadbasket corridor" — the agro-industrial complex along the Limpopo Valley — in order to precipitate Mozambican pressure on the Zimbabwean rebels to be reasonable in their negotiations with Britain. Although FRELIMO's outward support of the Zimbabwe cause never wavered, its behind-the-scenes lobbying no doubt helped push the Zimbabwean nationalists to conclude negotiations with Britain's foreign secretary and bring about the Rhodesian settlement.[10]

To the surprise of many observers, the end of the Rhodesian war has not brought peace to Mozambique. A rural insurgency against FRELIMO continues to disrupt many parts of the country and attract the government's concern. Anti-FRELIMO dissidents banded together soon after independence into what is now known as the RENAMO (formerly MNR, the Mozambique National Resistance). During the Zimbabwean war, the RENAMO began operations in the west central provinces of Manica and received support from the Rhodesian army, the South Africans, and conservative elements in Portugal. FRELIMO anticipated that RENAMO would collapse as soon as the Zimbabwean struggle ended and the white Rhodesians withdrew their logistical and training support. But the reverse happened. RENAMO's sabotage campaign spread into all of the country's ten provinces. Anti-government forces raked buses with machine gun fire, derailed trains, attacked local FRELIMO headquarters, mined roads, and blew up power lines.

The replacement of Rhodesian assistance with South African aid provides but a partial answer for the success of RENAMO. Another part of the explanation lies in FRELIMO's policies. Insurgents need at least some local support to carry on a guerrilla war against central authorities. FRELIMO actions, both before the end of the war for independence and after, contributed to rural alienation from the central government. FRELIMO's rapid drive into the central region of Mozambique in late 1973 and early 1974 had not allowed enough time for mobilization. As a consequence, the various ethnic communities of the region did not stand unified behind FRELIMO when the Portuguese army coup precipitated the collapse of Lisbon's colonial rule. Additionally, FRELIMO's post-independence efforts to collectivize and regiment rural life proved disruptive to traditional patterns. Corruption among local FRELIMO officials rubbed salt into wounds opened by governmental policies. There was also a measure of disillusionment among former FRELIMO fighters. Disappointed at the results of the revolution, some of them joined RENAMO.

RENAMO has lacked international legitimacy in the sense that it has enjoyed almost no support among Western academicians, who have widely deplored what they see as RENAMO's lack of an ideological foundation. (Discontented villagers, however, require no elaborate philosophical terminology in order to express their discontent.) Overall, however, RENAMO's resistance has proved surprisingly effective. RENAMO used tactics similar to those employed by ZANU in Zimbabwe in the struggle against the Ian Smith regime; small units began to disrupt the governmental infrastructure in the rural areas. According to a speech by Machel, by April 5, 1984 some 840 schools had been destroyed or closed, affecting more than 150,000 schoolchildren. Twelve health centers, over a score of maternity clinics, and 174 health posts had been wiped out. A total of 900 shops had been demolished, affecting supplies and sales for some 4.5 million people. A great number of rural people had been kidnapped or killed. Among the kidnapped were fifty-two foreign technicians and military advisors from the Soviet Union, Bulgaria, East Germany, Britain, and Brazil. Two East Germans were slain. The president catalogued the damage to Mozambique's economic infrastructure as including "bridges and roads, shops and warehouses, sawmills, plantations, agricultural and industrial machinery, electrical supply lines, petrol tanks, lorries and buses, locomotives and carriages."[11]

Mozambique's position became even more difficult because of FRELIMO's policy of providing operational centers for the African National Congress (ANC), the anti-South African movement. The ANC routinely used Mozambican territory to launch raids deep into South Africa. Occasionally, South African military forces retaliated or staged pre-emptive strikes against ANC facilities. These attacks resulted in casualties to Mozambicans as well as to South African expatriates and caused damage to Mozambican facilities. The Mozambican armed forces were in no condition to resist or repel South African attacks; in 1982 the armed forces consisted of 11,000 army personnel (including about 75 percent conscripts), 650 navy personnel, 1,000 airforce personnel, and 6,000 paramilitary border guards. Defense expenditure amounted to U.S. $0.2 billion (out of an estimated GNP of U.S. $2.95 billion).[12]

Mozambique's position has also worsened because of the country's inability to escape from its far-reaching economic dependence on South Africa. Mozambique has continued to supply labor to South African mines in return for hard currency. South Africans have assisted in Mozambican mining enterprises and in maintaining port facilities. South Africa has also purchased power from the Cabora Bassa hydroelectric plant.

The Nkomati accord, signed by South Africa and Mozambique in 1984, recognized the existing realities of power. The contracting parties concluded a nonaggression pact, vowing not to support guerrillas operating from each other's soil. From the ANC's standpoint, the new agreement was almost as fateful and as unexpected a departure from accepted policies in Africa as the Nazi-Soviet pact of 1939 had been in Europe. The Nkomati accord reflected much more than a policy change; it also embodied a change in political philosophy. Since Mozambique's independence, FRELIMO had challenged white rule first in Zimbabwe and then in South Africa. During the last decade, Mozambique has not only been considered the most thoroughgoing Marxist state in Africa, but has served as a Marxist Mecca for intellectuals with a grudge against capitalism and the West. Young professors, former school teachers, and graduate students have journeyed to Mozambique to build socialism in the sun. The Nkomati agreement has now dramatically confirmed FRELIMO's growing pragmatism toward individual entrepreneurship and foreign investment. Ideologically, the accord has been a step backwards. A Leninist might see it as little more than a tactical maneuver of "one step backwards, two steps forward," but it remains unclear whether FRELIMO will actually be able to take the two steps forward in the near future.

FRELIMO hoped that the Nkomati Accord would end the destructive operations of RENAMO, which were carried out almost at will over most of the country. Following the accord, however, RENAMO became, if anything, more vicious.[13] It targeted attacks close to the capital, striking a train only ninety kilometers from Maputo in late 1984. Motorists considered it unsafe to drive the first thirty miles from the South African border at Komatipoort to Maputo. Although FRELIMO leaders believed that the South African government was remaining faithful to the agreement, they charged the elements within the South African Defense Force were supporting the continuing violence and the efforts to overthrow the Maputo government. There were reports of captured RENAMO members who stated that they had crossed the South African border after the signing of the accord. Similarly, FRELIMO forces seized South African arms that had been landed by ship north of Beira — also after the signing of the accord.

The Nkomati Pact has seemed to negate the predictions of Western academicians, who expected South Africa's inevitable defeat in the revolutionary struggle, and who viewed South Africa's efforts at destabilizing Mozambique as dangerous both to South Africa's long-term interests and those of the United States.[14] For the time being, South Africa has achieved a major victory in the ongoing struggle. Socialism of the Mozambican kind has retreated on every front. But it is anyone's guess whether FRELIMO will abide by its present course, or whether its new policy of conciliation will prove as short-lived as the NEP in the Soviet Union sixty years ago.

ANGOLA: GOVERNANCE AND ECONOMY

In Angola a Marxist-Leninist apparatus was put together by hard-core elements in the MPLA and was subsequently used to monopolize power in the areas under its control. This formula derived from the roots of the MPLA, that is, from its affiliation with Soviet communist doctrine and the Portuguese Communist party. The first congress (held in December 1977) received and accepted the recommendations of the Central Committee "to study and decide upon a party guided by Marxism-Leninism, the ideology of the proletariat."[15] During the congress the MPLA reconstituted itself as the MPLA — *Partido do Trabalho*, or the MPLA — Labor Party. The delegates to the congress selected the party's first Central Committee, composed of forty-five members and ten alternate members. The Central Committee in turn elected the Political Bureau, which remained substantially the same as the MPLA Political Bureau chosen at the 1974 conference. The Central

Committee additionally formed a Secretariat. Because the constitution confirmed the primacy of the Central Committee and the Political Bureau over the government, many members of the party Secretariat held government ministerial posts. Therefore, members of the Political Bureau — most of whom hold positions on the Secretariat — *continue* to sit on the Council of Ministers (a body resembling a cabinet of ministries in Western governments).

As constituted, the Political Bureau is set up to exercise day-to-day decision-making power over the general policies laid down at the Central Committee meetings and the more infrequent party congresses. (The first of the party's extraordinary congresses convened in 1980.) In practice, the congresses serve as the party's sounding board. The senior party functionaries hold positions within the Central Committee — a body subdivided into fifteen departments and consisting of seventy-five members with a nine-member secretariat. The original party leader was Agostinno Neto. He died in 1979 and was replaced by Jose Eduardo dos Santos, a Soviet-educated petro-engineer who had served with the guerrilla forces in eastern Angola and, subequently, on the Central Committee. The MPLA-PT followed the Soviet model in all essential respects, (at least on paper) it created a political infrastructure appropriate to a Marxist-Leninist state. But the party lacked adequate numbers of politically trained and literate cadres to transform Angola into an African version of an East European state.

The MPLA-PT has formed mass organizations similar to those in other communist countries. These included organizations for youth and women, trade unions and militia units.[16] The Angolan Pioneers constitute the party's main recruitment vehicle for young people. Like the Soviet Union's Komsomol, the Angolan Pioneers admit most young people up to age twenty-five, after this age, the party scrutinizes the members' politics and commitment. Membership in the Pioneers therefore does not assure entrance into the party itself. The mobilization of women behind the party plays an important role in the support structure of the MPLA-PT regime. The Organization of Angolan Women serves as the chief instrument for enrolling female recruits and supporting the government's projects and policies. Of the three main mass organizations, however, it is the National Union of Angolan Workers (UNTA) that functions as the most powerful buttress of the MPLA-PT. According to party figures for 1982, 90 percent of all Angolan workers, including rural workers, belong to UNTA.[17] UNTA's first congress was held in April 1984.

In theory, the National Assembly is the supreme state body. In practice, it merely serves as a mouthpiece for the MPLA. (Twenty of the Assembly's 223 members are nominated by the Central Committee; the remaining members are chosen by electoral colleges composed of representatives elected by all loyal citizens.) The ruling party's Central Committee is subdivided into nine committees dealing with cadres (a vital function supervised directly by President dos Santos) organization, ideology, information and culture, defense and security, state and judicial bodies, economic and social affairs, production, foreign affairs, and administration and finance. Most power, however, rests with a nine-member Politbureau elected from the Central Committee.

Although committed to the Leninist doctrine of "democratic centralism," the MPLA has, in fact, suffered from serious internal dissent. One of the most prominent dissenters was Nito Alves, whose faction attempted a power grab in Luanda in 1976. Alves, a militant black-power advocate with strong pro-Soviet views, resented the hold of *mestiço* intellectuals on the top positions in the MPLA. Taking advantage of his post at the head of the Ministry of International Administration, Alves (along with fellow Central Committee member Jose Van Dunem) sought to advance his cause in the party by building support in the Luanda slums. The Political Bureau instituted an inquiry; its findings were presented to the Central Committee on May 20–21, 1976 and resulted in the expulsion of Alves and Van Dunem. The two subsequently fomented a coup against the party leadership. With the knowledge (and perhaps the encouragement) of elements in the Soviet embassy in Luanda, the Alves group (termed Nitists) staged their (abortive) coup on May 27. It was ruthlessly crushed by Cuban troops, but not before the Nitists had assassinated several top-level MPLA leaders.[18] This abortive coup was only one of several factional disputes that plagued the MPLA. (Before coming to power, the MPLA had expelled many of its leaders, including Gentil Viana, Joaquim Pinto de Andrade, and Daniel Chipenda; each had left the party with his followers.)

Subsequently, the Central Committee used the attempted Alves coup to enhance its (already successful) efforts to obtain a large representation on and an overriding influence over the Council of the Revolution. Nevertheless, the council itself eventually lost its prerogatives; the powers formally held by the council were transferred to the Central Committee.[19] Additionally, the 1977 constitutional amendments shifted the power to appoint government members from the council to the president.

This trend continued in 1982; dos Santos received special but undefined powers to deal with the ideological wing of the party, which had accused him of corruption and incompetence. (A play written by Coste Andrade served as one vehicle for their criticism.) Dos Santos embarked on a housecleaning. He publicized his efforts to centralize control in a speech at a public rally on December 10, 1982. "If there is not discipline; if the different echelons of the organizational structure do not function as one sole voice; under one sole command, the objectives of the revolution will not be logically implemented."[20] By early 1983 some thirty high officials had been purged. Among those suspended was Ruth Lara, former head of the party's political education program and wife of Lucio Lara, second in command in the leadership (purged in 1985).[21]

In both Angola and Mozambique the governments became increasingly dependent on the security apparatus for their power. Developed with the aid of the USSR and its allies (especially East Germany), these security systems attempted to penetrate every institution at every level; they collected information and policed the activities and attitudes of the people. The public section of the security apparatus sought social control by totally politicizing society, its institutions, and mass organizations. These social surveillance institutions, although much less developed than in most communist states, attempted to mold behavior by, for instance, eliminating any autonomous social organizations. The governments employed both recognizable officials and covert agents to carry out their security measures. Whereas party figures and uniformed officials performed their roles openly, the covert operatives reported on neighbors and coworkers in return for official favors. The authorities also created a widespread network of detention centers, prisons, and rural detention camps, where political prisoners were frequently held for long periods without charges or trials and subjected to every kind of humiliation and sadistic atrocity.[22] The MPLA, however, has lacked the efficiency of other communist parties; total power over the population has so far proved impossible to establish.

Angola's problems have been further complicated by its involvement in the ongoing guerrilla war against the South Africans in Namibia. Angola has harbored Namibian guerrilla detachments; in reply, Pretoria has supported UNITA and launched devastating counter-raids against southern Angola. Unlike FRELIMO in Mozambique, the MPLA regime has remained heavily dependent on the support of ca. 25,000 Cuban soldiers stationed in Angola and on Soviet and East German advisers. The Cubans, however, have refused to become involved in hostilities against South African forces, and neither the MPLA nor their Cuban allies have been able to defeat UNITA at existing troop levels.

In 1985 UNITA was headed by President Jonas Savimbi (a Swiss-educated political scientist and a veteran leader in the anti-colonial struggle) and Secretary-General Miguel Nzau Puna. According to its own statements, UNITA controlled about one-third of the country. Such statements, like similar claims made by other guerrilla movements in the past, are hard to verify. It is clear, however, that by 1985 support for UNITA had extended beyond the ranks of Savimbi's original supporters, the Ovimbundu people. In the struggle against the Portuguese, UNITA had been the only party that was not dependent on the support of kinsmen and backers outside Angola's borders. Accustomed to a reliance on its own resources, and committed to an extremely ruthless style of warfare, UNITA continued to fight after the breakdown of the tri-partite agreement of 1975. Whereas the FNLA has been largely eliminated as a fighting force, UNITA has developed into a dangerous challenge to MPLA's supremacy.

According to critics, UNITA's extreme dependence on the single figure of Savimbi makes the movement highly vulnerable. This vulnerability is heightened by UNITA's lack of an ideology to unite its adherents; the party is based only on antiwhite, antimestiço, anti-Soviet, and anti-Cuban sentiments. UNITA's published statements, however, reflect an ideology of sorts. The party condemns what it calls collusion between communism and specific sectors of foreign corporate enterprise — especially Gulf Oil, whose operations in Angola supply the MPLA regime with substantial revenue and which functions as an important pro-MPLA lobby in Washington. UNITA stresses the failures of socialist enterprise as practiced in Angola, advocates national self-sufficiency in food production, and objects to the anachronistic principles underlying the predominance of state monopoly and rigid state control of all economic activities. Instead, UNITA advocates a combination of economic planning with "a high degree of decentralization of control on all economic activities" and an increasing measure of private initiative in economic development at local and regional levels. It hopes to thus avoid "the creation of a counterproductive, cumbersome, unwieldy central government bureaucracy."[23]

The long struggle between UNITA and the government has resulted in a debilitating stalemate in the Angolan economy. An easy settlement is blocked by the presence of the Cuban proxies. The MPLA has insisted that it will not ask the Cubans to leave until Pretoria ends its support of UNITA and its raids. But extensive parts of Angola remain under the effective control of UNITA, which has come to dominate the country's southeastern regions. The Cubans have failed to protect Angola's threatened southern regions against South African incursions. (In 1984 Angola was forced to conclude an accord with South Africa — the so-called Lusaka agreement, signed February 16 — whereby South African forces were to withdraw from southern Angola in return for Angola's agreement to prevent the South West African People's Organization (SWAPO) or the Cubans from moving into the territory vacated by the South Africans.) The Lusaka agreement has seriously weakened SWAPO; The agreement may also have occasioned further disagreement within the MPLA on the question of whether to negotiate with UNITA or to continue the ongoing struggle.

Neither Angola nor Mozambique have found prosperity under Marxist-Leninist economic management. In and of itself, the anti-colonial war did not result in much physical destruction. But neither the MPLA nor FRELIMO attempted to formulate a consistent policy as long as the struggle lasted. The experience of the party cadres has mainly been acquired in guerrilla operations in the bush, in underground political organizations, or in academic and teaching positions. Few cadres had experience in economic management of any kind. MPLA and FRELIMO theoreticians had both opposed antiwhite racism. Nevertheless, they had been inclined to regard as enemies both the Portuguese bourgeoisie in the colonies and what they regarded as the Portuguese petty bourgeoisie and the Portuguese aristocracy of labor. Additionally, the MPLA and FRELIMO did not receive good advice from self-styled progressive scholars in the West, who were inclined to discount the value of the white settlers' economic role. Had the settler been as parasitic as asserted by anticolonial theoreticians, both Angola and Mozambique should have benefited from their mass exodus. In fact, both countries suffered from the loss of their economic experience and their willingness to accumulate capital.

The Marxist-Leninists' seizure of power in Angola had other unanticipated consequences. Instead of ending civil strife, revolution led to the outbreak of new civil wars — this time between contending factions. The economy suffered severely, even in areas untouched by insurgency. The once-prosperous coffee plantations almost ceased operations. Unable to market their produce at satisfactory prices, many villagers returned to subsistence cultivation. The government nationalized a broad range of enterprises engaged in production and distribution. These major public enterprises included the Empresa Nacional de Diamantes de Angola (which took over 77 percent of the shares of the Campanhia de Diamantes Angola) the Campanhia Geral dos Agodoes de Angola (which produced cotton textiles), the Empresa Nacional do Cafe, the Empresa de Pasca de Angola (a fishing enterprise) and the Empresa Nacional de Comercialização e Distribucião de Productos Agricolas (an agricultural marketing firm). Unfortunately, these firms tended to be overstaffed, inefficient, and poorly run.

The Angolan government proved unable to maintain either law and order or a stable public administration. The budgets operated at a deficit. (In 1980 Angola had an estimated revenue of 60,143 million kwanza and an expenditure of 87,172 million kwanza.) Inflation reached serious proportions. There was a constant trade deficit (growing from U.S. $11 million in 1978 to U.S. $60 million in 1980). Unable to either contain corruption or to develop an efficient planning mechanism, the government tried to cope with its manifold economic problems by means of coercion and a variety of administrative expedients. In mid-1983, for example, President dos Santos took control of additional ministries and reshuffled various cabinet positions. But overall, the economy declined. (Between 1960 and 1979 the GNP declined at an average annual rate of minus 2.1 percent (as compared with an annual growth rate of 2.9 percent in Malawi and 2.7 percent in Kenya).[24]

The exact extent of economic deterioration has remained hard to measure because the available statistics are unsatisfactory. Many are out of date, some are inadequate, and some are inaccurate as a result of administrative inefficiency or design. The Portuguese-created plantation economy has largely collapsed; consequences for the country's exports of coffee, sisal, cotton, sugar, and other cash crops have been disastrous. Large-scale cattle ranching, initiated by Europeans on irrigated land in southern Angola, has suffered from ongoing unrest. The fisheries have suffered from overfishing. Not surprisingly, Angola's ability to feed itself has progressively declined. In 1980–1981 Angola supplied no more than 56 percent of its domestic food requirements (as opposed to 90 percent at the end of the Portuguese era in 1974).

The Angolan government eventually tried to counteract the effects of Marxist dogmatism by once again encouraging foreign investment; in 1979 new legislation was passed that eased the foreign lender's lot. Nevertheless, the bulk of the economy remained state-controlled. In 1982 nationalized industries accounted for 58 percent of total production, the private sector for 29 percent, and joint ventures for 13 percent. This constituted a serious problem for the country because the state-controlled sector proved to be the least productive; it reached only 52 percent of its projected goals in 1982.[25] Oil was the factor that helped save the economy. It continued to be produced by a U.S. capitalist enterprise — the Cabinda Gulf Oil Company, a subsidiary of Gulf Oil Corporation. The Cabinda Gulf Oil Company worked in tandem with the socialist state; the nationalized corporation, SCNANGOL, held 51 percent of the Cabinda Gulf Oil Company's shares. The bulk of the oils was exported to the United States, where Gulf Oil (interestingly enough) became one of the main pro-Angolan lobbies in Washington. Gulf Oil provided the Angolan government with much of its revenue. It furnished the country with the lion's share of the hard currency used to import food and other necessities. As the world oil glut appeared in the 1980s, however, the once-lucrative oil revenue diminished. In 1983 Angola produced 180,000 barrels a day, but this figure already represented a sizable shortfall from her former production target of 250,000 barrels a day. In 1984 oil production declined even further, leaving Angola to face a host of apparently insoluble economic problems.[26]

POSTINDEPENDENCE INSTITUTIONS

Angola and Mozambique both claim to operate on the principles of Marxism-Leninism; accordingly, their ruling parties share common features. They began as popular movements dedicated to wars of liberation. Their original goal was "national democratic revolution," to be achieved in alliance with progressive elements from all social classes, including the "national bourgeosie." Once the

national democratic revolution had been achieved, the ruling front
or movement was to be transformed into a Marxist-Leninist cadre
party. It was to be founded on the principles of "democratic
centralism," as defined by Lenin, with rigid control from top to
bottom.[27] (In Angola the MPLA was restructured as a Marxist-
Leninist party in 1977. In the same year FRELIMO also structured
itself into a Marxist-Leninist vanguard party.) Both in Angola and
Mozambique, the ruling party presently acts as the central institution responsible for political, economic, and social leadership.
Both parties aim at a socialist revolution that will transform society
and ultimately create a "new person." In both countries, the head
of the ruling party also serves as president of the Republic, and the
party guides the various state organs.

The power arrangements in Angola and Mozambique (as in other
countries organized on Marxist-Leninist principles) are designed to
give the party a monopoly of power over the government and its
bureaucracy and provide protection against criticism for policy
mistakes and failures in running the state. Although the party is the
ultimate source of power, the delegates to the government bureaucracy deal directly with the economy and the people. The Marxist-
Leninist party leadership makes policy decisions; these are transmitted from the capital through provincial party committees to
city, town, and village authorities. Power is also passed horizon-
tally from party to government in the lower levels of the administrative structure down to and including the village level. Since
government officials are usually party members, party and
government offices frequently overlap.

Guinea-Bassau, once thought likely to become the most revolutionary state in Africa, failed to live up to political predictions. The
PAIGC's leader, Amilcar Cabral, impressed many young Africans
and some Western intellectuals as the continent's quintessential
Marxist thinker and revolutionary activist. His death in 1973 left a
vacuum in the party's leadership, which none of his followers could
fill. But even had Cabral lived, Guinea-Bissau's road to socialism
would still have been rocky. Barren of almost any resources, the
country offered few attractions. The annual rice production, for
example, has not reached preindependence levels. The offshore
archipelago of the Cape Verde Islands, which at least possesses
some strategic value, chafed at rule from the mainland. Its separation from Guinea-Bissau meant even this tenuous asset was lost.

On November 14, 1980, a quasi-military coup replaced president

Luís Cabral (brother of the assassinated Amilcar Cabral) with João Bernardo Viera. The coup leaders abolished the national assembly and state council and replaced the latter body with a nine-member revolutionary council, staffed largely by military men.

Shortly after the takeover, the new regime stated that the Cabral government had been guilty of widespread repression of its political enemies. As evidence, the Viera government took foreign journalists to the sites of mass graves of a reported 500 opponents, who had been executed in 1978. The coup's success constituted further evidence of how far Guinea-Bissau had drifted from the model of Marxism-Leninism. On paper the PAIGC appeared as a thoroughgoing vanguard party, although it referred to Guinea-Bissau as a "national revolutionary democracy" rather than a Marxist-Leninist state. Yet the party was sufficiently weak to allow a internal group backed by the military to seize power. The coup pointed to a further decline in revolutionary fervor and the passage of time confirmed that view.

Guinea-Bissau presently exists in the shadowy status of those African countries that hold to Marxist trappings but whose dictatorial leaders strive just to cling to power rather than to transform their poverty-ridden states into replicas of East European regimes. To legitimize the 1980 coup and strengthen his position, President Viera has pushed the development of a new constitution and abolished the post of prime minister. At the time of writing, there are no signs of a dramatic improvement in the economic conditions in Guinea-Bissau.

The bureaucratization so characteristic of twentieth-century Marxist revolutions has also overtaken the regimes in Portuguese-speaking Africa. The expansion of the state bureaucracy has accompanied the centralization of power typical of Marxist-Leninist parties in power. Centralization and concentration of power are necessary for the operation of a planned economy, a pervasive police and security system, and a regulated population. This pattern has been reinforced in Angola and Mozambique because the Marxist-Leninist parties need to reward faithful followers for years of struggle in the bush. They also need to implement a thoroughgoing revolutionary society in which new party cadre aspirants will seek government jobs as a means of upward mobility.

Both parties, however, face serious organizational difficulties. They are deficient in technical expertise. They have had to deal with serious factionalism and what the rulers call lack of party discipline. Because local, ethnic, and clan loyalties remain strong, hard cadres are difficult to find. Party membership (estimated in 1982 at 31,000 in Angola, and 110,000 in Mozambique) remains limited. The parties lack enough cadres to effectively administer the armed forces, the state, and the economy. Failure in the economic sphere has forced both FRELIMO and the MPLA to resort to African variants of Lenin's New Economic Policy; nevertheless, prosperity continues to recede into the distant horizon. Additionally, the prospects for revolutionary war and liberation in South Africa have dimmed.[28] The promises made by these revolutions in the 1960s have yet to be fulfilled in either the economic or the political sphere.

Notes

1. L. H. Gann, "Portugal, Africa, and the Future," *Journal of Modern African Studes* 13 (1975): 1–18.

2. Thomas H. Henriksen, *Mozambique: A History* (London: Rex Collings, 1978), pp. 100–103.

3. See for instance, Colin Legum, "A Letter on Angola to American Liberals," *New Republic*, January 31, 1976, pp. 15–19.

4. For further information, see Douglas L. Wheeler and René Pélissier, *Angola* (New York: Praeger, 1971), pp. 173–81.

5. Thomas H. Henriksen, *Revolution and Counterrevolution: Mozambique's War of Independence, 1964–1974* (Westport, Conn.: Greenwood Press, 1983), pp. 194–98.

6. Keith Middleman, "Independent Mozambique and Its Regional Policy," in John Seiler, ed., *Southern Africa Since the Portuguese Coup* (Boulder, Col.: Westview Press, 1980), p. 220.

7. *Central Committee Report to the Third Congress of FRELIMO* (London: Mozambique, Angola, Guinea Information Centre, 1978), p. 48.

8. René Pélissier, "Mozambique," in *Africa South of the Sahara, 1984–1985* (London: Europa Publications, 1984), pp. 614–17.

9. Godwin Matatu, "Mozambique: Machel's New War," *Africa*, no. 15 (May 1980): 14.

10. For more on the Rhodesian war, see L. H. Gann and Thomas H. Henriksen, *The Struggle for Zimbabwe: The Battle in the Bush* (New York: Praeger, 1981).

11. *Rand Daily Mail*, May 22, 1984.

12. See International Institute for Strategic Studies, *The Military Balance 1983–1984* (London, 1983), p. 71.

13. Benjamin Pogrund, "RNM Turns Screws on Embattled Mozambique," *Rand Daily Mail*, May 22, 1984.

14. See, for instance, Helen Kitchen, *U.S. Interests in Africa* (New York: Praeger Special Studies, Washington, D.C., 1983), pp. 63–67. For an opposing interpretation, see L. H. Gann and Peter Duignan, *Africa South of the Sahara: The Challenge to Western Security* (Stanford, Hoover Institution Press, 1981).

15. Michael Wolfers, "People's Republic of Angola," *Marxist Governments: A World Survey*, vol. 1 (London: Macmillan, 1981), p. 72.

16. Richard E. Bissell, "Angola," in Robert Wesson, ed., *Yearbook on International Communist Affairs* (Stanford: Hoover Institution Press, 1983), p. 7.

17. Bissell, "Angola," p. 8.

18. David Birmingham, "The Twenty-seventh of May: An Historical Note on the Abortive 1977 Coup in Angola," *African Affairs* 77, no. 309 (Oct. 1978): 554–64 and Political Bureau of the Central Committee, "How the Angolan Coup Was Crushed," *African Communist*, 71 (Fourth quarter 1977): 35–51.

19. Wolfers, "People's Republic of Angola," p. 77.

20. Luanda domestic service, December 11, 1982; *Foreign Broadcast Information Service* (Africa and Middle East), December 13, 1983.

21. Lisbon domestic service, December 30, 1982; *FBIS*, January 3, 1983.

22. For details see, for instance, Amnesty International, International Secretariat, *People's Republic of Angola: Background Briefing on Amnesty International Concerns* (London, December 1982), AI INDEX: AFR 12.01.83.

23. See UNITA, "The Angolan Road to National Recovery: Defining the Principles and Objectives" (Jamba, Angola, December 1983, Mimeographed), especially p. 132.

24. See World Bank, *Accelerated Development in Sub-Saharian Africa* (Washington, D.C., 1981), p. 143.

25. See Rene Pelissier, "Angola," *Africa South of the Sahara: 1982–1984* (London: Europa Publications, 1984), pp. 204–9.

26. See *Washington Post*, October 7, 1983.

27. Allen Issacman and Barbara Issacman, *Mozambique: From Colonialism to Revolution, 1900–1982* (Boulder, Col.: Westview Press, 1984), pp. 121–22.

28. Michael S. Radu, "Africa in the 1980s: The End of Innocence," in Richard E. Bissell and Michael S. Radu, eds., *Africa in the Post-Decolonization Era* (New Brunswick, N.J.: Transaction, 1984), pp. 229–33.

CONCLUSION

Robert H. Jackson

Much of sub-Saharan Africa has been politically independent for a quarter-century. In 1985 Namibia was the only remaining political dependency. The year of independence — 1960 — constitutes a political watershed in modern African history equal to the year of formal continental partition by European powers — 1884–85. Before 1960 Africa was the colonial continent par excellence, and for about a decade after, it was the archetypal region of new states. Until recently it has been difficult to characterize the emergent African states — primarily because insufficient time had elapsed to allow political events and problems to recur and become settled features of political life. At first — beyond formal sovereignty — it was not clear what "independence" signified. Much of the writing on African politics in the 1960s therefore concentrated more on theoretical possibilities like political development, nation-building, and modernization than on the actual course of political events that were just getting underway. After twenty-five years, however, African states have begun to register their own political histories, and their collective political experience is becoming historically discernible.

UNDERDEVELOPMENT

The United Nations christened the 1960s the "development decade" in the hope that a major political leap forward could finally overcome the lamentable backwardness of tropical Africa and some other parts of the newly emergent Third World.[1] In Africa, previous administrative governments of modest size were, in most cases, hastily equipped with new political superstructures: constitutions, legislatures, electoral systems, and so forth. Many observers hoped that these political institutions would take root and lead to governments conducted along democratic lines. Many of these same observers also hoped that the new African governments could become strategic instruments of national socio-economic development.

Significant — and, in some cases, impressive — progress in political and socioeconomic development has been achieved by some African countries. After an initial period of one-party authoritarianism, for the past decade Senegal has managed to operate a system of guided multiparty democracy. Botswana and The Gambia have been governed in accordance with democratic constitutions established at independence. Kenya has instituted an innovative system of one-party parliamentary democracy. The Ivory Coast, whose economy was capable of generating a per capita GNP of more than $1,000 in 1979, has been, until recently, an obvious success story in economic growth and substantially increased living standards. Agricultural development in Kenya, Malawi, Botswana and Swaziland has been noteworthy. By African standards, Tanzania has achieved a high rate of literacy, and Kenya, a high level of life expectancy. (Previous chapters contain other examples of African development.)

In tropical Africa as a whole, however, these cases constitute islands of development in an ocean of adversity and decay. Sub-Saharan Africa has recently acquired an image as the most impoverished and disordered region in the Third World. Moreover, political and socioeconomic adversity appears to be increasing. A 1984 World Bank report submitted to Western finance ministers indicated that living conditions were lower than they had been in 1970 and, even under the most optimistic assumptions, could be expected to fall still further during the coming decade. Per capita food production was 20 percent lower in 1984 than it was in 1960.[2] Many parts of sub-Saharan Africa are presently beset by extreme poverty, famine, civil wars, refugees, military coups, abusive dictatorships, massive corruption, and similar adversities. Moreover, many Africans suffer not only from nature but also from politics. The abuse of power is not new to Africa; it occurred both before and during the colonial era. What is new is the relative scale of politically induced adversity and the fact that it is taking place under African self-government.

At some risk of oversimplification, the socioeconomic and political adversities of black Africa can be classified as follows: (1) extreme socioeconomic underdevelopment, (2) incapable government administration, (3) discordant ethnic divisions and (4) insubstantial political institutions. The main concern of this concluding chapter is to summarize the black African political experience in these terms. South Africa is a major exception (although, to some extent, it also exhibits some of these characteristics).

If the African experience is any indication, extreme socioeconomic underdevelopment is difficult to overcome. In places where geographical adversities are at the root of backwardness, economic advancement is particularly difficult. Mali, Burkina Fasso (Upper Volta), and Chad are cases in point. In places where climatic adversities are increasing (as in the drought-stricken Sahelian countries) a decline, rather than a development, of living standards is a distinct possibility. Barring a sudden economic windfall — such as the discovery of oil or some other scarce mineral resource — the less-favored hinterland or drought-ridden countries may remain in an underdeveloped and poverty-stricken state for an indefinite period.

PROBLEMS OF GOVERNANCE

Most governments in sub-Saharan Africa remain deficient in organization and management; hence, they continue to have extraordinary difficulties in exercising their public functions. Because they are inadequately supplied with qualified personnel and poorly endowed with financial resources, equipment, and skills, many of these governments find it difficult to govern effectively. Governmental incapability cannot be attributed entirely to poverty and backwardness, however. Some countries that are comparatively poor by African standards are governed more effectively than some that are comparatively richer. In 1979 Malawi (which had a per capita GNP of $200) was probably governed far better than Ghana (which had a per capita GNP of $400); similarly, Nigeria (GNP $670) was probably not as well run as Kenya (GNP $380) or even Gambia (GNP $250).[3] Moreover, colonial governments were generally better organized and managed than their African successors (even though colonial economies were usually less developed). The Belgian Congo was far more effectively ruled than is modern Zaire; before independence, however, the economy was smaller, and other socioeconomic indicators (like health and education) were much lower. Governmental capability and socioeconomic development are undoubtedly related in complex and intimate ways. But the first is not entirely dependent on the second (and vice versa). There were capable governments in Europe and other parts of the world long before the modern commercial and industrial revolutions, and there have been incapable ones since.

A crucial ingredient of effective governance undoubtedly derives from the presence of competent and reliable officials — particularly at decision-making levels. Unfortunately, such personnel have been scarce in many sub-Saharan countries. In general, this shortage is related to material underdevelopment (which limits the supply of trained officials) and to ethnic norms (which interfere with the duty of officials to serve the public interest). Nevertheless, the shortage is also a specific consequence of colonial administrative practice (which restricted and even widely prevented the involvement of Africans in higher, nonclerical levels of administration) and a widespread policy of rapid and wholesale Africanization during and immediately following independence (which frequently entailed a decline of governmental capability by the replacement of more experienced European officials with less-experienced — and sometimes inexperienced — African personnel). More often than not the result was, in Crawford Young's term, a "deflation" of government capability. (Zaire is an extreme case in point, but the problem existed to a lesser degree in many other countries.) The few countries that defied this trend and Africanized more slowly and selectively — for example, the Ivory Coast, Malawi, and Botswana — tend to have more capable governments.

Rapid and wholesale Africanization has raised problems not only of efficiency but also of responsibility. In many African countries patronage and corruption are expected — and even accepted — modes of administrative behavior. In some countries malfeasance has virtually become a way of life for many people. For example, in Ghana, Nigeria, Zaire, and Uganda the authority and resources of nominally public offices are widely appropriated by their occupants for their own private benefit. The *locus classicus* is Zaire, where (according to Young) large amounts of public revenue are diverted to "patrimonial uses," and public authority is "mercantilized" into a commodity for sale. (See chapter on Zaire and Cameroon in this volume.) In short, rapid and wholesale Africanization has often had the unintended result of interfering with the capacity of the state to provide political goods to the general public. In many countries the "general public" was a political nonentity; it was kinship and ethnic groups that primarily influenced the behavior of government officials.

A government job has become the most highly valued occupation in societies in which the modern private sector is small (and sometimes very specialized). The power, prestige, and perquisites of administrative employment are legacies of colonial times. The usual route to government employment is via public education. Educational investments have been popular with the public and have been widely recommended by international development experts. As governments expanded educational opportunities, the number of graduates alienated from rural occupations and desirous of urban white-collar employment consistent with their new status increased. Consequently, employment in both the civil and military branches of government has increased in most African countries. In many countries, the expansion of government employment and expenditure has markedly outdistanced economic growth. In some — for instance, Chad, Somalia, and Ghana — the public sector has continued to expand even when the overall economy has declined.

Historically, such practices have not been confined to Africa, of course. As Barbara Jelavich writes of the newly independent Balkan states in the nineteenth century:

Domestic controversies involved not only this conflict between the ruler and the notables, but also the struggle for political power among the prominent men who joined competing factions or parties. Some organizations were formed around a strong leader, whereas others were based on issues, such as support of opposition to the prince, or questions of domestic reform. Victory in an election meant more than the triumph of a man or an idea. It gave the winning party the control of the bureaucracy and thus of the appointments to major posts, which in turn allowed access to sources of real profit . . . It was thought normal for a man to appoint members of his family to high offices when he gained power; it was a sign of his attachment and loyalty to those closest to him. Similarly, he was expected to reward friends and supporters. The assignment of public posts on the basis of political patronage rather than merit caused little violent outrage. Once in office, such officials regularly followed the Ottoman practices and took advantage of their positions. Again, many of their activities were accepted. Payments for services rendered were not regarded as unusual. The term *bakshish* covered both outright bribes and what the Western European would regard as tips. Officials in the lower branches of the bureaucracy were often so miserably paid that they had to augment their incomes through these practices. The total effect was unfortunate. Balkan states were not only impoverished, but also badly administered.[4]

In the late twentieth century, African states are in danger of becoming the super-Balkans of the globe.

Statism has exacerbated the problem of Africanization by multiplying the demands on the already limited and fairly inelastic supply of African manpower qualified for managerial positions (thereby further diluting the quality of governmental and parastatal administration). Crash programs to upgrade clerks into managers cannot overcome the problem. Like private managers and other occupations in which competence and judgment are at a premium, public managers ordinarily require not only training but a good deal of experience. This takes time. Crash programs assume that the problem is not inexperience but a shortage of skilled personnel — that public management is a technique that can be learnt from experts. The expansion of university education has been similarly ineffective in overcoming the problem. University graduates (even those trained in public administration) are not experienced public managers. Indeed, they have been trained by university professors who often have little or no relevant government experience themselves. Parastatalism usually compounds the problem. Parastatals typically suffer from overemployment and weak discipline and are usually run more like political establishments than commercial enterprises. Tanzania is an extreme case in point,[5] but most African countries have experienced similar problems.

Overstaffed and consumption-oriented governments have placed heavy and adverse economic pressures on many sub-Saharan countries in the form of inflation, accelerated international borrowing and indebtedness, declining productivity, low capital formation, and so forth. Ironically, these pressures have contributed significantly to the financial dependency of African countries; many have grown more dependent on foreign aid since independence. Food dependency has increased, governments have held down domestic food prices (to the advantage of their employees and other urban dwellers) and have encouraged the production of nonfood cash crops to earn foreign exchange. The political economics of food has therefore often resulted in a decline in production.[6] An increasing number of countries must import comestibles. In 1985 food deficits are rising, malnutrition is widespread, and famine is a fact in some places and a threat in others. Some countries depend on the charity of exporters for their food. Undoubtedly, many factors — particularly drought — have contributed to this alarming state of affairs. The growth of non-productive government is one of the most important contributors, however, and cannot be overlooked. Most sub-Saharan countries have been politically independent for a quarter-century, but during this time an increasing number of them (for instance Tanzania) have virtually become mendicant states.

Statism may work when government is staffed by people who are sufficiently experienced and reliable to make it productive; this is generally the case in Sweden, West Germany, Holland, the United Kingdom, Canada, the United States, and other countries (like South Africa) that have strong traditions of public service. (Even in many of these countries, however, statism entails certain ineffi-ciencies that, in recent years, have proved costly and have fre-quently resulted in reductions in the activities and establishments of government.) Statism works poorly when a government post is treated more as a sinecure than as a public trust and when govern-ment agents act for their own private — rather than the public — interest. Statism in Africa generally conforms more closely to the latter pattern.

TRIALS OF ETHNICITY

During the era of decolonization, many proponents of African independence predicted a lessening of interethnic tensions follow-ing the demise of the Western colonial empires. In practice, how-ever, independence often seemed to have exacerbated interethnic conflict. Popular expectations increased. The growth of the state machinery and the intrusion of the state into economic life also heightened ethnic tensions. As long as the state only concerned itself with raising taxes and arresting criminals, a villager could make his living no matter who controlled the government. But once the state began to regulate trade by means of marketing boards, prices by means of planning commissions, and credit by means of state banks, control of the state machinery itself became a matter of economic survival. Rival ethnic communities therefore acquired pressing interests in the command of political power. As more and more began to be expected of the government, it increasingly became a target of criticism for alienated students, intellectuals, and military officers who were convinced that they had not obtained their due share of political or economic benefits.

The political problems of postcolonial Africa were heightened by the fact that most of the new states consisted of ethnic mosaics originally put together by the colonial powers. In theory, the advocates of anticolonialism repudiated the permanence of the old colonial frontiers. In practice, the colonial frontiers stayed in place. Despite strong hostility to the colonial borders, a realignment of frontiers to correspond to the boundaries of indigenous ethnic groups was politically impossible. Realignments were not seriously considered (let alone attempted), and only Somalia and Morocco have refused to acknowledge the legitimacy of the colonial borders. Most other African governments have remained determined to affirm and uphold the sanctity of the colonial frontiers; they fear that to do otherwise would invite political chaos.[7]

The majority of new African states were insufficiently stable and unified to engage in boundary revisions that would, almost inevitably, have disrupted the precarious status quo among existing groups. For instance, the Nigerian government was opposed to the annexation of the Yoruba areas of neighbouring Benin, fearing such an action would upset the internal ethnic balance of the country by increasing Yoruba strength. Moreover, if secession based on ethnic self-determination were permitted, these realignments would threaten the integrity (and even the survival) of many other states by provoking numerous ethno-nationalist demands. Meeting these demands would radically reshape the existing political map. Hence the Nigerian government's forceful resistance of Biafran separatism was supported by most other African and non-African states. The weakness of African states and the insecurity of their governments has created a strong common interest in the preservation of the colonial frontiers, and the OAU has made this a cardinal principle of African international relations. The governments of Somalia and Morocco; Tigreans, Eritreans, and similar secessionists in Ethiopia; the southern Sudanese; Katangans in Zaire; Biafrans in Nigeria; and all other African separatists and irredentists have confronted an international political obstacle that, to date, has proved insurmountable. The OAU cannot recognize ethnic secessionists without violating its rules and threatening its existence. Consequently, the political map of Africa has remained virtually unchanged since colonial times.

The relative fixity of the postcolonial frontiers has had ambiguous results. The sanctity of the borders has helped to prevent international strife, maintained the existing jurisdictions, and kept border conflicts to a minimum; the result has been much less conflict than the extent of ethnic division might have been expected to produce. The only significant border conflicts involving military force have been the war between Somalia and Ethiopia for control of the Ogaden and the conflict between Morocco and the Polisario over the Western Sahara. The international legitimacy of borders has insured that force and conquest have been largely proscribed instruments of nation building in contemporary Africa. This situation is radically different from that which obtained in precolonial Africa (and in most other parts of the world). Many modern states in Europe and elsewhere were formed (at least in part) as a result of international violence; modern borders often represent lines where hostilities came to rest. The capacity to defend borders — alone or in alliance with others — is a prominent historical characteristic of modern state building. Since independence, however, no African borders have been permanently altered by force, and the future possibility of such changes is slight. In Africa, international law (as represented by OAU rules) is capable of maintaining existing state jurisdictions; there is therefore little need to defend them by force.

The rigidity of international frontiers, however, has neither strengthened the new states internally nor encouraged them to resolve existing ethnic problems. In fact, civil warfare has been common. But civil conflicts have not generally resulted in the foundation of strong national states. (As Kirk-Greene indicates, Nigeria is a rare exception.) In contemporary Africa, civil wars tend either to drag on without resolution or to subside periodically and then break out again. Such conflicts have beset countries as varied as Ethiopia, Sudan, Zaire, Chad, Uganda, Angola, and Mozambique. For example, Eritrean secessionists have been periodically at war with the Ethiopian government for decades, but they have no greater prospects of gaining international legitimacy in 1985 than at any time previously. Internal strife, with ethnic overtones, continues to trouble Angola. In none of these countries has the central government been able to permanently impose its will over its entire territory. And in none of them has a rebel force been able to capture the government or effectively rule the country to the extent of being able to achieve international legitimacy and a corresponding alteration of borders. Rebels have certainly escaped from the de facto control of central governments. Under current international law, however, this has not been sufficient for them to acquire international legitimacy. As a result, although the map of Africa has remained unchanged, countries like Ethiopia lack effective internal sovereignty and contain within their borders two or more ethno-regional governments that do not recognize one another.

The pluralistic society is a fact of political life in almost all of sub-Saharan Africa; it is a circumstance that can (at some risk) be ignored but cannot be eliminated. Ethnicity will not go away. The political problem, therefore, is to find ways to prevent ethnic conflicts from dividing the state and to take advantage of the support, stability, and other political goods that ethnic diversity can provide. Although international law can prevent formal secession, international law cannot produce ethnic collaboration with national governments; to achieve this end, some form of political accommodation is necessary. This is an easy concept to recognize in theory, but a difficult one to achieve in practice — especially in multiethnic African societies that lack common political traditions and institutions. To date, few African governments have established effective institutional mechanisms to politically accommodate the pluralistic society. The student of "consociational democracy," for example, would seek in vain for evidence of grand coalitions, joint vetoes, proportionality, multipartyism, and federalism in contemporary African politics.[8] Less-than-grand coalitions have been formed in Kenya and some other countries, a qualified multipartyism has been practiced in Senegal, and federalism has been attempted (with major disruptions) in Nigeria. These are exceptional cases, however.

In artificial countries it is hard to find institutions of political accommodation that can be accepted by most ethnic groups. Informal power sharing is probably easier to achieve. In countries where political accommodation has occurred, it has usually been at the discretion of equitable rulers and been based on a practice of "virtual representation." It has consisted of bringing important ethnic leaders into the government rather than keeping them outside — thereby including the ethnic groups whose members identify with their leaders. This is an ancient mode of representation that does not presume democracy or even constitutional government; for that reason alone it is probably attractive to African governments, which are often highly personal and discretionary.[9]

PRAETORIANISM AND FRAGILE CONSTITUTIONS

By the 1980s much of Africa had fallen into the hands of the military or of one-party dictatorships. The causes of military intervention have been as varied as their forms of leadership. African armies and their cadres differ widely in composition, training, discipline, and professional competence. Their relative place in the political scene and the powers that soldiers assert also vary. But when the military does stage coups, it usually justifies its proceedings by claiming that only the men in uniform can wipe out civilian corruption. The 1984 military takeover in Nigeria derived widespread support from popular impatience with corruption. Ethnic fears and rivalries have also encouraged military intervention — as have the weaknesses of African governments, their inabilities to rule effectively, and their failures to achieve economic development.

The structural weaknesses of African governments have provided an excuse for the military to replace the ballot box with the rifle. Coups are symptomatic of the failure on the part of politicians to establish effective and legitimate government. No military leader, however, has as yet achieved true legitimacy. It is the monopoly of armed force, combined with the use of bribes and payoffs, that has helped to keep the generals in power. (Furthermore, military intervention may increase corruption by teaching colonels, captains, and corporals in succession how to turn politico-military entrepreneurship to personal profit.)

In some cases the civilian elite encouraged the military to intervene. Generalization about military takeovers is difficult, however, because the military forces were as varied in their social characteristics as the leaders they replaced, and the forms and causes of intervention defy classification. No mold fits all cases or explains all coups. Given governmental instability, ethnic diversity, and the appalling problems faced by most independent African states, coups will probably continue to occur in many countries.

Why hasn't constitutional politics taken root in most countries of tropical Africa, and why has arbitrary rule — civilian or military — become widespread? There are no obvious and fully satisfactory answers to these difficult questions. Nevertheless, there are partial explanations that can be derived from the experience of countries in which constitutional rules have been successfully integrated into political life. In the European experience, constitutionalism and constitutional democracy usually followed the establishment of an effective government. In Britain, parliamentary rule successfully supplanted Tudor and Stuart absolutism; parliamentary democracy in turn replaced the constitutional aristocracy established by the Glorious Revolution. In this view, positive government capability must be established before issues of constitutional legitimacy can be resolved. Moreover, government capability may initially have to be purchased at the expense of constitutionalism. Many black African countries are still without solid governments, and, until these are established (perhaps by strong personal rulers), the possibility of constitutionalism cannot be great. Perhaps Kenya and Senegal are cases in point — countries in which Kenyatta and Senghor had to consolidate their power before some democratic rights could be instituted. In the Ivory Coast and in Malawi, government has functioned effectively, and perhaps we are witnessing the beginnings of constitutionalism in the holding of one-party elections.

According to Lord Lugard, "institutions and methods . . . in order to command success and promote the happiness and welfare of the people, must be deeprooted in their traditions and prejudices."[10] Burke and other constitutional conservatives have said the same. In most Western countries, and in non-Western ones like Japan, both the particular political institutions of the country and its territorial domain reflect indigenous political culture to a significant degree. National institutions are the handiwork of the people — particularly the most powerful people — living under them. In contrast, in most African countries these institutions are imported and are, moreover, significantly at odds not only with indigenous political culture but with the political ambitions of the most powerful people. Indeed, there is usually no single political culture or tradition in these countries. Consequently, until the new state gains much wider understanding and deeper acceptance (especially by the most important political actors) arbitrary rule will probably prevail, and constitutions will, at best, be formal rather than substantial features of political life.

Furthermore, there are at present few, if any, significant international pressures on African countries to engage in constitutional development or even civil politics (with the major exception of South Africa, which is being pressed to change its constitution rather than to adopt one). Ironically, by providing black African governments with an unqualified right to independence and self-determination (regardless of their internal political or socio-economic conditions), international society — and Western governments in particular — may well have contributed to their constitutional underdevelopment. (Admittedly, the former colonial governments all encountered strong pressures, both at home and abroad, to hand over power speedily — on the grounds that "self-government was better than good government.")

The international requirements of sovereignty soon became divorced from the ability of the successor governments to run their various countries in an effective manner. Subsequently, even the most tyrannical governments in Africa — such as Michael Micombero's genocidal regime in Burundi, Macias Nguema's dictatorship in Equatorial Guinea, Sekou Touré's despotism in Guinea, and Idi Amin's reign of terror in Uganda — escaped censure by the OAU and most of the rest of official international society, including the UN. The OAU did not condemn Amin. Instead, because the OAU is a club in which the members' first obligation is to respect each other's sovereignty, the organization condemned the invasion of Uganda and the overthrow of Amin's government by Nyerere's army. (In other words, what rulers do at home is their own affair, providing their actions do not adversely affect their colleagues' sovereignty.) As noted previously, with very few exceptions (Somalia, Morocco), black African governments exercise mutual recognition, forbearance, and toleration in their international relations.

The establishment of constitutional government undoubtedly takes time, and — if Western history is any example — a long time. In 1953 the Hansard Society pointed out that the triple process of state building — differentiation of a distinctive society; establishment of an effective central government; and popular legitimation of government — which took centuries in the West was being attempted in only a few generations in Africa. At the time this observation was made, it seemed more likely than it does today that African countries might be successful in telescoping the political duration of institution building. If the past quarter-century of African politics is any indication, however, in most cases institutional development promises to be a more prolonged process than originally assumed. In the meantime, some (and perhaps many) African countries will have to endure instability, disorder, violence, and similar hazards of nonconstitutional government. During this interim period, any achievements of civility in politics will probably owe more to the personal strength, self-restraint, and fairness of individual rulers and other powerful political actors than to the political institutions involved.

AFRICA BETWEEN EAST AND WEST

Almost immediately following independence many of the new African rulers began to express fears about the threat posed to Africa by the so-called neocolonialism of the West. Behind this fear was the belief that independence must be economic as well as political to be complete. But African independence was not a fundamental economic change. It did not and could not alter Africa's extreme underdevelopment and heavy dependence on external markets and capital. This is strikingly evident in southern Africa, where South Africa remains the major economic power of the region despite the expressed, and often determined, desires of many regional black African governments to become independent of it. Further, Europe did not cease to be crucial to African economies following independence. Instead, the European Economic Community (EEC) became Africa's most important trading partner and succeeded the former European empires in the provision of trade and tariff opportunities for Africa's exports. Indeed, the Economic Community of West African States (ECOWAS) was formed to provide African countries with, among other things, a complementary institutional relationship with the EEC.

The former imperial powers have not withdrawn entirely from the continent, however. France, in particular, has retained substantial, and often intimate, ties both with many former dependencies and with some colonies — such as Zaire — that had been dependencies of another European power. France has overshadowed Britain in its postindependence involvement in African affairs and is, in some important respects, the major Western actor in the region. The French presence in some countries is greater today than it was at independence. Frenchmen have played particularly important managerial roles in Ivory Coast, Cameroon, and Gabon. The widely noted economic success of Ivory Coast must be attributed in significant part to their presence. France has been instrumental in establishing and managing some crucial intra-African economic institutions. A good example is the comparatively stable Franc zone.

France has also retained a significant military presence; it has substantial troop establishments in Djibouti and the Central African Republic and smaller contingents in many other former colonies. Since independence, successive governments in Chad have almost always been supported by French forces, and France has intervened militarily in Gabon and the Central African Republic. The extent of French involvement after many of the current pro-Paris African rulers have been succeeded can only be speculated upon. Ruler successions in Gabon, Senegal, and Cameroon, however, have not significantly altered the role of France in these countries. It is likely that new leaders will be as unwilling as their predecessors to pay the political and economic price of reducing dependency on the former metropole. Whether or not Paris will reciprocate by continuing its involvement is also a matter of speculation. But the fact that the socialist government of President Mitterand assumed essentially the same African role held by its Gaullist predecessors indicates that the role has value regardless of party or ideological considerations and that it seems to be justified by a shared conception of the national interest.

If independence did not change Africa's dependency on the West, it did open the region to a new, unanticipated, and potentially destabilizing, neoimperial force: the Soviet Union and its clients (Cuba and East Germany). Africa increasingly became a new arena of the East-West conflict. In the early 1970s Soviet naval and air forces for the first time achieved the capacity to project military power into African civil and international conflicts on a scale sufficient to shift the balance of power. This can be seen perhaps most clearly in Angola and Ethiopia. In Angola, Cuban intervention on a massive scale in 1975–76 enabled the MPLA to gain control of the government following the collapse of Portuguese colonialism. In Ethiopia, Soviet airlift capacity and Cuban troops deployed in support of the Mengistu regime turned the tide of the war in the Ogaden in 1978 from an imminent Somali victory to a disastrous defeat. In both Angola and Ethiopia, avowedly Marxist-Leninist regimes have been maintained primarily by Russian and Cuban aid.

Soviet involvement in African affairs has been eclectic and expedient, as one would expect from a power with little previous experience in such affairs. In the early 1960s the Soviets registered modest success in influencing such radical and anticolonial — but not necessarily Marxist-Leninist — regimes as Nkrumah's Ghana,

Keita's Mali, and Touré's Guinea. Their political and military support often proved of far greater value to African clients than their economic aid, which was often technologically and institutionally unsuited to African conditions. Later, they became deeply involved in the support of liberation movements. The involvement has proved to be somewhat more successful in generating ideologically sympathetic client states — such as Angola, Mozambique, and (to some extent) Zimbabwe. They have also pursued control of strategic "chokepoints" — that is, places where important maritime routes converge. Ethiopia and southern Africa are of particular value in this regard, and the Soviets have expanded considerable resources and effort in attempting to exercise influence over them.

Soviet involvement has not been merely a traditional game of Machiavellian statecraft, however. It has also been inspired by a revolutionary international goal that seeks to place as much of Africa as possible in the Soviet camp. The first stage, according to Kremlin planners, was to encourage and support African "progressive movements" and fronts in the expectation that they could later be transformed into disciplined cadre parties that would become not only internationally loyal, but also ideologically correct, clients. Governments that professed Marxism-Leninism and accepted Soviet aid were expected to reciprocate by promoting the reorganization of their states in accordance with the Soviet model. (Something like this process can be discerned in Angola, Mozambique, the People's Republic of the Congo, and Ethiopia.) Revolutionary parties were expected to promote Marxism-Leninism — perhaps in a gradual fashion, as in the Mongolian and Cuban parties — and, similarly, governments were supposed to cement their international solidarity with the Soviet camp. The new "proletarian internationalism," as Soviet ideologists conceived it, would shift the historical balance of international forces to the advantage of "socialism" and to the disadvantage of "imperialism."

Revolutionary Soviet internationalism confronts major socioeconomic and political obstacles peculiar to Africa, however. Outside of South Africa, the industrial proletariat is very weak and extremely difficult to mobilize. In more than a few countries it is practically nonexistent. Likewise, peasants do not usually form a cohesive and militant class upon which a common-style revolutionary party or state can be built. The preindustrial and, in some cases, precommercial — that is, precapitalist — character of Africa and its still fairly widespread tribal mode of production either imposes a convoluted logic on orthodox communist theory or creates an unbridgeable gap between theory and practice. Multiethnic African cultures and widespread corruption usually render state cohesion, organization, and discipline of any kind (not only of a communist or socialist variety) extremely difficult to achieve. On close examination, the language of communism that is spoken in some African countries often proves, to be almost entirely lacking in substance.

Moreover, African governments have not proved to be the most reliable Soviet clients. Some that originally collaborated with the Soviets later decided to cooperate with the West. Sudan and Somalia are cases in point. The decision to move in the opposite direction is also possible, of course. Both possibilities underline the fact that African governments are sovereign and are able to determine their own course in international affairs. Instability also makes for unreliability, however. There is always the possibility that a client will be overthrown and that his successor will renounce any obligations to the Soviet Union. This situation occurred following the overthrow of Nkrumah in Ghana, Keita in Mali, and Macias in Equatorial Guinea. (It is also possible, of course, that the Soviets may conspire to overthrow regimes in an effort to install more manipulable successors.) Even when stable Afro-communist regimes are in power in a country, they may decide to chart a revolutionary course that is substantially different from the one desired by their Soviet patrons — as has happened in other parts of the world (most notably in China and Albania). In short, the Soviets are likely to be compelled by circumstances to resort to expediency, flexibility, conspiracy, and other nonideological canons of Machiavellian diplomacy in their attempted penetration of Africa.

POLITICAL ECONOMY: PROSPECTS AND POSSIBILITIES

A significant minority of African countries, including Cameroon, Ivory Coast, Kenya, Botswana, Gabon, Nigeria, and — above all — South Africa have made notewothy economic advances. In these instances, the main contributing factors have been a combination of reliable administration, mixed economies, ethnic peace, and pragmatic politics — or a windfall natural resource like oil (Gabon and Nigeria). But the performances of the majority of African countries have not matched the hopes of most planners and politicians. Indeed, according to the UN Economic Commission on Africa, the economies of thirty of the forty-nine independent African states have regressed since 1974. The UN Food and Agricultural Organization (FAO) has disclosed similar alarming findings. Statism has almost always been accompanied by economic deterioration. If these trends continue, tropical Africa could soon be reduced to a continent of beggar states desperately dependent on international charity. Most of them are facing a Malthusian crisis: their populations are increasing at a rate of 2.5 to 4 percent per year, whereas their food production is declining at about 1 percent per year. (South Africa is, of course, the most important exception. Between 1955 and 1977 — at a time when political analysts continued to predict turmoil and even collapse — South Africa's gross domestic product multiplied from less than 4 to more than 31 thousand million rands.)

It is hazardous to predict the future of countries, and this is not less true for the future of Africa, which is likely to have its share of surprises and contradictions. Social scientists are not prophets. To forecast a political future is, if anything, more difficult than to forecast an economic one, because economics is governed to a greater extent by general, more slowly changing, and relentless social forces. Politics is more subject to historical intervention by small numbers of powerful people, who may be fully capable of overturning a government or charting a new political course but may nevertheless be almost powerless when it comes to directing social forces.

Economically, we expect poverty and technological backwardness to persist (or to change only marginally) in many tropical African countries in the foreseeable future. The continent will probably continue to be the center of the Fourth World. Extremely underdeveloped areas like the Sahel have very limited prospects — unless oil or some other valuable resource is discovered. Nevertheless, because so little is known about the geology of Africa, resource discoveries can be expected. Resource discoveries could result in a significant improvement in general living standards if they occur in countries that have small populations and governments that are not excessively corrupt (as happened in Gabon as a result of oil discoveries). They could also result in the dislocation and desertion of more traditional economic sectors (as happened in

Nigeria). It is unreasonable to expect that Africa could be developed by resource economies alone, however. Of greater importance in the long run is the extent to which African countries will be able to generate the most crucial developmental capital: stable and economical government, entrepreneurship, hard work, thrift, and other traditional economic virtues. The economic significance of countries like Ivory Coast and Kenya — as compared to Gabon and Nigeria — is precisely that development has occurred in the absence of resource windfalls and has been primarily a result of such social or human capital.

Politically, we expect democracy to be obstructed by the perpetuation of one-party or military dictatorships. In this respect, the political future of tropical Africa may resemble the political history of Latin America. Most regimes will probably be sustained by coercion rather than by legitimacy and be changed by coups rather than by elections. In current African circumstances, it is not a hazardous exercise to predict the recurrence of coups and similar political usurpations. But to predict which countries might escape from them is almost impossible. The political experiences of Senegal, Kenya, and a few other countries, however, indicate that some degree of democratization is possible if a more self-confident and tolerant leadership develops. If the dominant political trend of the past quarter-century is anything to go by, this is not likely to be the main tendency. But whether it happens or not will depend largely on the will and abilities of leaders.

If a political economy lesson in the postindependence African experience has been outlined in this book, it is that heavy reliance on the state apparatus is far more likely to provoke stagnation and decay than to create development. If African governments are serious about improving the civil and socioeconomic conditions of their countries, they cannot avoid the conclusion that their experiments with statism — most often in the form of socialism — have, by and large, been failures. The results of these experiments have been almost exactly the opposite of their proposed goals. The only way to move away from the inefficiencies and corruptions of statism in countries where loyalty to the state is likely to remain weak or even nonexistent is to curtail state activities and allow capitalism to develop. A capitalist society would demand far fewer state regulations and restrictions and would therefore almost certainly increase efficiency and probity. Moreover, it would increase the opportunity of people to save, to invest, to move about, and, generally, to engage in a less fettered and paternalistic — and more self-reliant — pursuit of income and welfare.

The size of the state apparatus could be substantially reduced if many of its substantive economic management and regulatory activities were abandoned. This is difficult politically, but it is not impossible. Government would spend less and tax less if it were smaller and less intrusive; funds would therefore be liberated for private spending and investing. Contrary to the arguments of socialists, reducing the state apparatus would probably also result in a wider distribution of income and in an increased demand for less expensive goods that are more likely to be produced locally — in short, fewer automobiles and more bicycles. "Free enterprise" would be curtailed in the state sector — where it can gain expression only in the form of corruption and other abuses of state regulations — and would be liberated in the private sector — where it would be supportive, rather than destructive, of the public good. Black markets would decline because the free price system would be a legitimate method of allocating scarce resources. The free market might regain the significance it sometimes enjoyed during the colonial era, with corresponding increases in the standard of living.

The free market is far more likely than the state to induce entrepreneurship, hard work, thrift, and other economic virtues. A process of class formation based on real economic achievement — rather than on political power and privilege, as at present — would undoubtedly occur if statism were reduced. Historically, the middle class has been far more creative and progressive than have socialist, mercantilist, or other classes whose existence is dependent on statism. An entrepreneurial class might emerge to promote the wealth of nations — as has often happened when the state has reduced its involvement in the marketplace. A more prosperous and honest peasantry could develop in circumstances in which a free market price, rather than a state monopolized price, was allowed to determine the allocation of agricultural commodities — a peasantry that could produce in the expectation of a fair market return and could avoid resorting to smuggling or curtailing production under an artificially depressed state monopolized price. A peasantry like this existed in Ghana before Nkrumah's ill-fated move to socialism. It could exist there again, and in many other countries, if free markets were restored. Progressive farmers and middle-class businessmen are better equipped to develop Africa's economies than state functionaries, who are often intellectuals with little practical economic experience.

The state will of course, always retain an important and legitimate economic role. It will always be required to provide defense, law, order, and justice, without which a civil society and a market economy cannot function. In addition, it will be required to secure a stable currency, develop infrastructures, make extension services available, and so forth. In short, the state must be relied on to provide what the private sector is unable to. But the state must be limited in its economic role so that the economy is supported, but not exploited or weighed down, by government staff and regulations. It must also be limited in order to discourage corruption and black markets. The key to African development is the agricultural sector, which, in particular, must be loosed from the state and allowed to develop more spontaneously in response to free market forces.

Moreover, the state must henceforth secure legitimacy more by ruling efficiently and equitably than by resorting to extensive patronage and corruption — as is presently the case in most tropical African countries. A political change of this nature will obviously not be easy in circumstances in which many people are dependent on government for their power and privileges — circumstances which largely characterize the position of the educated urban class in Africa today. (The cynic would probably say it is impossible.) The alternative to a scaled-down state apparatus has become brutally clear, however: widespread suffering and hardship. Most people have not escaped from this alternative, including many members of the educated and urban classes. There is reason to believe that socialism, mercantilism, and other statist ideologies are widely discredited among people in most African countries today. Enlightened governments could take advantage of this attitude to promote African capitalism.

The Western democracies and the international financial and trading institutions they control (principally the EEC, the IMF, and the World Bank) could provoke African development by making their aid more conditional on economic liberalization and government reform. They could also induce these changes by promoting free trade for Third World exports. The extremely small size of many African economies makes it possible for moderate amounts of Western aid to constitute significant inducements. Loans to African governments must, however, by tightly supervised and confined to the legitimate economic activities of government. They should be procured on the basis of economic merit and should not be given as political bribes or conscience money. Every effort should be made to increase trade opportunities and thereby make African countries less dependent on aid. The Soviet Union is not in a strong position to obstruct this development process because it is not in the same economic league as the Western democracies. The West holds the trump cards in this international game. It should play them with a view to the greatest good of the greatest number of Africans and not to the pleasure of African regimes.

Although the West can substantially assist African development, the final responsibility rests with the African states and citizens themselves. Africans are by far the most important capital. African governments are sovereign. They — and not the West — have the final responsibilities, and they must take the crucial actions necessary to develop their countries rather than despoil them. In the final analysis, this is what the end of colonialism and political independence means.

Notes

1. See "Statistical Annex" in *Accelerated Development in Sub-Saharan Africa: An Agenda for Action* (Washington, D.C.: World Bank, 1981), pp. 142–86.

2. *The Observer* (London), 27 January 1985.

3. *Accelerated Development in Sub-Saharan Africa*, p. 143.

4. Barbara Jelavich, *History of the Balkans: Eighteenth and Nineteenth Centuries* (London: Cambridge University Press, 1983), pp. 298–99.

5. See Jon Moris, "Overall Institutional Performance," *Tanzania Agricultural Sector Report*, Background paper no. 6 (Washington D.C.: World Bank, 1982), Mimeographed).

6. For a general discussion, see Robert H. Bates, *Markets and States in Tropical Africa: The Political Basis of Agricultural Policies* (Berkeley, Los Angeles, and London: University of California Press, 1981).

7. Zdenek Cervenka, *The Organization of African Unity and its Charter* (New York and Washington: Praeger, 1969), pp. 92–94.

8. See Arend Lijphart, *Democracy in Plural Societies: A Comparative Exploitation* (New Haven and London: Yale University Press, 1977).

9. See Robert H. Jackson and Carl G. Rosberg, "Popular Legitimacy in African Multi-Ethnic States," *The Journal of Modern African Studies* 22, no. 2 (1984): 191–94.

10. Quoted in *Problems of Parliamentary Government in Colonies* (London: The Hansard Society, 1953), p. 4.

SELECT BIBLIOGRAPHY

Accelerated Development in Sub-Saharan Africa: An Agenda for Action. Washington, D.C.: The World Bank, 1981.

Adam, Heribert, and Giliomee, Herman. *The Rise and Crisis of Afrikaner Power.* Cape Town: D. Philip, 1979.

Adamolekun, 'Ladipo. *Public Administration: A Nigerian and Comparative Perspective.* Lagos: Longman, 1983.

—— *Sékou Touré's Guinea.* London: Methuen, 1976.

Adamu, Haroun, and Ogunsanwo, Alaba. *Nigeria: The Making of the Presidential System, 1979 General Elections.* Kano, 1983.

Albright, David E. *Communism in Africa.* Bloomington: Indiana University Press, 1980.

Arlinghaus, Bruce. *Military Development in Africa: The Political and Economic Risks of Arms Transfers.* Boulder, Colo.: Westview Press, 1984.

Austin, Dennis. *Politics in Africa.* Hanover, N.H.: Univeristy Press of New England, 1980.

Barkan, Joel D., and Okumu, John J., eds. *Politics and Public Policy in Kenya and Tanzania.* New York: Praeger, 1979.

Bates, Robert H. *Markets and States in Tropical Africa: The Political Basis of Agricultural Policies.* Berkeley and Los Ageles: University of California Press, 1981.

Bayart, Jean-François. *L'Etat au Cameroun.* Paris: Presses de la Fondation National des Sciences Politiques, 1979.

Biarnes, Pierre. *L'Afrique aux africains.* Paris: Armand Colin, 1980.

Bienen, Henry. *Armies and Parties in Africa.* New York: Africana Publishing Co., 1978.

Bissell, Richard E., and Crocker, Chester. *South Africa into the 1980s.* Boulder, Colo.: Westview Press, 1979.

Boateng, E. A. *A Political Geography of Africa.* Cambridge: Cambridge University Press, 1978.

Bond, Nguza Karl I. *Mobutu ou l'Incarnation du Mal.* London: Rex Collings, 1982.

Booth, Alan R. *Swaziland: Tradition and Change in a Southern African Kingdom.* Boulder, Colo.: Westview Press, 1983.

Brotz, Howard. *The Politics of South Africa: Democracy and Racial Diversity.* Oxford: Oxford University Press, 1977.

Callaghy, Thomas M. *South Africa: The Intensifying Vortex of Violence.* New York: Praeger Special Studies, 1983.

Carter, Gwendolen M., and O'Meara, Patrick, eds. *Southern Africa: The Continuing Crisis.* Bloomington: Indiana Univeristy Press, 1979.

Cartwright, John R. *Political Leadership in Africa.* New York: St. Martin's Press, 1983.

Caute, David. *Under the Skin: The Death of White Rhodesia.* Evanston Il.: Northwestern University Press, 1983.

Chazan, Naomi. *An Anatomy of Ghanaian Politics: Managing Political Recession, 1966-1972.* Boulder, Colo.: Westview Press, 1983.

Church, Ronald James Harrison. *Environment and Policies in West Africa.* New York: Van Nostrand, 1976.

Clapham, Christopher. *Haile-Selassie's Government.* London: Longman, 1969.

—— *Third World Politics.* London: Croom Helm, 1984.

Cliffe, Lionel, and Saul, John, eds. *Socialism in Tanzania: An Interdisciplinary Reader.* 2 vols. Nairobi: East African Publishing House, 1972.

Colclough, Christopher, and McCarthy, Stephen. *The Political Economy of Botswana: A Study of Growth and Distribution.* London: Oxford University Press, 1980.

Collier, Ruth Berins. *Regimes in Tropical Africa: Changing Forms of Supremacy, 1945–1975.* Berkeley: University of California Press, 1982.

Crespigny, Anthony de, and Schire, Robert. *The Government and Politics of South Africa.* Cape Town: Juta, 1978.

Cunningham, Simon. *The Copper Industry in Zambia: Foreign Mining Companies in a Developing Country.* New York: Praeger, 1981.

Davies, Robert H.; O'Meara, Dan; and Dlamini, Sipho. *The Struggle for South Africa: A Reference Guide to Movements, Organizations and Institutions.* London: Zed Books, 1984.

Decalo, Samuel. *Coups and Army Rule in Africa.* New Haven, Conn.: Yale University Press, 1976.

Dickson, A. Mungazi. *The Cross Between Rhodesia and Zimbabwe: Racial Conflict in Rhodesia, 1962–1979.* New York: Vantage Press, 1981.

Dismukes, Bradford, and McConnell, James. *Soviet Naval Diplomacy.* Elmsford, N.Y.: Pergamon Press, 1979.

Dudley, Billing J. *An Introduction to Nigerian Government and Politics.* Bloomington: Indiana University Press, 1982.

Dougherty, James E. *The Horn of Africa: A Map of Political-Strategic Conflict.* Cambridge, Mass.: Institute for Foreign Policy Analysis, 1982.

Gann, L. H. *Central Africa: The Former British States.* Englewood Cliffs, N.J.: Prentice-Hall, 1971.

Gann, L. H., and Duignan, Peter. *Africa South of the Sahara: The Challenge to Western Security.* Stanford, Calif.: Hoover Institution Press, 1981.

——— *Why South Africa Will Survive.* New York: St. Martin's Press, 1981.

Gann, L. H., and Henriksen, Thomas. *The Struggle for Zimbabwe: Battle in the Bush.* New York: Praeger, 1981.

Gellar, Sheldon. *Senegal, An African Nation Between Islam and the West.* Boulder, Colo.: Westview Press, 1982.

Gifford, Prosser, and Louis, William Roger. *The Transfer of Power in Africa: Decolonization, 1940–1960.* New Haven, Conn.: Yale University Press, 1982.

Grundy, Kenneth W. *Soldiers Without Politics: Blacks in the South African Armed Forces.* Berkeley: University of California Press, 1983.

——— *The Rise of the South African Military Establishment: An Essay on the Changing Locus of State Power.* Cape Town: South Africa Institute of International Affairs, 1983.

Hall, Richard. *Zambia, 1890–1964: The Colonial Period.* London: Longmans, 1976.

Halpern, Jack. *South Africa's Hostages: Basutoland, Bechuanaland, and Swaziland.* Harmondsworth, England: Penguin Books, 1965.

Hanf, Theodor; Weiland, Heribert; and Viertag, Gerda. *Südafrika: Friedlicher Wandel? Möglichkeiten Demokratischer Konfliktregelung.* Mainz: Matthias Grünewald Verlag, 1979.

Hatch, John. *Two African Statesmen: Kaunda of Zambia and Nyerere of Tanzania.* London: Secker and Warburg, 1976.

Hazelwood, Arthur. *The Economy of Kenya: The Kenyatta Era.* New York: Oxford University Press, 1979.

Henriksen, Thomas H. *Mozambique: A History.* London: Rex Collings, 1978.

——— *Revolution and Counterrevolution: Mozambique's War of Independence, 1964–1974.* Westport, Conn.: Greenwood Press, 1983.

Hodder, B. W. *Africa Today: A Short Introduction to African Affairs*. London: Methuen, 1978.

House, Arthur H. *The U.N. in the Congo: The Political and Civilian Efforts*. Washington: University Press of America, 1978.

Hyden, Goran. *Beyond Ujamaa in Tanzania: Underdevelopment and an Uncaptured Peasantry*. Berkeley and Los Angeles: University of California Press, 1980.

International Bank for Reconstruction and Development. *Zaire: Current Economic Situation and Constraints*. Washington, D.C., 1980.

Jackson, Robert H., and Rosberg, Carl G. *Personal Rule in Black Africa: Prince, Autocrat, Prophet, Tyrant*. Berkeley: University of California Press, 1982.

Johnson, R. W. *How Long Will South Africa Survive?* New York: Oxford University Press, 1977.

Joseph, Richard. *Radical Nationalism in Cameroun*. Oxford: Clarendon Press, 1977.

Kalb, Madeleine G. *The Congo Cables, the Cold War in Africa — from Eisenhower to Kennedy*. New York: Macmillan, 1982.

Kanza, Thomas. *Conflict in the Congo*. Harmondsworth, England: Penguin Books, 1972.

Karis, Thomas, and Carter, Gwendolen, et al. *From Protest to Challenge: A Documentary History of African Politics in South Africa, 1882–1964*. 4 vols. Stanford, Calif.: Hoover Institution Press, 1972–1977.

Kirke-Greene, Anthony, and Rimmer, Douglas. *Nigeria Since 1970*. New York: Holmes & Meier, 1981.

Kitchen, Helen. *U.S. Interests in Africa*. New York: Praeger Special Studies, 1983.

Kotecha, Ken C., and Adams, Robert. *African Politics: The Corruption of Power*. Lanham, Md.: University Press of America, 1981.

Lamb, David. *The Africans*. New York: Vintage Books, 1984.

Lawson, Kay, ed. *Political Parties and Linkages: A Comparative Perspective*. New Haven and London: Yale University Press, 1980.

Lefort, Rene. *Ethiopia: An Heretical Revolution?* London: Zed Press, 1983.

Legum, Colin, ed. *Africa Contemporary Record: Annual Survey and Documents*. New York: Africana Publishing Co.

Legum, Colin; Zartman, William; Langdon, Steven; and Mytelka, Lynn K., eds. *Africa in the 1980s: A Continent in Crisis*. Council on Foreign Relations 1980s Project. New York: McGraw-Hill, 1979.

Legum, Colin, and Lee, Bill. *Conflict in the Horn of Africa*. New York: Africana Publishing Co., 1977.

Lemarchand, René, ed. *American Policy in Southern Africa: The Stakes and the Stance*. Washington, D.C.: University Press of America, 1978.

LeVine, Victor T. *The Cameroon Federal Republic*. Ithaca, N.Y.: Cornell University Press, 1971.

————— *Political Corruption: The Ghana Case*. Stanford, Calif.: Hoover Institution Press, 1975.

Lewis, I. M. *A Modern History of Somalia*. London: Longman, 1980.

Lodge, Tom. *Black Politics in South Africa Since 1945*. London: Longman, 1983.

Mahiou, Ahmed. *L'Avenement du parti unique en Afrique noire*. Paris: R. Pichon and R. Durand-Auzias, Librairie Générale de Droit et de Jurisprudence, 1969.

Marnham, Patrick. *Fantastic Invasion: Notes on Contemporary Africa*. New York: Harcourt Brace Jovanovich, 1980.

Maasdorp, Gavin C. *SADCC, a Post-Nkomati Evaluation*. Braamfontein: South African Institute of International Affairs, 1984.

Meredith, Martin. *The First Dance of Freedom: Black Africa in the Postwar Era*. New York: Harper & Row, 1984.

Nghunda, Lukombe. *Zairianisation, Radicalisation, Rétrocession en République du Zaire*. Kinshasa: Presses Universitaires du Zaire, 1979.

Nwabueze, B. O. *The Presidential Constitutionalism*. New York: St Martin's Press, 1982.

Oberschall, Antony R. *African Businessmen and Development in Zambia*. Princeton, N.J.: Princeton University Press, 1979.

Oquaye, M. *Politics in Ghana, 1972–1979*. Accra, 1980.

Ottaway, David. *Afrocommunism*. New York: Holmes & Meier, 1981.

Oyediran, Oyelaye, ed. *Nigerian Government and Politics Under Military Rule*. New York: St. Matin's Press, 1979.

Parson, Jack. *Botswana: Liberal Democracy and the Labor Reserve in Southern Africa*. Boulder, Colo.: Westview Press, 1984.

Péan, Pierre. *Affaires africaines*. Paris: Fayard, 1983.

Pearson, Roger, ed. *Sino-Soviet Intervention in Africa*. Washington, D.C.: Council on American Affairs, 1977.

Potholm, Christian P. *The Theory and Practice of African Politics*. Englewood Cliffs, N.J.: Prentice-Hall, 1979.

Price, Joseph Henry. *Political Institutions of West Africa*. 2d ed. London: Hutchinson, 1975.

Prouzet, Michael. *Le Cameroun*. Paris: Librairie Générale de Droit et de Jurisprudence, 1974.

Race Relations as Regulated by law in South Africa, 1948–1979. Compiled by Muriel Horrell. Johannesburg: South African Institute of Race Relations, 1982.

Rivière, Claude. *Guinea*. Ithaca, N.Y.: Cornell University Press, 1977.

Robertson, Ian, and Whitten, Phillip, eds. *Race and Politics in South Africa*. New Brunswick. N.J.: Transaction Books, 1978.

Ronen, Dov. *Dahomey Between Tradition and Modernity*. Ithaca, N.Y.: Cornell University Press, 1975.

Rosberg, Carl G., and Callaghy, Thomas M., eds. *Socialism in Sub-Saharan Africa: A New Assessment*. Berkeley, Calif.: Institute of International Studies, 1979.

Samuels, Michael A., ed. *Africa and the West*. Boulder, Colo.: Westview Press, 1980.

Schatzberg, Michael G. *Politics and Class in Zaire*. New York: Africana Publishing Company, 1980.

Schwab, Peter. *Ethiopia, Politics, Economics, and Society*. Boulder, Colo.: Lynne Rienner Publishers, 1985.

Seidman, Ann Wilcox. *Outposts of Monopoly Capitalism: Southern Africa in a Changing Global Economy*. Westport, Conn.: L. Hill, 1980.

Seiler, John, ed. *Southern Africa Since the Portuguese Coup*. Boulder, Colo.: Westview Press, 1980.

Selwyn, Percy. *Industries in the Southern African Periphery: A Study of Industrial Development in Botswana, Lesotho, and Swaziland*. London: Croom Helm, 1977.

Shaw, Timothy. *Towards a Political Economy for Africa: The Dialectics of Dependence*. London: Macmillan, 1985.

Shorter, Aylward. *East African Societies*. London: Routledge and Kegan Paul, 1974.

Sonkosi, Zola. *African Opposition in South Africa from 1948–1969: An Analysis of the African National Congress of South Africa's Non-Violent and Violent Actions*. West Berlin: Sonkosi, 1975.

South Africa: Time Running Out. Report of the Study Commission on U.S. Policy Toward Southern Africa. Berkeley: University of California Press, 1981.

Stahl, Michael. *Ethiopia: Political Contradictions in Agricultural Development*. Stockholm: Raben & Sjogren, 1974.

Thompson, Leonard, and Prior, Andrew. *South African Politics*. New Haven, Conn.: Yale University Press, 1982.

Tordoff, William. *Government and Politics in Africa*. London: Macmillan, 1984.

Tötemeyer, Gerhard. *South West Africa/Namibia: Facts, Attitudes, Assessment and Prospects*. London: Rex Collings, 1977.

van der Horst, Sheila T., ed. *Race Discrimination in South Africa: A Review*. Cape Town: David Philips, 1981.

van Zyl Slabbert, Frederick, and Welsh, David. *South Africa's Options: Strategies for Sharing Power*. New York: St. Martin's Press, 1979.

Walshe, Peter. *The Rise of African Nationalism in South Africa: The African National Congress, 1912–1952*. Berkeley: University of Calinfornia Press, 1971.

Were, Gideon S. *Leadersip and Underdevelopment in Africa*. Nairobi: The author, 1983.

Wheeler, Douglas L., and Pellissier, Rene. *Angola*. New York: Praeger, 1971.

Whitaker, Jennifer Seymour, ed. *Africa and the United States: Vital Interests*. New York: New York University Press, 1978.

——— *Conflict in Southern Africa*. New York: Foreign Policy Association, 1978.

Wilson, Derek A. *A History of South and Central Africa*. London Cambridge University Press, 1975.

Woodward, Calvin A. *Prospects for Political Stability in Botswana, Lesotho and Swaziland*. Pretoria: Africa Institute, 1984.

Young, Crawford. *Ideology and Development in Africa*. New Haven, Conn.: Yale University Press, 1982.

INDEX

Adoula, Cyrille 133, 134
African National Congress (ANC)
167, 292–3, 295–6, 300,
334–40, 352, 372
Africanization 15, 26, 411
agriculture 1, 13–15, 413
  Angola 402–3
  Botswana 365, 369
  Cameroon 155
  Ethiopia: imperial 263–4;
    revolutionary 269–70, 280
  Ghana 42–3
  Kenya 234–5
  Lesotho 372–3
  Malawi 193–4
  Mozambique 390–1
  Namibia 358
  neglect 1, 12, 13–15, 65
  Somalia 280
  South Africa 321
  Swaziland 372–3
  Tanzania 210, 211–13
  Uganda 224
  Zambia 186–7
  Zimbabwe 182
Ahidjo, Ahmadou 94, 109–10,
  150–4
Amin, Idi 218, 220–5
Angola 377–86 *passim*, 396–403,
  403–6 *passim*
  agriculture 402–3
  anticolonial wars 383–6
  colonial legacy 378–83; economy
    378–80; government 381–3
  economy 401–3
  government 396–8
  guerrilla war 400–1
  independence 385
  oil 403
  parastatals 402, 403
  politics 397–9
  security apparatus 399
apartheid 297–8, 301–2
Azikiwe, Nnamdi 49

Banda, Hastings Kamuzu 168, 191–4
Benin 78–118 *passim*
  ethnicity 98

military intervention 98–9
  see also West Africa (formerly
    French)
Boesak, Allen 300
Botha, P. W. ("Piet") 287–9, 291,
  307–8, 314, 329
Botswana 345–7, 364–70
  agriculture 365, 369
  bureaucracy 369
  economy 367–8
  ethnicity 364
  industry 369–70
  military 367
  mining 369
  politics 366–7
bureaucracy 17–21, 411–14
  Botswana 369
  Cameroon 152
  Ethiopia 259–60
  Ghana 40
  Mozambique 384–8, 391
  Namibia 352–5
  Nigeria 54–5
  South Africa 302–8
  Tanzania 210–17
  West Africa (formerly French) 92
  Zimbabwe 179–80
Burkina Faso 78–118 *passim*
  ethnicity 98
  military intervention 99, 101
  see also West Africa (formerly
    French)
Buthelezi, Gatsha 298, 372

Cameroon 78–118 *passim*, 120–2,
  149–57
  agriculture 155
  bureaucracy 152
  coup attempt 155
  economy 10
  ethnicity 94, 150–1, 152–4
  oil 110, 150, 155
  one-party rule 150, 151
  patrimonialism 151, 154
  personal rule 151–2
  politics 109–11, 150, 153
  regionalism 150–1, 152–4
  religion 153

435